# Studies in Consumer Demand — Econometric Methods Applied to Market Data

# Studies in Consumer Demand — Econometric Methods Applied to Market Data

*by*

JEFFREY A. DUBIN
*Division of the Humanities and Social Sciences*
*California Institute of Technology*
*Pasadena, California*

SPRINGER SCIENCE+BUSINESS MEDIA, LLC

**Library of Congress Cataloging-in-Publication**

Dubin, Jeffrey A.
Studies in consumer demand econometric methods applied to market data / by Jeffrey A. Dubin.
p. cm.
Includes bibliographical references and index.
ISBN 978-1-4613-7593-7 ISBN 978-1-4615-5665-7 (eBook)
DOI 10.1007/978-1-4615-5665-7
1. Consumption (Economics)—Econometric models. 2. Marketing research—econometric models. I. Title.
HB820.D8 1998
339.4'7'015195--dc21 98-26792
CIP

---


Originally published by Kluwer Academic Publishers in 1998
Softcover reprint of the hardcover 1st edition 1998
This printing is a digital duplication of the original edition.


*Printed on acid-free paper.*

This book is dedicated in loving
memory to my father
Sidney Dubin.

# Contents

# List of Figures

# Preface

*He wants most decidedly to be inspired by the burning practical problems of the day; this realistic orientation is indeed an essential characteristic of econometrics.*

–Ragnar Frisch, *Econometrica*, January, 1946.

The chapters in this monograph collect some of my empirical research conducted during the last ten years. Often these projects required significant time and resources to complete. The compilation of this research and the exposition of the ideas and results took place during the last three years. The majority of the word-processing and type-setting was accomplished during the last year.

In writing this book, I was in part motivated by Frank Fisher's collected works in theoretical and applied econometrics. When I am thinking about a new project, choosing an econometric specification, or building an economic model, I will frequently consult my former professor's book as it provides many useful examples and techniques. It's possible that there is no better way to learn the art of applied econometrics than to be immersed in someone else's study. I therefore hope that these chapters will serve a similar role and provide by example my approach to the modeling of consumer demand.

Much of this work was the result of projects conducted for or in the legal arena. In all cases, I have only relied on the non-confidential aspects of these projects as summarized in final reports or my own testimony. These chapters therefore do not reveal data that is proprietary to the parties. The opinions provided in these chapters are solely mine.

Certain individuals deserve mention for their assistance in the research for this book. While it's impossible to mention everyone, I need to pay to special attention to a few. For Chapter 1, I would like to thank Al Vlietstra and Louis O'Brien of Canada Post. For Chapter 2, I thank W.B. Peale and John Kakinuki. For Chapter 3, I thank Charles Cicchetti. For Chapter 4, I would like to thank David Abbott, Colin Long, David Moes, and especially my close friend Doug Rivers who aided in the development of the theory. Thank you

Doug for being there for me. For Chapter 5, I thank my research assistant Mary Elizabeth Vault. For Chapter 6, I thank Jim Akers and especially acknowledge the contribution of Tim Bresnahan. For Chapter 8, I thank Mike Ceramella and Mike McMahon of Koch Industries.

To bring this text to life, I must thank my secretary Victoria Mason. Victoria has done a fabulous job with this book and with the intricacies of LaTeX. Without a doubt, this project would not have been completed without her. Victoria was aided by Abbey Dellman who also deserves my thanks. Paula Scott served as my line and copy editor. I thank Paula for her help with the exposition. Bob Turring, in Caltech's illustration department, did a wonderful job with the illustrations. Finally, I thank my editor at Kluwer, Ranak Jasani, who made this such a simple project on the production side. Of course, in a manuscript of this complexity, some errors will remain and I retain the ultimate responsibility for these.

On a more personal note, I must thank my wife Jackie and my children Andrew and Ethan for their patience and support. They're not always sure what I'm working on, but they know I'm working.

I also take this opportunity to reiterate my life-long respect and thanks to Dan McFadden who was principal among so many other terrific teachers at MIT in showing me how to do good applied work. His standards are those I always aspire to but frequently cannot reach. Finally, I thank my friend, partner, and mentor Charles Cicchetti. In one way or another Charlie has touched each and every chapter in this book. During the last ten years, I have learned to be an economist from Charlie which is often different than being an economics professor. Most importantly, he taught me that sometimes you don't choose the problems, they choose you.

JEFFREY DUBIN

# INTRODUCTION

This monograph contains eight previously unpublished studies of consumer demand. Each study stands on its own as a complete econometric analysis of the demand for a well-defined consumer product. The econometric methods range from simple regression techniques applied in the first four chapters, to the use of logit and multinomial logit models used in chapters 5 and 6, to the use of nested logit models in chapters 6 and 7, and finally to the discrete/continuous modeling method used in chapter 8. Emphasis is on applications rather than econometric theory. In each case enough detail is provided so that the reader can understand the purpose of the analysis, the availability and suitability of data, and the econometric approach to measuring demand. A summary of each chapter follows.

*The Demand for Addressed Admail and Complementary Products in Canada*

This chapter sets out a model of the demand for addressed admail in Canada. Addressed admail is a form of third class mail principally used by businesses in their advertising of consumer products. An important business decision for the Canadian Postal Authority, as for any business, is product pricing. The issue at hand is the degree to which addressed admail is elastically demanded in Canada, that is, the degree to which substitutes are available to customers of the Canadian Postal Service. In reaching a conclusion regarding the efficacy of a price increase, it is necessary to model the demand for secondary or complementary products whose demand follows that of admail. Econometric models are therefore constructed for complementary products such as letter, publication, and parcel mail. A definition of a product multiplier is given and related to the cross-elasticity of demand. Finally, the efficacy of a price increase for addressed admail is considered after quantifying the direct and indirect effects on the demand for Canada Post's full product line. The data in this chapter are monthly time-series compiled for a fifteen-year period.

*The World Demand for Fractional Horsepower Direct-Current Motors*

This chapter focuses on the demand for an intermediate good used in the production of consumer appliances such as hair dryers, hair scissors, and children's toys. The intermediate good is a micro-motor that is also used extensively by the worldwide automobile manufacturing community to control automobile side-view mirrors, rear-mirrors, door-locks, and air-vents. Millions of these motors are produced each year and find their way into consumer products and automobiles. After reviewing the theory of derived demand, an econometric model is constructed to analyze the historical demand for motors supplied by two major motor manufacturers. At issue is the degree to which worldwide prices have been eroded by the entry of one manufacturer into production—such entry having been alleged to be illegal and in violation of the patents held by the first manufacturer. The data in this chapter is monthly data and was derived from the invoices of the companies. Exogenous factors to explain demand were constructed using estimates of the uses of these motors and were quantified from surveys of car and small appliance producers.

*The World Demand and Supply of Acetic Acid*

Acetic acid is a top-ten commodity produced from very basic raw materials including methane gas. This chemical is a commercial industry staple. For example, acetic acid is a major ingredient in the production of vinyl acetate monomer (VAM), which itself is used to make latex paint and various construction adhesives. This chapter builds a worldwide demand model for acetic acid. As classical issues of demand system identification present themselves here, it is necessary to identify the demand curve. A new approach to identification is developed in which an engineering estimate of the supply curve is derived from physical production capacities and from marginal costs of production for each existing producer of acetic acid in the world marketplace. Identification is achieved using estimated supplies as instruments for demand. Equilibrium market prices are calculated by solving for the intersection of supply and demand, and estimates of market prices are compared to actual market prices. The analysis is based on worldwide monthly production data for a ten-year period.

*The Demand for Branded and Unbranded Products—An Econometric Method for Valuing Intangible Assets*

This chapter develops an econometric method for valuing intangible assets. Specifically, a method is developed to measure the value to a license holder of owning a branded consumer product. While it is well known that brands confer values to their owners, existing methods for establishing the brand values via comparable, profit, or income methods are often fraught with imprecision or are frequently based on untested assumptions. An economic approach to brand valuation is developed in which the demand for branded goods is estimated and compared to the demand for comparable unbranded goods including both private label and generic commodities. Assuming that the brand holder were to operate in the unbranded market segment, that is without the benefit of his brand, a profit comparison is conducted comparing actual and hypothetical demand. The economic analysis relies on oligopoly pricing models and certain assumptions regarding the opportunity use of the brand holder's fixed investment. The model developed extends existing royalty-based methods that attempt to establish the relevant royalty rate and extends and corrects the valuation method known as the price-premium method. This chapter is divided into three sections. The first section reviews existing methods of intangible value measurement. The second section develops the economic theory for measurement of intangible value. The third section develops econometric models of demand for five products: coffee creamer, evaporated milk, instant breakfast, dog food, and cat food. The data in this chapter are based on Nielsen survey data taken from a large number of major market centers across the U.S. The data are both time-series and cross-sectional in character and are derived from source documents available circa 1984 for a ten-year historical period.

*The Demand for Recreational Fishing in Montana*

In this chapter I consider the demand for recreational fishing in Montana. Specifically I examine how consumers reveal their values for specific rivers by their willingness to travel to one river for fishing versus another. The modeling approach combines survey data taken at nineteen river locations with characteristics of the rivers and information obtained from mapping software on the distances traveled to the chosen rivers and distances avoided for the rivers not chosen. Using the raw survey data it is possible to build logistic demand models for location choice. Willingness-to-pay measures are constructed based upon the estimated demand models. This chapter extends existing travel cost methodology conducted using aggregate trip choice data to a travel cost model for the choices made by individuals. I estimate the multinomial logit model using the weighted exogenous sampling method. Consumer surplus calculations for discrete choice models are reviewed and extended for the WESML estimation method. At issue is an estimate of the lost consumer surplus suffered by individuals from environmental damage at a single river in Montana. The data for this chapter are taken from approximately one thousand survey respondents. The survey response micro-data are merged with river characteristic data taken from government surveys.

*The Demand for Commercial Fishing in California*

This chapter develops a demand model for commercial fishing activity in the Pacific Ocean waters near southern California. The empirical analysis is based on a model of location choice by commercial fishermen and emphasizes the "travel profit" aspects of selecting one area over another in the ocean when deciding to fish for anchovy and jack mackerel. Biological data on fish abundance from surveys of one-kilometer ocean grids is considered along with the travel cost of reaching certain locations. A nested logit model is developed to help understand why certain species are fished rather than others, and why fisherman travel to one area of the ocean versus another. At issue is the contamination of an area of the ocean due to PCB and DDT deposits and the consequences of losing these waters for commercial fishing activity. The lost producer surplus is calculated based upon the nested logit estimates. The data for this chapter come from surveys of commercial fishermen and from recorded logs of catch data by type of fish and by location. Exogenous measures of biological activity by area are taken from government sources.

### *The Demand for Cameras by Consumers–A Model of Purchase, Type Choice, and Brand Choice*

This chapter considers consumer choices for a simple consumer durable good—the photographic camera. Using household surveys combined in a panel format, I develop a nested logit model for camera choice in order to understand the decision in a given period to purchase a camera, and if purchased, the type (conventional, instant, 35mm, etc.) and brand purchased (Kodak, Polaroid, etc.). The demand for cameras is revealed by consumer choices made over time. Brand effects for camera purchase are measured by the incidence of consumer "repeat buying" of a given brand. At issue, in this analysis, are the increased sales of instant cameras that Polaroid Corporation would have made had Kodak not illegally infringed on the market for instant cameras. Based upon the nested logit models it is possible to quantify the degree of substitutability between camera brands and types. Using the historical survey data, it is possible to estimate the degree to which Polaroid would have captured Kodak's infringing sales in the but-for world in which infringement had not occurred. This chapter has three subsections. In the first the infringement issues are presented. In the second, the nested logit model is introduced with reference to the National Family Opinion survey data available to track camera purchases made over time. In the third section, the estimated models are presented and the but-for infringement sale diversions are calculated. An appendix to this chapter considers the introduction of consumer heterogeneity in nested logit models and demonstrates the empirical consequences of introducing heterogeneity in the estimated models. The data for this chapter are based upon the choices of approximately 30,000 individuals over a four-year timespan.

### *The Demand for Transportation Services in Natural Gas Markets—The Market Power of a Natural Gas Pipeline*

This chapter considers the market power of a natural gas pipeline. Market power is defined as the ability to raise prices by a sustained, significant, non-transitory amount. Currently regulation determines the maximum price that a pipeline may charge for its transportation services. In the absence of regulation, a natural gas pipeline could raise prices to a small or large degree. For reasons of economic efficiency deregulation is an appropriate course if it is found that a particular economic entity lacks market power. In order to analyze the issue of market power, this chapter develops the demand for transportation services for a specific pipeline. Using historical transaction data I determine the elasticity of demand for transportation services at specific times and locations for this pipeline. Examination of the elasticity of demand reveals whether it is in the economic interest of the pipeline to raise its prices significantly and for sustained periods. In this chapter, I propose various measures of competition. These include concentration measures, market share measures, and the costs of connection (i.e., bypass costs) for nearby competitors. An empirical analysis of the decision by the pipeline to discount its rates from the maximum tariff levels is performed using a logit analysis. The different measures of competition are compared and tested to determine the degree to which they assist in predicting the historical discounts offered by the pipeline. While previous research has attempted to link Herfindahl concentration to industry profitability, this section provides a new analysis of whether the concentration measure is a good predictor of the competitive response taken by a single producer. A discrete/continuous econometric system is estimated which links the discount decision of the producer with the demand for the producer's transportation services. Using regression techniques with selection corrections to account for the potentially endogenous discount decision, a number of demand models are estimated for each of the main products provided by the pipeline. After the demand functions are estimated, elasticity estimates are derived and the issue of market power is considered. The data for this chapter are taken from a large natural gas pipeline operating in the United States. The data are monthly aggregates of activity at approximately sixteen hundred specific metering points on the pipeline system. The company's data is augmented with time specific macro-economic data and location specific factors which were developed using a graphical information system.

# 1 THE DEMAND FOR ADDRESSED ADMAIL AND COMPLEMENTARY PRODUCTS IN CANADA

## 1.1 Introduction

The purpose of this chapter is to establish the relationships among addressed admail pricing, volume, and profitability in Canada. Addressed admail is advertising by mail that includes both short-long (small, flat mail such as business envelopes) and oversized (larger or irregularly shaped items) pieces. Canada Post Corporation (CPC) sets the pricing on its admail product. In order to determine the efficiency of a proposed price increase, this chapter addresses the elasticity of advertised admail and its resulting multiplier effects. A multiplier effect exists when product complementaries are present. In discerning the revenue and profit consequences of a proposed price increase on admail, the effects on related products such as letters, parcels, and so forth must be analyzed. For example, the demand for parcels and packages may change as a result of a change in admail if consumers purchase fewer products through the mail as a consequence of receiving fewer mail order catalogs.[1]

In the next section I discuss econometric methods, multiplier effects including cross-price and cross-quantity multipliers, and their interrelationships. In

[1]Few published articles on mail demand exist. A study of parcel-post mail demand using time-series methods appears in Nissen and Lago (1975). The demand for first-class mail is analyzed in Taylor (1993) using a quarterly time series from 1971–1986.

the following sections, I review data collection, econometric results, and simulations of the multiplier effects.

## 1.2 Econometric Methods and Multiplier Measurement

In this section I discuss the basic econometric method for measuring multiplier and elasticity effects. I compare two versions of multiplier measurement–a cross-price method and a cross-quantity method.

The demand function for CPC products has the general form

$$\log Q_t = \alpha + \beta_l \log P_t + X_t'\gamma + \varepsilon_t$$

where:

- $Q_t$ denotes sales in time period $t$,
- $P_t$ denotes selling price in period $t$,
- $X_t$ denotes a vector of factors other than selling price, and
- $\varepsilon_t$ denotes the random component in demand.

All measurements are taken in time period $t$ which in our analysis is a specific monthly period. Observations of this relationship range from $t = 1$ (April 1984) through $t = 142$ (January 1996). The factors in the vector $X_t$ include seasonal indicator variables, paper and printing costs, trend terms, and the retail sales level. All nominal dollar costs are adjusted for inflation prior to estimation. In the equation above, the relationship between $\log Q_t$ and $\log P_t$ is an "own-price" relationship since the selling price of the product affects its own volume sold. When the prices of substitute or complementary products are included in the vector $X_t$, above, the demand equation estimates the elasticities of demand with respect to these prices. These effects are known as cross-price elasticities.

### *1.2.1 Multiplier Effects*

Economic goods are complements when a price increase in one product causes the demand for that product to decline and simultaneously causes the demand for a related product to decline. For example, if a price increase in addressed admail causes a decline in addressed admail volume which in turn causes a subsequent decline in the volumes of related products such as letter mail, publications, or packages (perhaps with a lag), then addressed admail and related products are economic complements.

Addressed admail volumes will have a multiplier effect in related (or secondary) products to the extent that they are economic complements. A multiplier between commodities quantifies the change in the quantity of the secondary good resulting from the change in the quantity of the primary good. From an economic perspective, the multiplier need not in fact be measured. All that is required for economic analysis is a measurement of the cross-elasticity of demand for secondary products when changes in price of the primary product occur. In my study, I nonetheless consider two distinct (but related) approaches to measure elasticity multipliers.

### 1.2.2 *Cross-Price Elasticity Multipliers*

The demand function for a CPC secondary product (i.e., letters, publications, or packages[2]) depends both on the price of the secondary product as well as on the price of the complementary primary product (i.e., addressed admail). The demand relationship for letter mail, for example, can be written:

$$\log Q_t^{\text{letter}} = \alpha + \beta_1 \log P_t^{\text{letter}} + \beta_2 \log P_t^{\text{admail}} + X_t'\gamma + \varepsilon_t.$$

This equation determines the own-price elasticity of letter mail with respect to its own price, $P_t^{\text{letter}}$, and determines the cross-price elasticity of letter mail with respect to the price of the primary good, $P_t^{\text{admail}}$. In this case, the own and cross-price elasticities are:

$$\begin{aligned} elas\left(Q^{\text{letter}}, P^{\text{letter}}\right) &= \beta_1 \quad \text{and} \\ elas\left(Q^{\text{letter}}, P^{\text{admail}}\right) &= \beta_2 \end{aligned}$$

where $elas(Q,P)$ denotes the elasticity of $Q$ with respect to $P$.[3] As $\beta_1$ is an own-price elasticity, we expect the coefficient $\beta_1$ to be negative, and we should similarly expect the cross-price effect $\beta_2$ to be negative (since admail is a complementary product).

In other words, an increase in letter mail price causes a decrease in letter mail volume. Similarly, an increase in the admail price causes a decline in admail volumes and a consequent decline in letter mail volume. Hence the coefficient $\beta_2$ is expected to be negative, since it affects demand in a manner that is complementary to the letter mail price.[4]

In the empirical analysis presented below, I consider separate equations for letter mail, publications, and packages. Each equation includes an own-price effect for the good in question and the price of addressed admail. In double-log form, the coefficient of admail's log price determines the cross-elasticity multiplier. As shown in the simulation section below, the latter is a necessary component in determining the revenue impacts on all CPC products as the price of addressed admail is increased.

### 1.2.3 *Cross-Quantity Multiplier*

I now consider a second procedure for measuring the multiplier effect. Here the multiplier is measured directly by estimating the effect of the quantity of

[2]Packages are defined as parcels and books.

[3]I use the notation $\epsilon(Q,P) = elas(Q,P) \equiv (\partial Q/\partial P) \cdot (P/Q)$.

[4]A substitute good's price would appear in the demand equation with a positive sign. This follows since an increase in a substitute's price leads to an increase in the demand for the good in question.

the primary good on the quantity of the secondary good ultimately demanded. Thus, I expect that changes in admail's historical levels induce changes in letter mail, publication, and package quantities (perhaps with a lag).

Using letter mail again as the example, the demand relationship specified by this method would be:

$$\log Q_t^{\text{letter}} = \alpha + \beta_1 \log P_t^{\text{letter}} + \beta_2 \log Q_t^{\text{admail}} + X_t'\gamma + \varepsilon_t.$$

This equation determines letter mail's own-price elasticity with respect to its own price, $P_t^{\text{letter}}$, and simultaneously determines letter mail's cross-quantity elasticity with respect to the admail quantity, $Q_t^{\text{admail}}$. In this case:

$$elas\left(Q^{\text{letter}}, Q^{\text{admail}}\right) = \beta_2$$

is the letter mail's cross-quantity elasticity with respect to a change in addressed admail quantity. With the exception that this relationship is quantified as a percentage change in letter mail with respect to a percentage change in admail (i.e., elasticity), this method directly measures the quantity multiplier. Indeed, the definition of the pure quantity multiplier is $\partial Q^{\text{letter}} / \partial Q^{\text{admail}}$.

Using this definition of the elasticity we obtain:

$$\frac{\partial Q^{\text{letter}}}{\partial Q^{\text{admail}}} = \beta_2 \cdot \left[\frac{Q^{\text{letter}}}{Q^{\text{admail}}}\right]$$

which shows that the cross-quantity elasticity can be reexpressed as a pure quantity multiplier. The latter value may be useful if one is interested in the quantity of letter mail that is ultimately induced by a change in the quantity of addressed admail. Adjusted for price differences in the product lines, I provide such estimates below.

### *1.2.4 The Relationship Between Cross-Price and Cross-Quantity Multipliers*

The cross-price and cross-quantity multipliers are related in a very straightforward manner. The cross-price elasticity multiplier is simply the cross-quantity multiplier multiplied by the admail demand's own-price elasticity. This can be seen using the definitions:

$$\frac{\partial \log Q^{\text{letter}}}{\partial \log Q^{\text{admail}}} \cdot \frac{\partial \log Q^{\text{admail}}}{\partial \log P^{\text{admail}}} = \frac{\partial \log Q^{\text{letter}}}{\partial \log P^{\text{admail}}}.$$

Hence, it follows that:

$$\begin{aligned} & elas\left(Q^{\text{letter}}, P^{\text{admail}}\right) \\ & = elas\left(Q^{\text{letter}}, Q^{\text{admail}}\right) \cdot elas\left(Q^{\text{admail}}, P^{\text{admail}}\right). \end{aligned}$$

As I discuss further below, I compute the cross-price multiplier using estimates of the cross-quantity multiplier and the relationship just derived.

## 1.3 Data

The three primary sources of data for the econometric models were Canada Post, Statistics Canada, and Nielsen.

### *1.3.1 Canada Post Data*

The basic data for the time-series analyses were provided by Canada Post. This data contain volumes and revenues for short-long and oversized admail, letter mail and publications. The data range over approximately twelve years from 1984 to 1996.

### *1.3.2 Nielsen Data*

Nielsen provided monthly information on five media types (daily papers, magazines, out-of-home advertising, radio advertising, and television advertising). The data were provided as Canada country totals. Data were available only from 1986 forward. Using Nielsen data in the regression analysis therefore curtails available observations by approximately twenty-two months.[5]

### *1.3.3 Statistics Canada Data*

Statistics Canada provided information on an annual, quarterly, and monthly basis for such factors as consumer price indices, gross domestic product, printing, paper, and publishing price indices, newsprint production, telephone service and telephone operating revenue, commodity prices, price indices for paper and paper stock, population, wood pulp production, retail sales by source, sales in the telecommunications and print-publishing service, time lost in work stoppages, and other factors.

## 1.4 Econometric Models and Results

This section presents the estimated econometric models for addressed admail, letter mail, publications, and packages. The models for addressed admail represent primary demand, while the models for related products represent secondary demand. The latter models are necessary to measure and quantify multiplier effects.

### *1.4.1 Addressed Admail*

The basic addressed admail model has the form:

[5] While I had attempted to gather price information from Nielsen, all that was ultimately available was expenditure information. Therefore, one does not know with certainty whether historical increases in real advertising expenditures represent a larger quantity and lower price of an elastically-demanded commodity or a higher price and lower quantity of an inelastically-demanded commodity.

$$\begin{aligned}\log(\text{quantity}) = \alpha \quad & + \delta_1 s1 + \delta_2 s2 + \ldots + \delta_{11} s11 \\ & + \gamma_1 \ \log(\text{pi\_mnppr/cpi}) \\ & + \gamma_2 \ \log(\text{price/cpi}) \\ & + \gamma_3 \ \log(\text{ret\_m\_al/cpi}) \\ & + \gamma_4 \ \log(\text{trend}) + \varepsilon.\end{aligned}$$

The demand equation specifies a double-log relationship. The dependent variable is the natural logarithm of admail quantity purchased in a given month, log(quantity). The independent variables consist of a constant term, a set of eleven seasonal indicators $s_1, s_2, \ldots s_{11}$, the logarithm of the inflation adjusted price of paper and printing, log(pi_mnppr/cpi), the logarithm of the inflation adjusted level of retail sales, log(ret_m_al/cpi), and the logarithm of a time trend variable, log(trend). The regression also includes an inflation adjusted own-price variable, log(price/cpi).

The model employs an intercept, time trend, and eleven seasonal indicator effects. One seasonal indicator is excluded as a normalization. These eleven seasonal indicators are defined so that their joint effects sum to zero over a full year. The variable $s_1$ has the value one in January and minus one in December, $s_2$ has the value one in February and minus one in December and so on. Hence:

$$\sum_{j=1}^{11} \delta_j s_j = \sum_{j=1}^{11} \delta_j - (\delta_1 + \delta_2 + \cdots + \delta_{11}) = 0.$$

The January seasonal effect is measured with the coefficient $\delta_1$, the February seasonal effect is measured with the coefficient $\delta_2$, and so forth. The December seasonal effect is implicitly $-(\delta_1 + \delta_2 + \ldots + \delta_{11})$. Since the model specifies the dependent variable in logarithms, the seasonal indicators provide a multiplicative scaling of demand. The average scaling over a year is one. Below, I graph the multiplicative seasonal effects for the total admail model.

The trend term is defined as a continuous combination of year and month with trend = year + [(month-1)/12]. Hence, January 1984 has a trend value 84.0 while December 1984 has trend value 84.92. The coefficient of the log(trend) term provides a direct estimate of the percentage change in sales with respect to time. This follows since: $d\log(\text{quantity})/d\,\text{trend} = \gamma_4/\text{trend}$. Therefore, 100 $\Delta Q/Q \doteq \gamma_4$ when $d$trend is one year and trend is approximately 100. Table 1.1 presents the estimated models for all addressed admail. Variable definitions are summarized in a variable glossary in table 1.2.

The model is relatively precisely estimated. Approximately 90 percent of the variation in the dependent variable is explained by the regressors. This precision is revealed in figure 1.1, which shows the actual and predicted volumes for total addressed admail.

As can be seen in figure 1.1, the demand for addressed admail is strongly seasonal. The individual $t$-statistics for seasonality coefficients in table 1.1 show that this seasonality is well estimated by the regression. Figure 1.2 shows the multiplicative seasonal effect.

**Figure 1.1: Predicted versus Actual Volumes for Admail**

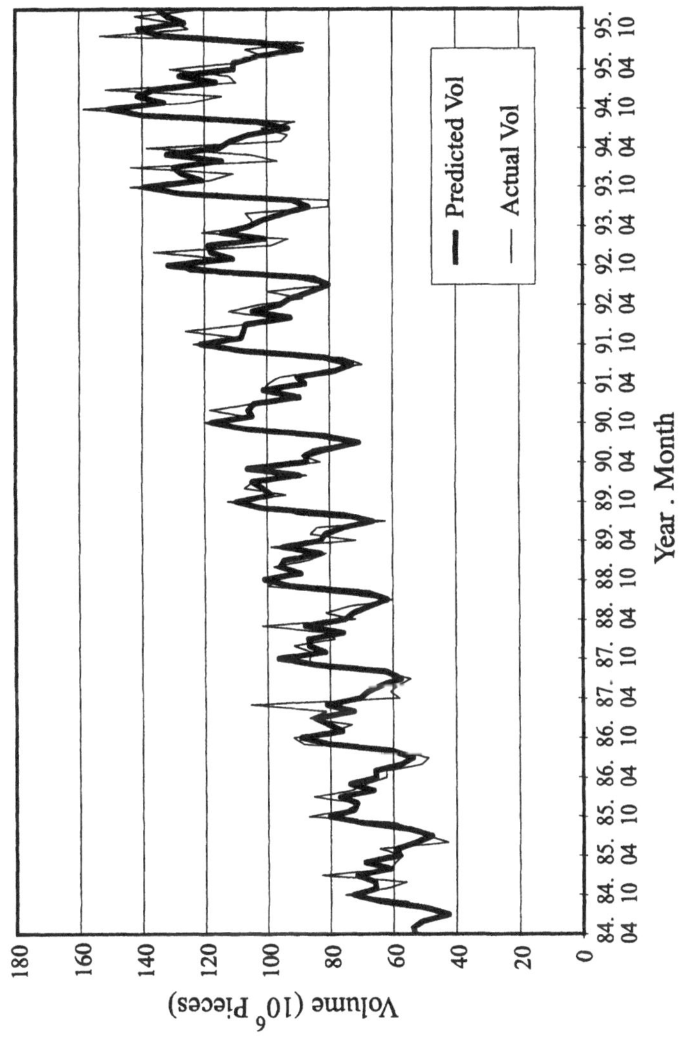

**Figure 1.2: Admail Seasonality**

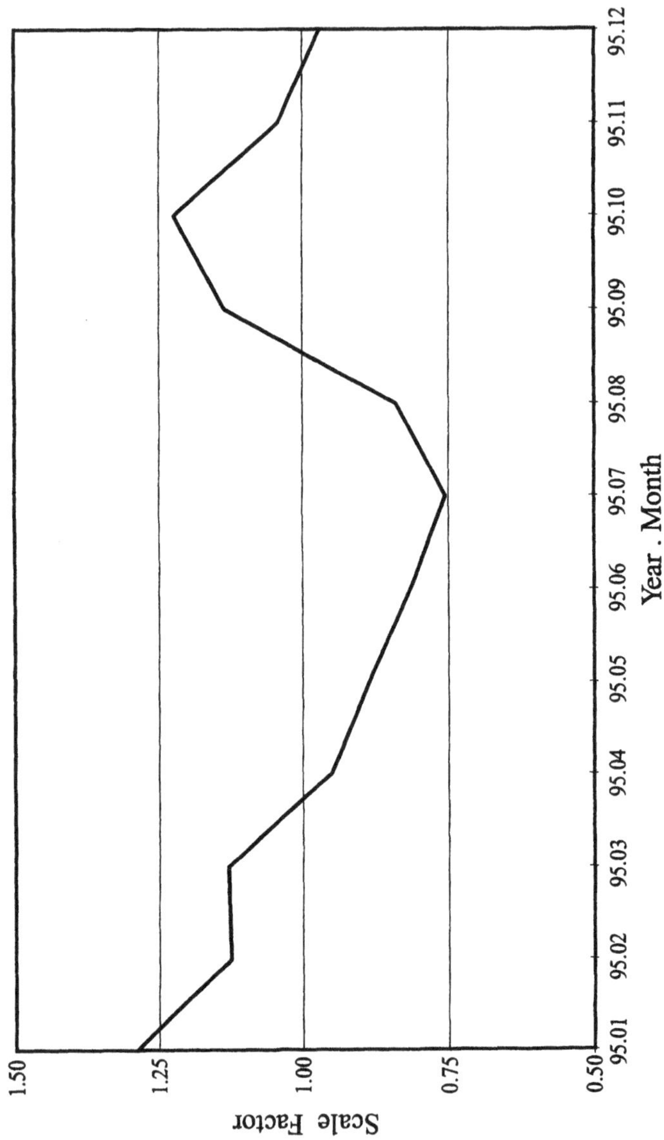

**Table 1.1.** Addressed Admail

| Dep Variable: | Admail All (log(all_ad_v)) |
|---|---|
| (1) | −20.13294<br>(−8.23) |
| s1 | 0.25315<br>(5.98) |
| s2 | 0.11759<br>(2.56) |
| s3 | 0.12204<br>(4.09) |
| s4 | −0.050945<br>(−1.82) |
| s5 | −0.12055<br>(−3.90) |
| s6 | −0.2045<br>(−6.75) |
| s7 | −0.28132<br>(−9.99) |
| s8 | −0.17471<br>(−6.21) |
| s9 | 0.12654<br>(4.49) |
| s10 | 0.20114<br>(7.13) |
| s11 | 0.042117<br>(1.41) |
| (log(pi_mnppr/cpi)) | −0.32069<br>(−3.27) |
| (log(all_ad_p/cpi)) | −0.42267<br>(−1.87) |
| (log(ret_m_al/cpi)) | 0.70182<br>(4.05) |
| (log(trend)) | 5.6549<br>(20.69) |
| Observations | 142 |
| Corrected R-squared | 0.87775 |
| Mean of Dep Variable | 11.38478 |

For comparison purposes, December has an estimated multiplicative effect approximately equal to one. Therefore, figure 1.2 shows that October is one peak in the year with approximately 20 percent more volume than December. January is another peak with 30 percent more volume than December. Con-

**Table 1.2.** Variable Glossary

| | |
|---|---|
| all_ad_v | Admail total volume |
| all_ad_p | Admail total price |
| all_lt_v | All letter volume |
| all_lt_p | All letter price |
| all_pb_v | All publication volume |
| all_pb_p | All publication price |
| all_pk_v | All package volume |
| all_pk_p | All package price |
| pi_mnppr | Industrial production index newsprint and paper stock |
| ret_m_al | Retail sales–all stores |
| cpi | Consumer price index 1986 = 100 |
| n_tv | Television advertising expenditure (Nielsen) |
| n_mag | Magazine advertising expenditure (Nielsen) |
| Volume in thousands of pieces; prices are in Canadian dollars per piece. | |

versely, July is a trough with only approximately 80 percent of December's volume.

The trend effect demonstrates a steady increase in demand over the time period (April 1984–January 1996). An historical growth of approximately 4 percent in addressed admail is indicated which is not accounted for by other factors. Typically, trend variables in econometric models serve as proxies for omitted factors. For example, in Canada trend might be indistinguishable from the national population level, because the national population rises in the same manner as trend.

The factor for paper and printing costs, pi_mnppr, reveals steady increases in the nominal price level until the rapid increase and subsequent fall in cost in 1995. The estimated price elasticity for this factor reveals a value of $-0.32$ ($t$-statistic $-3.3$) indicating that an increase in the real cost of paper and printing drives down the demand for addressed admail, and that customers are partially captive to this cost due to the measured inelasticity.

Retail sales have a positive and statistically significant effect on admail demand. A percentage increase in retail sales leads to a 0.70 percentage increase in the demand for addressed admail.

Finally, the own-price effect has a measured elasticity of $-0.42$ ($t$-statistic $-1.87$) showing that an increase in the cost per piece of addressed admail causes addressed admail volumes to decline. As the measured effect is less than one in absolute value, the model indicates that the demand for admail is generally inelastic. This is an expected result given that addressed admail has few close substitutes.

### 1.4.2 Discussion

The inelasticity estimated by the model indicates that an increase in the price of CPC addressed admail products will result in lower volume, but higher overall revenues. Profitability will also increase as costs decline with the lower total volumes. Of course, a complete analysis requires that multiplier effects be considered as well. I will return to the multiplier topic below.

The specification I used for the demand for addressed admail does not include all factors that possibly explain admail. However, it arguably includes the majority, if not all, of the important ones. In some cases, factors were examined that were not statistically significant determinants of addressed admail volumes (such as work stoppages). In other cases, certain factors were not distinguishable from trend effects. In still other cases, the factors employed acted similarly to included variables in that independent effects for the additional variables could not be separately measured (for example, gross domestic product was significant in the model only if retail sales were excluded).

### 1.4.3 Nielsen Factors

In table 1.3, I consider the demand equation for total addressed admail in which I include additional control variables taken from the Nielsen data. The two factors I add to the basic addressed admail demand model are real expenditures on television and magazine advertising. Available degrees of freedom decline by twenty-two (almost two full years) due to the missing Nielsen data in the 1984–1985 period. The results presented in table 1.2 show that television advertising is a substitute, to a degree, for addressed admail and that magazine advertising appears to be complementary. The measured own-price elasticity for addressed admail volumes reveals an elasticity of $-0.39$ ($t$-stat $= -1.68$). This estimate is not dissimilar to that obtained earlier and, with the lost degrees of freedom, the model is probably no more useful with the Nielsen data than it is without it.

### 1.4.4 Robustness of Price Elasticities Measure

The price variable all_ad_p shows that addressed admail experienced a 58.6 percent increase in the nearly twelve-year period represented in the time-series data. On average, the nominal price for addressed admail rose 4.95 percent per annum. However, during this period, addressed admail's real cost rose less than one-tenth of one percent per annum. Thus, in real terms, addressed admail costs have been essentially flat. The data period has, nevertheless, seen some relatively large price increases and decreases. For example, prices rose as much as 24 percent in one annual period and declined as much as 8 percent in another. The maximum monthly change in nominal price was just over 16 percent, while the largest single monthly decline was just under 8 percent. Of course, the regression modeling utilizes the month-to-month variations in real prices in order to reliably estimate the price effect in the demand equation.

**Table 1.3.** Addressed Admail with Nielsen

| Dep Variable: | Admail All (log(all_ad_v)) |
|---|---|
| (1) | −16.06652 (−6.25) |
| s1 | 0.19285 (3.76) |
| s2 | 0.013246 (0.24) |
| s3 | 0.094777 (3.12) |
| s4 | −0.079099 (−2.62) |
| s5 | −0.12137 (−3.34) |
| s6 | −0.14938 (−4.75) |
| s7 | −0.20095 (−5.32) |
| s8 | −0.072293 (−1.71) |
| s9 | 0.098428 (3.04) |
| s10 | 0.13873 (3.84) |
| s11 | −0.00857 (−0.23) |
| (log(pi_mnppr/cpi)) | −0.23855 (−2.28) |
| (log(all_ad_p/cpi)) | −0.38955 (−1.68) |
| (log(ret_m_al/cpi)) | 0.13901 (0.64) |
| (log(trend)) | 5.24572 (12.62) |
| (log(n_tv/cpi)) | −0.059016 (−0.76) |
| (log(n_mag/cpi)) | 0.2142 (3.73) |
| Observations | 120 |
| Corrected R-squared | 0.8536 |
| Mean of Dep Variable | 11.45181 |

In order to insure that the price elasticity results were robust across the time period and over all price ranges, I performed two statistical tests. The tests examined whether the price elasticity of demand varied either over time or over the historical price range. In neither test were there pronounced or statistically significant differences. Therefore, I conclude that the estimated specification is valid over the entire period and all price changes (large and small or positive and negative).

At price levels which are much larger than those experienced historically, the prediction confidence interval will be larger. In other words, the forecasted demand for addressed admail will be known with less confidence at price levels that differ markedly from historical levels.

### *1.4.5 Letter Demand, Publication Demand, and Package Demand*

For each of the three secondary products, I estimate three basic models. In the first model, for each secondary product, I measure the own-price effect for the product. In the second model, I include a cross-price variable for addressed admail in order to estimate cross-price effects. In the third model, I include the volume of addressed admail to directly measure the cross-quantity multiplier. The three variations are presented together in tables organized by type of secondary product.

These models were estimated in auto-regressive form to measure the cross-elasticity and multiplier effects. The auto-regressive form includes the lagged dependent variables as an explanatory variable in the demand equation. This is known as the Koyck lag adjustment or the partial adjustment form. The partial adjustment specifies that demand will change from period to period by a fraction of the difference between the desired demand level and the actual demand level. This is, therefore, a dynamic specification of demand. The models estimated here do not include explanatory factors beyond own-price, retail sales, and trend effects.

The basic auto-regressive specification employs a six-period lag for the dependent variable, and a three period lag for price effects. The lag structure was chosen by investigating alternative dynamic models and by specification testing. The resulting models are relatively stable and exhibit dynamics that are relatively short-lived.

The basic model in auto-regressive form may be written:

$$\log(Q_t) = \lambda \log(Q_{t-6}) + X_t\gamma + \varepsilon_t$$

where $Q_t$ denotes a secondary quantity; $Q_{t-6}$ denotes the six-period lagged value of $Q_t$, and $X_t$ denotes a vector of other explanatory variables.

In steady state and provided a stability condition holds such that $|\lambda| < 1$, the model becomes:

$$(1 - \lambda) \log Q_t = X_t\gamma + \varepsilon_t$$

so that the long-run coefficients are $\gamma/(1 - \lambda)$, while the short-run coefficients are simply $\gamma$.

Table 1.4 presents the letter mail demand models. The first column shows that the own-price inelasticity is −0.32 in the short run and −0.32/(1 − .46) = −0.59 in the long run. Both own-elasticities are estimated in the inelastic range. The trend effect has a relatively small positive coefficient, while the coefficient on the retail sales variable is statistically significantly different from zero and positive. In table 1.4 the specification and results are similar with the exception of the factor included to measure addressed admail's cross-price elasticity. The estimated coefficient is positive (although not statistically different from zero.) This is troubling as economic theory dictates a negative coefficient in order for the multiplier to be present. In column 3, I determine a multiplier measurement based upon the six-period lag value of addressed admail. The cross-quantity elasticity is 0.12 in the short run and statistically significant at the 90 percent level. The long-run or steady state effect is 0.12/(1 − .32) = 0.18. The $R^2$ for these equations are consistently around 70 percent; however, the autoregressive structure constrains the $R^2$ measurement and interpretation.

In table 1.5, I present the estimated secondary demand models for publications. The own-price elasticity for publications is inelastic in the short run at −0.25 (*t*-stat = −2.31) and also inelastic in the long-run with elasticity −0.25/(1 − 0.49) = −0.49. The model in column 2 of table 1.5 shows a positive elasticity on addressed admail's cross-price. Again, theory suggests that this coefficient must be negative for a multiplier to be present. Proceeding to the volume multiplier estimate in column 3, we see that the coefficient on lagged admail volume has an estimated short-run value of 0.054 and a steady state value of 0.054/(1 − .46) = 0.10. The measured elasticity is not in fact statistically different from zero in this case. The $R^2$ values in the publication regression models are approximately 73 percent.

In table 1.6, I present the estimated secondary demand models for packages. The own-price elasticity is estimated to be positive, which does not follow our theoretical expectations. The trend in the estimated regression has a negative coefficient. The decline in the real price of packages could have led to an estimated positive correlation between price and volume if the included explanatory variables were insufficient to capture the trend effects. While the own-price is positive and statistically significant, the cross-price effect is negative with elasticity −0.24 in the short run and −0.24/(1−0.197) = −0.20 in the long run. The volume multiplier is determined in column 3. Here, the lagged volume of addressed admail has an estimated value 0.078 in the short run and 0.078/(1 − 0.168) = 0.09 in the long run. As was the case for publications, the estimated quantity multiplier has a relatively large 95 percent confidence interval, indicating that the quantity multiplier was not well determined within these regressions.

### 1.4.6 *Summary of Secondary Demand Models*

The secondary demand models estimated in auto-regressive form have mixed success in their ability to determine multiplier effects. The cross-price specifications either produced coefficients of the wrong sign or, in the case of packages,

**Table 1.4. Letter Demand Models**

| Dep Variable: | Letter (log(all_lt_v)) | With Admail Cross Price (log(all_lt_v)) | With Lagged Admail Volume (log(all_lt_v)) |
|---|---|---|---|
| (1) | 2.75541<br>(1.58) | 3.95205<br>(1.99) | 5.43019<br>(2.35) |
| s1 | 0.1221<br>(4.96) | 0.1224<br>(4.99) | 0.14983<br>(5.14) |
| s2 | 0.11209<br>(3.90) | 0.11388<br>(3.97) | 0.11707<br>(4.09) |
| s3 | 0.068965<br>(3.49) | 0.067471<br>(3.42) | 0.04425<br>(1.83) |
| s4 | 0.015314<br>(0.84) | 0.012161<br>(0.66) | −0.008757<br>(−0.39) |
| s5 | −0.014523<br>(−0.73) | −0.016009<br>(−0.80) | −0.028286<br>(−1.33) |
| s6 | −0.14562<br>(−6.27) | −0.14217<br>(−6.10) | −0.13731<br>(−5.84) |
| s7 | −0.074607<br>(−3.89) | −0.073606<br>(−3.84) | −0.079895<br>(−4.15) |
| s8 | −0.13081<br>(−7.32) | −0.12981<br>(−7.28) | −0.12366<br>(−6.80) |
| s9 | −0.078221<br>(−4.40) | −0.076697<br>(−4.31) | −0.087047<br>(−4.74) |
| s10 | 0.010251<br>(0.60) | 0.009359<br>(0.55) | 0.02005<br>(1.12) |
| s11 | 0.03866<br>(−2.23) | −0.039678<br>(−2.29) | −0.031201<br>(−1.77) |
| (log(all_lt_v[−6])) | 0.45766<br>(5.29) | 0.4453<br>(5.12) | 0.32625<br>(2.85) |
| (log(all_lt_p[−3] /cpi[−3])) | −0.32451<br>(−1.16) | −0.42789<br>(−1.46) | −0.38818<br>(−1.38) |
| (log(ret_m_al/cpi)) | 0.20764<br>(2.00) | 0.20602<br>(1.98) | 0.20927<br>(2.03) |
| (log(trend)) | 0.3172<br>(1.59) | 0.18528<br>(0.82) | −0.2907<br>(−0.72) |
| (log(all_ad_p[−3] /cpi[−3])) | —<br>— | 0.1619<br>(1.25) | —<br>— |
| (log(all_ad_v[−6])) | —<br>— | —<br>— | 0.12266<br>(1.74) |
| Observations | 136 | 136 | 136 |
| Corrected R-squared | 0.65108 | 0.65272 | 0.65688 |
| Mean of Dep Variable | 12.90844 | 12.90844 | 12.90844 |

**Table 1.5.** Publications Demand Model

| Dep Variable: | Publications (log(all_pb_v)) | With Admail Cross Price (log(all_pb_v)) | With Lagged Admail Volume (log(all_pb_v)) |
|---|---|---|---|
| (1) | 3.78764 | 6.95361 | 5.58173 |
| | (1.18) | (2.04) | (1.33) |
| s1 | 0.045342 | 0.033829 | 0.059545 |
| | (1.36) | (1.02) | (1.51) |
| s2 | 0.070033 | 0.060783 | 0.076168 |
| | (1.84) | (1.62) | (1.94) |
| s3 | 0.065354 | 0.060369 | 0.060152 |
| | (2.70) | (2.54) | (2.37) |
| s4 | −0.002971 | −0.007631 | −0.012442 |
| | (−0.12) | (−0.32) | (−0.45) |
| s5 | −0.02744 | −0.022913 | −0.030113 |
| | (−1.10) | (−0.93) | (−1.19) |
| s6 | −0.015377 | −0.009329 | −0.022562 |
| | (−0.63) | (−0.39) | (−0.85) |
| s7 | −0.054386 | −0.054717 | −0.062081 |
| | (−2.32) | (−2.38) | (−2.38) |
| s8 | −0.090669 | −0.08673 | −0.090477 |
| | (−3.63) | (−3.53) | (−3.61) |
| s9 | −0.029106 | −0.026723 | −0.032353 |
| | (−1.25) | (−1.17) | (−1.36) |
| s10 | 0.050721 | 0.050412 | 0.054685 |
| | (2.29) | (2.32) | (2.38) |
| s11 | 0.036273 | 0.037393 | 0.04053 |
| | (1.61) | (1.70) | (1.73) |
| (log(all_pb_v[−6])) | 0.49336 | 0.46716 | 0.46523 |
| | (6.45) | (6.17) | (5.33) |
| (log(all_pb_p[−3] /cpi[−3])) | −0.25646 | −0.30466 | −0.24427 |
| | (−2.32) | (−2.76) | (−2.17) |
| (log(ret_m_al/cpi)) | 0.09993 | 0.022834 | 0.1063 |
| | (0.71) | (0.16) | (0.75) |
| (log(trend)) | −0.13315 | −0.2229 | −0.59114 |
| | (−0.22) | (−0.38) | (−0.65) |
| (log(all_ad_p[−3] /cpi[−3])) | — | 0.3886 | — |
| | — | (2.42) | — |
| (log(all_ad_v[−6])) | — | — | 0.054314 |
| | — | — | (0.67) |
| Observations | 136 | 136 | 136 |
| Corrected R-squared | 0.69031 | 0.70237 | 0.6889 |
| Mean of Dep Variable | 10.62816 | 10.62816 | 10.62816 |

**Table 1.6.** Packages Demand Model

| Dep Variable: | Packages (log(all_pk_v)) | With Admail Cross Price (log(all_pk_v)) | With Lagged Admail Volume (log(all_pk_v)) |
|---|---|---|---|
| (1) | 10.49094<br>(5.45) | 8.02963<br>(3.06) | 12.31064<br>(4.48) |
| s1 | 0.051662<br>(1.33) | 0.053878<br>(1.39) | 0.069718<br>(1.61) |
| s2 | 0.078373<br>(1.75) | 0.077883<br>(1.74) | 0.086459<br>(1.89) |
| s3 | 0.099479<br>(3.73) | 0.10073<br>(3.79) | 0.089744<br>(3.13) |
| s4 | 0.006467<br>(0.25) | 0.010003<br>(0.39) | −0.009545<br>(−0.31) |
| s5 | −0.064411<br>(−2.23) | −0.065546<br>(−2.28) | −0.06774<br>(−2.32) |
| s6 | −0.14548<br>(−4.55) | −0.14882<br>(−4.66) | −0.14721<br>(−4.59) |
| s7 | −0.12322<br>(−4.81) | −0.12159<br>(−4.76) | −0.134<br>(−4.76) |
| s8 | −0.15771<br>(−6.23) | −0.15761<br>(−6.25) | −0.15544<br>(−6.10) |
| s9 | −0.052409<br>(−2.01) | −0.052938<br>(−2.04) | −0.057057<br>(−2.15) |
| s10 | 0.034905<br>(1.44) | 0.036158<br>(1.50) | 0.03919<br>(1.59) |
| s11 | 0.086987<br>(3.46) | 0.087388<br>(3.49) | 0.091484<br>(3.57) |
| (log(all_pk_v[−6])) | 0.19909<br>(2.25) | 0.1972<br>(2.24) | 0.16836<br>(1.78) |
| (log(all_pk_p[−3] /cpi[−3])) | 0.035811<br>(0.56) | 0.034071<br>(0.54) | 0.042821<br>(0.67) |
| (log(ret_m_al/cpi)) | 0.22544<br>(1.35) | 0.25319<br>(1.51) | 0.23041<br>(1.38) |
| (log(trend)) | −0.8519<br>(−2.32) | −0.66978<br>(−1.72) | −1.38216<br>(−2.03) |
| (log(all_ad_p[−3] /cpi[−3])) | —<br>— | −0.24279<br>(−1.38) | —<br>— |
| (log(all_ad_v[−6])) | —<br>— | —<br>— | 0.075895<br>(0.93) |
| Observations | 136 | 136 | 136 |
| Corrected R-squared | 0.57413 | 0.57731 | 0.57364 |
| Mean of Dep Variable | 9.50725 | 9.50725 | 9.50725 |

a coefficient that is inconsistent with the quantity multiplier estimated for the same model. From these results, one could conclude that the multiplier is small or statistically poorly determined; or that the econometric method fails due to colinearity in the movement of historical prices; or that the method fails due to some other misspecification. The quantity multiplier, on the other hand, is more precisely determined and consistently positive. Based on these results and attempts to determine multipliers using other specifications, I rely upon the quantity multipliers for the simulations to follow. Table 1.7 summarizes the estimated elasticities in the various models.

**Table 1.7.** Summary of Elasticity Results

| | Short-Run | Long-Run |
|---|---|---|
| **Addressed Admail:** | | |
| Own-price | −0.423 | −0.423 |
| **Letter Mail:** | | |
| Own-price | −0.324 | −0.598 |
| Cross-price | 0.162 | 0.292 |
| Quantity Multiplier | 0.123 | 0.182 |
| **Publications:** | | |
| Own-price | −0.256 | −0.505 |
| Cross-price | 0.387 | 0.726 |
| Quantity Multiplier | 0.054 | 0.101 |
| **Packages:** | | |
| Own-price | 0.036 | 0.045 |
| Cross-price | −0.243 | −0.303 |
| Quantity Multiplier | 0.076 | 0.091 |

### *1.4.7 Selecting Multipliers for Simulations*

Based on the discussion above, I use the quantity multiplier estimates for the simulations. I also use the steady-state values for the calculations done in the simulation section. A full simulation model would require that the dynamics be evaluated period by period. However, as the lagged effects are relatively short-lived, the long-run quantity multiplier estimates should be adequate for the simulations.

To estimate the elasticity of secondary demand with respect to primary price in the quantity multiplier method, I multiply the own-price elasticity by the estimated quantity-multiplier elasticity. The final elasticities to be used in the simulations are summarized in table 1.8.

**Table 1.8.** Simulation Elasticities

| | | |
|---|---|---|
| **Addressed Admail:** | | |
| elas($Q^A$, $P^A$) | = | −0.423 |
| **Letter Mail:** | | |
| elas($Q^L$, $P^A$) | = | −0.077 |
| **Publications:** | | |
| elas($Q^{Pub}$, $P^A$) | = | −0.043 |
| **Packages:** | | |
| elas($Q^{Pack}$, $P^A$) | = | −0.038 |
| $Q^A$ = Addressed admail quantity | | |
| $Q^L$ = Letter mail quantity | | |
| $Q^{Pub}$ = Publication quantity | | |
| $Q^{Pack}$ = Package quantity | | |
| $P^A$ = Price of addressed admail | | |

### *1.4.8 Interpreting Quantity Multipliers*

The quantity-multiplier elasticities can easily be converted to conventional quantity multipliers. By definition:

$$dQ^L/dQ^A = (Q^L/Q^A) \cdot elas(Q^L, Q^A).$$

The change in a secondary quantity for a unit change in admail volume is, therefore, a quantity-multiplier elasticity multiplied by the ratio of the secondary product's volume to addressed admail volume. The volumes for fiscal year 1994–1995 are presented in table 1.9.

Performing these calculations, I find:

$$dQ^L/dQ^A = [(4,564,050 \ / \ 1,425,010) \cdot 0.182] = 0.583;$$

$$dQ^{Pub}/dQ^A = [(429,287 \ / \ 1,425,010) \cdot 0.101] = 0.030;$$

$$dQ^{Pack}/dQ^A = [(135,298 \ / \ 1,425,010) \cdot 0.091] = 0.009.$$

To combine these quantity changes, I weight by each piece's average revenue per piece (ARP) and sum the ARP weighted volumes. I then divide that total

**Table 1.9.** Volumes (000)

| Fiscal Year 1994–1995 | Volume |
|---|---|
| Addressed Admail | 1,425,010 |
| Letter Mail | 4,564,050 |
| Publications | 429,287 |
| Packages | 135,298 |
| Source: CPC Annual Report and CPC | |

by the ARP for addressed admail to convert to admail quantity equivalents. The ARPs, revenues, and revenue share for admail and secondary products are presented in table 1.10.

**Table 1.10.** Volumes and ARP (000)

| **Fiscal Year 1994–1995** | **Volume** | **ARP** | **Revenue** | **Rev. Share** |
|---|---|---|---|---|
| Addressed Admail | 1,425,010 | 0.253 | 361,000 | 0.118 |
| Letter Mail | 4,564,050 | 0.465 | 2,122,000 | 0.691 |
| Publications | 429,287 | 0.225 | 97,000 | 0.031 |
| Packages | 135,298 | 3.633 | 492,000 | 0.160 |
| Source: CPC Annual Report and CPC | | | | |

Therefore, the combined multiplier for all secondary demand is:

$$\frac{P_L}{P_A}\frac{Q^L}{Q^A}\varepsilon(Q^L,Q^A) \quad + \frac{P^{Pub}}{P^A}\frac{Q^{Pub}}{Q^A}\varepsilon(Q^{Pub},Q^A)$$

$$+ \frac{P^{Pack}}{P^A}\frac{Q^{Pack}}{Q^A}\varepsilon(Q^{Pack},Q^A).$$

The price-adjusted components of the total multipliers are:

$$\frac{P^L}{P^A}\frac{Q^L}{Q^A}\varepsilon(Q^L,Q^A) = [(0.465 \;/\; 0.253)\cdot 0.583] = 1.071;$$

$$\frac{P^{Pub}}{P^A}\frac{Q^{Pub}}{Q^A}\varepsilon(Q^{Pub},Q^A) = [(0.225\ /\ 0.253)\cdot 0.030] = 0.027;$$

$$\frac{P^{Pack}}{P^A}\frac{Q^{Pack}}{Q^A}\varepsilon(\alpha^{Pack},Q^A)\ [(3.633\ /\ 0.253)\cdot 0.009] = 0.129.$$

The overall multiplier (price adjusted) is therefore (1.071 + 0.027 + 0.129) = 1.23.

An additional addressed admail piece creates (with some lag) 0.583 pieces of letter mail, 0.030 publications, and 0.009 packages. However, each secondary product is not equally valuable to CPC. Adjusting for the price differentials and converting back to addressed admail units, I determined that one piece of addressed admail results in the dollar equivalent of 1.2 pieces of addressed admail in the future. Therefore, I conclude that the addressed admail multiplier is approximately 1.2.

If the price elasticity of admail demand were unit elastic (so that a price increase or decrease would have no effect on admail revenues), then a 1 percent increase in the price of admail would lead to a 1.2 percent decrease in the revenues from secondary products expressed relative to addressed admail's revenue base. At the actual own-price elasticity for admail of −0.42, revenue gains from increasing the price of admail will be almost completely offset by secondary multiplier revenue losses. The revenue elasticity is estimated to be approximately 0.007 percent of combined revenues.

## 1.5 Simulations

In this section, I derive the formulas which relate CPC's revenue, costs, and profit levels to the price level set by CPC for addressed admail. I express these results in terms of elasticities, that is, the percentage change in revenue, costs, or profit with respect to a percentage change in the price of addressed admail. In the following section, I apply the elasticity results and incremental cost estimates to determine the combined primary elasticity and secondary multiplier effects.

### *1.5.1 Theory*

Assume that revenue is derived from the primary good (addressed admail) with demand $Q_A(P_A)$ and from $M$ secondary sources denoted $j = 1, 2, \ldots, M$ whose demands $Q_j$ depend on their own price and the primary good's price. The demand function for secondary good $j$ is denoted $Q_j(P_A, P_j)$, and receives ARP at the exogenous price level $P_j$. In this notation, $j$ indexes the products: letter mail, publications, and packages. Total revenue for the primary and secondary commodities is therefore:

$$R = Q_A(P_A)\cdot P_A + \sum_{j=1}^{M} Q_j(P_A, P_j)\cdot P_j.$$

Differentiating both sides of this equation with respect to addressed admail's price, we obtain:

$$\begin{aligned}\frac{\partial R}{\partial P_A} &= Q_A + P_A Q_A'(P_A) + \sum_j P_j \frac{\partial Q_j}{\partial P_A} \\ &= Q_A + Q_A \frac{P_A}{Q_A}\frac{\partial Q_A}{\partial P_A} + \sum_j P_j Q_j \frac{1}{Q_j}\frac{\partial Q_j}{\partial P_A} \\ &= Q_A(1+\varepsilon(Q_A, P_A)) + \sum_j \frac{P_j Q_j}{P_A}\varepsilon(Q_j, P_A).\end{aligned}$$

Hence,

$$\frac{P_A}{R}\frac{\partial R}{\partial P_A} = \frac{P_A Q_A}{R}(1+\varepsilon(Q_A, P_A)) + \sum_j \frac{P_j Q_j}{R}\varepsilon(Q_j, P_A)$$

which implies

$$\varepsilon(R, P_A) = S_A(1+\varepsilon(Q_A, P_A)) + \sum_j S_j \varepsilon(Q_j, P_A), \qquad (1)$$

where:

| | | |
|---|---|---|
| $\varepsilon(R, P_A)$ | = | elasticity of revenue with respect to price of addressed admail, |
| $\varepsilon(Q_A, P_A)$ | = | addressed admail own-price elasticity, |
| $\varepsilon(Q_j, P_A)$ | = | cross-price elasticity multiplier for secondary good $j$, |
| $S_A$ | = | percentage of total revenue from addressed admail, and |
| $S_j$ | = | percentage of total revenue from secondary good $j$. |

We see that the revenue elasticity with respect to a change in the price of addressed admail is a revenue weighted average of the cross-price elasticities for the secondary products and a term which is one plus the own-price elasticity.

Provided the own-price elasticity is inelastic, $|\varepsilon(Q_A, P_A)| < 1$, the term $(1+\varepsilon(Q_A, P_A))$ will be positive. The secondary multiplier effects will lead to $\varepsilon(Q_j, P_A) < 0$ since addressed admail is a complement to its secondary products. Under these conditions, an increase in the price of addressed admail will increase the revenue from addressed admail. However, the multiplier effect will lead to a simultaneous decrease in the revenues derived from the secondary products.

The total costs for admail and the secondary products may be written:

$$C = C_A(Q_A) + \sum_j C_j(Q_j)$$

where $C_A$ is the total cost function for addressed admail and $C_j$ is the total cost function for secondary good $j$. For simplicity (and to be consistent with the total unit cost estimates produced by CPC for their different product lines) I have assumed that total costs are additively separable across products. Differentiating this definition of total cost we see that:

$$\frac{\partial C}{\partial P_A} = C'_A \frac{\partial Q_A}{\partial P_A} + C'_j \frac{\partial Q_j}{\partial P_A}.$$

An increase in addressed admail's price will lower total costs at the rate $\partial C/\partial P_A$. Costs will fall since total primary and secondary product output declines.

As I showed above, an increase in addressed admail's price changes revenue at the rate $\partial R/\partial P_A = \varepsilon(R, P_A) \cdot R/P_A$. The change in profitability occurs at the rate $\partial \pi/\partial P_A = \partial(R-C)/\partial P_A = \partial R/\partial P_A - \partial C/\partial P_A$. Profits will therefore increase at the margin provided $\partial R/\partial P_A > \partial C/\partial P_A$ (i.e., provided the marginal revenue from both primary and secondary goods exceeds the marginal production cost of the primary and secondary goods). Since $\partial C/\partial P_A$ is a negative quantity, profits will rise if either $\partial R/\partial P_A$ is positive or even if it is negative but still greater than the decline in marginal cost.

The above discussion assumes a single homogeneous type of addressed admail. In fact, CPC has discretion over all its addressed admail products (short-long versus oversized for instance). Therefore, CPC can adjust each product's price differently. In principle, the demand for each addressed admail product depends on the array of all addressed admail products because each is a substitute for the others. Moreover, the cross-price elasticities will, in principle, depend on the type of primary addressed admail product. This would occur if the multiplier effects for secondary products respond differently depending on the primary addressed admail source. An example would be the response of letter mail or packages to short-long admail versus oversized admail.

The above analysis can be generalized to encompass multiple primary goods, even while maintaining the assumption that each primary good has a uniform effect on secondary demand. The formulas for marginal total revenue and marginal total costs are similar to those derived above. An optimal pricing solution in this case is similar to the general Ramsey pricing model. As it is likely that addressed admail products are economic substitutes, Ramsey pricing theory suggest that an optimal pricing policy will set a price for an addressed admail product such that its Lerner index ((price – marginal cost) / price) exceeds the inverse of its own-price elasticity. In this case, the optimal price may exceed that set by a monopolist, who sets pricing policy only with respect to a single primary addressed admail product.

### *1.5.2 Simulation Results*

In this section, I consider how price increases in addressed admail affect profitability. I do this first excluding multiplier effects and follow with an analysis including multiplier effects.

**Profit Simulations Without Multiplier Effects.** If multiplier effects are not considered, then equivalently $\varepsilon(Q_j, P_A) = 0$. Using results from the previous section, we have:

$$\begin{aligned} dR/dP_A &= Q_A\,(1 + \varepsilon(Q_A, P_A)) \\ dC/dP_A &= \tfrac{C'_A}{P_A} \cdot Q_A \tfrac{P_A}{Q_A} \tfrac{\partial Q_A}{\partial P_A} \\ &= Q_A\,(C'_A/P_A) \cdot \varepsilon(Q_A, P_A), \end{aligned}$$

where $R$ in this case is addressed admail revenue only, $P_A \cdot Q_A$.

Hence,

$$\frac{d\Pi}{dP_A} = Q_A \left[ (1 + \varepsilon(Q_A, P_A)) - \left( \frac{C'_A}{P_A} \right) \cdot \varepsilon(Q_A, P_A) \right]$$

which implies:

$$\frac{d\Pi}{R} \Big/ \frac{dP_A}{P_A} = \left[ (1 + \varepsilon_A) - \left( \frac{C'_A}{P_A} \right) \cdot \varepsilon_A \right].$$

This shows that the percentage change in profits, relative to total addressed admail revenue for a percentage change in price, consists of two components. As discussed above, if the own-price elasticity is inelastic $|\varepsilon_A| < 1$, then the revenue component $(1 + \varepsilon_A)$ will be positive and the incremental cost component will also be positive, since $C'_A > 0$ and $\varepsilon_A < 0$.

**Profit Simulations with Multiplier Effects.** In the previous section, I showed that:

$$\frac{dR}{dP_A} = Q_A(1 + \varepsilon_A) + \sum_j P_j Q_j \varepsilon_j / P_A$$

where $\varepsilon_A = \varepsilon\,(Q_A, P_A)$ and $\varepsilon_j = \varepsilon\,(Q_A, P_j)$. I also showed that:

$$\begin{aligned} \frac{dC}{dP_A} &= C'_A \frac{\partial Q_A}{\partial P_A} + C'_j \frac{\partial Q_j}{\partial P_A} \\ &= Q_A \frac{C'_A}{P_A} \varepsilon_A + \sum_j \frac{Q_j C'_A}{P_A} \varepsilon_j. \end{aligned}$$

Combining these results, we have an expression for how profits change as addressed admail's price changes.

$$\begin{aligned}\frac{d\Pi}{dP_A} &= \frac{dR}{dP_A} - \frac{dC}{dP_A} \\ &= Q_A(1+\varepsilon_A) + \sum_j P_j Q_j \varepsilon_j / P_A - Q_A \frac{C'_A}{P_A}\varepsilon_A \\ &- \sum_j Q_j C'_j \varepsilon_j / P_A.\end{aligned}$$

To calculate an expression for the profit-elasticity I divide both sides of this equation by (combined revenue) $R$ and multiply by $P_A$ to obtain:

$$\begin{aligned}\frac{P_A}{R}\frac{d\Pi}{dP_A} &= \frac{P_A Q_A}{R}(1+\varepsilon_A) + \sum_j \frac{P_j Q_j}{R}\varepsilon_j \\ &- \frac{P_A Q_A \varepsilon_A C'_A}{R P_A} - \sum_j P_j Q_j \varepsilon_j C'_j / R P_j\end{aligned}$$

so that:

$$\begin{aligned}\frac{d\Pi/R}{dP_A/P_A} &= S_A(1+\varepsilon_A) + \sum_j S_j\varepsilon_j - S_A\varepsilon_A C'_A/P_A - \sum_j S_j \varepsilon_j C'_j/P_j \\ &= S_A\left[1+\varepsilon_A(1 - C'_A/P_A)\right] + \sum_j S_j\varepsilon_j(1 - C'_j/P_j) \\ &= S_A(1+\varepsilon_A M_A) + \sum_j S_j \varepsilon_j M_j \qquad (2)\end{aligned}$$

where:

$$\begin{aligned} S_j &= P_j Q_j / R, \\ S_A &= P_A Q_A / R, \\ M_j &= (P_j - C'_j)/P_j, \quad \text{and,} \\ M_A &= (P_A - C'_A)/P_A. \end{aligned}$$

The components $S_j$ and $S_A$ are revenue weights while the components $M_j$ and $M_A$ are economic margins relative to sales price. Margins have been calculated by product line and were based on incremental cost estimates from CPC.

The revenue weights are based on the fiscal year 1994–1995 revenues shown in table 1.10.
From equation (2) we obtain:

$$\frac{d\Pi/R}{dP_A/P_A} = 0.078.$$

Hence, a percentage change in the price of addressed admail will lead to a 0.078 percentage change in profitability relative to overall sales (i.e., sales combined for addressed admail, letters, publications, and packages).

### *1.5.3 Discussion*

With the secondary demand effects included, the predicted increase in profits is approximately 0.78 percent of overall revenues if addressed admail prices were raised only 10 percent. A 15 percent increase in addressed admail prices is predicted to lead to a 1.17 percent profit increase of combined revenues. Based on fiscal year 1994–1995 figures, this amounts to an additional $35.9 million dollars in profit.

## 1.6 Conclusions

The forecasted consequences of an increase in addressed admail prices depend heavily on the multiplier effect. Without secondary demand effects, price increases in addressed admail are predicted to have financial consequences which are very substantial and profitable. Once the secondary demand effects are included, the efficacy of a price rise is reduced. This underscores how important it is to precisely determine the multiplier. Further, because letter mail produces such a large fraction of total revenue, even small estimated multipliers in the letter mail equation have important implications for the profit elasticity results. This emphasizes the importance of precisely determining a single effect—addressed admail's impact on resultant letter volume.

The trend in addressed admail growth is unlikely to continue forever. Interviews with members of the Canadian Direct Marketing Association indicate that customers are already seeking alternatives to admail and that addressed admail may already be in the mature stage of its product life. As prices are increased, it is likely that CPC will shift customers into the more elastic portion of the demand curve. In other words, price increases will encourage customers to develop alternatives. Hence, reestimation of these models and reevaluation of these conclusions is suggested.

# 2 THE WORLD DEMAND FOR FRACTIONAL HORSEPOWER DIRECT-CURRENT MOTORS

## 2.1 Introduction

The purpose of this chapter is to analyze the worldwide demand for and pricing of fractional horsepower direct-current motors. I refer to this type of motor as a micro-motor in this chapter. Micro-motors have numerous applications in automobiles for power mirrors, door locks, and air-conditioning dampers, as well as applications in children's toys and in small appliances such as blow dryers, hair clippers, and shavers. These motors operate on direct current at fractions of a horsepower. Typically, single piece motors sell for about thirty-five to seventy-five cents, with an average of over 30 million pieces sold per year.

Micro-motors provide an excellent example of a good that has a derived demand. Consumers or end-users do not demand micro-motors directly. Instead, consumers demand products such as appliances and automobiles which use the micro-motors. Automobile accessories such as power door locks and power mirrors utilize micro-motors. In modeling the derived demand for a good it is necessary to account for the desired output level of the final product in which that good is contained. Here, the number of cars and the number of appliances using micro-motors, determine, in large part, the demand for micro-motors.

Production of micro-motors in the world economy has been largely provided by the Japanese manufacturer Mabuchi. Mabuchi developed some of the key technology for miniature motors and has enjoyed the benefit of its patented inventions. However, in the mid-1980s the Hong Kong manufacturer Johnson entered the micro-motor market with an allegedly infringing substitute product. I use the growth in Johnson's market share to discern the price erosion effect of Johnson's entry. To do this I first specify and estimate a pricing-to-market model for Mabuchi's worldwide pricing.

My analysis is confined to two basic motor types known as the 100 Series and the 200 Series. These series have equivalents at both the Mabuchi and Johnson corporations. Within the series types are subtypes for shape, finish, and other characteristics. The 100 Series motors are largely used in non-automotive applications while the 200 Series motors are primarily used in automobile manufacturing. Interestingly, most production of 200 Series motors has been sold to non-U.S. auto manufacturers while American-made automobiles more often use U.S. manufactured miniature motors. Mabuchi 200 Series motors are therefore found in BMWs, SAABs, Volvos, and other high-end European automobiles.

In the next section I review data sources and econometric methods. I then specify the econometric models and present their results. Finally, I analyze worldwide pricing behavior in this market.

## 2.2 Econometric Analysis of Micro-Motor Demand

In figure 2.1, I show Johnson's unit sales of 100 and 200 Series motors on a worldwide basis. The data is depicted over quarterly periods with a smoothed line drawn to provide an easy visual cue to the general trend in sales over time. Johnson began selling 100 Series micro-motors in July 1985. These sales rose over a four or five-year period, ultimately achieving a 20 percent worldwide market share. Johnson began selling 200 Series micro-motors in September 1987. Their sales of these motors peaked approximately two years later.

In figure 2.2, I depict the unit sales of Mabuchi 100 and 200 Series micro-motors. This figure shows how Mabuchi's sales rose over time commencing in early 1982. Figure 2.3 shows the combined 100 and 200 Series micro-motors sales by Mabuchi and Johnson. One of the purposes of my econometric analysis is to determine the causes of the general sales increase. In so doing I distinguish between movements along and shifts in the underlying demand curve and am therefore able to determine the elasticity of demand.

I rely upon three main factors to explain the worldwide demand for 100 and 200 Series micro-motors. To model demand for micro-motors, I use factors for the size of the relevant automobile and appliance markets, the inflation-adjusted worldwide micro-motor price, and a time trend to control for general trends in demand not accounted for by the other factors.

### *2.2.1 Demand Dynamics*

Car and appliance manufacturing requires some planning and time. Cars available for sale in a given year may rely on assembled components ordered and procured in previous periods. This potential difference in the timing between component orders and final product manufacture implies that auto and appli-

Figure 2.1: Unit Sales of Johnson 100 and 200 Series Motors

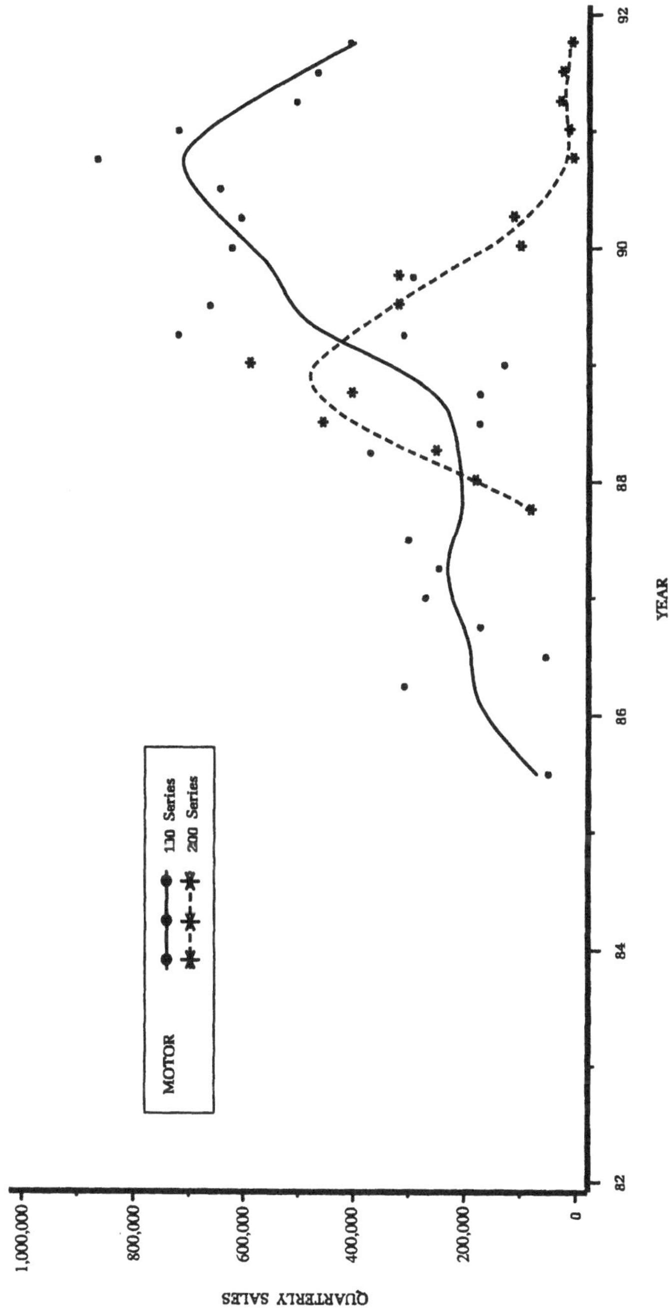

**Figure 2.2: Unit Sales of Mabuchi 100 and 200 Series Motors**

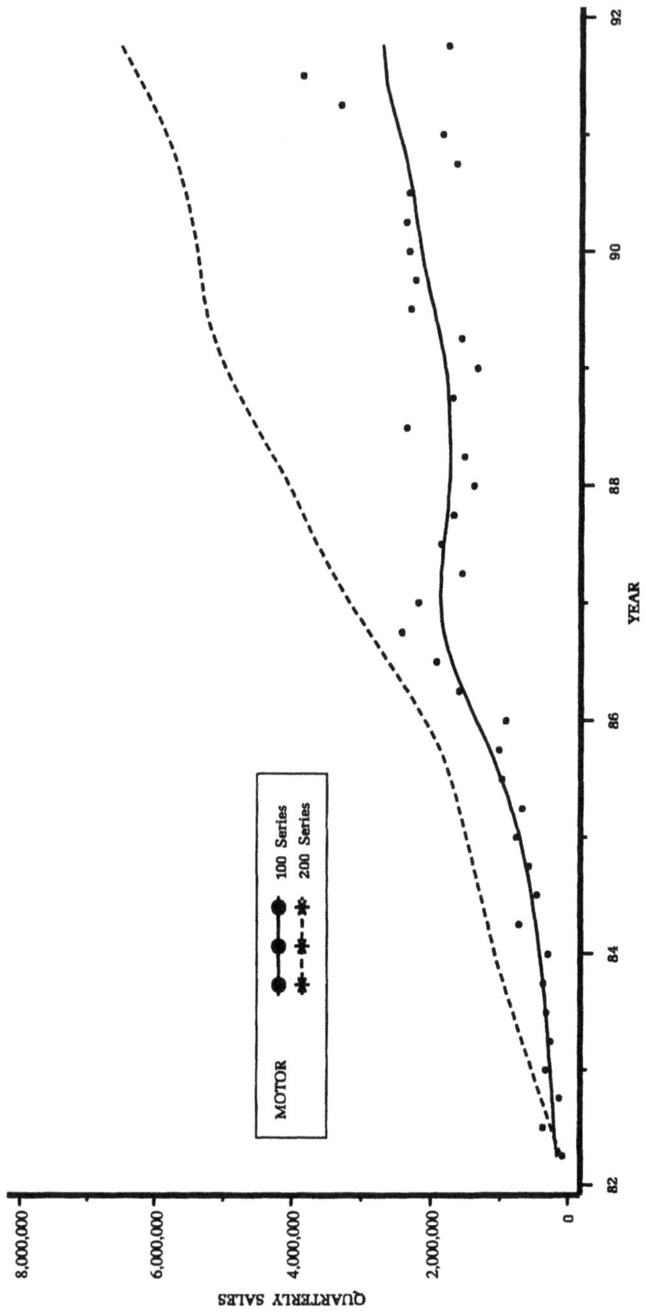

Figure 2.3: Worldwide Sales of 100 and 200 Series Motors

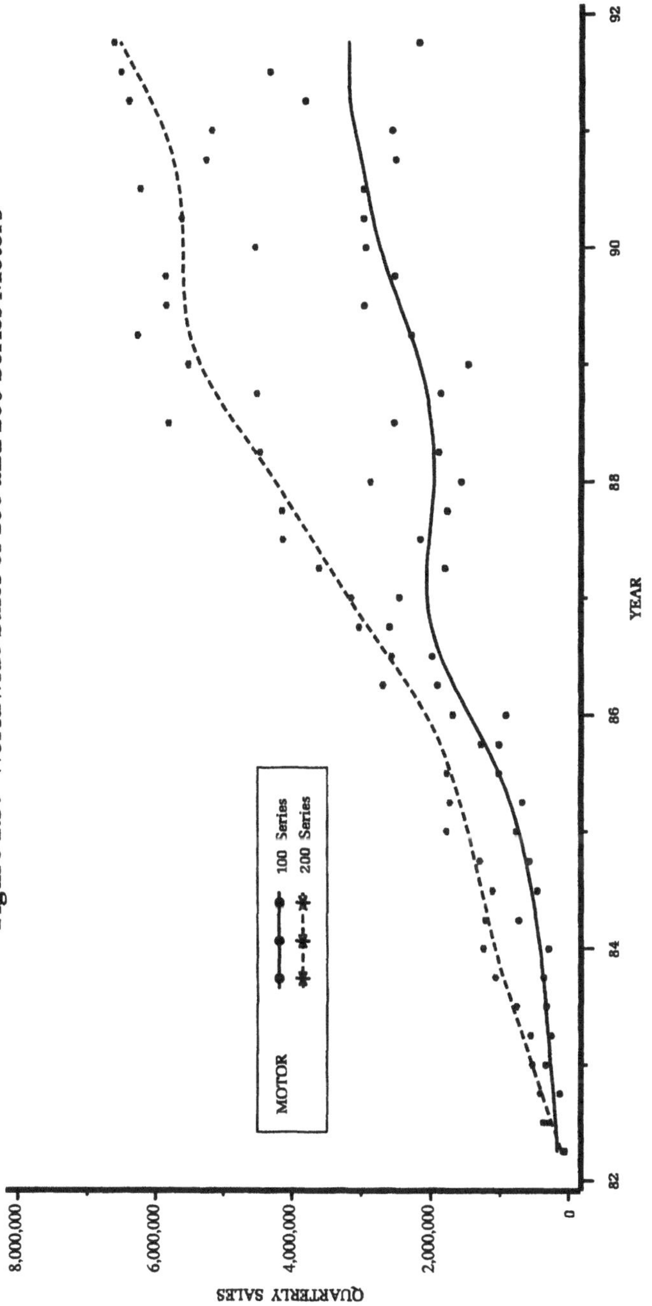

ance sales will not, in general, be perfectly contemporaneously correlated with micro-motor sales. To allow for this possibility, I fit the demand for micro-motors as a distributed lag in historical automobile sales and other factors.

The form of this specification is:

$$Y_t = \alpha + \sum_{i=1}^{k} \beta_i X_{t-i} + \varepsilon_t$$

where $Y_t$ denotes sales of motors in period $t$ and the quantities $X_{t-i}$ denote historical automobile sales. The term $\alpha$ represents other factors which affect demand, including most importantly the own-price effect, a time trend, and appliance uses of micro-motors.

In the estimation, I use the polynomial lag structure suggested by Almon (1965). The Almon lag structure assumes that the coefficients $\beta_i$ may be written:

$$\beta_i = \alpha_0 + \alpha_1 i + \alpha_2 i^2 + \cdots + \alpha_p i^p.$$

I use the Almon lag structure of order $p$ (where $p = 3$) so that the lag coefficients achieve a smooth cubic shape. I also use a lag length of $k$ (where $k = 12$) to allow for seasonality and other lagged effects in the monthly data.

The coefficients $\alpha_i$ may be determined by including four constructed variables of the form:

$$Z_{jt} = \sum_{i=0}^{k} X_{t-i} * i^j \qquad j = 0, 1, \cdots, 3$$

Coefficients are determined by least squares regression. In steady-state, the equilibrium multiplier between automobile uses and motors is given by:

$$\overline{Y} = \alpha + \left( \sum_{i=0}^{k} \beta_i \right) \overline{X}$$

where $\overline{Y}$ and $\overline{X}$ are, respectively, the steady-state values for micro-motors demanded and automobile uses. I calculate the lag coefficients from the estimated coefficients $\alpha_i$ and then form their sum to determine the equilibrium multiplier effect.

### *2.2.2 Company Data on Prices and Quantities*

The basic data for my analysis were derived from source documents provided by Mabuchi and Johnson. I augmented this data with information from publicly available sources. For example, *Ward's Automotive Yearbooks*,[1] detail

[1] Ward's Automotive Yearbook, Fifty-Fourth Edition, Ward's Communications, 28 West Adams, Detroit, MI, 48226.

micro-motor automotive uses, while international trade statistics for import and export yield information pertaining to small household appliances. My goal in constructing a database for Mabuchi and Johnson sales was to track monthly sales over a roughly ten-year period and to ascertain the quantities and prices at which transactions took place.

The company data reflected the actual invoiced sales of micro-motors to producers. For each transaction, I was able to determine the model number of the motor sold, the prices and quantities involved, the currency used when the transaction occurred, the customers location, and the basic application or use of the motor. I aggregated the data to form average monthly prices and revenues for the approximately ten-year period from 1982 to 1992.

### *2.2.3 Construction of Explanatory Factors*

The explanatory factors used in the demand analysis, other than worldwide price and trend terms, consist of estimates of automobile and appliance micro-motor uses.[2] In table 2.1, I summarize the data sources used in the analysis. In the next section, I summarize how I constructed the factors used in the econometric model.

### *2.2.4 Automotive Data*

For the period 1982 through 1992, I collected data on certain specific car models. This data provide information regarding import sales within the United States, as well as United States domestic production and worldwide production. For each car model that I analyzed, I collected information on the percentage of such cars using 200 Series micro-motors. These uses include operating air-conditioning dampers, power mirrors, and power door locks. I also collected information on the percentage of two-door cars manufactured, as compared with four-door cars, as this would affect the number of door lock motors used. I used *Ward's Automotive Yearbooks* for the years 1982-1992 to obtain this information. *Ward's* tracks specific car models and their features. This data was collected to approximate the number of 200 Series micro-motors likely to be in use in automobiles worldwide over the ten-year period.

The approximation contains several basic steps. First, for the period 1981–1991, in each month and for thirty-five car models, I recorded the air-conditioning, power door lock, and power mirror uses for 200 Series micro-motors. Second, for an additional eleven car models produced domestically during the same period, I recorded the air-conditioning, power door lock, and power rearview

---

[2]An empirical model of the Japanese television market and related discussion appears in Karp and Perloff (1989). The Karp and Perloff model bears some similarity to mine in its specification of worldwide demand.

**Table 2.1.** Data Used in Analysis

**Automotive Data 1981–1991:**
- *Import Car Sales in the United States
- *Domestic Car Production in the United States
- *Percentage of Import Air Conditioning, Power Mirrors, and Power Locks
- *Percentage of Export Air Conditioning, Power Mirrors, and Power Locks
- *Worldwide Car Production
- *Percentage of Two-Door Cars Manufactured

  Source: *Ward's Automotive Yearbook*, 1982–1992

**Appliance Data 1981–1991:**
- *Appliance Shipments in the United States

  Source: Toy Manufacturers of America, Inc., Shipments—National Statistics Program, 1982–1992; and Appliance Magazine Annual Appliance Industry Forecasts, 1982–1992.
- *Appliances Imported to the United States 1981–1991

  Source: U.S. Import for Consumption—UTSUSA Commodity by County of Origin, Pub. No. FT247, 1982–1992.
- *Appliances Exported from Specific Countries to the United States 1986–1991

  Source: Hong Kong Trade Statistics; Japan Exports & Imports Commodity by Country; and Monthly Statistic of Exports, The Republic of China Taiwan District, 1987–1992.

**Foreign Exchange Rates 1981–1991**

Source: Board of Governors of the Federal Reserve System, Foreign Spot Exchange Rates, Monthly Time Series, 1971-1992.

**Consumer Price Index 1981–1991**
- *Consumer Price Index, Hong Kong, Japan, France, Germany, and United States

  Source: *International Financial Statistics Yearbook* 1992.
- *Consumer Price Index, Taiwan

  Source: Asia 1991-1992 Measures and Magnitudes

**Japanese Interest Rates 1981–1992**

Source: Main Economics Indicators-Historical Statistics, 1969–1988, O.E.C.D., and Main Economics Indicators-Historical Statistics, September 1992.

mirror uses for 200 Series micro-motors. Finally, I estimated the total micro-motor uses in automobiles by combining the data across car models.[3]

Based on information supplied by Mabuchi, I further restricted my micro-motor automobile-use accounting. Specifically, I considered Alfa Romeo only in the years of 1990 and 1991. I considered Jaguar, Peugeot, Porsche, SAAB, and Volvo only for power door locks. I examined BMW only for power mirrors and power door locks.

In accounting for power door locks, I used the percentages of two-door and four-door automobiles produced to count the power door locks employed (two-door cars were assumed to have two power door locks if they had power door locks at all). For power mirrors, based on information provided to me by Mabuchi, I assumed that a single power mirror required two motors. Finally, using the ratio of worldwide car production to U.S. domestic production, I estimated the total number of 200 Series micro-motors used in automobile power mirrors worldwide. The basic idea here was to determine micro-motor use in the U.S. market from imports and domestic production and then extrapolate to the world market.

In figure 2.4, I show the historical worldwide production of those automobiles which used or potentially used Mabuchi 200 Series micro-motors. The graph displays monthly automobile production over the ten-year period. In figure 2.5, I display my estimate of the number of 200 Series micro-motors used in these car models. The graph demonstrates that in 1982, there was an average of 3.5 motors used per car. This increased to 4.5 motors per car by 1987, and then to approximately five 200 Series motors per car by 1991.

In figure 2.6, I display my approximation of the total number of 200 Series micro-motors used in automobiles worldwide over the 1981–1991 decade. As can readily be seen by examining figures 2.4 through 2.6, more automobiles were being manufactured in later years. Consequently, the increased number of automobiles, coupled with increased uses for micro-motors in them, led to an accelerating worldwide demand for micro-motors. This increase in worldwide demand for micro-motors caused the demand curve for micro-motors to shift.

### 2.2.5 *Appliance Uses*

Using information provided by the Toy Manufacturers of America and *Appliance Magazine*, I estimated the number of hair dryers, electric toothbrushes, juicers, and electric trains and cars shipped into the United States. I selected these products based both on data availability and on the potential uses of Mabuchi and Johnson 100 Series micro-motors in household appliances.

It was not possible to track every toy and hobby application such as uses of micro-motors in hobby cars and dolls. Further, I did not attempt to extrapolate small household appliance micro-motor use to the worldwide level.

---

[3]Company information reveals that only Mabuchi supplied motors in the 200-Series to the automobile market. Mabuchi motors were used in Alfa Romeo, BMW, Jaguar, Peugeot, Porsche, SAAB, and Volvo cars.

**Figure 2.4: Worldwide Production of Autos Using 200 Series Motors**

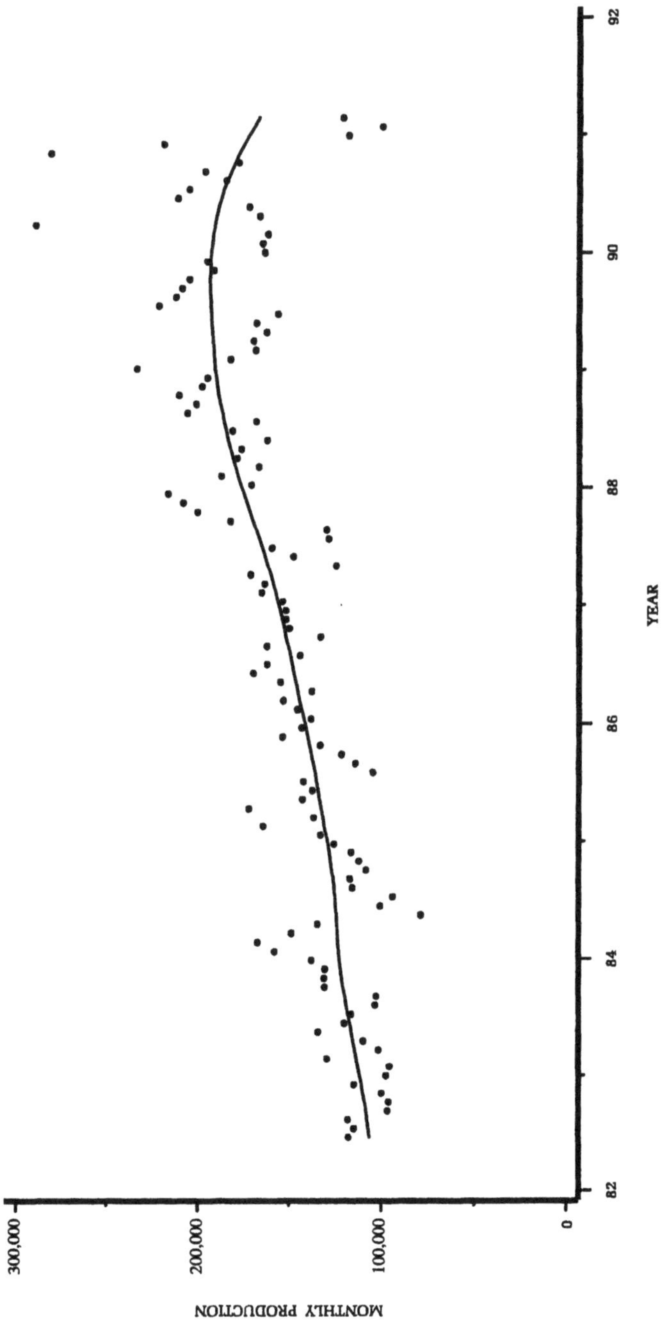

Figure 2.5: 200 Series Motors per Automobile

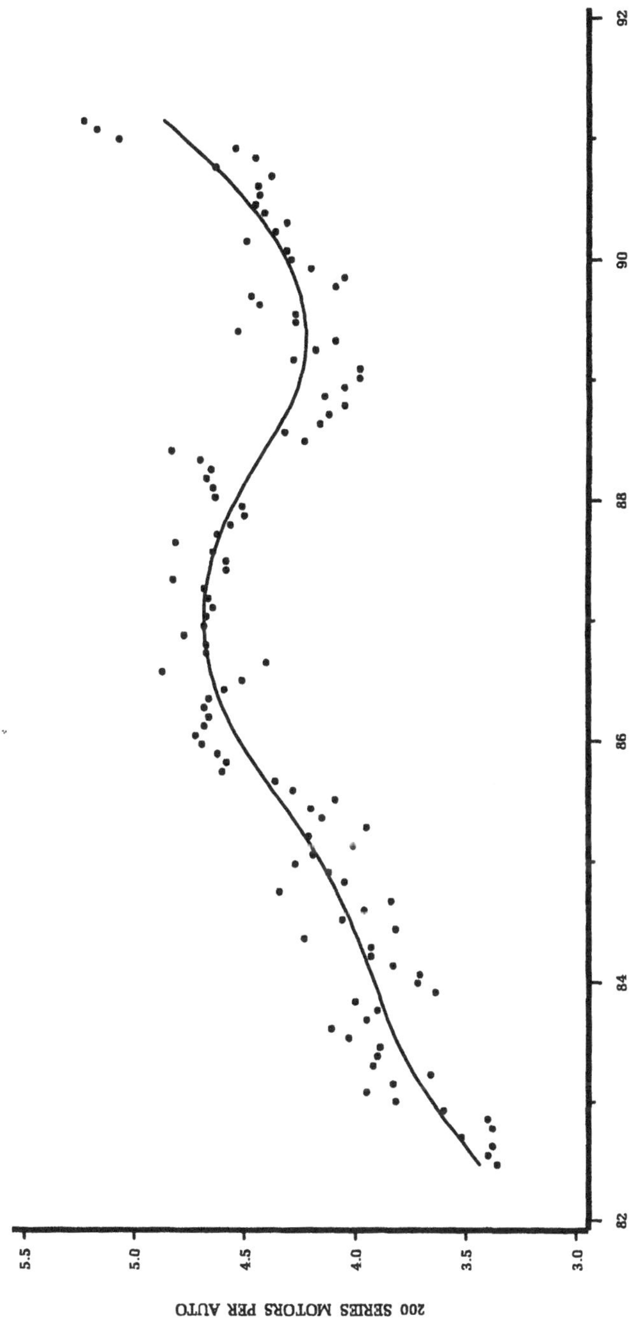

**Figure 2.6: Worldwide Demand for 200 Series Motors Used in Automobiles**

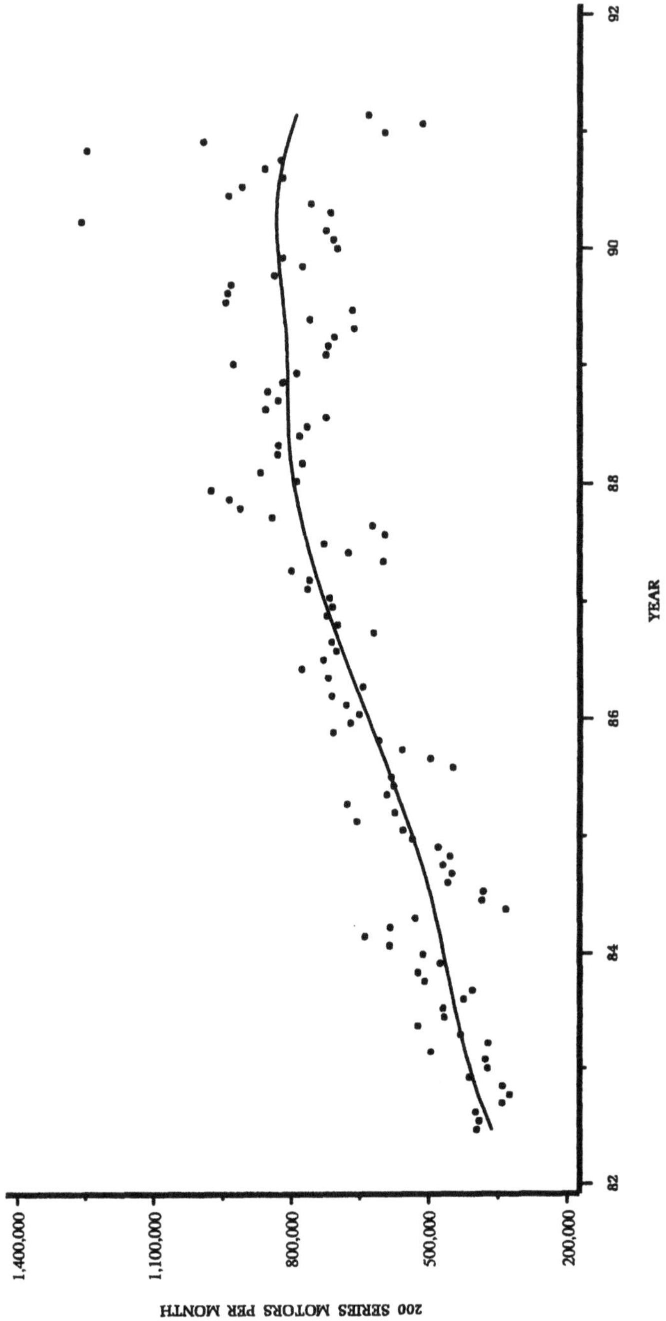

Thus, my estimates of total appliance uses tend to understate total 100 Series micro-motor use. However, I did collect information on the percentage of all small household appliances imported into the United States from specific countries, and the percentage of small household appliance production, by specific country, exported to the United States.

These figures demonstrate that, in 1985, approximately 68 percent of all small household appliances using micro-motors were imported into the United States from Hong Kong. However, this percentage declined to approximately 11 percent by 1991. Similarly, 65 percent of Hong Kong's total household appliance production was exported to the United States in 1985. This percentage declined to approximately 22 percent by 1991. Combining import and export information and using the information on small household appliance shipments, I conclude that appliances using micro-motors purchased worldwide are at least 50 percent greater than those purchased in the United States. However, this calculation only accounts for consumption in five countries outside the United States and is, therefore, downwardly biased. For this reason, I relied only on U.S. consumption of small household appliances in the econometric analysis.

The total number of small household appliances shipped into the United States or produced within the United States for domestic consumption reflects a general, and often substantial, increase in production over time.

### *2.2.6 Worldwide Micro-Motor Prices*

Figure 2.7 displays the worldwide prices charged by Johnson for 100 Series and 200 Series micro-motors. Because both Johnson and Mabuchi sell their products worldwide and receive payment in foreign currencies, I have converted all prices to a common currency—the Japanese yen. Thus, I conduct my demand analysis on a worldwide basis. The available data did not permit me to perform a more disaggregate demand analysis.

Figure 2.8 displays the prices Mabuchi charged worldwide for 100 and 200 Series micro-motors. The Mabuchi price data are present over a longer time period than is the Johnson price data because Mabuchi was selling their product as early as 1982. Again, the worldwide prices are shown using the yen as a normalizing currency. The general deflation in prices reflects, in part, changes in relative exchange rates as well as the price erosion effects associated with Johnson's entry into the market.

In figure 2.9, I show the worldwide prices charged by Johnson and Mabuchi for 100 Series micro-motors. The figure displays a clear pattern. Johnson's prices are generally lower than Mabuchi's by approximately 15 to 20 percent. Figure 2.10 shows the worldwide prices charged by Johnson and Mabuchi for 200 Series micro-motors. This figure displays a period of lower 200 Series micro-motor prices offered and sold by Johnson followed by a period in which the prices were more similar to those charged by Mabuchi. Figure 2.11 displays the worldwide prices of 100 and 200 Series micro-motors by combining both Johnson and Mabuchi sales. As shown, prices for both the 100 and 200 Series micro-motors declined over time.

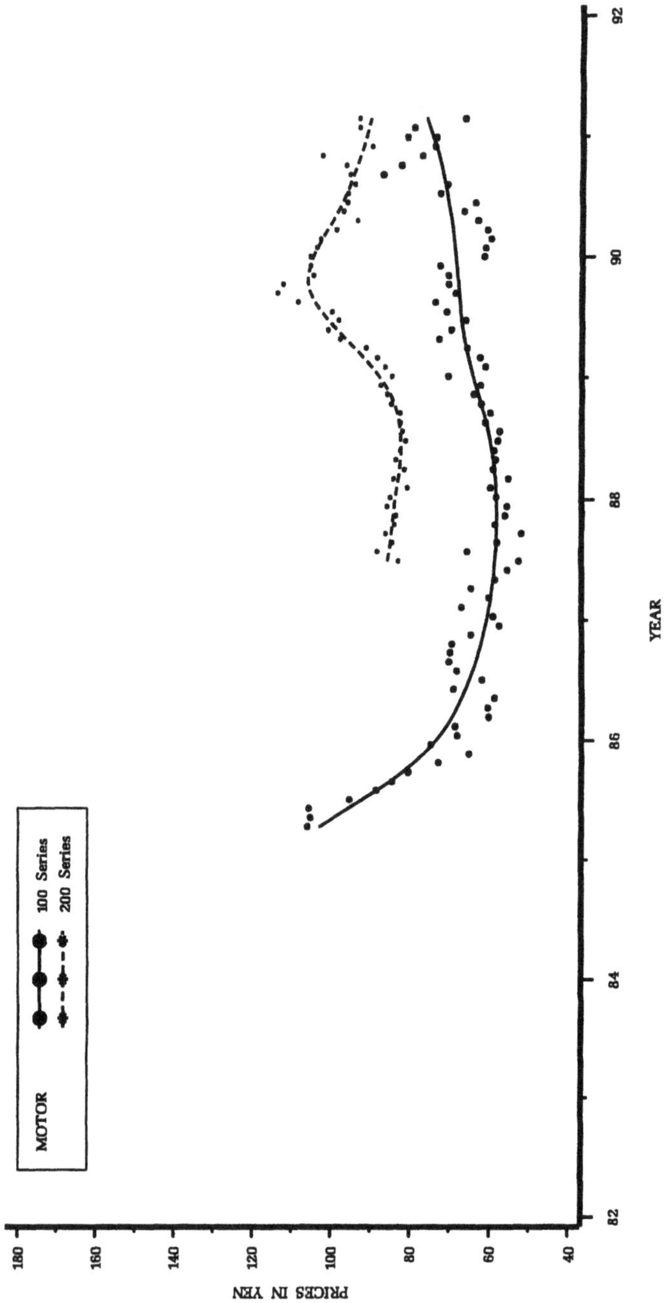


**Figure 2.7: Worldwide Prices of Johnson 100 and 200 Series Motors**

Figure 2.8: Worldwide Prices of Mabuchi 100 and 200 Series Motors

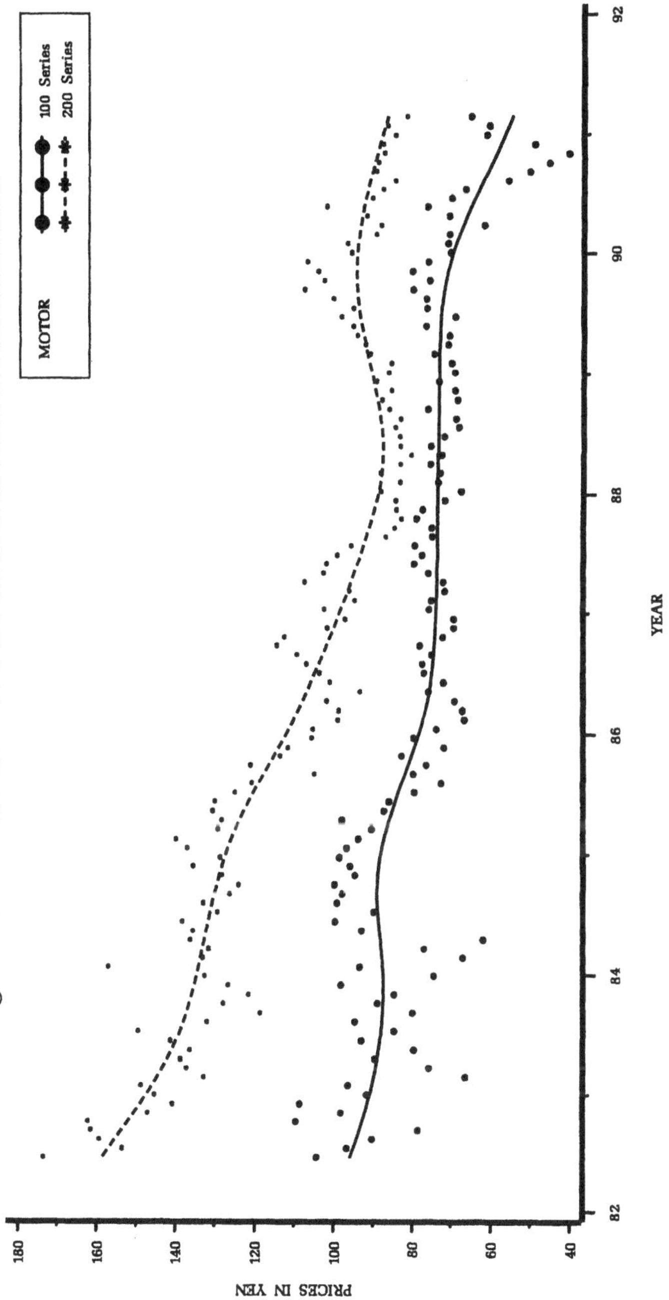

**Figure 2.9: Worldwide Prices of 100 Series Motors by Manufacturer**

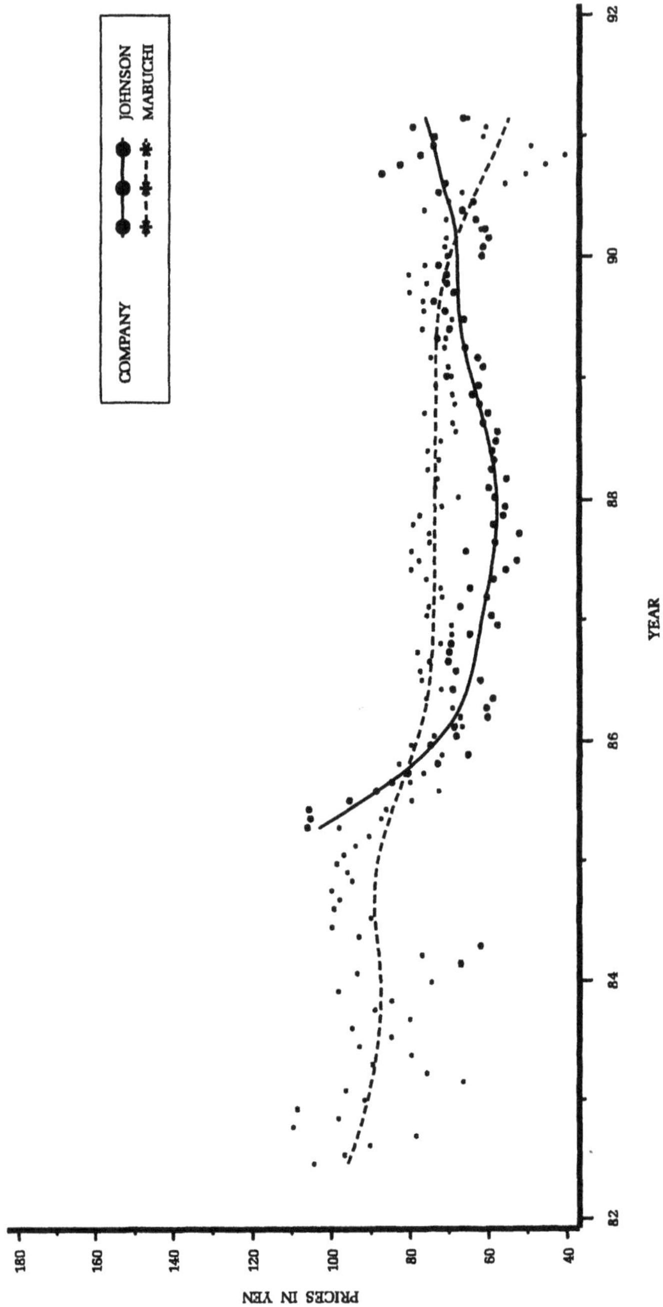

Figure 2.10: Worldwide Prices of 200 Series Motors by Manufacturer

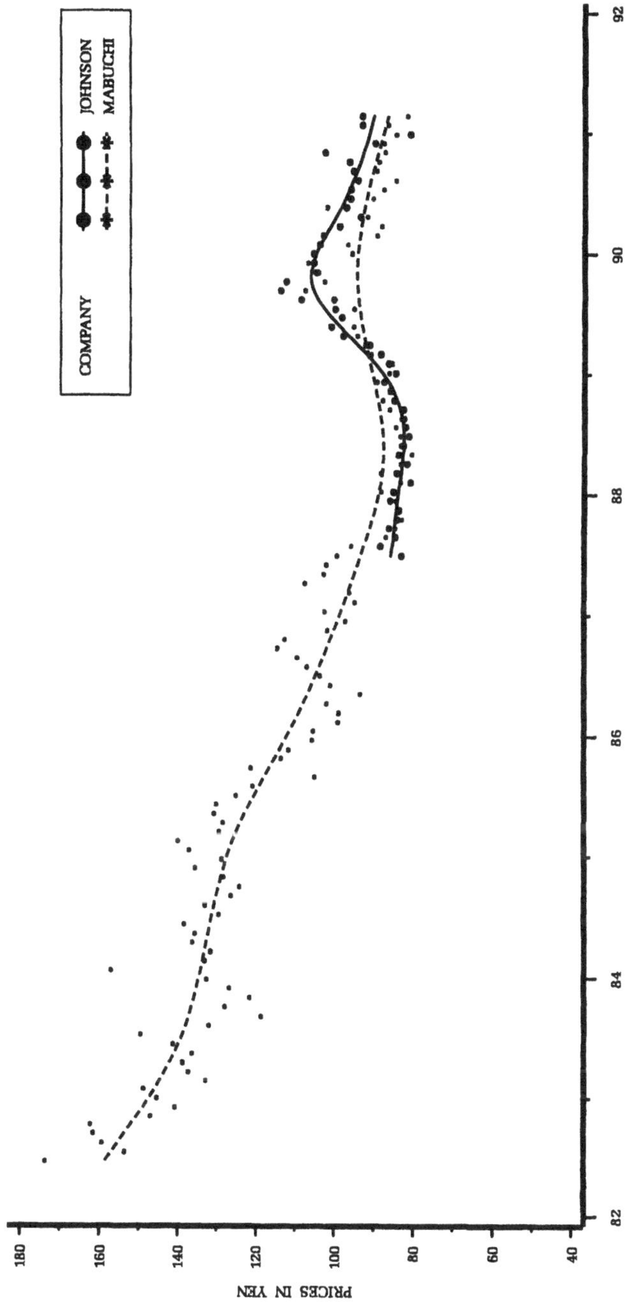

Figure 2.11: Worldwide Prices of 100 and 200 Series Motors

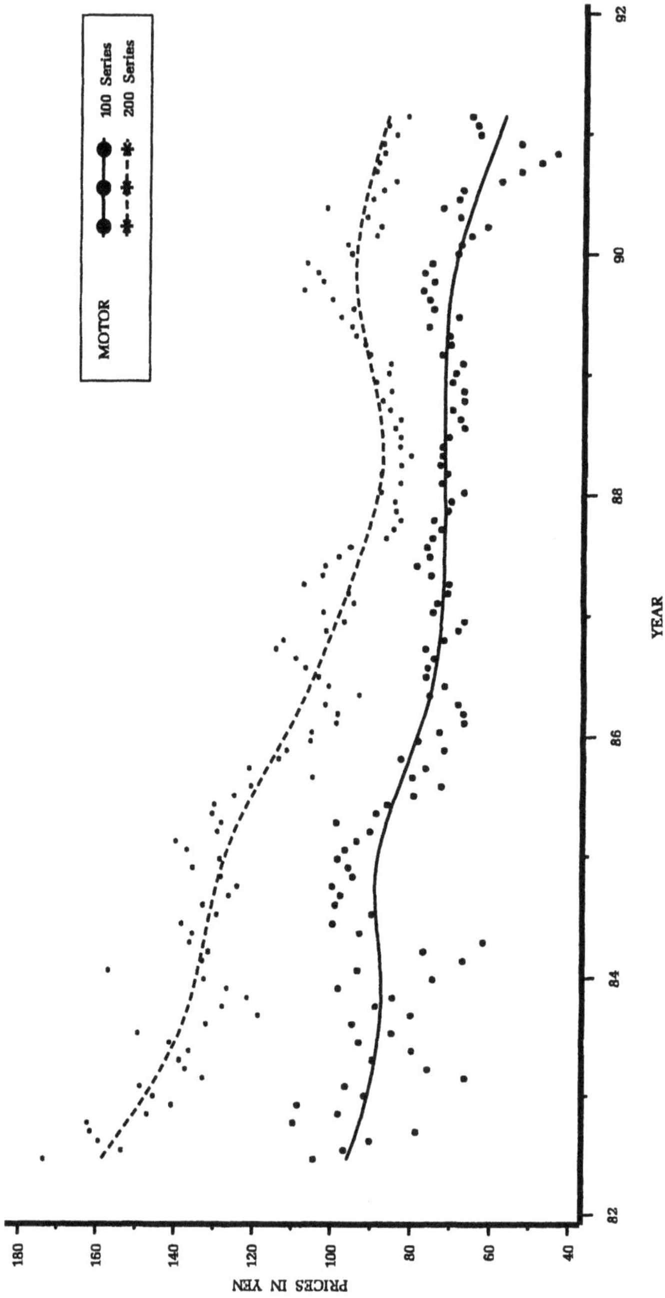

## 2.3 Econometric Results for Worldwide Demand

I conducted my demand analysis separately for 100 and 200 Series micro-motors. The results of the analyses are presented in tables 2.2 and 2.3 respectively. In general, the models fit well. The models explain 78 percent of the variation in 100 Series micro-motor sales, and 90 percent of the variation in 200 Series sales. The models reveal that historical automobile uses predict the demand for 200 Series micro-motors with an equilibrium multiplier of 1.8. This implies that my accounting somewhat underestimates all 200 Series micro-motor use. Predicted and actual worldwide sales of 100 Series micro-motors are displayed in figure 2.12. Predicted and actual worldwide sales of 200 Series micro-motors are shown in figure 2.13.[4]

Turning to price effects, I find that the elasticity (at means) for 100 Series micro-motors is −0.52. Therefore, I conclude that demand for these 100 Series micro-motors is inelastic. This result is significant at standard levels ($t$-stat = −1.9). The regression is based on 115 monthly observations over the eleven-year period for which I had data on 100 and 200 Series micro-motor sales. The results for the 200 Series micro-motors price effects show complete inelasticity. Therefore, I cannot reject the hypothesis that 200 Series micro-motor prices had a statistically insignificant effect on 200 Series micro-motor demand.[5]

In figure 2.14, I illustrate the estimated demand curve with all other factors held constant at their mean values for 1985 and 1990. The line delineated as 1985 represents the estimated demand function for 100 Series micro-motors in that year. I have indicated on this line the average price and average monthly production in 1985. Similarly, I also show in this graph the 1990 average price and mean monthly production. As can be seen clearly, by 1990, prices fell by roughly a third (as denominated in yen) while production rose from roughly four hundred thousand units per month to approximately nine hundred thousand units per month.

My demand analysis demonstrates that some of this quantity increase is due to lower prices (approximately one hundred and fifty thousand units per month). However, my demand analysis also shows that the remaining quantity increase (three hundred and fifty thousand units per month) is due to a shift in the demand schedule as the world goods production utilizing 100 Series micro-motors increased.

Figure 2.15 reveals the same pattern for the 200 Series micro-motors. Again, there is a price decline between 1985 and 1990. However, this price decline results in no predicted change in demand from movements solely on the demand curve. This is true because the demand curve for 200 Series micro-motors is totally inelastic in the data's relevant range. Meanwhile, there is a substantial quantity increase from five hundred and fifty thousand units per month to

[4]The data on historical appliance usage aided in the estimation but proved to be somewhat less predictive of 100 Series micro-motor demand than I had expected. This probably resulted from the difficulties in measuring all 100 Series micro-motor uses worldwide.
[5]The results using a log-linear specification were similar.

Figure 2.12: Actual versus Predicted Worldwide Sales of 100 Series Motors

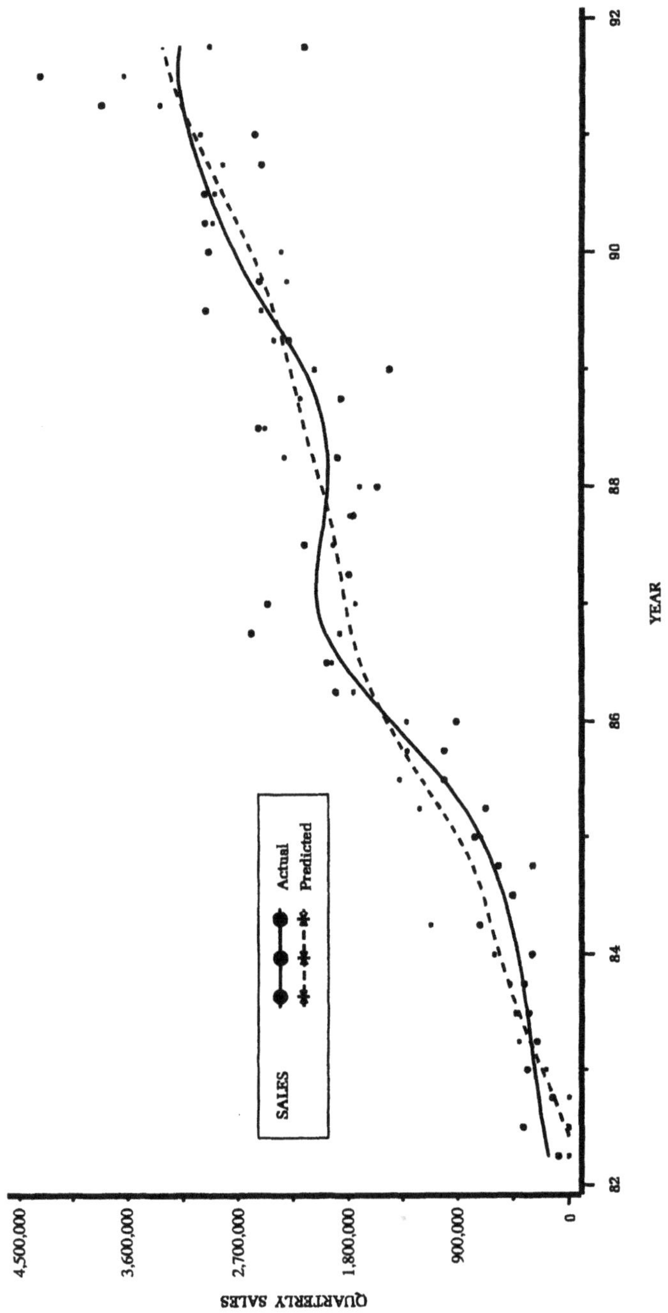

**Figure 2.13: Actual versus Predicted Worldwide Sales of 200 Series Motors**

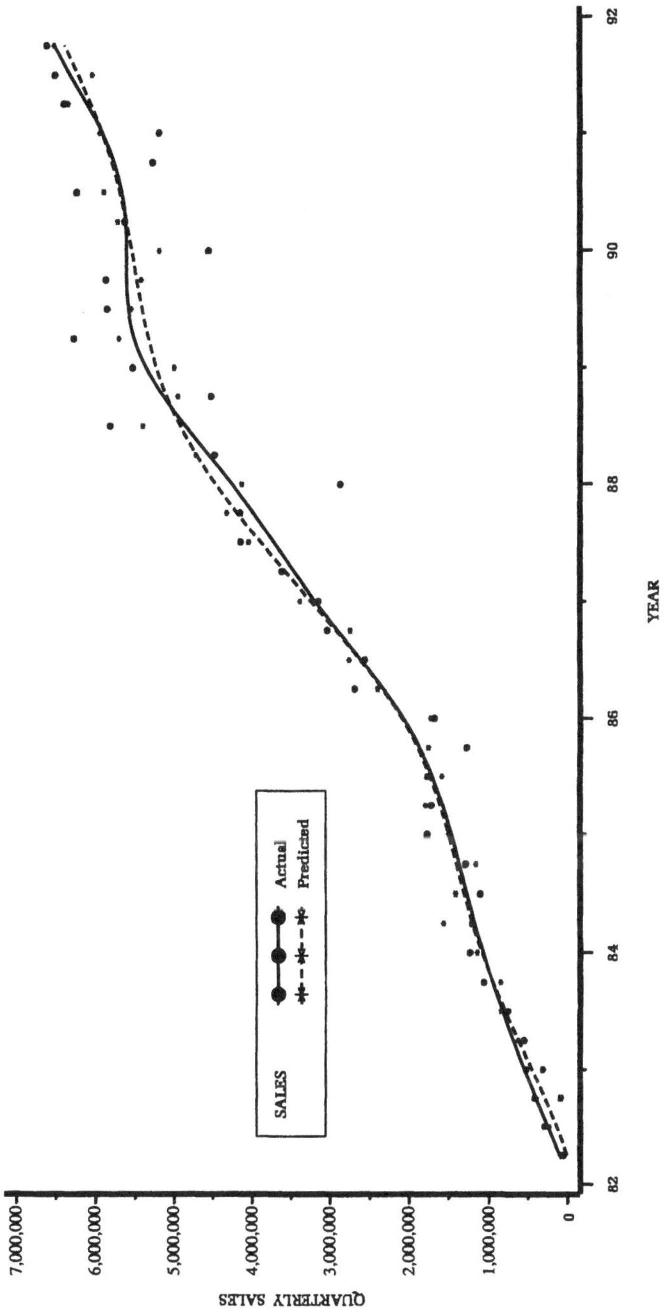

**Figure 2.14: Demand Curves for 100 Series Motors 1985 versus 1990**

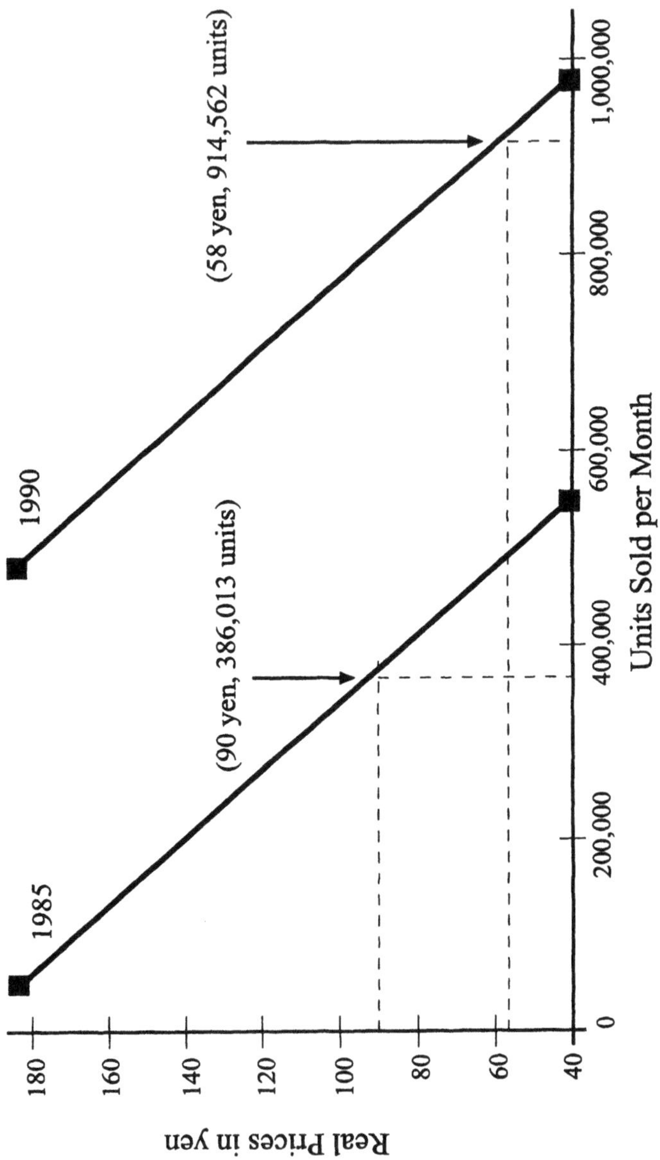

**Table 2.2.** Worldwide Demand for 100-Series Motors

| Independent Variables | |
|---|---|
| Z0 | 0.34 (2.94) |
| Z1 | −0.083 (−0.92) |
| Z2 | 0.00016 (0.008) |
| Z3 | 0.00038 (0.38) |
| Constant | −6,758,730.00 (−2.78) |
| Appliance (U.S.) | −0.137 (−1.21) |
| Real Worldwide Price of 100-Series Motors | (−387,676.00) (−1.88) |
| Trend | 85,844.00 (2.87) |
| Number of Observations | 115.00 |
| $R$-squared | 0.78 |
| Mean price elasticity | −0.52 |

Ordinary least square regression estimates with $t$-statistics in parenthesis. Observations are monthly. Z0, Z1, Z2, and Z3 are terms in the Almon lag as described in the text.

approximately 1.8 million units per month by 1990. This increase is completely accounted for by a shift in the derived demand for the 200 Series micro-motors.

## 2.4 Discussion of Results

We have seen that increased small household appliance production and increased imported automobile production resulted in shifts in the demand curve

**Figure 2.15: Demand Curves for 200 Series Motors 1985 versus 1990**

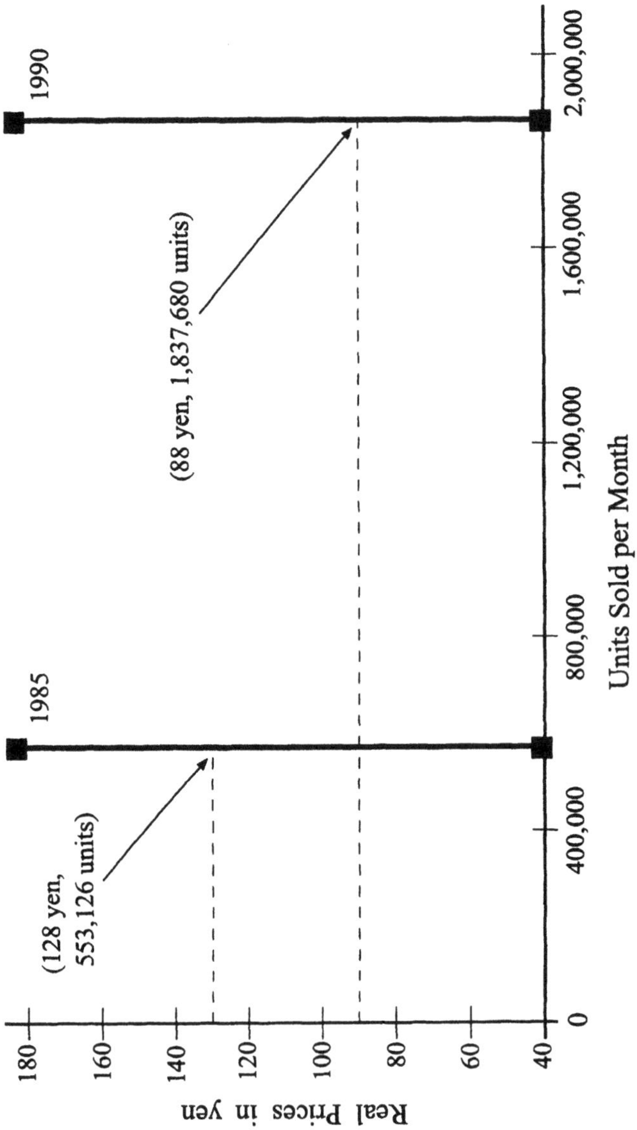

**Table 2.3.** Worldwide Demand for 200-Series Motors

| Independent Variables | |
|---|---|
| Z0 | 0.0785<br>(0.50) |
| Z1 | 0.191<br>(1.61) |
| Z2 | −0.055<br>(−2.30) |
| Z3 | 0.0036<br>(2.67) |
| Constant | −8,547,010.00<br>(−3.02) |
| Appliance (U.S.) | 0.465<br>(2.92) |
| Real Worldwide Price of 100-Series Motors | (58,194.00)<br>(0.25) |
| Trend | 89,754.00<br>(2.46) |
| Number of Observations | 115.00 |
| $R$-squared | 0.90 |
| Mean price elasticity | 0.00 |

Ordinary least square regression estimates with $t$-statistics in parenthesis. Observations are monthly. Z0, Z1, Z2, and Z3 are terms in the Almon lag as described in the text.

for the 100 and 200 Series micro-motors. We have also seen that demand for the 100 and 200 Series micro-motors is very price inelastic. These results are to be expected. A change in the price of a good that represents a large fraction of an individual's budget may lead to a substantial change in that individual's demand. Conversely, when a good represents a relatively small fraction of an individual's budget, demand will generally be less elastic. These observations, which follow economic theory and are basic empirical regularities, are also observed in micro-motor demand. The 100 Series micro-motors represent a larger fraction of the cost of producing toys and appliances than the 200 Series micro-motors do in relation to the cost of producing an automobile. Therefore, a greater price sensitivity is discerned for the 100 Series micro-motors. In contrast, whether a high-end European import car has one or ten 200 Series micro-motors operating its subsystems, the total price of these motors is insignificant in comparison to the car's total price. Thus, consumer demand for cars dictates the derived demand for micro-motors used in cars.

A relatively small change in the micro-motor price would have no discernible effect on the demand for these motors because, even if the price increase were passed on to automobile purchasers, the increase in the micro-motor price would have no noticeable effect on the car's price. Therefore, the price increase associated with the micro-motor would not affect the demand for the automobile. And, as the demand for the micro-motors is derived from consumer demand for the car, the demand for the micro-motor is also unaffected.

## 2.5 Mabuchi's Historical Pricing Behavior and Johnson's Entry

In this section, I examine the effects that Johnson's entry into the market for 100 and 200 Series micro-motors had on worldwide pricing. In this analysis, I compare Mabuchi's pricing behavior for its micro-motors sold in its domestic market (Japan) with its pricing behavior in foreign markets. In its domestic market, Mabuchi was effectively a monopolist, facing no competition for its micro-motors. By contrast, in its foreign markets, Mabuchi faced both real and potential competition. In those markets, if Mabuchi raised its prices sufficiently, it would encourage both Johnson and possibly other micro-motor manufacturers to enter the market.

In analyzing Mabuchi's pricing behavior, I rely on the theory known as "pricing to market" developed by Marston (1990) and others.[6] A discussion, similarly on point, was provided by Prutzman (1992) writing in the *New York Times.* Prutzman noted that circa 1985, the dollar weakened significantly against foreign currencies, including the German mark. Therefore, it was expected that the U.S. foreign trade imbalance would improve. This would occur because U.S. goods would become relatively less expensive to foreign purchasers and import goods would become simultaneously more expensive, causing imports to decline and U.S. exports to rise. Prutzman observed that the decline in the dollar value "didn't do the job" in improving the trade imbalance problem. This occurred, despite the dollar's weakness, because German companies (including BMW) raised U.S. prices only 4.5 percent, even though the increase in the mark's value against the dollar should have resulted in a 10 percent price increase.

Marston's theory explains this phenomenon. Marston's pricing to market model considers a firm producing and selling in a domestic market and ex-

[6]For related discussion see Giovannini (1988) and Dohner (1984).

porting its goods to a foreign market. Marston observes that the firm will generally find it in its interest to set different prices in its domestic and foreign markets even when the foreign price is expressed in domestic currency by applying an exchange rate. The reason for this is that demand elasticities in the two countries (being affected in part by differentials in the degree of product substitution) will necessitate differential markups. However, prices will not be completely independent in the two countries since each is tied to a common incremental production cost when all manufacturing occurs domestically. Marston observes that a good's foreign currency price will increase as the exchange rate declines. The extent to which the relative price of goods destined for foreign and domestic markets is affected by movements in the exchange rate is called the "pass-through effect." Marston shows that the pass-through effect is often inelastic, that is, that foreign producers will not raise their product's price in the U.S. to the full extent suggested by changes in the exchange rate alone. This is precisely the phenomenon observed by Prutzman in the *New York Times* article.

To compare Mabuchi's pricing behavior in foreign markets with its pricing behavior in its domestic market (Japan), I follow Marston's empirical model. This model postulates that the ratio between foreign and domestic prices (after exchange) will, in part, follow changes in the real exchange rate and, in part, be determined by differences in the competitive factors that influence the relative demand elasticities.

In the case at hand, I introduce a factor for Johnson's competitive strength, measured by its market share, as an additional explanatory factor in the pricing to market theory. This additional factor proxies changes in the demand elasticity for Mabuchi's product in its foreign markets.[7] By comparing Mabuchi's pricing behavior before and after Johnson's entry into the market, and by measuring Johnson's competitive growth over time and its effect on Mabuchi prices, I am able to determine the degree to which Mabuchi lowered its prices in response to Johnson's market entry.

In figure 2.16, I display Mabuchi's pricing of 100 and 200 Series micro-motors sold in Japan. We see that prices were virtually constant for the 200 Series micro-motors and approximately constant for the 100 Series micro-motors after 1986. Mabuchi's pricing behavior in its domestic market serves as a baseline or "control" in the pricing to market theory of foreign market pricing.

In figure 2.17, I compare Mabuchi's pricing for its 100 Series micro-motors sold in Japan with its prices set worldwide. I generally observe that, after about 1985, prices were lower in foreign markets than they were in Japan. In figure 2.18, I compare Mabuchi's pricing for its 200 Series micro-motors sold in Japan with its prices set worldwide. I observe that until about mid-1985, Mabuchi set its prices in foreign markets at a higher level than they did domestically. Subsequent to mid-1985, Mabuchi's price for the Series 100 and

[7]As discussed above, it was not possible to derive price elasticities of demand for individual countries based on the available company data.

**Figure 2.16: Prices for Mabuchi 200 Series Motors Sold in Japan**

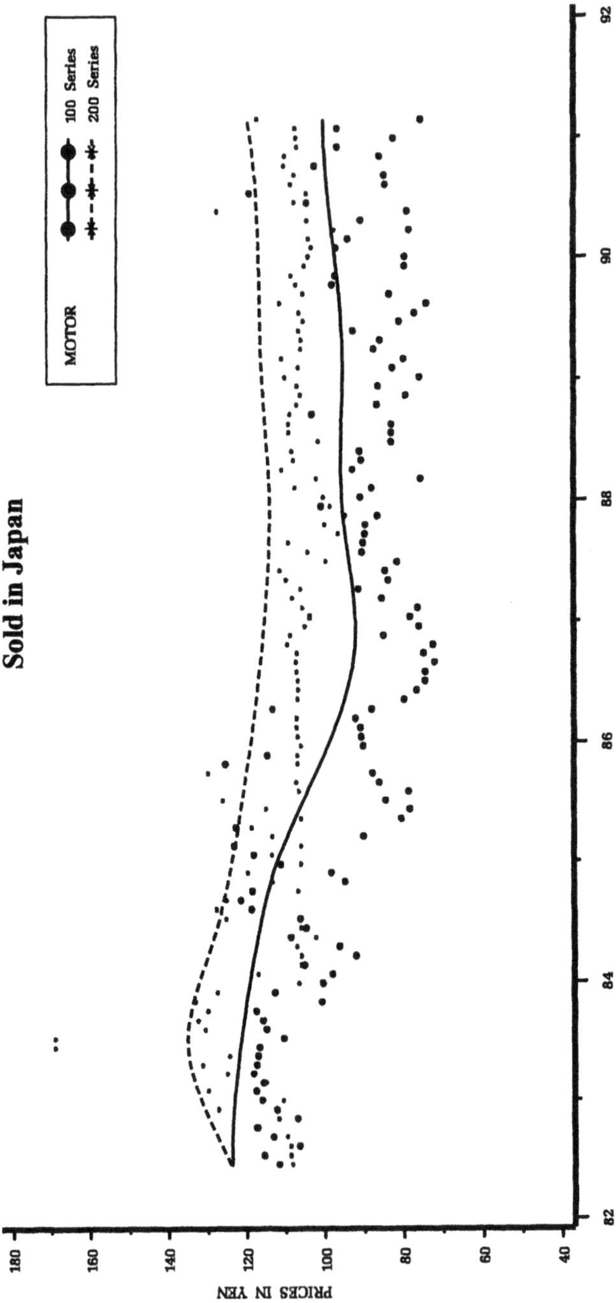

200 micro-motors sold in foreign markets declined substantially compared to the prices in Japan.

To sort out the degree to which the relative price differences for motors sold by Mabuchi in Japan and its foreign markets are related to Johnson's entrance in the market, I conducted a regression analysis based on the pricing to market theory. The analysis explains the price differences between 100 and 200 Series micro-motors sold in Hong Kong, Taiwan, Germany, France, and the United States relative to the price of the same micro-motors sold in Japan.

Following Marston's pricing to market theory, I have constructed the real exchange differential between the Japanese yen and the currencies of these other countries. To form a real (inflation adjusted) exchange rate differential, I utilize measures of relative inflation levels between Japan and these countries. My analysis allows for country specific shifts in relative pricing levels and includes a time trend to account for general trends in pricing not explained by other factors. Finally, I construct a measure of Johnson's economic presence in the marketplace using Johnson's market share in 100 and 200 Series micro-motors. Other measures of market concentration would produce similar results given the essentially two-supplier nature of the market.

I display Johnson's market share by micro-motor type in figure 2.19. I observe that Johnson's competitive rise in the 100 Series micro-motor market occurred over an approximately five-year period. Ultimately, Johnson captured a 20 percent market share. Johnson's rise in the 200 Series micro-motor market took a shorter time to reach an approximate 10 percent market share. In my empirical analysis, I assume that some threshold effect exists before Johnson's market share has an empirically discernible effect on Mabuchi's behavior. My assumption is that this threshold was reached after November 1987 when Johnson began to sell significant quantities of both 100 and 200 micro-motors. Hence, I assume, with respect to this analysis, that prior to November 1987, Johnson's sales of 100 and 200 Series micro-motors did not have an empirically discernible effect on Mabuchi's pricing behavior. Therefore, this analysis does not attempt to examine Johnson's influence on Mabuchi's pricing prior to November 1987.

## 2.6 Conclusions

The regression analysis, presented in table 2.4, explains 97 percent of the historical variation in Mabuchi's worldwide pricing behavior. The regression results demonstrate the partial pass-through effect as described by Marston (the pass-through elasticity is measured at 0.43). Hence, as the yen appreciated relative to other currencies, Mabuchi increased its foreign price but not to the full extent implied by the change in exchange rates.

The degree of Mabuchi's price pass-through was incomplete in order for Mabuchi to maintain market share. However, once Johnson began selling substantial quantities of 100 and 200 Series micro-motors, the competitive effect of Johnson's sales forced Mabuchi to lower its price in foreign markets. Thus, Johnson's entry caused worldwide price erosion. The measured degree of price

Figure 2.17: Mabuchi Prices for 100 Series Motors Sold in Japan versus Mabuchi Prices for 100 Series Motors Sold Worldwide

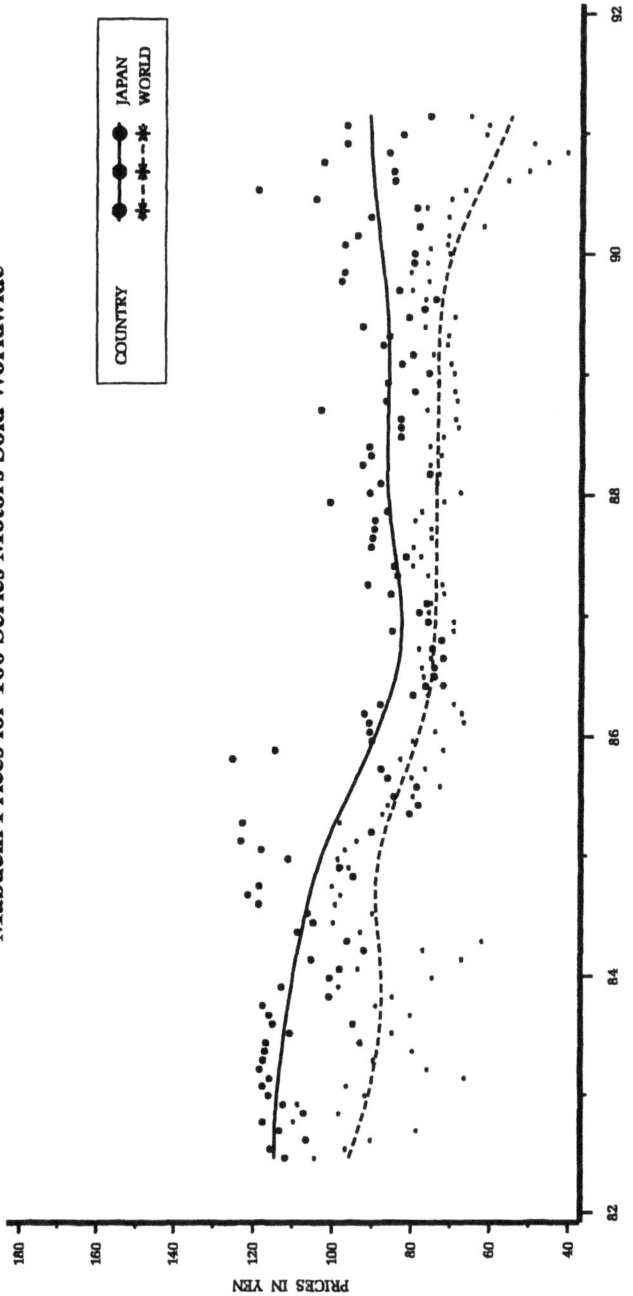

**Figure 2.18: Mabuchi Prices for 200 Series Motors Sold in Japan versus Mabuchi Prices for 200 Series Motors Sold Worldwide**

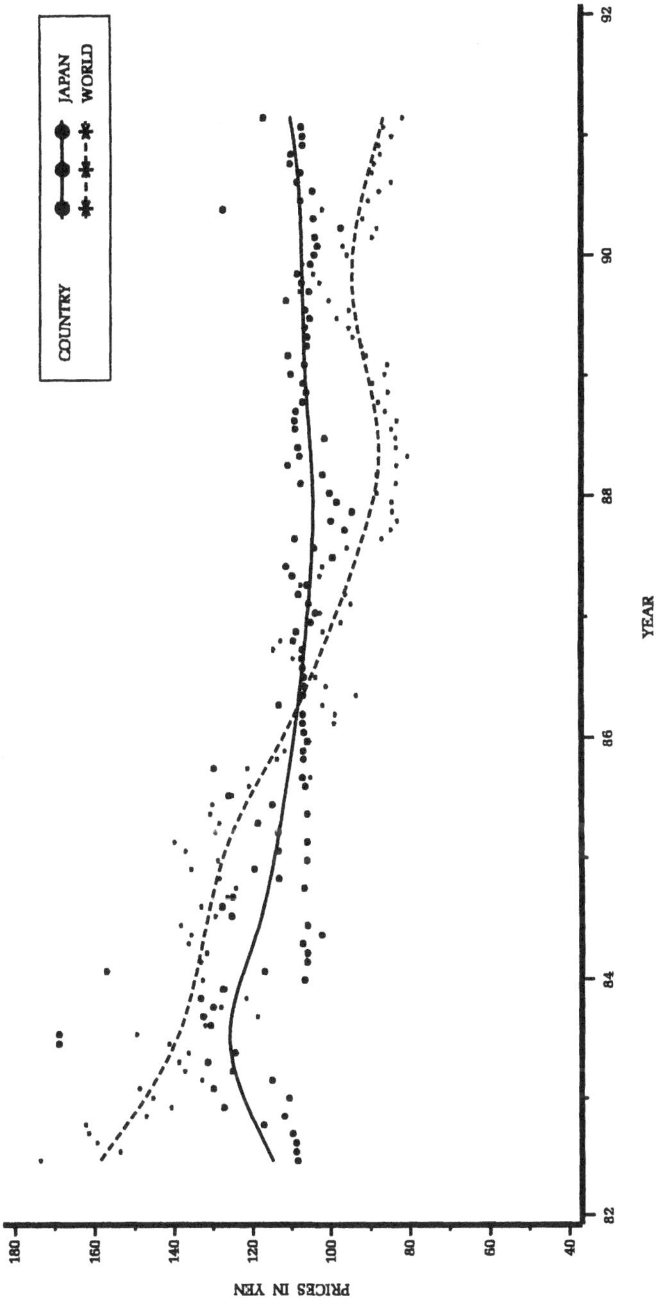

**Figure 2.19: Johnson's Share of 100 and 200 Series Motors**

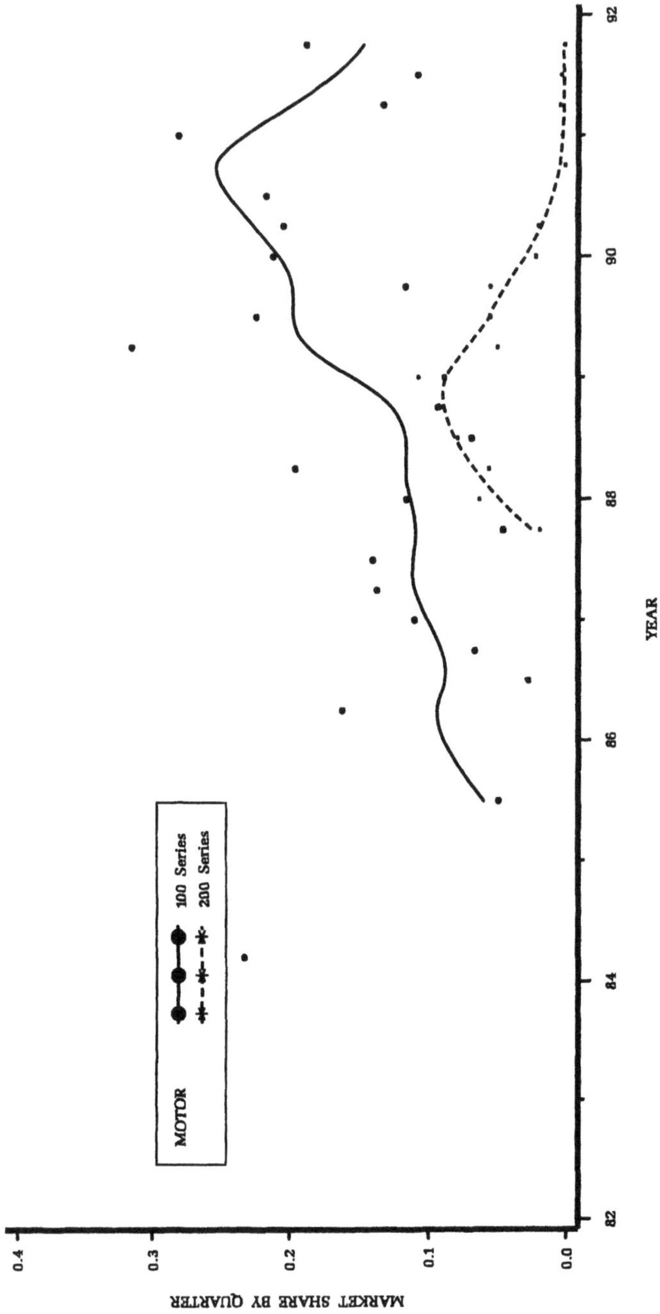

**Table 2.4.** Worldwide Pricing Analysis

| Independent Variables | |
|---|---|
| Logarithm of real exchange ratio worldwide relative to Japan | 0.43<br>(8.59) |
| Time period | 0.06<br>(9.87) |
| Johnson's market share after November 1987 | −0.45<br>(3.75) |
| Number of Observations | 557.00 |
| $R$-squared | 0.965 |

(i) Ordinary least square regression; $t$-statistics in parentheses.
(ii) Observations are monthly and were pooled over the countries France, Germany, Hong Kong, the United States, and Taiwan.
(iii) Country specific dummy variables were included in the regression analysis but omitted from the table.
(iv) Dependent variable is the logarithm of Mabuchi micromotor prices worldwide relative to Japan.

erosion caused by Johnson's entry depended on Johnson's market share in the 100 and 200 Series micro-motor markets. On average, I calculate a 6.5 percent decline. My analysis has accounted for historical differences in prevailing real exchange rates and general trends in worldwide pricing behavior. Based on this analysis, I conclude that Johnson had a measurable and statistically determinant effect on worldwide pricing. The entry of a second competitive supplier led to a substantial lowering of micro-motor prices worldwide.

With lower worldwide prices demand increased, but only to a small degree given the inelasticity in underlying demand. Historical volumes were found to increase nonetheless. The increase in volume was almost entirely attributable to shifts in worldwide demand as uses of micro-motors increased relative to historical levels.

# 3 ESTIMATION AND IDENTIFICATION OF THE WORLDWIDE DEMAND FOR ACETIC ACID

## 3.1 Introduction

The purpose of this chapter is to estimate the worldwide demand for acetic acid. Identification of the demand function proceeds along two paths. First, a classical instrumental variable approach is utilized as the simultaneity of demand and supply causes prices to be endogenous. Here, I rely on exclusion restrictions to create instruments for worldwide price. Second, I use technological estimates of incremental cost for acetic acid production to construct a technological supply curve. The supply curve is used both to generate instruments for identification of the demand function, and in a simulation to demonstrate the consequences of reducing worldwide production by discretely altering the production capabilities of individual suppliers.

The chapter first discusses the uses of acetic acid and its production. I discuss both the raw material inputs for the production of acetic acid and the major chemicals manufactured using acetic acid. I review data sources for production and worldwide market price and discuss the construction of the technological supply curve. I then present econometric estimates of supply and demand for acetic acid and show how changes in the supply relationship affect worldwide pricing.

## 3.2 Review of the Basic Products

Acetic acid is used in the production of cellulose acetate products including acetate fiber, cigarette filters, photographic film, and vinyl acetate monomer (VAM). Approximately 60 percent of all acetic acid goes into the production of VAM and about 80 percent of VAM production is used in construction. Applications in the construction industry using VAM include many types of adhesives. In the U.S. alone, over four billion pounds of acetic acid are produced each year, making acetic acid a leading raw material in domestic production.

### *3.2.1 Uses of Vinyl Acetate Monomer*

A major use of VAM is in the production of latex paints which can be thinned with water, cleaned up easily, and will dry quickly. VAM is also used in making adhesives including packaging and wood glue, and paper coatings (*Kirk-Othmer Encyclopedia of Chemical Technology* [1983]). VAM is an excellent emulsifier and can be combined with a wide variety of modifying agents including solvents, plasticizers, and tackifying resins. VAM emulsions work well in gluing applications since the emulsion quickly dries and sets-up rapidly.

### *3.2.2 VAM Production*

There are several VAM production processes in use, including liquid-phase and vapor-phase processes. The process most widely used to produce vinyl acetate monomer is the addition of acetic acid to ethylene in the presence of a palladium catalyst. In some instances the more expensive material acetylene may by substituted for ethylene in the production process but the ethylene feed method is estimated to be 20 percent less expensive.[1]

### *3.2.3 Acetic Acid*

Acetic acid is an organic acid found in ocean water and brines and is central to all biological energy pathways.[2] The process of fermenting fruit and vegetable juices yields a weak acetic acid solution better known as vinegar. Most of the production of acetic acid takes place in the U.S., Germany, Britain, Japan, Canada, and Mexico. Annual production of acetic acid in these countries is in excess of four million tons.

---

[1]Feed stock disruptions (the explosion of the Hoechst Celanese acetic plant in Pampa, Texas in November 1987 and explosions at Shell's plant and Texaco's plant in 1988) kept U.S. producers from increasing exports of VAM. Increased production was generally expected as the dollar weakened during 1988. However, these expectations were not realized. The Hoechst Celanese plant was off line for approximately eighteen months. Explosions at an ethylene plant in January 1988 further affected VAM production while the start of the Gulf War in July 1990 caused disruptions in supplies and temporary spikes in energy prices.

[2]For a complete discussion on acetic acid see *Kirk-Othmer Encyclopedia of Chemical Technology* (1991).

### 3.2.4 *Acetic Acid Production*

Commercial production of acetic acid has changed significantly in the past twenty years.[3] A variety of processes exist to manufacture acetic acid including butane liquid-phase oxidation, direct ethanol oxidation, and the by-product recovery process. Use of the butane liquid-phase oxidation process has declined significantly in recent years in favor of the methanol carbonylation technology.

The preferred production process, methanol carbonylation, is based on a patented technology from the 1920s which involves adding carbon monoxide to methanol under high temperature and pressure. In 1968, the methanol carbonylation process was improved by using a rhodium catalyst.[4] This process allowed lower carbon monoxide pressures and reaction temperatures.[5] About half of the world's production of acetic acid is currently based on methanol carbonylation and about one-third on the acetaldehyde oxidation process (this method is also based on ethanol and metallic catalysts).

### 3.2.5 *Methanol*

Methanol is commercially manufactured by reacting pressured synthesis gas with a metallic catalyst. Synthesis gas is composed of carbon monoxide, hydrogen, and small amounts of other gases. A major input in the production of methanol is energy. Modern production processes require approximately one hundred thousand BTUs per gallon of methanol produced.[6]

### 3.2.6 *Summary*

Vinyl acetate monomer is principally derived from acetic acid and ethylene. Acetic acid is principally derived from the combination of methanol and carbon monoxide. These four chemicals rank among the top forty chemicals produced each year in the United States. Ethylene production ranks fourth, methanol production ranks twenty-first, acetic acid production ranks thrity-fourth, and vinyl acetate production ranks thirty-ninth. VAM pricing should follow closely the pricing of its major component ingredients. On a weight adjusted basis, nearly equal proportions of acetic acid and ethylene are used to manufacture VAM. To gain some notion of relative prices, VAM sells for forty cents per pound, ethylene for twenty-two cents per pound, and acetic acid for eighteen cents per pound (*Chemical Week*, January 1–8, 1992).

---

[3] Acetic acid production and worldwide capacity is discussed in Wheeler (1988).

[4] The rhodium catalytic reaction has only been recently understood due to advances in basic surface chemistry (Friend [1993]).

[5] Other technologies, which are not as economically attractive at current raw material prices, include the direct liquid-phase oxidation of butane in the presence of metallic ions (cobalt, chromium, etc.), and a recent fermentation process which produces low-concentration acetic acid from inexpensive sugars.

[6] Capacities and production worldwide are discussed in Wheeler and Abshire (1988).

## 3.3 Data

The analysis of the market for acetic acid requires data on production, prices, and capacity. In addition, similar data on inputs (e.g. methanol) and end-uses (e.g. vinyl acetate monomer) are needed.

The best general source of data on acetic acid and related chemicals is the *Chemical Economics Handbook* which contains a wealth of data on production, prices, and capacity for several countries including the United States. Annual U.S. production and sales data are reported in *Synthetic Organic Chemicals.* Quarterly data on production are published in the *Preliminary Report on U.S. Production of Selected Synthetic Organic Chemicals.* Both reports are published by the International Trade Commission (ITC). *Chemical Week* publishes a weekly report on U.S. and European spot and contract prices on thirty-eight chemicals including acetic acid. *Chemical and Engineering News* publishes an annual statistical summary on the chemical industry which reports annual data on production of acetic acid, methanol, and VAM in the major industrial countries. These data are based on a variety of sources including the ITC, the United States Bureau of the Census, the British Plastics Federation, Ministry of International Trade and Industry (MITI), and other government sources. The *Chemical Marketing Reporter* publishes price data on a weekly basis.

I collected Data on acetic acid, methanol, and VAM for the period from 1986 to 1993. For each chemical, I collected spot and list prices from the *Chemical Marketing Reporter* and production data from the ITC reports. The observations of price and quantities produced were collected on a monthly basis.

## 3.4 Incremental Capacity

Using data from the *Chemical Economics Handbooks* and other sources I compiled the 1993 worldwide production capacity for acetic acid. Table 3.1 shows the production of acetic acid by company, country of origin, technological process, nameplate capacity, and estimated incremental cost of production. The production processes used in 1993 were the oxidation process ($CH^3CHO$), the light hydrocarbon liquid-phase oxidation process (butane/naphtha), and the methanol carbonylation process (MeOH).

Estimates of incremental cost were derived from the *Chemical Economic Handbooks.* These estimates are based on the technological process involved and on the prices for butane, natural gas, methanol, ethylene, oxygen, power, and steam. The units in table 3.1 show total nameplace capacity in thousands of metric tons per year and incremental cost in dollars per ton.[7]

[7]There are 2,027 pounds in a metric ton.

**Table 3.1.** Acetic Acid Incremental Cost and Capacity 1993

| Company | Country | Process | Nameplate Capacity $10^3$ (metric tons/year) | marginal cost $/ton |
|---|---|---|---|---|
| BPCL | UK | MeOH | 180 | 86.6 |
| Celanese | USA | MeOH | 590 | 97.2 |
| Sterling | USA | MeOH | 280 | 115.4 |
| BPCL | UK | MeOH | 270 | 115.6 |
| Daicel | Japan | MeOH | 320 | 116.2 |
| Quantum | USA | MeOH | 400 | 116.6 |
| State | Russia | MeOH | 150 | 126.3 |
| Rhone-Poulenc | France | MeOH | 330 | 127.4 |
| SS-BP | Korea | MeOH | 165 | 130.3 |
| CPDC | Taiwan | MeOH | 80 | 138.5 |
| MSK | Yugoslavia | MeOH | 100 | 142.1 |
| Celanese | Mexico | $CH^3CHO$ | 115 | 143.3 |
| Berol | Sweden | $CH^3CHO$ | 10 | 145.8 |
| Celanese | Mexico | $CH^3CHO$ | 63 | 146.2 |
| Celanese | USA | Butane | 335 | 154.4 |
| BPCL | UK | Naphtha | 338 | 158.9 |
| State | Romania | $CH^3CHO$ | 40 | 161.7 |
| Lonza | Switzerland | $CH^3CHO$ | 45 | 168.8 |
| Nippon Gohesei | Japan | $CH^3CHO$ | 148 | 177.7 |
| Showa Denko | Japan | $CH^3CHO$ | 130 | 178.7 |
| Eastman | USA | $CH^3CHO$ | 160 | 184.6 |
| Daicel | Japan | Naphtha | 34 | 194.9 |
| Hoechst | Germany | $CH^3CHO$ | 160 | 197.3 |
| Basf | Germany | MeOH | 40 | 209.5 |
| Hoechst | Germany | $CH^3CHO$ | 150 | 212.7 |
| Wacker | Germany | $CH^3CHO$ | 80 | 219.7 |
| Celanese | Canada | Butane | 78 | 219.9 |
| Rhodia | Brazil | $CH^3CHO$ | 70 | 221.7 |
| Norquissa | Brazil | $CH^3CHO$ | 60 | 222.5 |
| Cloroetil | Brazil | $CH^3CHO$ | 13 | 233.5 |
| Huels | Germany | $CH^3CHO$ | 50 | 289.2 |
| State | Poland | $CH^3CHO$ | 30 | 325.6 |
| State | Russia | $CH^3CHO$ | 200 | 393.6 |
| State | Russia | $CH^3CHO$ | 25 | 403.8 |
| State | Russia | $CH^3CHO$ | 20 | 405.4 |

## 3.5 Econometric Estimation

### *3.5.1 Specification*

The worldwide demand for acetic acid is specified to depend on the worldwide price of acetic acid, and on the worldwide price of the good for which acetic acid is a basic precursor, vinyl acetate monomer. As the price of acetic acid increases, the demand for acetic acid will fall, other things equal. Based on the discussion of the technologies involved, we should expect that as the price of VAM increases the production of VAM precursors will increase, causing the derived demand for acetic acid to rise. The basic demand equation has the form:

$$\begin{aligned} \text{PRODWW} &= \alpha + \beta\text{TREND} + \gamma_1\text{QTR1} + \gamma_2\text{QTR2} + \gamma_3\text{QTR3} \\ &\quad + \chi_1\text{PRHAC} + \chi_2\text{PRVAM} + \varepsilon \end{aligned} \tag{1}$$

where:

PRODWW = the worldwide demand for acetic acid;
TREND = time trend;
QTR1 = January, February, March quarter indicator;
QTR2 = April, May, June quarter indicator;
QTR3 = July, August, September quarter indicator;
PRHAC = the worldwide price of acetic acid; and
PRVAM = the worldwide price of VAM.

The worldwide price of acetic acid, PRHAC, is constructed as a weighted average (using quantity weights) of the prices in dollars per ton of acetic acid in the Far Eastern, North American, and Western European markets. The worldwide price of vinyl acetate monomer, PRVAM, is also a weighted average of the prices in these three regions, with the exception that the European price component was taken to be the average of the European high and low prices. The unit of observation is one month and the time period for the analysis is 1986 through 1993. There were approximately eighty monthly periods used in the econometric analysis.

### *3.5.2 Estimation*

Ordinary least squares regression estimates of the parameters of equation (1) are presented in table 3.2.

Inspection of the regression results shows a positive trend in the demand for acetic acid as well as the presence of some seasonality, with higher demand in the third quarter. The price coefficient is negative indicating that as the price of acetic acid rises, the demand falls. The price of VAM also appears in the regression correctly signed. The regression explains about 75 percent of the variation in worldwide demand for acetic acid.

### *3.5.3 Identification*

The results of the ordinary least squares regression, while suggestive, are subject to simultaneous equation bias. In particular, we should expect the price of acetic acid to be endogenously determined by the supply and demand for worldwide acetic acid. An unobserved effect causing a shift in the demand for acetic acid will also cause a simultaneous movement in the worldwide price.

**Table 3.2.** Acetic Acid Demand Equation (OLS)

| Dependent Variable | PRODWW |
|---|---|
| Constant | 318.87 (25.17) ** |
| Trend | 8.83 (10.83) ** |
| Quarter 1 | −2.15 (−0.62) |
| Quarter 2 | 2.16 (0.63) |
| Quarter 3 | 6.58 (1.90) * |
| PRHAC | −0.17 (−2.91) ** |
| PRVAM | 0.13 (4.86) ** |
| Number of Observations | 84 |
| Corrected $R$-Squared | 0.75 |

* denotes significance at 90 percent level.
** denotes significance at 95 percent level.
$t$-statistics in parentheses.

This results in a correlation between the disturbance in equation (1) and the price of acetic acid and therefore leads to inconsistent estimates using ordinary least squares.

One solution to the problem of identifying the demand curve relies on the technique of instrumental variables. The first variable I use as an instrument is the worldwide price of methanol, PRMET. The price of methanol should be correlated with the acetic acid price since methanol is a basic ingredient in to the production of acetic acid. On the other hand, the price of methanol does not itself appear in the demand equation for acetic acid and thus can be used as an instrument.

A second instrumental variable can be constructed from the supply curve.[8] As discussed above, the technological supply curve in 1993 was constructed by measuring the nameplate capacity of all worldwide facilities which produce acetic acid and arranging them in order of increasing incremental cost of production. Sorting the incremental costs, in this way, identifies the worldwide supply curve for acetic acid in 1993 since we can calculate which plants operate with positive economic margins at a given worldwide price. In order to construct an exogenous instrument from this supply curve, we first construct a reduced-form prediction of worldwide demand which does not depend on the endogenous price of acetic acid. Equation (2) gives the reduced form predicted quantity:

$$\begin{aligned}\text{PRODWW} &= \alpha^* + \beta^*\text{TREND} + \sum_j \gamma_j^* QTR_j + \chi_1^*\,\text{PRVAM} \\ &\quad + \chi_2^*\,\text{PRMET} + \varepsilon^*. \end{aligned} \tag{2}$$

The reduced-form production equation is estimated consistently by ordinary least squares. These estimates are presented in table 3.3.

While structural interpretations of reduced-form coefficients are not usually made, it is worth noting that all coefficients in the reduced-form have the expected sign, including the coefficient of the variable PRMET–which serves as a proxy for the endogenous price. Using predicted demand from equation (2), we calculate the estimated supply price of acetic acid consistent with that level of predicted demand. The predicted price is determined by equation (3)

$$\text{PPRHAC} = S(\text{PPRODW} \cdot 12) \tag{3}$$

where

PPRHAC = the predicted supply price in dollars per metric ton;
PPRODW= the predicted demand from the reduced-form demand equation given in (2); and
S(·) = the supply function.

The shape of the supply function is an increasing step function with constant incremental costs over the incremental capacity of each producer of acetic acid. The factor of twelve appearing in equation (3) converts the monthly sales demand to an annual volume.

In calculating the predicted supply price, I make the simplifying assumption that the monthly demand level would persist unaltered for a twelve month period. To simplify the analysis, I have also approximated the non-linear supply schedule in the relevant range using a quadratic approximation. The quadratic approximation has the form $P_j = AQ_j^2 + BQ_j + C$ where $Q_j$ is the midpoint of

[8] A similar technique for estimating demand functions with endogenously determined prices is given in McFadden, Puig, and Kirshner (1977).

**Table 3.3.** Acetic Acid Demand Equation (Reduced-Form)

| Dependent Variable | PRODWW |
|---|---|
| Constant | 283.36 |
| | (38.22) ** |
| Trend | 6.25 |
| | (9.73) ** |
| Quarter 1 | 0.85 |
| | (0.26) |
| Quarter 2 | 6.36 |
| | (1.91) ** |
| Quarter 3 | 7.47 |
| | (2.32) ** |
| PRVAM | 0.14 |
| | (7.77) ** |
| PRMET | −0.30 |
| | (−5.20) ** |
| Number of Observations | 82 |
| Corrected $R$-Squared | 0.79 |

* denotes significance at 90 percent level.
** denotes significance at 95 percent level.
$t$-statistics in parentheses.

quantity range for the $j$th block in the non-linear supply schedule and $P_j$ is the corresponding price. The approximate supply curve is presented in table 3.4.

The simple correlation between the prices PPRHAC and PRHAC, the predicted and actual prices of acetic acid, is 0.80 so that PPRHAC should be a good instrument for PRHAC. To verify that PRMET and PPRHAC will be good instruments for PRHAC, we consider the first stage of the two-stage least squares estimation method. The specification for equation (4) is:

$$\begin{aligned} \text{PRHAC} &= \alpha^{**} + \beta^{**}\text{TREND} + \sum_j \lambda_j^{**}\text{QTR}_j + \chi_1^{**}\text{PPRHAC} \\ &\quad + \chi_2^{**}\text{PRVAM} + \chi_3^{**}\text{PRMET} + \varepsilon^{**}. \end{aligned} \tag{4}$$

**Table 3.4.** Acetic Acid Supply Schedule (Quadratic Approximation)

| Dependent Variable | PRHAC |
|---|---|
| Constant | 109.47 (8.15) ** |
| Quantity | −0.00147 (−1.45) |
| Quantity$^2$ | 0.00000864 (4.96) ** |
| Number of Observations | 32 |
| Corrected $R$-Squared | 0.88 |

* denotes significance at 90 percent level.
** denotes significance at 95 percent level.
$t$-statistics in parentheses.

The estimated first-stage regression is presented in table 3.5. The predicted price from equation (4), denoted by HPRHAC, is next used in the second stage of the two-stage least squares regression as an exogenous proxy for PRHAC. The second-stage equation is estimated using:

$$\begin{aligned} \text{PRODWW} &= \alpha^{***} + \beta^{***}\text{TREND} + \sum_j \lambda_j^{***}\text{QTR}_j \\ &\quad + \chi_1^{***}\text{HPRHAC} + \chi_2^{***}\text{PRVAM} + \varepsilon^{***}. \end{aligned} \tag{5}$$

The second-stage regression is estimated by ordinary least squares and the estimation results are presented in table 3.6.

While the coefficients in table 3.6 are consistently estimated, the standard errors and auxiliary statistics are not correct. Instead, I rely on an instrumental variables method treating PRHAC as an endogenous variable and using PPRHAC and PRMET as instruments. All other variables in equation (1) are treated exogenously including the price of VAM. The instrumental variables estimates are presented in table 3.7.

The estimates given in table 3.7 for the structural coefficients of the demand equation are qualitatively similar to the least squares estimates. However, the magnitude of the difference between the ordinary least squares and the instrumental variable estimates allows us to conclude (using a Hausman test for endogeneity, $t = -3.50$) that PRHAC is endogenous in the demand equation. The consistently estimated demand equation shows that approximately 71 percent of the variation in acetic acid demand is explained by the model.

The elasticity of demand is given by equation (6):

**Table 3.5.** Acetic Acid Price Equation (OLS)

| Dependent Variable | PRHAC |
|---|---|
| Constant | 116.29 |
| | (5.91) * * |
| Trend | 8.17 |
| | (4.79) * * |
| Quarter 1 | −2.25 |
| | (−0.45) |
| Quarter 2 | −5.24 |
| | (−1.02) |
| Quarter 3 | 2.13 |
| | (0.43) |
| PRVAM | 0.21 |
| | (2.36) * * |
| PRMET | 0.18 |
| | (5.58) * * |
| PPRHAC | 0.77 |
| | (8.59) * * |
| Number of Observations | 82 |
| Corrected $R$-Squared | 0.95 |
| * denotes significance at 90 percent level. | |
| ** denotes significance at 95 percent level. | |
| $t$-statistics in parentheses. | |

$$\varepsilon = \frac{d\,\text{PRODWW}}{d\,\text{PRHAC}} \frac{\text{PRHAC}}{\text{PRODWW}} = \chi_1 \frac{\text{PRHAC}}{\text{PRODWW}} \tag{6}$$

We evaluate the elasticity of demand at the mean values for PRHAC and PRODWW using the consistent estimate of the price coefficient $\chi_1$. The estimated price elasticity is −0.45. Since this value is less than one in magnitude, I conclude that the worldwide demand for acetic acid is inelastic.

Finding that the demand for acetic acid is inelastic is in accord with our expectations. Acetic is a product which has a derived demand. For the most part, the demand for acetic acid is caused by its use in the production of

**Table 3.6.** Acetic Acid Demand Equation (2SLS)

| Dependent Variable | PRODWW |
|---|---|
| Constant | 340.0<br>(29.5) ** |
| Trend | 10.43<br>(10.98) ** |
| Quarter 1 | −0.59<br>(−0.18) |
| Quarter 2 | 4.04<br>(1.21) |
| Quarter 3 | 8.57<br>(2.55) ** |
| PRVAM | −0.36<br>(−4.6) ** |
| HPRHAC | 0.210<br>(6.19) ** |
| Number of Observations | 82 |
| Corrected $R$-Squared | 0.78 |

* denotes significance at 90 percent level.
** denotes significance at 95 percent level.
$t$-statistics in parentheses.

VAM. VAM production is, in turn, determined by exogenous factors such as the strength of the construction industry and the economy.

### *3.5.4 Simulating the Model*

I now consider the determination of equilibrium price in the acetic acid market using the estimated demand equation and the technologically-derived supply function. The demand and supply curves we use correspond to the 1992–1993 period. At the intersection of supply and demand we estimate a 1992–1993 market clearing price of $422 per metric ton. The quantity produced at this price level is approximately 4,831 metric tons per year.

To simulate the effects of a shift in supply, we assume hypothetically that all production at a single facility (the Celanese Clear Lake plant) would have

**Table 3.7.** Acetic Acid Demand Equation (IV)

| Dependent Variable | PRODWW |
|---|---|
| Constant | 340.0<br>(25.6) ** |
| Trend | 10.43<br>(9.55) ** |
| Quarter 1 | −0.59<br>(−0.15) |
| Quarter 2 | 4.04<br>(1.05) |
| Quarter 3 | 8.57<br>(2.21) ** |
| PRHAC | −0.36<br>(−4.0) ** |
| PRVAM | 0.21<br>(5.38) ** |
| Number of Observations | 82 |
| Corrected $R$-Squared | 0.71 |

* denotes significance at 90 percent level.
** denotes significance at 95 percent level.
$t$-statistics in parentheses.

ceased.[9] Eliminating the Celanese Clear Lake plant would cause its annual production capacity of 210 metric tons per year to be removed from the marketplace.

The consequences of losing 210 metric tons per year of production are modeled by a shift in the supply curve. Specifically, the supply curve shifts by an amount of 210 metric tons for all production that is at least as costly as that at the Clear Lake plant. To approximate this shift in the supply schedule, I reestimated the supply function without the incremental capacity of the Celanese plant. The results of the quadratic approximation after the shift in supply are given in table 3.8.

[9]The choice of the Celanese Clear Lake plant is not material to the presentation.

**Table 3.8.** Acetic Acid Supply Schedule (After Supply Shift)

| Dependent Variable | PRHAC |
|---|---|
| Constant | 118.75<br>(6.14) ** |
| Quantity | −0.0027<br>(−1.75) |
| Quantity$^2$ | 0.0000122<br>(4.42) ** |
| Number of Observations | 33 |
| Corrected $R$-Squared | 0.80 |

* denotes significance at 90 percent level.
** denotes significance at 95 percent level.
*t*-statistics in parentheses.

The shift in the supply curve relative to the actual supply curve is shown in figure 3.1. The shift in the supply curve of 210 metric tons per year results in a change in the equilibrium price from $422 per metric tons to $457 per metric ton and a decrease in annual production from 4,831 metric tons per year to approximately 4,681 metric tons per year. The price level rises by approximately 8.3 percent while production is predicted to fall by 150 metric tons per year or approximately 3.1 percent.

## 3.6 Conclusions

In this chapter I have estimated the worldwide demand for and supply of acetic acid. Demand estimates follow from classical instrumental variables estimation techniques while supply estimates were derived by technological identification of the underlying incremental costs of production. In figure 3.2 I display both predicted and actual production over the period from 1986 to 1993. As the figure shows, the overall fit of the models is quite good

I conclude that the demand for acetic acid is inelastic with an elasticity of −0.4. To illustrate the consequences on worldwide production from the loss of just one production facility (a facility that nevertheless provides infra-marginal capacity), I considered a simple experiment which eliminated the production of the Celanese Clear Lake plant. The resulting loss of 210 metric tons per year in production capacity is predicted to increase the world price of acetic acid by approximately 8 percent. Meanwhile total consumption of acetic acid is predicted to fall by 150 metric tons as the higher price curtail demand on a worldwide basis.

**Figure 3.1: Equilibrium Acetic Acid Price**

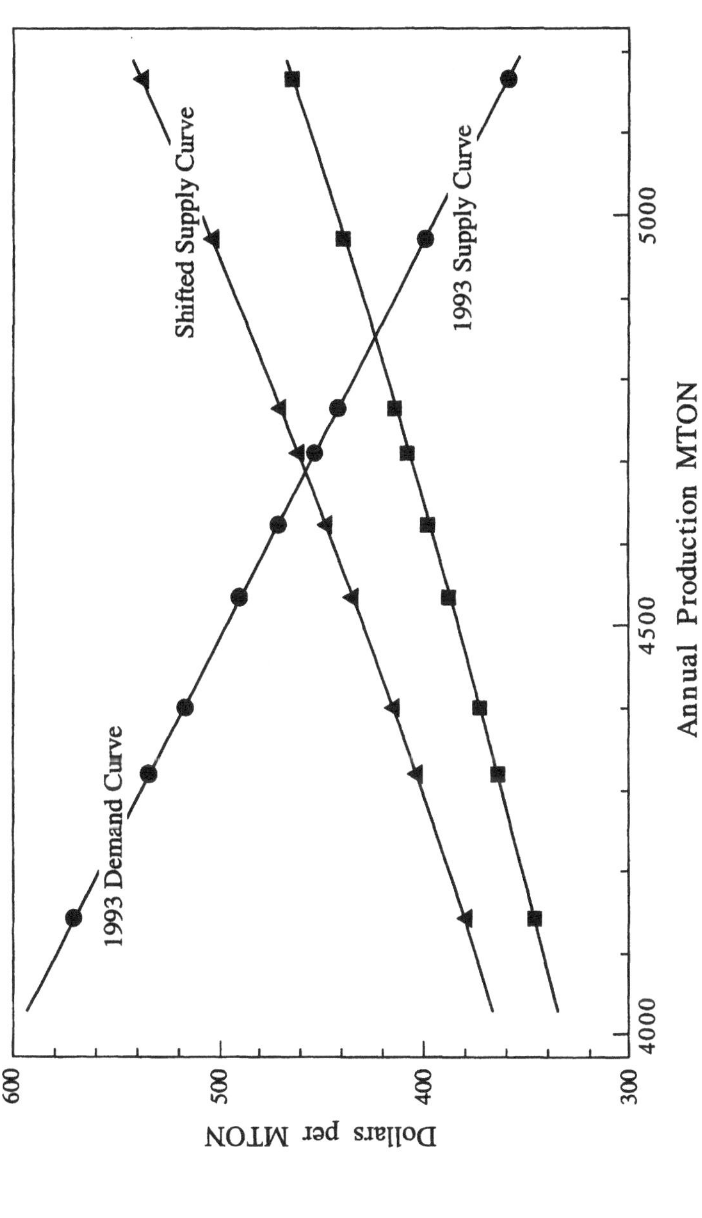

**Figure 3.2: Predicted versus Actual Demand of Acetic Acid**

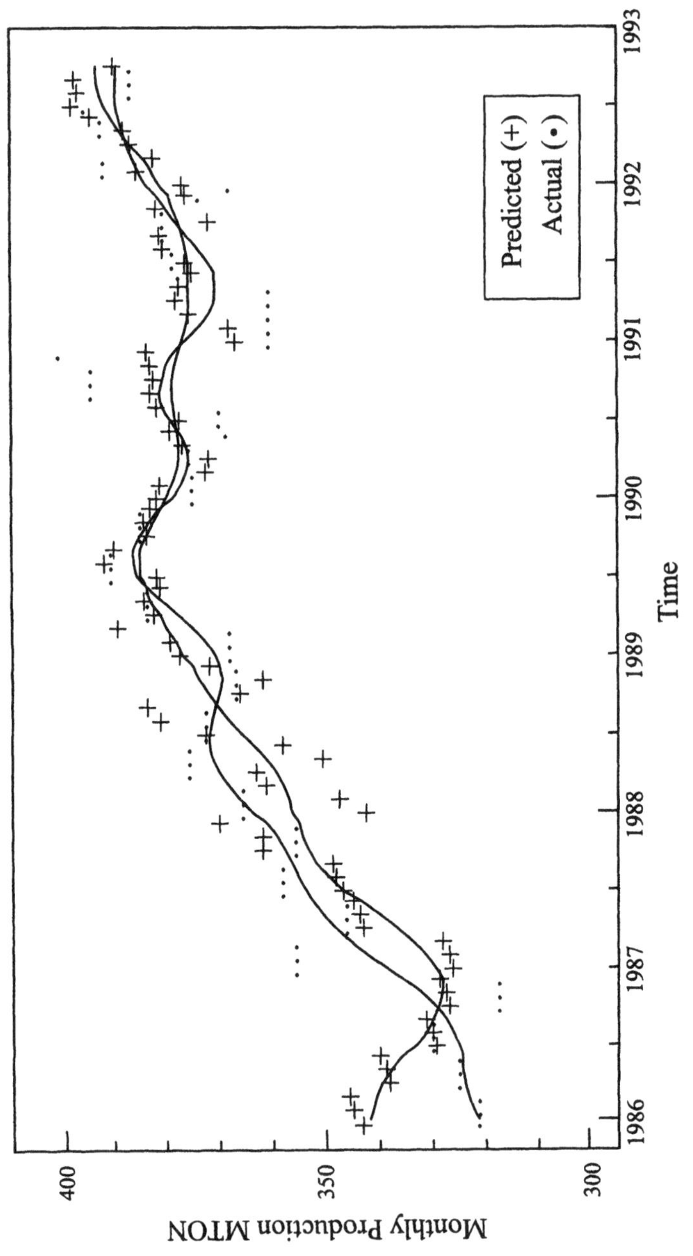

# 4 THE DEMAND FOR BRANDED AND UNBRANDED PRODUCTS—AN ECONOMETRIC METHOD FOR VALUING INTANGIBLE ASSETS

In this chapter I consider the economic value of certain intangible assets such as trademarks and brand values. Specifically I develop an economic analysis to estimate the values for five trademarks of the Carnation Company circa 1985—Coffee-mate, Carnation Evaporated Milk, Carnation Instant Breakfast, Mighty Dog (dog food), and Fancy Feast (cat food). These five brands were among Carnation's best known brands; each has a relatively large market share, and each commands a price premium relative to its unbranded competitors.

For this group of brands, there was both sufficient data to estimate product demand reliably, and enough variety among the products to illustrate the nature and range of trademark values. The tools of demand analysis are used to quantify these characteristics and to calculate the trademark's economic value. These values are expressed as percentages of operating income and sales.[1]

In brief, there are two basic components to the economic analysis of trademark value. First, historical sales data on these brands and their competitors are used to estimate the demand for these products. The demand function can

[1]The purpose of this analysis is not to predict a reasonable royalty rate for these trademarks per se since a number of factors may enter into the valuation of these trademarks in negotiations between an owner and a user. A negotiated value may be higher or lower than the economic value. Nevertheless, the economic value of the trademark presents a useful guidepost since it seeks to determine objectively the incremental revenues earned by use of the trademark.

be used, with knowledge of production costs to determine the profitability of a product under alternative pricing strategies. The demand function summarizes all relevant information about the market for a product such as special population segments that purchase a particular product, seasonal variations in purchases, levels of advertising spent, and characteristics of similar products in the same market. In appendix 4.6.2 to this chapter, I present a product review which provides the basis for the additional information included in each demand analysis.

The second component of the economic analysis is a method for calculating the value of a brand trademark from the demand functions for the brand and its competitors. From an economic perspective, the value of a brand trademark to a producer is the difference between the profits that it would earn operating with the trademark and the profits it would earn operating without that trademark.[2]

A formula giving the appropriate split of total profit between the trademark and non-trademark components is derived in section 4.2. The fraction of total profits attributable to the trademark, that is the "trademark fraction," is shown to depend on the market shares of the trademark brand versus that of the unbranded product (private label and generic goods) and their respective price elasticities.[3] In general, the greater the price elasticity of the branded good relative to the price elasticity of competing unbranded goods, the lower the fraction of profit which should be allocated to the brand trademark.

The remainder of this chapter is divided into five sections and two appendices. Section 4.1 provides a basis for the economic analysis and reviews the existing literature on brand, trademark, and intangible valuation. Section 4.2 describes the economic theory underlying my approach to brand valuation and shows how knowledge of the demand functions for a brand and its competitors can be used to determine the value for a trademark. Section 4.3 describes the data used to estimate demand functions for the above mentioned products and their competitors. Section 4.4 explains how these demand functions were estimated and presents the key parameter values required for the economic value calculations. Section 4.5 concludes the chapter with a discussion of the economic value calculations. Appendix 4.6.1 reviews certain results from oligopoly theory. Appendix 4.6.2 provides background information on the specific brands that I evaluated.

---

[2]The value of a trademark can also include other attributes of value, such as long-term profit or growth potential, but this difference in current profits represents a useful floor on such overall values.

[3]The distinction between private label and generic commodities is discussed in Burke (1979). Burke notes that generics, while different from private label commodities in packaging and marketing, account for less than 1 percent of total food sales. In my analysis I do not distinguish between private label and generic commodities.

## 4.1 The Basis for the Demand Approach

Traditionally, several approaches have been used to value intangible assets such as patents and trademarks. My approach to determining the value of particular trademarks is to use economic demand analysis.

### *4.1.1 Economic Value of Brand Trademarks*

The economic value of a brand or trademark reflects a manufacturer's ability to command a higher selling price and/or market share for the branded good than it would attain for an essentially identical unbranded good. Uncertainty about the quality of, or lack of familiarity with unbranded alternatives makes many consumers reluctant to purchase such products even when they sell at a considerable discount to branded goods. This has two consequences which will be demonstrated mathematically below. First, because consumers prefer the branded good to its unbranded competitors, the branded good can be sold at a higher price than the unbranded good. Second, despite the price premium, the producer of the branded good is usually able to sell larger quantities than the unbranded producer. The combination of price premium and increased market share determines the relative profitability of branded and unbranded goods.

From an economic perspective, the appropriate value for a trademark relates to the loss in profit that would ensue if the branded producer were denied use of the trademark.[4] The purpose of demand analysis is to estimate what price the producer of a branded good would charge if forced to sell the identical good without the brand label, and what quantity it would be able to sell at that price. If these prices and quantities can be estimated with sufficient accuracy, then it is possible to determine the value to the holder of the brand trademark, as a portion of profit or sales.

Demand analysis was regularly employed by the Carnation Company itself in setting its pricing strategies (see appendix 4.6.2 below). For example, company studies indicated that the demand for evaporated milk was very price elastic. Indeed, a 1984 survey found canned and powdered milk to be the most price elastic of 116 products studied.

### *4.1.2 Other Approaches to Brand Valuation*

An economic approach to brand valuation is certainly not the only approach that has been applied to this problem. While brand names and trademarks have long been recognized to have values for their owners there have been only a few attempts to estimate these brand values. Two studies which review the most common techniques are Farquhar (1989) and Lipman (1989). In this

[4]The long-run advantage created by a trademark is identical to that created by a patent. Trademarks and patents are analytically similar because they confer some degree of monopoly power to their owners. However, trademarks identify the origin or source of the products to which they are affixed while patents may be more generally applicable to technologies that apply to several products.

section I summarize some of the literature and alternative methodologies to brand valuation.

### *4.1.3 Price Premium Approach*

The price premium approach is based on a comparison of the price of a branded commodity with the price of an unbranded good. Intuitively the price differential between the two commodities reflects a value attributable to the branded good. As Simon and Sullivan (1993) have noted, the price premium will usually result in biased estimates of brand equity. They note that the price premium may exist due to quality differences or different production costs, and will generally fail to reflect the expected future profits from owning the brand. Importantly they note that the price premium reflects the elasticity of demand as a proxy for brand loyalty. The price premium method is clearly not capable of distinguishing between the value that consumers place on branded products as apposed to cost savings or other competitive advantages that differentiate the brand holder from the producer of the non-branded good. Interestingly, in actual implementation, the price premium method is often employed utilizing a series of subjective adjustments to apportion the price differential into brand equity and other components. These adjustments may be made by "experts" in valuation, but are frequently simply subjective restatements which lack any quantitative basis.[5]

Recently a hedonic decomposition of the price premium has been provided by Wiggins and Raboy (1996). Their approach determines brand effects for the banana market. Market elasticity concentration and other factors are not included in their analysis.[6]

### *4.1.4 Consumer Valuation Method*

Another technique for valuing brand equity is to survey customers and ask their opinions regarding the factors that influence purchase decisions. An example of using scanner data to devise measures of consumer loyalty and perceived values by customers is given in Kamakura and Russell (1991). As noted by Simon and Sullivan (1993), the consumer valuation method suffers from the inability to

[5]Another potential issue raised by a price premium approach results from the fact that the historical price charged by unbranded producers may be different from the price at which a particular brand producer would sell its product if it were deprived of its trademark. The selling price chosen by a particular producer depends on its cost of production as well as consumer demand for its product. However, unbranded competitors may face different production costs than the branded producer and would choose different sales strategies, even if they face the same demand curve. For example, if the brand producer's own costs are lower and it is forced into the unbranded market, it may be more profitable for the formerly branded producer to sell more units at a lower price than at the price historically charged by unbranded producers.

[6]An analysis of margin as it relates to market structures is provided in Connor and Peterson (1992).

use the consumer data to quantify a brand's equity.[7] While it has apparently not been proposed to date, a contingent valuation technology would seem to be relevant to the determination of a brand's equity. Specifically, consumers might be asked to rank order hypothetical goods which varied over limited qualitative dimensions but which varied in brand name or trademark. Consumer responses to such hypothetical questions could be used to establish the values of a brand, much in the same way that the contingent valuation method is used to measure the value consumers place on environmental goods.

### *4.1.5 Brand Replacement Cost*

In the brand replacement cost method, historical expenditures to develop the brand are added together with some accounting for the time value of money. When done correctly the brand replacement cost method should account for the randomness inherent in creating a successful brand. In this regard the actual costs of developing a successful technology should include the cost of research and development of projects or technologies that are not successful. This method is far from perfect. It suffers because the analyst often does not know how much of historical advertising expenditure was used to "build" the brand, as opposed to simply maintaining its position or image. The method also does not take into account future sale possibilities, instead relying solely on the historical costs of brand development, which may be very different from a brand's current marketability.

### *4.1.6 Income Method*

The income method, or brand-earnings multiplier method, attempts to forecast the future profit stream arising from sales of a given branded product, and then to determine the fraction of this profit stream that is attributable to the brand. Again, this approach can be highly subjective and results in the application of certain rules of thumb. A more detailed description of the income method is given in Wentz and Martin (1989). Below we discuss one rule of thumb for approximating a product's sales into brand and non-brand components. This rule has come to be known as Goldschilder's method.

### *4.1.7 Profit-Split Methods*

The profit-split method divides the operating profits for a particular product between licensor and licensee and then discounts the resulting after-tax income stream to present value. The method is supposed to approximate the way license agreements are actually negotiated. A licensee is willing to pay a portion

[7] The logit model of Guadagni and Little (1983) uses past purchase behavior to measure consumer "loyalty." Carpenter and Lehmann (1985) and Zufryden (1986) use the previous brand purchases as controls for segmentation of customer classes. See also Grover and Srinivasan (1989) who use loyalty variable within a logit model for estimating market shares within product group segments.

of his operating profits to a licensor because of the contribution made by the trademark to the profits generated in the licensee's business.

Goldschilder's application of the profit-split concept utilizes a rule of thumb (typically 25 to 30 percent) for allocating a proportion of operating profits to the trademark. The determination of this fraction is apparently arbitrary.

### *4.1.8 Comparables*

Another method to measure the value of an intangible asset is the comparables method. In the comparables method, the sales of a brand, or a royalty payment made for the use of a brand or trademark for a comparable product, is used as a guide to the value of the good at issue. Unfortunately, as the market for trademarks is quite thin, few truly comparable trademarks exist in the marketplace limiting the usefulness of the technique.

### *4.1.9 Value in Acquisition*

A technique described by Mahajan et al. (1990) attempts to value a brand by the acquisition premium that an acquiring company is willing to pay to utilize the branded good owned by the acquired company. This method is fraught with difficulties in identifying which aspect of the acquisition value can be associated with the products being acquired, and in identifying the synergies or cost savings present in the merger.

### *4.1.10 The Financial Approach*

In an important study, Simon and Sullivan (1993) introduce two new techniques for valuing brand equity. They also review many of the techniques discussed here but leave out Goldschilder's technique and the comparables method. Interestingly, their article recognizes the empirical content of the elasticity approach but stops short of actually embracing that method as a standard.

Simon and Sullivan first decompose the intangible assets of a firm into three components: (1) brand equity, (2) the value of other firm-specific factors not associated with brand equity, and (3) market-specific factors that lead to imperfect competition. In their discussion of this decomposition four factors are assumed to explain the brand equity component.[8]

The first factor assumed to affect brand equity is advertising. Advertising effects on brand value have been studied by Stigler (1961), Nelson (1974), Farquhar (1989), Bass and Clarke (1972), and Montgomery and Silk (1972). These studies conclude that advertising can create or change perceived value,

[8]Firm-specific factors, which affect the firm's intangible value but not its brand equity, are due in part to "superior technologies and specialized knowledge" according to Simon and Sullivan. These aspects are measured by the firm's share of patents relative to its competitors, and the firm's share of research and development expenditures. The imperfect competition factors are measured by the four-firm concentration ratio (the sum of the market shares of the top four firms) and an indicator for the presence or absence of regulation.

and therefore shape consumer demand. In my study, advertising is assumed to directly affect consumer demand and is introduced as a measured factor in the demand equation.

Another factor assumed to affect brand equity by Simon and Sullivan is the share of a firm's own advertising relative to the advertising conducted by the firm's competitors. This relationship was demonstrated by Little (1979) and Thomas (1989). These studies argue that a competitor's advertising influences its own demand as well as the advertising of its rival's brands. In my analysis the own-advertising and the advertising of the competing brands are allowed to affect the demand for the firm's branded product.

The final two factors proposed by Simon and Sullivan are the age of the brand and the competitive positioning of the brand. In this regard, Simon and Sullivan rely on the work of Ries and Trout (1986) on brand age-effects, and on the work of Schmalensee (1982), Robinson and Fornell (1985), and Urban et al. (1986) on strategic positioning. In the case of brand age it is assumed that older brands have greater product awareness and loyalty. It is also hypothesized that strategic advantages accrue to the pioneering brand.[9]

Simon and Sullivan then present two techniques for measuring a firm's brand equity. These methods are derived from financial market estimates of brand-related profits. In their first method, Simon and Sullivan decompose the value of a firms intangible assets into three components: the value of brand equity, the value of non-brand factors that reduce the firm's costs relative to its competitors, and the value of industry-wide factors which permit monopoly or super-competitive profits (such as a favorable regulatory climate). Using a Tobin's Q approach, they first measure a firm's intangible assets. Then they relate the firms intangible value to the three components described above. The objective is to isolate the value of brand equity from the values determined by industry structure or from cost advantage.

In their second approach, Simon and Sullivan apply an event-type methodology to the stock prices for specific firms over a defined event horizon. For instance the introduction of Diet Coke by Coca-Cola is hypothesized to affect the brand equity of the Coca-Cola company. The change in brand equity is hypothesized to be due to the introduction of the new brand into the marketplace and may be discernible in the price of Coca-Cola's stock.

[9]In my study some of these effects are not measurable given that they are constant over time and constant within the product categories I study. For instance, Carnation may have introduced their coffee creamer Coffee-mate before there was any substitute. Nonetheless, the age of the Coffee-mate brand is nearly synonymous with the age of the competing creamers, and the "pioneering advantage" associated with the Coffee-mate brand is captured by the constant term in the Coffee-mate demand equation. Therefore, while Simon and Sullivan measure and utilize factors for the age of a brand and for the order in which that brand entered the marketplace, I omit such factors in my analysis.

### *4.1.11 Brand Valuation with Econometrics*

The econometric method determines a royalty or value based on the market impact of the producer's losing the right to use the trademark. The premise of this method is that the economic value of a trademark equals the difference between the economic profits a producer could earn with the trademark and the profits gained without the trademark.

The two items of relevant information for the branded producer if its trademark expired (or otherwise were unavailable) would be: (1) consumer demand for unbranded goods (which can be determined from historical data on unbranded sales) and (2) the branded producer's own costs of production (*not* the costs or historical quantities sold by the unbranded producer). Demand analysis uses this information, in combination with an assumption of profit maximization, to estimate what the profits of the branded producer would be if it were forced to sell its goods without benefit of the brand trademark.

The econometric method maintains two assumptions. First, that consumers would perceive that unbranded goods produced by the branded producer were identical to other private label goods. Second, that the branded producer's unit costs are the same whether it produces branded or unbranded goods. If the branded product is, in fact, superior to private label alternatives, then the branded producer may be able to lower its costs by producing goods equivalent to those currently sold under private label. On the other hand, the branded producer may possess technological advantages which allow it to produce superior products at little or no additional cost, so that it could eventually reestablish its brand advantage over private label products.

Quality differences in many goods are often in the eye of the beholder.[10] To the extent that quality or technological differences exist or are perceived, the value of these is reflected in the valuation conclusions reached below, because any such differences are incorporated in consumer demand.

In summary, demand analysis can be used to estimate the hypothetical profits of a branded producer selling without its brand trademark. Using this method, the value of the trademark (expressed as a percentage of sales) due to the holder is equal to the difference between its actual (with the brand) economic profits and its hypothetical (without the brand) economic profits, divided by total actual sales revenue. These percentages of revenues may be compared with other methods of determining trademark values based upon

[10]Examples concerning cosmetics are discussed in *Money*, October 1975. Pharmaceutical drugs are discussed in Harris, *The Real Voice* (New York: The MacMillan Company, 1964) pp. 30–40 and 72–79 and Gumbhir and Rodowskos (1974). For gasoline see "Meanings Posted Octane Ratings," Federal Trade Commission, 14 October 1969, pp. 179–204. The similarity in qualities between branded and private label commodities was also addressed in the context of price discrimination by the United States Court of Appeals. The Court found that branded and private label goods were often of "like grade and quality." See the Borden Company v. Federal Trade Commission, 339 F. 2d 133; 1964 Trade Cas. (CCH) P71,308, December 4, 1964.

royalty rates. Under these methods, the actual value of the trademark is equal to the discounted present value of this stream of royalties.

## 4.2 Demand Analysis and Brand Profitability

This section describes the underlying economic theory for brand valuation, as well as the details of calculating a portion of profits attributable to use of a trademark. Consumer demand for branded and unbranded goods determines the relative profitability of operating with and without benefit of a brand trademark. Assuming that firms operate to earn maximum profits, the formulas derived below show that the appropriate portion of profit attributable to the trademark depends on the respective market shares and price elasticities of the branded and unbranded producers. The formula derived in this section will be used below to obtain an estimate of the economic value of several Carnation brands.

The holder of a brand trademark has a monopoly in the market for its brand, though the existence of close substitutes—other branded and unbranded goods—constrains its ability to set prices. As a monopolist, the branded producer is free to set prices to maximize its profits.

In figure 4.1, the demand curve labeled $D$ represents demand for a branded good. The second curve in figure 4.1, labeled $D'$, represents the demand for a similar unbranded good. When the price of the unbranded good is $P'$ consumers will purchase $Q'$ units of the unbranded good. Reflecting pure brand preference by consumers in the aggregate, the two demand curves in figure 4.1 are drawn so that when the branded and unbranded goods are offered at the same price, the quantity demanded of the branded good exceeds that of the unbranded good.

In drawing the figure, I have also assumed common and constant marginal costs of $C$ per unit (the simplest case, but not a necessary assumption for the development which follows), shown by the flat curve $MC$. Regardless of whether, in fact, different producers have different cost structures, this assumption is valid because if the branded producer were deprived of its brand trademark, it would retain its same marginal cost curve $MC$, but would face the unbranded demand curve $D'$ in place of its old demand curve $D$.

In figure 4.1, the marginal cost curve is represented by $MC$ and the demand curve is $D$. By setting its price equal to $P$, the branded producer sets marginal cost equal to marginal revenue. If, instead, the branded producer faced the unbranded demand curve $D'$, it should set price equal to $P'$ and sell $Q'$ units so that $MR' = MC$ in order to maximize its profits.

The maximum profit earned by the branded producer is given by the lightly shaded rectangle in figure 4.1 which represents price (set to maximize profits) in excess of cost at a volume determined by the demand function. The area of this rectangle is equal to

$$\pi = Q(P - C), \tag{1}$$

Figure 4.1: The Demand for Branded and Unbranded Commodities

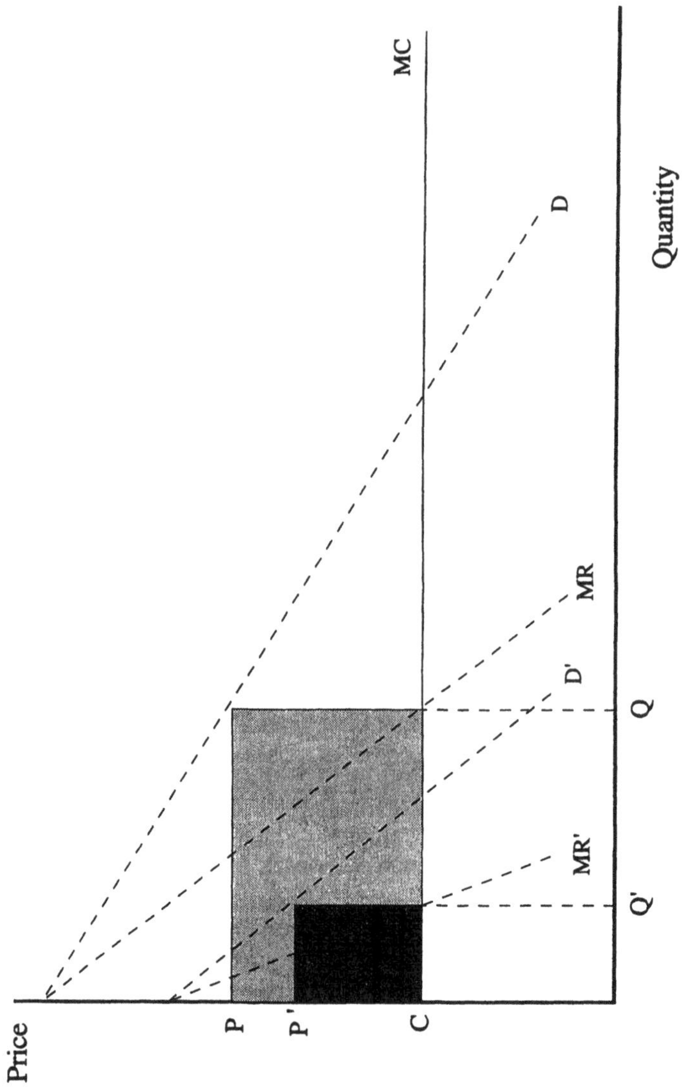

that is, the quantity sold ($Q$) multiplied by the per-unit profit ($P - C$). Similarly, the profit earned by the branded producer while selling unbranded goods is given by the smaller, darkly shaded rectangle which has an area equal to

$$\pi' = Q'(P' - C), \tag{2}$$

that is, the quantity sold ($Q'$) multiplied by its per-unit profit ($P' - C$).

Figure 4.1, therefore, graphically illustrates the value of a brand name to its holder. The economic value of the brand trademark is the difference between what the producer can earn selling the branded product ($\pi$), versus what the producer could earn without the trademark ($\pi'$). This difference may be expressed as:

$$V = \pi - \pi'. \tag{3}$$

Substituting equations (1) and (2) into (3) and rearranging, this equation can be reformulated as:

$$V = Q(P - C) - Q'(P' - C) = Q(P - P') + (Q - Q')(P' - C). \tag{4}$$

Note that the last formulation of this calculation has two components which are added together. The first component, $Q(P - P')$, is the per unit price premium associated with the brand, $(P - P')$, multiplied by sales quantity, ($Q$), of the branded good. In effect, this first component equals the total value of the price premium for the brand. The second component, $(Q - Q')(P' - C)$, represents the increase in sales volume attributable to the brand trademark, $(Q - Q')$, times per unit profits of the unbranded producer, $(P' - C)$. The second component therefore represents the value of increased market share. These two components are represented graphically on figure 4.1 as the result of the darkly shaded area expanding in both a vertical (price premium) and horizontal dimension (market share increase) to fill the lightly shaded area.

From figure 4.1, it is apparent that the value of a brand trademark in contributing to operating profits generally should be less than the total operating profits from selling the branded good. The reason for this is that even without use of the brand trademark, the producer would still be expected to earn some economic profit. Put another way, not all profits of the branded producer are attributable to ownership of the brand trademark. The portion shown in the darkly shaded area can be realized without the trademark. Only the portion of profit shown as outside the darkly shaded area is attributable to the trademark.

Figure 4.1 presents an idealized case in that it assumes that the branded producer will be able to act as a monopolist in the unbranded market. However, the unbranded market is, in fact, an oligopoly when there are multiple producers each able to earn only a share of the overall profits. Therefore, in reality, the shaded box representing the branded producer's share of unbranded profits will be smaller than that shown in figure 4.1.

For a monopolist (such as the branded producer), profit maximization requires that price and volume be set at levels where marginal revenue will be equated to marginal cost. Using Lerner's rule, it follows that for the monopolist:

$$MR = P\left(1 - \frac{1}{\varepsilon}\right) = C \tag{5}$$

where $\varepsilon$ is the price elasticity of demand for the brand market. Rearranging terms, the monopolist's percentage markup (per unit profit $P - C$ divided by selling price) equals:

$$\frac{P - C}{P} = \frac{1}{\varepsilon} \tag{6}$$

As noted above, if the branded producer were to switch to production of unbranded goods, it would no longer be a monopolist. The branded producer, because of the scale of its production, would still have market power in the unbranded market, but competition with other unbranded producers would tend to reduce its markup rate $(P' - C)/P'$. It is shown in appendix 4.6.1 that the markup rate for an oligopolist is

$$\frac{P' - C}{P'} = \frac{S'}{\varepsilon'} \tag{7}$$

where $S'$ is the branded firm's quantity share (where a 100 percent market share would equal one) in the unbranded market and $\varepsilon'$ is the price elasticity of demand in the unbranded market. The oligopoly theory we rely on assumes Nash-Bertrand conditions.[11]

With these results, the appropriate value for a product trademark as a portion of sales can be expressed as a function of the relative demand elasticities and relative market shares for that product and its unbranded competitors. The economic value of the trademark ($R$), determined as a percentage of revenues equals

$$R = \frac{V}{PQ} = \frac{Q(P - C)}{PQ}\left[1 - \frac{Q'(P' - C)}{Q(P - C)}\right] \tag{8}$$

[11] In an analysis similar to mine Hausman, Leonard, and Zona (1994) consider the elasticity of specific brands of beer using monthly transaction data collected at the individual metropolitan (SMSA) level. Their analysis is applied to the issues in a hypothetical merger. Hausman, et al. rely on a Nash-Bertrand assumption, as do I, in order to calculate the equilibrium price levels that attain post-merger. See also Hausman, Leonard, and Zona (1991) for a similar application by these authors. Price-cost margins are discussed in relation to market structure in Cowling and Waterson (1976) and Nickell and Metcalf (1978)

which represents the per period value of the trademark divided by the per period total sales revenue.

As can been seen from the structure of equation (8), the value $R$ is the product of two factors. The first factor, $Q(P - C')/PQ$, is the economic operating margin (total economic profits divided by total revenues). The second factor:

$$G = 1 - \frac{Q'(P' - C)}{Q(P - C)} \tag{9}$$

is the proportion of economic profits realized due to the brand trademark (i.e., the "trademark fraction"). According to equation (8), the trademark fraction $G$ is multiplied by the economic operating margin to derive the per period economic value of the trademark. Substituting equations (6) and (7) into (9) gives

$$G = 1 - \frac{P'Q'S'/\varepsilon'}{PQ/\varepsilon} = 1 - S'\frac{\alpha_0' T' P' \varepsilon}{\alpha_0 T P \varepsilon'} \tag{10}$$

where $\alpha_0$ and $\alpha_0'$ are the branded producer's shares of total industry unit sales (including other branded goods as well as unbranded goods) before and after its switch to unbranded production, and $T$ and $T'$ are total industry unit sales before and after the switch.[12]

It is useful to consider the intuitive nature of equation (10), because the proportion of profits attributable to the brand trademark, equal to $G$ and given by equation (10), embodies a number of common sense considerations in valuing a trademark.

- First, the greater the price difference between the branded and unbranded products (i.e., the lower the ratio of $P'$ to $P$), the higher is $G$.

- Second, the greater the difference between the branded producer's market shares before and after the switch to unbranded production (i.e., the lower the ratio of $\alpha_0'$ to $\alpha_0$ which is also part of the subtraction in the equation), the higher is $G$. In other words, higher market shares demonstrate higher brand values.

- Third, the greater the branded producer's prospective share of unbranded production (i.e., the higher $S'$ ), the lower is $G$. This occurs because the branded producer, due to its scale of production, would dominate the unbranded market and still earn substantial profits even without its trademark, thereby reducing the stand alone value of the trademark.

- Fourth, the greater the drop in total industry unit sales resulting from the switch to non-branded production (i.e., the lower the ratio of $T'$ to $T$), the

[12] In other words $Q' = \alpha_0 T'$ and $Q = \alpha_0 T$.

higher is $G$, though to some extent, the decline in industry sales would be shared by other producers.

- Fifth, the more elastic branded demand is to unbranded demand (i.e., the higher the ratio of $\varepsilon$ to $\varepsilon'$), the lower is $G$. Very elastic demand is usually thought to be a sign of weak consumer brand loyalty.

Equation (10) can be simplified using relationships developed previously in this chapter; that is, the $P$ and $P'$ variables can be expressed as functions of elasticities and market shares which are already variables in the equation. Specifically, the price ratio $P'/P$ in (10) can be written in terms of elasticities and market shares. Equations (6) and (7) are equivalent to[13]

$$\frac{C}{P} = 1 - \frac{1}{\varepsilon} \text{ and } \frac{C}{P'} = 1 - \frac{S'}{\varepsilon'}. \tag{11}$$

Therefore,

$$\frac{P'}{P} = \frac{C/P}{C/P'} = \frac{1 - \frac{1}{\varepsilon}}{1 - \frac{S'}{\varepsilon'}}. \tag{12}$$

Therefore (10) can be reformulated as

$$\begin{aligned} G &= 1 - S' \frac{\alpha_0'}{\alpha_0} \frac{T'}{T} \frac{1 - \frac{1}{\varepsilon}}{1 - \frac{S'}{\varepsilon'}} \frac{\varepsilon}{\varepsilon'} \\ &= 1 - S' \frac{\alpha_0'}{\alpha_0} \frac{T'}{T} \frac{\varepsilon - 1}{\varepsilon' - S'}. \end{aligned} \tag{13}$$

The analysis is completed by making two reasonable assumptions about aggregate market response to the elimination of a brand. The first assumption is that total industry unit sales are unaffected by a brand elimination. According to this view, consumers will simply move their purchases to other competing products in the same category. Therefore:

$$T' = T. \tag{14}$$

For products that make up a small portion of a consumer's total expenditures (highly likely for the products in my study) and whose price varies in a narrow range, this assumption should provide an accurate approximation. Equation (13) can then be simplified to:

[13]It is important to note that equation (11) shows that merely comparing elasticities in the branded and unbranded markets may not be revealing of relative profits to the producer without also considering market share in the unbranded market. Moreover, a comparison of total profitability must take into account quantity differences.

$$G = 1 - S' \frac{\alpha_0'}{\alpha_0} \frac{\varepsilon - 1}{\varepsilon' - S'}. \tag{15}$$

Next, it is necessary to make some assumptions about how relative market shares change in response to the elimination of a brand. In the marketing literature (see Bell, Keeney, and Little (1975), and Barnett [1976]), it is often assumed that each brand has a level of attractiveness and that consumers purchase products in proportion to their attractiveness. The resulting market share model is then a multinomial logit. If there are $n+1$ goods in the market and $A_i$ denotes the attractiveness of the $i$th good ($A_i > 0, i = 0, 1, 2, \ldots, n$), the market share or relative attractiveness of product $i$ can be expressed as:

$$\alpha_i = \frac{A_i}{\sum_{j=0}^{n} A_j} \tag{16}$$

where $\sum_{j=0}^{n} A_j$ represents the sum of all values of $A_j$ for goods zero through $n$ in the product category (i.e., the total attractiveness of all products on the market). Without loss of generality, let $A_0$ denote the attractiveness of the brand that will be eliminated, $A_1$ the attractiveness of all unbranded goods, and $A_2, \ldots A_n$ the attractiveness of all remaining competing branded goods.

If brand zero is eliminated, and the former brand zero consumers redirect their choices uniformly to all other products,[14] then the total quantity share of all unbranded goods (including those unbranded goods now produced by the formerly branded producer) will rise from

$$\alpha_1 = \frac{A_1}{\sum_{j=0}^{n} A_j} \tag{17}$$

to

$$\alpha_1' = \frac{A_1}{\sum_{j=1}^{n} A_j} = \frac{A_1 / \sum_{j=0}^{n} A_j}{\sum_{j=1}^{n} A_j / \sum_{j=0}^{n} A_j} = \frac{\alpha_1}{\sum_{j=1}^{n} \alpha_j} = \frac{\alpha_1}{1 - \alpha_0}. \tag{18}$$

The change in unbranded market share arises solely because of the different denominators in equations (17) and (18). The numerators are unchanged because the attractiveness of unbranded goods ($A_1$) remains unchanged. The elimination of brand zero is reflected by the elimination of its attractiveness ($A_0$) from the total attractiveness of all products in the market. In essence, this analysis shows that the percentage shares of the total market enjoyed by producers may increase when another brand is eliminated.

[14]If, in fact, this is not the case and a higher proportion of the former product zero consumers remain with the other branded products, then this assumption would be untrue. This would occur if market shares followed a nested logit model for instance. If so, the estimate of the branded producer's loss of market share would be conservative.

Let $S$ denote the branded producer's quantity share of its own sales and of the unbranded sales prior to the expiration of its trademark. I assume that the relative shares of the formerly branded producer and the unbranded producers will remain the same, in other words, $S' = S$. Therefore, the formerly branded producer captures a share of the expanded unbranded market, expressed as:

$$S' = S = \frac{A_0}{A_0 + A_1} = \frac{\alpha_0}{\alpha_0 + \alpha_1}. \tag{19}$$

Therefore, the quantity share of the total market of the formerly branded producer becomes, in the expanded unbranded market,

$$\alpha_0' = S'\alpha_1' = \frac{\alpha_0\alpha_1}{(\alpha_0 + \alpha_1)(1 - \alpha_0)}. \tag{20}$$

Finally, substituting equations (14), (19) and (20) into (15) yields the conclusion

$$\begin{aligned} G &= 1 - S'\frac{\alpha_0'}{\alpha_0}\frac{\varepsilon - 1}{\varepsilon' - S'} \\ &= 1 - \left(\frac{S'}{\alpha_0}\right)(\alpha_0')\left(\frac{\varepsilon - 1}{\varepsilon' - S'}\right) \\ &= 1 - \left(\frac{1}{\alpha_0 + \alpha_1}\right)\left(\frac{\alpha_0}{(\alpha_0 + \alpha_1)}\frac{\alpha_1}{(1 - \alpha_0)}\right)\left(\frac{\varepsilon - 1}{\varepsilon' - S'}\right) \\ &= 1 - \frac{\alpha_0}{\alpha_0 + \alpha_1}\frac{\alpha_1}{\alpha_0 + \alpha_1}\frac{1}{1 - \alpha_0}\left(\frac{\varepsilon - 1}{\varepsilon' - S'}\right) \\ &= 1 - \frac{S(1 - S)}{1 - \alpha_0}\frac{\varepsilon - 1}{\varepsilon' - S}. \end{aligned} \tag{21}$$

If we refer back to equations (8) and (9) we see that $G$ is the portion of operating income that is attributable to the existence of the trademark. Therefore, equation (21) can be used to compute the economic value of the brand's trademark.

### 4.2.1 *Discussion*

If the branded producer were forced to compete in the unbranded market, it would necessarily have lower overall production of its formerly trademarked goods. This is demonstrated in the following theorem.

**Theorem 4.1** *$Q > Q'$ if and only if $\alpha_0 + \alpha_1 < 1$.*

*Proof*: We need to compare the quantities $Q$ and $Q'$ as defined above. Recall that $Q$ is the branded producer's output while $Q'$ is the output of the branded producer in the unbranded market.

$Q$ will be larger than $Q'$ if and only if $\alpha_0 T > \alpha_0' T'$, following the definitions in footnote twelve. From equation (14), this can happen if and only if $\alpha_0 > \alpha_0'$, that is, whenever

$$\frac{\alpha_0'}{\alpha_0} > 1.$$

To show that the latter is true we use equation (20):

$$\frac{\alpha_0'}{\alpha_0} = \frac{\alpha_1}{(\alpha_0 + \alpha_1)(1 - \alpha_0)}$$

Therefore $\alpha_0/\alpha_0' > 1$ whenever $(\alpha_0 + \alpha_1)(1 - \alpha_0) > \alpha_1$. Multiplying out, this happens if and only if

$$(\alpha_0 + \alpha_1) - \alpha_0(\alpha_0 + \alpha_1) > \alpha_1$$

or

$$\alpha_0 > \alpha_0(\alpha_0 + \alpha_1)$$

or

$$1 > (\alpha_0 + \alpha_1).$$

*Q.E.D.*

Thus, provided that the combined market share of the branded producer and the unbranded producers is less than one (i.e., the entire market), the branded producer will produce less quantity under competition in the unbranded market than it had in the branded market. This is always the case for the goods I study since there exist other branded producers besides Carnation. This also explains that the value of the trademark as derived in equation (4) consists of two positive components: the first is the price premium component and the second is the sales volume component.

Figure 4.1 illustrates a special case in which Carnation does not face competition by others producers in the unbranded market. This special case violates the necessary and sufficient conditions in the theorem stated above. Suppose for instance, that Carnation were the only producer in the branded market, that they had no competition in the unbranded market, and that there were no other branded producers. Then Carnation has 100 percent of the market in both the actual and hypothetical worlds. In this case, $\alpha_0 = \alpha_0'$ and $Q = Q'$, as Carnation produces the entire market under the maintained assumption $T = T'$.

Figure 4.1 therefore fails to properly illustrate a special case, but one that is only of theoretical interest. It does correctly depict the situation that we more generally expect wherein $P$ exceeds $P'$ and $Q$ exceeds $Q'$ provided that Carnation faces competition in the unbranded market. The proper interpretation of the demand curve $D'$ in figure 4.1 is that it is the demand that Carnation would face if it were forced to compete in the unbranded market.

## 4.3 Data Description

This section describes the data used in the demand analysis in the subsequent sections of this chapter. There are three categories of variables used in the demand analysis: sales data, macroeconomic and demographic indicators, and product specific variables. Data on sales (quantity sold and average selling price) are drawn from two different sources, the "Nielsen Research Report to Carnation Company Inc." (Nielsen Research 1979–1984) and the " SAMI Basic/Special Report" (Selling Area Marketing, Inc. 1979–1984), found in Carnation's marketing files. The use of Nielson and SAMI data for elasticity determination is similar to elasticity measurement based on store-level scanner data (Hoch, Kim, Montgomery, and Rossi [1995]). Hoch et al. find that elasticities determined at the store level depend on both consumer demographic variables and competitor variables. My analysis controls for demographic factors in the demand analysis and computes product-level rather than store-level elasticities. Area demographic and macroeconomic indicators are obtained from government sources. A variety of different sources are consulted for variables anticipated to affect the demand of particular products. These sources are discussed at length in appendix 4.6.2. Variable sources and definitions are described for each category of data below.

### *4.3.1 General Data*

**Nielsen Reports.** The primary source for data on selling prices and quantities is a series of surveys conducted by the A. C. Nielsen Company. Nielsen uses a national probability sample of 1,050 stores in the continental United States to calculate its estimates. The data are obtained bimonthly through in-store audits. During each store visit, Nielsen personnel count all products on the shelf, in displays, and in the back room or storage area (Carnation Company Marketing Research Department [1982–1983]). Sales volume is computed as the sum of purchases from warehouses, brokers, or other distributors over a two-month period (as shown on invoices), less the increase in inventory from the previous visit. Shelf prices are recorded as the retail price after adjustment for any promotional pricing that may have been in effect on the day of the visit. Data are reported on total pounds or cases sold, retail price, percent of volume sold with retail advertising support (local advertising, special prices, ad coupons, and displays), total and visual inventory quantities, and total store sales for those selling the particular product or brand (called "all commodity volume" or ACV). Various measures can be derived from these such as product market share and sales per million dollars of ACV.[15]

[15]The Nielsen sample is stratified by region, county size, and store size. The continental U.S. is divided into ten geographical regions. Within each region, counties are classified by size ("A" through "D", where "A" denotes Standard Metropolitan Statistical Areas and "D" denotes very rural and unpopulated areas). Four store sizes are defined (chains doing over $2 million a year in business, large independents, medium independents, and small independents). Together, the combination of region, county size, and store size results in

**SAMI Reports.** An alternative source of sales data for some of the products are reports on warehouse withdrawals compiled by the Strategic Areas Marketing, Inc. (SAMI) service (a division of Time-Life until the late 1980s, but subsequently sold to Information Resources, Inc.). SAMI reports average shelf price and case volume every four weeks for fifty-four market areas.[16]

The SAMI data are not based on a probability sample. Instead, SAMI personnel collect data on withdrawals made by individual retail stores from participating food distributor warehouses in each of the fifty-four markets. The data cover approximately 80 percent of the total ACV in each market, so that any bias introduced by the lack of full coverage is expected to be small.

**Socioeconomic Data.** The product review (in appendix 4.6.2) identifies a number of demographic variables anticipated to affect demand. To account for these effects, as well as shifts in consumer demand caused by unemployment and population growth, area demographic and economic indicators are collected from various editions of the *State and Metropolitan Area Data Book* (U.S. Department of Commerce, Bureau of the Census 1982, 1986, 1991). These variables include: total population,[17] percent of population of Hispanic origin, and per capita personal income.[18] The variables are collected for each metropolitan statistical area (MSA) for the period 1979 through 1984 on an annual basis, though not every year is available. (Missing data are interpolated.) Data are then matched to either Nielsen or SAMI regions as appropriate.

---

160 strata (i.e., ten regions times four county sizes times four store sizes), though there are no stores in some strata. Stores are sampled from each strata with probability proportional to estimated ACV. The sample is weighted to be representative of all grocery stores in the continental U.S. The reports compiled by Nielsen for Carnation divide the continental U.S. into thirty-two districts for which aggregates were computed.

The thirty-two districts are: Atlanta, Baltimore, Birmingham, Boston, Buffalo, Charlotte, Chicago, Cleveland, Columbus, Dallas, Denver, Detroit, Houston, Indianapolis, Jacksonville, Kansas City, Los Angeles, Memphis, Miami, Minneapolis, New Orleans, New York, Omaha, Philadelphia, Phoenix, Pittsburgh, Portland, Salt Lake City, San Francisco, Seattle, Spokane, and St. Louis.

[16]The fifty-four market areas are: Albany, Atlanta, Baltimore, Birmingham, Boston, Buffalo, Charleston/Huntington, Charleston/Savannah, Charlotte, Chicago, Cinci/Dayton/Colum, Cleveland, Dallas, Denver, Detroit, El Paso, Grand Rapids, Green Bay, Gransville, Hartford, Houston, Indianapolis, Jacksonville, Kansas, Los Angeles, Louisville, Memphis, Miami, Milwaukee, Minneapolis, Nashville, New Orleans, New York, Norfolk, Oklahoma, Omaha, Peoria, Philadelphia, Phoenix, Pittsburgh, Portland OR, Portland ME, Quad Cities, Raleigh, San Francisco, Seattle, St. Louis, Salt Lake City, Shreveport, Spokane, San Antonio, Scranton/Wilkes-Barre, Syracuse, and Wichita.

[17]Population variables used in conjunction with SAMI sales data are calculated from the U.S. Department of Commerce *State and Metropolitan Area Data Books* based on Selling Areas Marketing, Inc. SAMI Reports (1985) map and socioeconomic statistics. The ratio of the 1984 SAMI districts' population to the State and Metropolitan Area population was applied to the other periods for which SAMI sales data was used.

[18]Additional variables collected include: percent of population by age segment (under age 5, ages 5-24, ages 25-44, ages 45-64, and age 65 and over); birthrate per thousand population, total personal income, total civilian labor force, unemployment rate, number of retail food establishments, and amount of retail food sales.

**Leading National Advertisers Data.** Leading National Advertisers (LNA) tracks multimedia advertising expenditures across the U.S. in six major media: consumer magazines, newspaper supplements, network television, spot television, network radio, and outdoor billboards. LNA publishes quarterly breakdowns of spending in these media by brand and company in its "LNA Multi-Media Report Service" (Leading National Advertisers 1979–1984). LNA includes only companies which spend over twenty-five thousand dollars in all six media combined. Bimonthly expenditures are interpolated from the quarterly totals.

**CPI Data.** Prices in this study are deflated using a monthly consumer price index[19] for four Census regions,[20] published by the U.S. Department of Commerce, Bureau of Labor Statistics (1979–1984).

### *4.3.2 Product Specific Data*

For each product under review, I describe the precise nature of the sales data along with any product specific variables that are used in the estimation of demand functions.

**Coffee Creamer Sales.** Data on powdered non-dairy coffee creamer sales are taken from Nielsen research reports (described above), covering the time period from December 1978–January 1979 to October–November 1984. The analysis is limited to sixteen and twenty-two ounce sizes of Coffee-mate, Cremora, and Private Label creamer. Sales are reported in thousands of pounds. Retail support is measured by the percentage of sales involving displays of the product, coupons, or special prices.

**Coffee Consumption.** Coffee consumption is derived from two sources of data: Nielsen research reports (1979–1984) and the "United States of America Coffee Drinking Study—Winter 1987," published by the International Coffee Organization (1987). The Nielsen report has the same format as described above. The Coffee Drinking Study is conducted annually and the 1987 report, which was available for use, contains historical data for 1984. It is based on telephone interviews with approximately seventy-five hundred persons aged ten and over and representative of the population in the continental U.S.

**Evaporated Milk Sales.** Bimonthly quantity, price, and advertising data for thirteen districts are taken from the Nielsen reports described above for

[19]Several consumer price indexes are available. The most common index of the cost of living, used here, is the consumer price index for all urban consumers (CPI-U). It is an index of the cost of a fixed basket of consumer goods in which the weight assigned to each commodity is the share of expenditures on that commodity by consumers in eighty-five urban areas during 1982–84.

[20]The four regions are North East, North Central, South, and West.

tall sizes of Carnation, Pet, and all other evaporated milk.[21] Quantities are reported on a case basis. Retail support is measured by the percentage of sales involving displays, local ads, or special pricing.

**Instant Breakfast Sales.** Sales of six and ten-packet Carnation Instant Breakfast and competing six-packet Private Label products are taken from the SAMI Basic Report covering the period from August 1983 through January 1985. Quantities are reported on a per pound basis.

**Dog Food SAMI Data.** SAMI sales data are used to estimate demand functions for different types of dog food. Monthly data on case volume and sales revenue are available for thirty-seven different brands in forty-eight districts[22] from 1980 to 1984. In view of the large volume of data and to simplify data entry, sales data from every other four-week period are used in the regression analysis. Since there are numerous minor brands of all-meat and maintenance dog food, brands are aggregated into six categories: Mighty Dog, Kal Kan, Alpo, Cycle, Private Label, and Other All-Meat Brands and Maintenance.

To correct for differences in case size, the average number of ounces per case is calculated for each brand in each region in January and August 1982 (a preliminary analysis indicated little variability in ounces per case over time). The number of ounces sold and price per ounce is estimated for each brand by multiplying the number of cases sold by the average number of ounces per case.

**Small Dog Population.** Limited data are available on the size of the dog population. It is therefore necessary to interpolate survey estimates of the percentage of households owning dogs in various regions.[23]

**Cat Food SAMI Data.** The cat food demand model is estimated using monthly SAMI reports from January 1980 to January 1985. As with dog food, there is a large number of brands (forty-five) and it is necessary to multiply case volume by the average number of ounces per case (computed for each brand and region for the months of February 1982 and September 1982) to make sales quantities comparable. Brands are grouped into seven categories (Fancy Feast, Friskies Buffet, Nine Lives, Kal Kan, Bright Eyes, Private Label, and All Other Gourmet and Maintenance).

---

[21] Complete data was available for only thirteen of the 32 possible districts. These districts are: Baltimore, Atlanta, Birmingham, Charlotte, Jacksonville, Miami, New Orleans, Indianapolis, Denver, Dallas, Houston, Memphis, and Phoenix.

[22] Data are not available for Columbus, Green Bay, Omaha, Peoria, Portland ME, and Shreveport.

[23] Dog ownership percentages, which indicate historical data for earlier years, are based on historical data for 1980 and 1984 contained in an internal Carnation memorandum prepared by R. Plante for J. Brown (May 1988). This data is corroborated by the Pet Food Institute (1987). Household data is obtained from the 1992 U.S. Department of Commerce, Bureau of the Census, *Statistical Abstract of the United States.*

**Cat Population.** Estimates of the cat population are based on the sources referred to above in computing the dog population. Survey estimates of the proportion of households owning cats are interpolated.

## 4.4 Analysis

As shown in section 4.2, to estimate an economic value for the trademarks at issue, I rely on the brand price elasticity and the price elasticities for the unbranded competitors. The demand elasticities used to calculate the trademark fraction are estimated using retail price data. If distributors and retailers use equiproportional markups across brands, then these are the demand elasticities faced by brand manufacturers. Connor and Weimer (1986) present evidence that the gross margins of food manufacturers are highly correlated with the markups of grocery wholesalers and retailers. Such practices are encouraged by competitive pressures in grocery markets.

### *4.4.1 Coffee Creamer*

The demand models for coffee creamer have been estimated for sixteen ounce size products.[24] The basic demand equation relates the logarithm of the bimonthly sales of creamer to the logarithms of the real price per pound for the creamer in question and to the logarithms of the real prices of substitute creamers.[25] The demand equation also allows for trend and seasonality in the consumption pattern as well as for regional effects. Finally, the demand equation specifies that creamer sales are potentially influenced by (1) the level of real income per capita, (2) the frequency of coffee consumption (measured in coffee cups consumed per day per capita), (3) the total volume of all sales in the region (all commodity volume), (4) real advertising of branded creamers, and (5) retail support, including in-aisle displays, in-ad coupons, or special pricing.

The demand function has the log-linear form:

$$\log Q_{bsrt} = \alpha + \log P_{bsrt}\beta_1 + \log P'_{bsrt}\beta_2 + X_{bsrt}\gamma + \varepsilon_{bsrt}$$

where $Q_{bsrt}$ is the bimonthly quantity of creamer sold by brand $b$, in size category $s$, in region $r$, in period $t$. The price of the creamer is $P_{bsrt}$ and denotes the average selling price for the brand $b$, in size $s$, sold in region $r$, at time period $t$. The price vector $P'_{bsrt}$ captures the prices of substitute brands and sizes in the same period and region. The explanatory factors $X_{bsrt}$ depend

---

[24] While Carnation markets Coffee-mate in a variety of sizes, the sixteen ounce size is the highest sales volume commodity in the product line and, moreover, is marketed primarily in the retail distribution channel. The sixteen ounce commodity therefore provides the best basis for comparison between branded and unbranded consumer demand.

[25] Our empirical specifications are similar to Gius (1993). Gius considers the demand for branded liquor products. Using historical time-series data, he estimates the demand for both premium and non-premium liquors in order to determine the extent of the product market. Gius also uses Leading National Advertisers data as a measure of advertising, price divided by the consumer price index, and a trend term in his demand equations.

on the brand, size in question, location, and time period. The vector $X_{bsrt}$ includes seasonal effects, time trend, advertising, real income per capita, cups per day per capita, special promotions, etc. The form of the specified demand curve has a simple interpretation for the demand price elasticities. The own-price elasticity, that is the price elasticity of quantity-demanded of a particular brand with respect to its own price, holding all other prices fixed, is:

$$\varepsilon = \frac{\partial \log Q_{bsrt}}{\partial \log P_{bsrt}} = \frac{P_{bsrt}}{Q_{bsrt}} \cdot \frac{\partial Q_{bsrt}}{\partial P_{bsrt}} = \beta_1$$

The price elasticities of quantity-demanded of a particular brand with respect to the prices of substitute goods are similarly the coefficients $\beta_2$.

In table 4.1, I summarize the dependent and explanatory variables for the various coffee creamer demand models.

The model for coffee creamer estimates the demand for sixteen ounce creamer as a function of the prices of sixteen ounce creamersand the prices of twenty-two ounce creamers. (This reduces the number of observations from 1008 to 404 since not all markets allow consumers to choose from among all three products and both sizes.) Table 4.2 shows the regression results for the sixteen ounce models.

**Discussion.** The demand for Coffee-mate sixteen ounce dry creamer depends significantly on relative prices. As the price of sixteen ounce Coffee-mate creamer rises, consumers are predicted to purchase less sixteen ounce Coffee-mate creamer. The other price effects reveal that sixteen ounce Private Label and twenty-two ounce Coffee-mate creamer are economic substitutes for Coffee-mate sixteen ounce creamer. (This can be seen in table 4.2 in the column marked "CM#1" and the row marked "lppl16." For example, the variable "lppl16" represents the relative price of sixteen ounce Private Label. Its value, 0.359, has a sign opposite to the value for sixteen ounce Coffee-mate which is −2.006.) As the prices of these goods rise, the demand for sixteen ounce Coffee-mate increases.

The pattern of seasonal effects reveals that significantly more sixteen ounce Coffee-mate creamer is purchased in the February–March bimonth as compared with the June–July and August–September periods. Additionally, the summer periods show generally lower demand than either the fall or winter periods. These results are consistent with a commodity which is consumed with coffee where the seasonality of coffee consumption leads to the seasonality of creamer consumption.[26]

In the sixteen ounce Coffee-mate model, the per capita real income and coffee consumption per day variables were not statistically significant from zero (the $t$-statistic are .798 and 1.148 respectively). The all commodity volume

[26]The addition of weather-related variables such as the actual number of heating degree days for the period in the region did not significantly improve the precision of the model once the seasonal effects were included in the model.

**Table 4.1.** Variable Definitions for Coffee Creamer Model

| | |
|---|---|
| lscm16 | logarithm of sales of 16 ounce Coffee-mate, pound basis |
| lscr16 | logarithm of sales of 16 ounce Cremora, pound basis |
| lspl16 | logarithm of sales of 16 ounce Private Label, pound basis |
| lpcm16 | logarithm of price of 16 ounce Coffee-mate |
| lpcr16 | logarithm of price of 16 ounce Cremora |
| lppl16 | logarithm of price of 16 ounce Private Label |
| lpcm22 | logarithm of price of 22 ounce Coffee-mate |
| lpcr22 | logarithm of price of 22 ounce Cremora |
| lppl22 | logarithm of price of 22 ounce Private Label |
| trend | linear time trend |
| seas1 | December–January period |
| seas2 | February–March period |
| seas3 | April–May period |
| seas4 | June–July period |
| seas5 | August–September period |
| lrinc | logarithm of real personal income |
| lcpd | logarithm of cups of coffee consumed per day |
| lacv16 | logarithm of all commodity volume |
| rscmdis | retail support displays Coffee-mate |
| rscmiac | retail support in-ad coupons Coffee-mate |
| rscmsp | retail support special prices Coffee-mate |
| rscrdis | retail support displays Cremora |
| rscriac | retail support in-ad coupons Cremora |
| rscrsp | retail support special prices Cremora |
| rspldis | retail support displays Private Label |
| rspliac | retail support in-ad coupons Private Label |
| rsplsp | retail support special prices Private Label |
| ladcar | logarithm of real advertising expenditure for Coffee-mate (LNA derived) |
| ladcrm | logarithm of real advertising expenditure for Cremora (LNA derived) |

for the region in the time period was highly significant, indicating that areas with larger markets will also sell more creamer. (See table 4.2 showing the variable "lacv16" in the column marked "CM#1." The coefficient on this variable has a positive value of 0.139 and a $t$-statistic of $-2.639$.) The retail support variables indicate that of the three forms–displays, in-ad coupons, or special prices–only in-ad coupons and special prices have a significant impact

**Table 4.2.** Estimated Coffee Creamer Demand Models

| | CM #1 LSCM 16 | CM #2 LSCR 16 | CM #3 LSPL 16 |
|---|---|---|---|
| trend | −0.024 | 0.028 | −0.064 |
| | (−1.747) | (1.299) | (−4.372) |
| lpcm 16 | −2.006 | −0.023 | 0.145 |
| | (−6.555) | (−0.049) | (0.344) |
| lpcr16 | 0.220 | −1.491 | 0.236 |
| | (1.079) | (−4.630) | (0.841) |
| lppl16 | 0.359 | 0.123 | −1.441 |
| | (1.832) | (0.398) | (−5.310) |
| lpcm22 | 0.918 | 0.254 | 0.605 |
| | (3.310) | (0.591) | (1.596) |
| lpcr22 | −0.058 | −0.160 | −0.066 |
| | (−0.344) | (−0.604) | (−0.372) |
| lppl22 | 0.232 | 0.255 | 0.675 |
| | (1.301) | (0.913) | (2.728) |
| seas1 | 0.020 | −0.278 | −0.330 |
| | (0.342) | (−3.105) | (−4.199) |
| seas2 | 0.166 | −0.109 | −0.173 |
| | (4.204) | (−1.788) | (−3.184) |
| seas3 | −0.007 | 0.000 | −0.105 |
| | (−0.203) | (−0.008) | (−2.156) |
| seas4 | −0.154 | 0.244 | −0.036 |
| | (−2.261) | (2.299) | (−0.381) |
| seas5 | −0.166 | 0.059 | 0.025 |
| | (−2.653) | (0.610) | (0.291) |
| lrinc | 0.118 | 0.935 | 0.169 |
| | (0.798) | 4.028) | (0.807) |
| lcpd | 0.419 | 2.562 | 1.939 |
| | (1.148) | (4.413) | (3.820) |
| lacv16 | 0.139 | 0.070 | 0.176 |
| | (2.639) | (0.850) | (2.435) |
| racmdis | −0.003 | – | – |
| | (−1.776) | | |
| rscmiac | 0.007 | – | – |
| | (2.050) | | |
| rscmsp | 0.003 | – | – |
| | (3.414) | | |
| rscrdis | – | −0.003 | – |
| | | (−1.202) | |
| rscriac | – | −0.001 | – |
| | | (−0.331) | |
| rscrsp | – | 0.005 | – |
| | | (3.082) | |
| rspldis | – | – | 0.001 |
| | | | (0.757) |
| rspliac | – | – | −.002 |
| | | | (0.238) |
| rsplsp | – | – | −0.001 |
| | | | (−0.752) |
| ladcar | 0.001 | 0.037 | 0.016 |
| | (0.189) | (3.631) | (1.826) |
| ladcrm | 0.020 | −0.045 | 0.002 |
| | (1.927) | (−2.757) | (0.143) |
| $R$-Squared | 0.892 | 0.894 | 0.823 |
| Number of Observations | 404 | 404 | 404 |
| Std. Error of the Regression | 0.179 | 0.280 | 0.247 |

on the demand for sixteen ounce Coffee-mate product. The presence of each of these leads to higher sales in the period and region. Finally, the LNA advertising variables suggest that advertising for Coffee-mate does not significantly increase the demand for Coffee-mate. However, it is interesting to note that advertising for Cremora actually increases the demand for Coffee-mate, attesting to the strength of the Coffee-mate brand capturing increased sales from increased consumer awareness, even if not directed specifically to Coffee-mate. The regression model provides an excellent fit to the historic pattern of sales as 89 percent of the variation in demand is explained by the model.

The demand price elasticities and market shares are summarized in tables 4.3 and 4.4, respectively.[27]

**Table 4.3.** Coffee Creamer: Summary of Price Elasticities

| Product | Price Elasticity |
|---|---|
| 16 oz. Coffee-mate | -2.01 |
| 16 oz. Cremora | -1.49 |
| 16 oz. Private Label | -1.44 |

**Table 4.4.** Coffee Creamer: Summary of the Market Shares (1984)

| Product | Market Share |
|---|---|
| 16 oz. Coffee-mate | 51.3% |
| 16 oz. Cremora | 20.5% |
| 16 oz. Private Label | 28.2% |

### *4.4.2 Evaporated Milk*

The demand model for evaporated milk is estimated for tall size evaporated milk products. The basic demand equation relates the logarithm of bimonthly sales of evaporated milk to the logarithms of the prices of evaporated milk products. The demand equation also allows for a time trend, seasonality in the consumption pattern, and regional effects. Finally, the demand equation specifies that evaporated milk sales are potentially influenced by (1) the level of real income, (2) the percent of the population that is Hispanic, (3) real advertising of branded evaporated milk products, and (4) retail support, including

[27] According to the "SAMI Million Dollar Brand Report" (1990), the Coffee-mate product had a market share of of 39 percent in 1984 based on total tonnage. The SAMI report does not provide a separate market share for the sixteen ounce product.

in-aisle displays, local advertising, and special prices.[28] In table 4.5, I present the variable definitions for the evaporated milk regression models.

**Table 4.5.** Variable Definitions for Evaporated Milk Model

| | |
|---|---|
| lqcar | logarithm of sales of tall Carnation Evaporated Milk (case basis) plus logarithm of sales of tall PET Evaporated Milk (case basis) plus logarithm of sales of tall All Other Evaporated Milk (case basis) |
| lp1 | logarithm of real price of tall Carnation Evaporated Milk (can basis) |
| lp2 | logarithm of real price of tall PET Evaporated Milk (can basis) |
| lp3 | logarithm of real price of tall All Other Evaporated Milk (can basis) |
| lp12 | logarithm of real price of tall PET Evaporated Milk plus logarithm of real price of tall Carnation Evaporated Milk |
| lp13 | logarithm of real price of tall PET Evaporated Milk plus logarithm of real price of tall All Other Evaporated Milk |
| lp23 | logarithm of tall All Other Evaporated Milk plus logarithm of real price of tall PET Evaporated Milk |
| trend | linear time trend |
| seas1 | December–January period |
| seas2 | February–March period |
| seas3 | April–May period |
| seas4 | June–July period |
| seas5 | August–September period |
| lrinc | logarithm of real personal income |
| spanorg | percentage of population in region who are Hispanic |
| retd | retail support display for all products |
| retl | retail support local ads for all products |
| rets | retail support special price for all products |
| ladcar | logarithm of real advertising expenditure for Carnation Evaporated Milk (LNA derived) |
| ladpet | logarithm of real advertising expenditure for PET Evaporated Milk (LNA derived) |

The demand for evaporated milk is considered for the two major branded commodities (Carnation and PET) and for the class of all other unbranded evaporated milks. Demand is assumed to depend on seasonal effects, a linear time trend, Nielsen measures of retail advertising (including local advertising, special pricing, and special displays), LNA advertising measured for Carnation and PET, the percentage of the region's population which is Hispanic, the logarithm of real income, and the prices of three commodities. Due to the

[28] A comparison of the regression models for coffee creamer and for evaporated milk reveals that different explanatory factors have been used in each model and that the number of available observations of demand differ in the two cases. In all respects this should be expected. The set of factors which help explain the differences in coffee creamer consumption between regions, such as coffee consumption per day, are not expected to be related to the consumption of evaporated milk.

relatively small number of observations available in the Nielsen data, I pool the separate demand equations and impose cross-equation restrictions in accord with economic theory. The cross-equation restrictions specify that certain socioeconomic effects have a uniform or product level effect rather than an effect differentiated by brand. In addition, the cross-equation restrictions impose symmetry in the cross-price elasticities (Varian 1992). Table 4.6 shows the regression results for the pooled models.[29]

**Discussion.** After controlling for seasonal, trend, and regional indicators, I find that the demand for evaporated milk is positively associated with increases in retail support when conducted primarily through displays and local advertising. Carnation's overall level of advertising increases the demand for evaporated milk (as can be seen in table 4.6 in row "ladcar" and column "EVAP#1" where the coefficient of the variable for Carnation advertising is 0.022 with a significant $t$-statistic of 2.013) while PET's advertising was not a significant determinate of demand (i.e., row "ladpet" and column "EVAP#1" show a coefficient of −0.035 and an insignificant $t$-statistic of −1.329). While I had expected a positive correlation between the Hispanic population and the demand for evaporated milk, I did not, in fact, find evidence for this correlation. On the other hand, increases in real per capita personal income (denoted "lrinc") were positively related to the demand for evaporated milk. The price effects were relatively precisely determined. PET and Private Label commodities are revealed to be economic substitutes for Carnation's evaporated milk and all other cross-price effects were estimated with the expected signs. Overall, greater than 77 percent of the variation in evaporated milk demand was explained by the pooled regression model.

The demand price elasticities and market shares are summarized in tables 4.7 and 4.8, respectively.[30]

### *4.4.3 Instant Breakfast*

The demand for instant breakfast is analyzed for six-packet size boxes, since it was determined that too few markets provide both six- and ten-packet packages of instant breakfast for brands other than Carnation. The basic demand equation relates the logarithm of four-week sales of a six-packet instant breakfast product to the logarithms of its own price and the prices of substitute instant breakfast products. The demand equation also allows for trend and seasonality in the consumption pattern, as well as for regional effects. Table 4.9 shows the variable definitions for the regression models.

---

[29]The logarithm of All Commodity Volume variable was found to be insignificant and therefore has not been included in the results reported.

[30]According to the "SAMI Million Dollar Brand Report" (1990), Carnation Evaporated Milk had a 28.5 percent market share in 1984 based on total tonnage. The slight discrepancy in my finding and the SAMI report finding results from the SAMI report measuring all sizes of Carnation Evaporated Milk rather than just the tall size.

**Table 4.6.** Estimated Evaporated Milk Demand Models

| | EVAP #1 LQCAR | EVAP #2 LQPET | EVAP #3 LQAOT |
|---|---|---|---|
| trend | −0.068 | −0.068 | −0.068 |
| | (−2.860) | (−2.860) | (−2.860) |
| lpcar | −2.032 | 0.996 | 0.604 |
| | (−3.848) | (2.434) | (1.773) |
| lppet | 0.996 | −0.877 | 0.191 |
| | (2.434) | (−1.919) | (0.604) |
| lpaot | 0.604 | 0.191 | −1.22 |
| | (1.773) | (0.604) | (−3.656) |
| lrinc | 0.408 | 0.408 | 0.408 |
| | (1.839) | (1.839) | (1.839) |
| spanorig | −2.882 | −2.882 | −2.882 |
| | (−0.491) | (−0.491) | (−0.491) |
| retd | 0.010 | 0.010 | 0.010 |
| | (4.448) | (4.448) | (4.448) |
| retl | 0.005 | 0.005 | 0.005 |
| | (3.181) | (3.181) | (3.181) |
| rets | 0.001 | 0.001 | 0.001 |
| | (0.319) | (0.319) | (0.319) |
| seas1 | 0.189 | 0.189 | 0.189 |
| | (4.182) | (4.182) | (4.182) |
| seas2 | −0.019 | −0.019 | −0.019 |
| | (−0.377) | (−0.377) | (−0.377) |
| seas3 | −0.015 | −0.015 | −0.015 |
| | (−0.292) | (−0.292) | (−0.292) |
| seas4 | −0.006 | −0.006 | −0.006 |
| | (−0.115) | (−0.115) | (−0.115) |
| seas5 | −0.030 | −0.030 | −0.030 |
| | (−0.623) | (−0.623) | (−0.623) |
| ladcar | 0.022 | 0.022 | 0.022 |
| | (2.013) | (2.013) | (2.013) |
| lapet | −0.035 | −0.035 | −0.035 |
| | (−1.329) | (−1.329) | (−1.329) |
| $R$-squared | 0.772 | 0.772 | 0.772 |
| Number of Observations | 888 | 888 | 888 |
| Standard Error of Regression | 0.341 | 0.341 | 0.341 |

**Table 4.7.** Evaporated Milk: Summary of Price Elasticities

| Product | Price Elasticity |
|---|---|
| Tall Evaporated Milk Carnation | -2.03 |
| Tall Evaporated Milk PET | -0.88 |
| Tall Evaporated Milk All Other | -1.22 |

**Table 4.8.** Evaporated Milk: Summary of the Market Shares (1984)

| Product | Market Share |
|---|---|
| Tall Evaporated Milk Carnation | 30.8% |
| Tall Evaporated Milk PET | 21.4% |
| Tall Evaporated Milk All Other | 47.8% |

**Table 4.9.** Variable Definitions for Instant Breakfast Model

| | |
|---|---|
| lqpl6 | logarithm of sales of 6-packet Private Label (pound basis) |
| lqcar6 | logarithm of sales of 6-packet Carnation (pound basis) |
| lppl6 | logarithm of real price of 6-packet Private Label (pound basis) |
| lpcar6 | logarithm of real price of 6-packet Carnation (pound basis) |
| lpcar10 | logarithm of real price of 10-packet Carnation (pound basis) |
| trend | linear time trend |
| seas1 | December–January period |
| seas2 | February–March period |
| seas3 | April–May period |
| seas4 | June–July period |
| seas5 | August–September period |

**Discussion.** The demand for instant breakfast is specified to depend on regional indicators, a time trend, seasonal effects, and the prices of six-packet Private Label, six-packet Carnation, and ten-packet Carnation Instant Breakfast. Table 4.10 shows the regression results. While a trend away from six-packet Carnation Instant Breakfast is revealed in the analysis, no trend effect is found in the demand for the six-packet Private Label commodity. After controlling for seasonal and regional effects, I find that the own-price elasticities are relatively precisely determined and that the six-packet Private Label product has a complementary demand with the demand for six-packet Carnation Instant Breakfast. Also, I find that the ten-packet Carnation product has a complementary demand to that of 6-packet Private Label commodity. While some of the cross-price elasticities are either imprecisely determined or not in accord with my expectation that these products should act as economic substitutes, it is likely that some price collinearity is present. Overall, greater than 97 percent of the variation in demand is explained by the model.

**Table 4.10.** Estimated Instant Breakfast Demand Models

| | Instant #1 (Carnation) | Instant #1 (Private Label) |
|---|---|---|
| trend | −0.194 | 0.035 |
| | (−3.402) | (1.010) |
| seas1 | −0.135 | −0.157 |
| | (−2.630) | (−5.046) |
| seas2 | −0.126 | −0.007 |
| | (−2.850) | (−0.277) |
| seas3 | −0.054 | −0.008 |
| | (−1.094) | (−0.268) |
| seas4 | −0.141 | −0.082 |
| | (−2.592) | (−2.485) |
| seas5 | −0.074 | −0.017 |
| | (−1.709) | (0.642) |
| ladcar6 | −1.472 | 0.067 |
| | (−1.873) | (0.140) |
| lpcar10 | −0.370 | −0.801 |
| | (−0.506) | (−1.807) |
| lppl6 | −1.178 | −1.739 |
| | (−2.292) | (−5.579) |
| $R$–squared | 0.975 | 0.974 |
| Number of Observations | 140 | 140 |
| Standard Error of Regression | 0.162 | 0.098 |

Data was collected from LNA for major media advertising for all product classes. However, according to LNA, for the regions and time periods specified, there was no advertising by Carnation of its instant breakfast product. Therefore, I did not use this factor. Additionally, changes in real income (denoted "lrinc" in the other models) were not found to be significant (determinate) for six-packet Carnation Instant Breakfast or for six-packet Private Label and therefore were removed from the model.

Tables 4.11 and 4.12 summarize the price elasticities and market shares of the Carnation and Private Label products.[31]

**Table 4.11.** Instant Breakfast: Summary of Price Elasticities

| Product | Price Elasticity |
|---|---|
| Carnation 6-packet | −1.47 |
| Private Label 6-packet | −1.74 |

**Table 4.12.** Instant Breakfast: Summary of the Market Shares (1984)

| Product | Market Share |
|---|---|
| Carnation 6-packet | 80.3% |
| Private Label 6-packet | 17.6% |

### 4.4.4 *Dog Food*

The demand for wet dog food, including Mighty Dog and Private Label, is specified to depend on the prices of the major branded dog foods, the price of Private Label dog food, and the price of all other canned dog foods. In addition to prices, the demand is specified to depend on the logarithm of real income, the logarithm of the number of small dogs, the logarithm of LNA-determined advertising, trend, and seasonal effects. In table 4.13, I summarize the dependent and explanatory variables for the dog food models.

### 4.4.5 *Discussion*

A review of table 4.14 shows that there was a general decline in demand for Mighty Dog dog food between 1979 and 1984 (as can be seen in the "trend" variable whose coefficient, −0.033, is negative and *t*-statistic, −2.165, is significant) after controlling for other factors. A seasonal pattern to demand is not revealed in the estimation. The number of small dogs is highly significant in the demand model (which is revealed by the coefficient, 0.933, for the variable "lsdog" and its *t*-statistic of 36.335). Real per-capita personal income was found to increase the demand for both Mighty Dog and Private Label commodities.

[31] According to the "SAMI Million Dollar Brand Report" (1990), Carnation Instant Breakfast had a 76.8 percent market share in 1984. The slight discrepancy in the SAMI report finding and my finding results from the SAMI report measuring all sizes of Carnation Instant Breakfast rather than just the six-packet size.

**Table 4.13.** Variable Definitions for Dog Food Model

| | |
|---|---|
| lcv1 | logarithm of Mighty Dog 4-week case volume |
| lcv5 | logarithm of Private Label 4-week case volume |
| seas1 | December–January period |
| seas2 | February–March period |
| seas3 | April–May period |
| seas4 | June–July period |
| seas5 | August–September period |
| trend | linear time trend |
| lpr1 | logarithm of real price of Mighty Dog |
| lpr2 | logarithm of real price of Alpo |
| lpr3 | logarithm of real price of Kal Kan |
| lpr4 | logarithm of real price of Cycle |
| lpr5 | logarithm of real price of Private Label |
| lpr6 | logarithm of real price of All Remaining All-Meat Brands plus Total Maintenance |
| ldog | logarithm of small dog population |
| lrinc | logarithm of real personal income |
| ladmd | logarithm of real advertising expenditure for Mighty Dog (LNA derived) |
| ladcy | logarithm of real advertising expenditure for Cycle (LNA derived) |
| ladal | logarithm of real advertising expenditure for Alpo (LNA derived) |
| ladkk | logarithm of real advertising expenditure for Kal Kan (LNA derived) |

The advertising variables did not show any determinate effect on the demand for these two products. The price variables show that Alpo, Kal Kan and All Other are viewed as substitutes for Mighty Dog while Cycle and Private Label work as complements. Mighty Dog also reveals a significant own-price elasticity. The price effects for Private Label demand show that Alpo, Kal Kan and Cycle are viewed as substitutes for the Private Label commodity while Mighty Dog and All Other are revealed as complement commodities. The regression model provides a good fit to the historic pattern of sales as over 78 percent of the variation in demand is explained by the model.

In tables 4.15 and 4.16, I summarize the demand price elasticities and market shares, respectively.[32]

[32]According to the "SAMI Million Dollar Brand Report" (1990), Mighty Dog had a market share of 5.3 percent in 1984.

**Table 4.14.** Estimated Dog Food Demand Models

| | Dog Food #1 LCV1 (Mighty Dog) | Dog Food #2 LCV5 (Private Lbl.) |
|---|---|---|
| trend | −0.033 | −0.049 |
| | (−2.165) | (−1.586) |
| seas1 | −0.059 | −0.010 |
| | (−0.887) | (−0.070) |
| seas2 | −0.012 | −0.082 |
| | (−0.161) | (−0.527) |
| seas3 | 0.006 | 0.004 |
| | (0.098) | (0.028) |
| seas4 | −0.019 | −0.059 |
| | (−0.257) | (−0.393) |
| seas5 | 0.031 | 0.026 |
| | (0.412) | (0.167) |
| lpr1 (log of Mighty Dog price) | −2.424 | −4.542 |
| | (−0.003) | (−8.306) |
| lpr2 (log of Alpo price) | 0.331 | 0.583 |
| | (2.288) | (1.962) |
| lpr3 (log of Kal Kan price) | 0.678 | 1.677 |
| | (3.566) | (4.289) |
| lpr4 (log of Cycle price) | −1.456 | 1.371 |
| | (−5.007) | (2.294) |
| lpr5 (log of Private Label price) | −0.704 | −2.251 |
| | (−5.575) | (−8.672) |
| lpr6 (log of All Other price) | 0.146 | −0.550 |
| | (1.325) | (−2.421) |
| lsdog | 0.933 | 1.038 |
| | (36.335) | (19.663) |
| lrinc | 0.867 | 1.003 |
| | (6.226) | (3.505) |
| ladmd | −0.011 | 0.005 |
| | (−0.465) | (0.100) |
| ladcy | −0.001 | −0.001 |
| | (−0.166) | (−0.071) |
| ladal | 0.022 | 0.059 |
| | (1.150) | (1.499) |
| ladkk | −0.014 | −0.017 |
| | (−0.516) | (−0.309) |
| $R$-Squared | 0.785 | 0.563 |
| Number of Observations | 836 | 836 |
| Standard Error of the Regression | 0.395 | 0.812 |

**Table 4.15.** Dog Food: Summary of Price Elasticities

| Product | Price Elasticity |
|---|---|
| Mighty Dog | -2.42 |
| Private Label | -2.25 |

**Table 4.16.** Dog Food: Summary of the Market Shares (1984)

| Product | Market Share |
|---|---|
| Mighty Dog | 5.9% |
| Private Label | 2.2% |

### 4.4.6 *Cat Food*

The demand for canned cat food, including Fancy Feast and Private Label, is specified to depend on the price of major branded cat food, the price of Private Label cat food, and the price of all other canned cat food. The demand is also specified to depend on the logarithm of real income, the logarithm of the number of cats in the region, the logarithm of the advertising for Fancy Feast, trend, and seasonal factors. In table 4.17, I summarize the dependent and explanatory variables for the cat food models.

### 4.4.7 *Discussion*

Inspection of table 4.18 shows that the demand for Fancy Feast was falling during the early 1980s while that of Private Label was increasing. The number of cats has a positive effect on both the demand for Fancy Feast and Private Label cat foods (as can be seen in table 4.18, the variable "lcat" whose coefficient, 32.159, is positive and *t*-statistic is 7.002). There is also revealed to be a negative relationship between increases in real income and the demand for Private Label cat food. After controlling for seasonal and regional effects, the own-price elasticities were relatively precisely determined but cross-price effects were generally not significant. Overall, the model explains greater than 67 percent of the variation in demand for Fancy Feast.

The demand price elasticities and market shares are summarized in tables 4.19 and 4.20, respectively.[33]

[33] According to the "SAMI Million Dollar Brand Report" (1990), Fancy Feast had a market share of 3.9 percent in 1984.

**Table 4.17.** Variable Definitions for Cat Food Model

| | |
|---|---|
| lcv1 | logarithm of Fancy Feast 4-week case volume |
| lcv6 | logarithm of Private Label 4-week case volume |
| seas1 | December–January period |
| seas2 | February–March period |
| seas3 | April–May period |
| seas4 | June–July period |
| seas5 | August–September period |
| trend | linear time trend |
| lpr1 | logarithm of real price of Fancy Feast |
| lpr3 | logarithm of real price of Friskies Buffet |
| lpr4 | logarithm of real price of Nine Lives |
| lpr5 | logarithm of real price of Kal Kan |
| lpr6 | logarithm of real price of Private Label |
| lpr7 | logarithm of real price of Bright Eyes |
| lpr8 | logarithm of real price of All Remaining Gourmet Brands plus Total Maintenance |
| lcat | logarithm of cat population |
| lrinc | logarithm of real personal income |
| ladff | logarithm of real advertising expenditure for Fancy Feast (LNA derived) |

## 4.5 Conclusions

To calculate the percentage of profits and of sales for each of the commodities, based upon the economic value of the trademark to the owner, I use elasticity values from the branded and Private Label estimated regression models. For coffee creamer I take the elasticities from table 4.3 for sixteen ounce sizes of Carnation and Private Label. For evaporated milk, I use the price elasticities for the tall sizes from the pooled models. In the case of instant breakfast, I take the price elasticities from the regression for six-packet Carnation and Private Label. In the dog food analysis, I use the price elasticities for Mighty Dog and Private Label. Lastly, in the cat food analysis, I use the price elasticities for Fancy Feast and Private Label. These elasticities are listed in tables 4.3, 4.7, 4.11, 4.15, and 4.19 and are summarized below in table 4.21 for convenience.

Comparing these results to those obtained in the literature is difficult since few studies have either isolated these products or bothered to compare branded and unbranded product elasticities. For instance, Lee, Brown, and Schwartz (1986) have estimated the demand for branded and unbranded frozen orange juice. Their specification included seasonal factors, regional indicators, and socio-economic variables. Using panel data for 1981–1982, their conclusion was that the price elasticity for frozen orange juice is −0.34 for national brand de-

**Table 4.18.** Estimated Cat Food Demand Models

| | Cat Food #1 LCV1 (Fancy Feast) | Cat Food #2 LCV6 (Private Lbl.) |
|---|---|---|
| trend | −0.442 | 0.065 |
| | (−2.071) | (1.202) |
| seas1 | 0.114 | −0.064 |
| | (0.561) | (−1.240) |
| seas2 | 0.478 | −0.099 |
| | (2.260) | (−1.849) |
| seas3 | 0.413 | −0.125 |
| | (2.095) | (−2.510) |
| seas4 | 0.682 | −0.110 |
| | (3.690) | (−2.356) |
| seas5 | 0.412 | −0.109 |
| | (2.441) | (02.561) |
| lpr1 (log of Fancy Feast price) | −4.271 | 0.240 |
| | (−3.466) | (0.770) |
| lpr3 (log of Friskies Buffet price) | 0.236 | 0.209 |
| | (0.278) | (0.972) |
| lpr4 (log of Nine Lives price) | −0.072 | −0.057 |
| | (−0.243) | −0.759) |
| lpr5 (log of Kal Kan price) | −1.210 | 0.203 |
| | (−1.270 | (0.843) |
| lpr6 (log of Private Label price) | −.019 | −1.607 |
| | (−0.036) | (−12.165) |
| lpr7 (log of Bright Eyes price) | 0.016 | −0.066 |
| | (0.041) | (−0.658) |
| lpr8 (log of All Other price) | 0.091 | −0.011 |
| | (0.101) | (−0.048) |
| lcat | 32.159 | 3.699 |
| | (7.002) | 3.184) |
| lrinc | 2.750 | −1.196 |
| | (0.993) | (−1.707) |
| ladff | −0.061 | 0.018 |
| | (−1.529) | (1.748) |
| $R$-Squared | 0.672 | 0.942 |
| Number of Observations | 666 | 666 |
| Standard Error of the Regression | 1.032 | 0.261 |

**Table 4.19.** Cat Food: Summary of Price Elasticities

| Product | Price Elasticity |
|---|---|
| Fancy Feast | -4.27 |
| Private Label | -1.60 |

**Table 4.20.** Cat Food: Summary of the Market Shares (1984)

| Product | Market Share |
|---|---|
| Fancy Feast | 3.9% |
| Private Label | 8.7% |

mand and −0.21 for private label. While the result that the branded product shows more price elasticity than the unbranded product is qualitatively consistent with our results, the magnitude of these elasticities is inconsistent with the optimizing behavior of a monopolist with respect to its differentiated product. (Monopolists should always operate in the elastic portion of the demand curve unless marginal costs are negative.)

Inspection of table 4.21 reveals that the elasticities for branded goods exceed the elasticities for unbranded or private label goods in all but one case. Since elasticity is often associated with brand loyalty I digress to explain this pattern.

### *4.5.1 Branded and Unbranded Goods–Elasticity Results*

Should we expect that branded goods are less elastically demanded than their counterpart unbranded goods? At first thought this would appear to be the case, since branded goods are more highly differentiated from their competitors and would therefore tend to have lower price elasticities of demand. Under this line of argument, branded products have fewer substitutes than do unbranded products and therefore customers are less likely to purchase lower-priced competing (and possibly inferior) products when faced with a price increase. Does the evidence reveal this pattern? The answer found in our analysis and in other similar studies is no.

For example Russell and Bolton (1988, p. 237) citing Blattberg and Wisniewski (1985) state that "Marketing theory suggests that consumers on private label brands are more price sensitive than consumers of national brands. In fact, the estimated stick margarine in price elasticity of Blattberg and Wisniewski (1985) show that private label brands are less price elastic." Citing Telser (1962), Russell and Bolton (1988, p. 221) state, "For example, an early study by Telser (1962) found that the market share price elasticities of low price brands of frozen orange juice were greater than that of high price brands. How-

**Table 4.21.** Summary of Market Shares and Price Elasticities

| | Coffee-mate 16 oz. Creamer | Carnation Evaporated Milk | Carnation Instant Breakfast 6-packet | Mighty Dog Dog Food | Fancy Feast Cat Food |
|---|---|---|---|---|---|
| Market Share of the Branded Commodity | 51.3% | 30.8% | 80.3% | 5.9% | 3.9% |
| Market Share of the Private Label Commodity | 28.2% | 47.8% | 17.6% | 2.2% | 8.7% |
| Elasticity of the Branded Commodity | 2.01 | 2.03 | 1.47 | 2.42 | 4.27 |
| Elasticity of the Private Label Commodity | 1.44 | 1.22 | 1.74 | 2.25 | 1.61 |

ever, the opposite relationship held for the other categories in Telser's study (regular coffee, instant coffee, and margarine)."

The confusion apparent in these examples results from comparing elasticities without first considering the degree of competition arising from those producers who share the market. The comparison of branded and unbranded elasticities (without further adjustment) does not make an allowance for the degree of competition in the unbranded market. This comparison overstates the economic value to any single producer in the unbranded market and therefore makes the elasticity results seemingly paradoxical.

Thus, it is not possible to simply compare the elasticities of branded and unbranded commodities without a consideration of market share. Since there are typically multiple producers of the unbranded product (or at least multiple sellers), any single producer can only extract a portion of the total profitability in the unbranded market. It is more valuable to be a monopolist facing a more elastic demand curve than to be a oligopolist who will have to compete for the profits achievable from a less elastic demand curve.

Shapouri et al. (1981) analyze the demand for wine using similar data and methods to those in our study. In one of the few papers comparing firm-level and industry-level demand, these authors find that the firm-level demand elasticities are, in almost every case, larger than the industry-level elasticities. Analogously, I have shown that the elasticity of the firm selling a branded commodity is almost always larger than the elasticity for the industry segment selling the unbranded commodity.[34]

### *4.5.2 Trademark Valuation Percentage*

In order to calculate the trademark value as a percentage of revenues using the formulas derived in section 4.2, it is necessary to calculate economic operating margins. Accounting operating margins do not include a charge for a "normal" rate of return on plant, equipment, and other assets that have alternative uses. As a result, I have utilized the identifiable fixed assets for each division of the Carnation Company, plus an allocation of the general corporate assets, times a rate of return for alternative uses of capital, to obtain an economic operating margin. These figures are listed in table 4.22.

For example, with Coffee-mate sixteen ounce creamer, in 1984 the fixed assets associated with the Instant Division of the Carnation Company as a percent of sales were 25.8 percent. Adding Corporate Assets of 3.3 percent to this results in a total of 29.1 percent. Finally, assuming a weighted average

[34]Pagoulatos and Sorensen (1986) cite Becker (1971, p. 13) in arguing that price elasticity of demand will be greater the lower the degree of competition since colluding firms will attempt to restrict output and raise prices to reach a more elastic portion of the demand curve. This view is also consistent with the empirical evidence that an unbranded market segment will have smaller demand elasticities than would otherwise be expected. Bellizi et al. (1981) citing Burke (1979) states that private label (unbranded) buyers have been a small but loyal group. The loyalty demonstrated by private label or generic buyers may also translate into lower price elasticities of demand.

cost of capital of 13.0 percent leads to a reduction in the accounting operating margin by 3.8 percent. The calculations for royalty rates are summarized in table 4.23.

For example, selecting the numbers for Coffee-mate sixteen ounce Creamer gives us:

$\alpha_0$ = market share of the Branded Commodity = 51.3%
$\alpha_1$ = market share of the Private Label Commodity = 28.2%
$\varepsilon$ = elasticity of the Branded Commodity = 2.01
$\varepsilon'$ = elasticity of the Private Label Commodity = 1.44

Using these numbers in equation (19) results in:

$$S = \frac{\alpha_0}{\alpha_0 + \alpha_1} = \frac{0.513}{0.513 + 0.282} = 0.645$$

then applying this result to equation (21) results in:

$$\begin{aligned} G &= 1 - \frac{S(1-S)}{1-\alpha_0} \frac{\varepsilon - 1}{\varepsilon' - S} = 1 - \frac{0.645(1-0.645)}{1-0.513} \frac{2.01-1}{1.44-0.645} \\ &= 1 - 0.470 \cdot 1.270 = 0.403 \end{aligned}$$

This value of 40.3 percent corresponds to the value listed in table 4.23 under "Coffee-mate 16 ounce Creamer" for its Trademark Fraction Percentage of Economic Profit.

The trademark fraction is then multiplied by the economic operating margin reported in table 4.23 in order to arrive at a royalty rate.

As can be seen from table 4.23, the economic value of the trademark, expressed as a percentage of revenues, ranges from 1.3 percent for evaporated milk to 26.4 percent for Carnation Instant Breakfast. The percentage value for Coffee-mate, Mighty Dog, and Fancy Feast are 17.5 percent, 18.5 percent, and 11 percent, respectively. These royalty rates are consistent with our expectations. The most unique and differentiated products have the higher royalty rates, while the least differentiated products (such as evaporated milk) have the lowest royalty rates.

**Table 4.22.** Summary of Capital Charge Calculation

| | Coffee-mate 16 oz. Creamer | Carnation Evaporated Milk | Carnation Instant Breakfast 6-packet | Mighty Dog Dog Food | Fancy Feast Cat Food |
|---|---|---|---|---|---|
| Fixed Assets (as a percentage of sales) | 25.8% | 11.8% | 25.8% | 11.3% | 11.3% |
| General Corporate Assets (as a percentage of sales) | 3.3% | 3.3% | 3.3% | 3.3% | 3.3% |
| Resulting Total Assets (as a percentage of sales) | 29.1% | 15.1% | 29.1% | 14.6% | 14.6% |
| Weighted Average Cost of Capital | 13.0% | 13.0% | 13.0% | 13.0% | 13.0% |
| Margin Attributable to return on Fixed Assets (as a percentage of sales) | 3.8% | 2.0% | 3.8% | 1.9% | 1.9% |

**Table 4.23.** Summary of Trademark Fraction Calculations

| | Coffee-mate 16 oz. Creamer | Carnation Evaporated Milk | Carnation Instant Breakfast 6-packet | Mighty Dog Dog Food | Fancy Feast Cat Food |
|---|---|---|---|---|---|
| Accounting Operating Margin (as a percentage of sales) | 39.8% | 5.2% | 46.5% | 25.0% | 26.9% |
| Rate of Return on Fixed Assets (as a percentage of sales) | 3.8% | 3.0% | 3.8% | 1.9% | 1.9% |
| Economic Operating Margin (as a percentage of sales) | 36.0% | 2.2% | 42.7% | 23.1% | 25.0% |
| Trademark Fraction Percentage of Economic Profit | 40.3% | 57.2% | 61.8% | 80.3% | 43.8% |
| Percentage of Revenues | 14.5% | 1.3% | 26.4% | 18.5% | 11.0% |

## 4.6 Appendices

### 4.6.1 *Oligopoly Profits*

The standard Cournot-Nash analysis of oligopoly assumes that producers simultaneously choose their quantities (or capacities) and prices adjust to equilibrate the market. Suppose, for example, that there are two producers of a homogeneous good with constant marginal costs of productions $C_1$ and $C_2$, respectively. If they produce $Q_1$ and $Q_2$ units, total production is $Q = Q_1 + Q_2$ and, for the market to be in equilibrium, $Q = D(P)$. Let $D^{-1}(\cdot)$ be the inverse demand function, so

$$P = D^{-1}(Q) = D^{-1}(Q_1 + Q_2). \tag{22}$$

The profit for firm $i$ is

$$\begin{aligned} \pi_i(Q_1, Q_2) &= Q_1(P - C_i) \\ &= Q_i[D^{-1}(Q_1 + Q_2) - C_i]. \end{aligned}$$

If firm one takes firm two's output as given, the first-order conditions for profit maximization are

$$\begin{aligned} 0 &= \frac{\partial \pi_1(Q_1, Q_2)}{\partial Q_1} \qquad (23) \\ &= [D^{-1}(Q_1 + Q_2) - C_1] + Q_1 \frac{\partial D^{-1}(Q_1 + Q_2)}{\partial Q_1} \\ &= P - C_1 + Q_1/D'(P). \end{aligned}$$

Rearranging terms yields

$$\frac{P - C_1}{P} = -\left(\frac{Q_1}{Q}\right)\frac{Q}{P}\frac{1}{D'(P)} = \frac{S_1}{\varepsilon} \tag{24}$$

where $S_1 = Q_1/Q$ is the market share (in quantities) of firm one and $\varepsilon = -Q/PD'(P)$ is the price elasticity of demand in the market.

Equation (24) is a straightforward generalization of equation (6). If firm one is a monopolist (i.e., $Q_2 = 0$), then $S_1 = 1$ and equation (24) reduces to equation (6). At the other extreme, as $S_1$ approaches zero, so that firm one has no significant market power, then economic profits fall to zero. These results have been derived under a model of duopoly, but are equally valid with any number of firms where $Q$ is interpreted as the total production quantity of all firms in the industry.

### 4.6.2 *Product Review*

This appendix provides an overview of the five products that were studied—Coffee-mate, evaporated milk, instant breakfast, Mighty Dog, and Fancy Feast. I identify characteristics of buyers, brands, and product categories that may be relevant to the demand analysis in section 4.4. For example, in determining demand for dog or cat food, the quantity of pet food consumed over time should be considered in light of any changes in population trends for dog and cat ownership which may have occurred over time as well. Another good example may be seasonal variations in coffee consumption in the analysis of coffee creamer demand. The variations, unless accounted for, may make comparisons of sales data among different seasons misleading. This product review assists in identifying the important factors to include in the analysis. This information is drawn primarily from Carnation's marketing files and from interviews with those individuals who were marketing the products during the early to mid-1980s.

**Coffee-mate.** According to a survey study (Carnation Consumer Research Department [1991]), 37 percent of all cups of coffee are whitened. Fresh milk was used in one-half of these cups. Non-dairy powdered creamerswere the second most popular whitening product and were used in approximately 20 percent of all cups of coffee consumed.[35] Carnation's Coffee-mate is the top-selling non-dairy powdered creamer. Its major branded competitor is Cremora, which is manufactured by Borden. Private Label products, some of which are manufactured by Dean Foods, are also available. Other substitutes for non-dairy powdered creamers, in addition to fresh milk, include fresh cream, evaporated milk, and powdered milk.

Since coffee is a complementary product for powdered creamers, trends and fluctuations in coffee consumption affect the demand for powdered creamers. There has been a long-term decline in per capita daily consumption of coffee in the United States. Between 1962 and 1985, the average number of cups of coffee consumed by adults declined from 3.1 to 1.8. The proportion of the population drinking coffee also declined from 75 percent to 55 percent over the same period. However, these two downward trends have been offset by increases in the total U.S. population so that the total amount of coffee consumed has increased. Between 1980 and 1985, for example, there was a 4.4 percent increase in total coffee consumption (Rhum 1987).

Average per capita consumption rates vary by season, region, gender, and age. Since coffee is traditionally a hot beverage, its consumption fluctuates seasonally and peaks during the colder months. Consumption rates are also higher in colder climates. The Midwest has the highest per capita rate of coffee consumption at 2.3 cups per day during 1984. Consumption rates were lowest in the South (at 1.8 cups per capita per day). The Northeast and West regions

[35]This 1991 research review cites a 1989-90 "National Eating Trends Survey of Coffee Creamer Usage" as the source for these statistics.

had roughly equal levels of consumption and tended to be close to the national average (Rhum 1987).

Coffee drinkers who use coffee creamerstend to be of lower socioeconomic status than other coffee drinkers. According to a Carnation marketing study, Coffee-mate consumption was highest among those coffee drinkers with incomes under $10,000, with no more than a high school education, employed in blue collar occupations, living in smaller cities or rural areas, and who are African-American. The only age-related skew of Coffee-mate users is that males aged 30 to 34 were relatively less likely to purchase the product. The results of the study for all coffee creamer users showed a similar demographic profile for users of other brands (Carnation 1991).

Although not used in the demand analysis, it is noteworthy that Coffee-mate commands a higher degree of brand loyalty than its competitors. In 1985, Coffee-mate satisfied 62 percent of its purchasers' product requirements.[36] In comparison, Cremora fulfilled only 39 percent of its purchasers' product requirements. This rate was significantly lower than Coffee-Mate's and, in addition, Cremora consumers were more likely to make their purchases on deals. In 1985, 41 percent of Cremora units were purchased using a manufacturer's coupon (with an average value of seventy-three cents). Only 17 percent of Coffee-mate sales were made with coupons and the average coupon value was forty-seven cents (Carnation 1985).

**Carnation Evaporated Milk.** The Carnation Company's origins are in the evaporated milk business. Today, as in 1985, Carnation Evaporated Milk is the leading national brand. It competes against several other national brands (Sweetened Condensed, Pet, Eagle, and Milnot) as well as Private Label and generic products.

Evaporated milk has commonly been used as a creamer in coffee and in everyday foods such as soups, potatoes, and sauces. Evaporated milk is also used in recipes for traditional holiday foods (such as pies), and for seasonal foods (such as ice cream and hot cereals). The two uses of evaporated milk—everyday and special occasion—create two distinct market segments. These segments have different purchasing patterns, brand preferences, and demographic profiles.

A small number of heavy users make the bulk of evaporated milk purchases. According to a 1987 Carnation study, only 13 percent of all evaporated milk consumers make five or more purchases per year, but they represent 61 percent of total category sales volume (Carnation 1987). Sixty percent of evaporated milk consumers make only one purchase per year (representing 15 percent of sales volume). Carnation sales are more concentrated among light users than its competitors. Specifically, 69 percent of Carnation purchasers (representing 28

[36]Purchasers' product requirements are defined as the total proportion of category volume that a brand represents among its buyers. For example, if all Coffee-mate purchasers bought a total of one hundred dollars worth of dry creamer and sixty dollars of the total was Coffee-mate creamer then, Coffee-mate satisfies 60 percent of its purchasers' product requirements.

percent of Carnation sales volume) make only a single purchase per year, while only 8 percent of Carnation purchasers (representing 41 percent of sales volume) make five or more purchases of evaporated milk per year (Carnation 1987).

Hispanics and African-Americans are believed to comprise a relatively significant proportion of the heavy user category. These two demographic groups are more likely to use evaporated milk to prepare everyday and holiday foods that are unique to their cultures than are other demographic groups. Data from a 1983–85 panel study indicated that non-whites (including both Hispanics and African-Americans) were twice as likely to have used evaporated milk within the past year than whites (Carnation 1987).[37]

Since both the Hispanic and African-American populations are geographically concentrated, evaporated milk purchases tend to be higher in regions where these groups make up a larger proportion of the population. More than four out of five Hispanics reside in the Southwest, while blacks comprise about a quarter of the population in the South. Not too surprisingly, the West South Central and South Atlantic regions have the highest percentage of households purchasing evaporated milk.

There is considerable seasonal variation in other uses for evaporated milk. About a third of evaporated milk consumption between 1980 and 1982 was with coffee (which is somewhat more likely to be consumed during the winter). Pies comprised 9 percent of the total number of end dishes using evaporated milk; of the total uses for pies, 59 percent occurred between October and December. Other popular uses include potatoes, sauces, soups, or hot cereals. Of the total of these end dishes, 38 percent were prepared between January and March.[38]

There are clear demographic differences between the purchasers of different brands of evaporated milk. Households purchasing Private Label products tend to be those of young families (with five or more members and with children under eighteen) (Carnation 1987). The households also tend to be less affluent, to be less well-educated, to live in mobile homes, and to hold blue collar jobs. Finally, Private Label consumers are more likely to reside in the Mountain States and in rural areas (Carnation 1987).

[37]Some of the traditional Hispanic uses include *atole* (a corn beverage), *elote* (creamed corn), *three milks* (a dessert), *morir sanando* (a beverage with orange juice), *coquito* (a rum drink), and *maizena* (a corn dish). A study of evaporated milk usage found that Hispanics were 49 percent more likely than non-Hispanics to use canned milk. Even though Hispanics accounted for only 9 percent of the evaporated milk category buyers, Hispanic sales volume is believed to be much greater because of the large variety of uses of evaporated milk in Mexican cooking. A 1987 study estimated that the Hispanic population might purchase as much as 70 percent of the evaporated milk category sales volume (Carnation 1987). African-Americans also tend to be heavy buyers of evaporated milk for use in a number of traditional southern dishes. Evaporated milk is often used in cooking cornbread and as batter for chicken and pork chops. According to the previously cited 1987 study, African-Americans comprised about 12 percent of all evaporated milk purchasers (Carnation 1987).

[38]These statistics are based on a Market Research Corporation of American panel study conducted between July 1980 and June 1982 that is cited in the 1987 Carnation Research Review.

Although a brand loyalty variable is not used in the demand analysis, it is useful to note that brand loyalty is weak among evaporated milk buyers. A 1982–83 survey showed that evaporated milk users are generally willing to purchase multiple brands. For each of the evaporated milk brands (Carnation, Pet, Sweetened Condensed, Eagle, Milnot, Private Label, and generic), buyers allocated 60 to 70 percent of their purchases to brands other than their primary choice. For example, Carnation consumers purchased the Carnation brand 37 percent of the time, Private Label 25 percent, Eagle 14 percent, and Pet 10 percent (Carnation 1987).

**Carnation Instant Breakfast.** Carnation Instant Breakfast (CIB) was introduced in 1965 and its sales peaked soon thereafter. Between 1968 and 1983, sales declined by about 60 percent as a number of products with similar features were introduced. Competing products include Pillsbury and Private Label instant breakfasts as well as granola bars, diet snacks and beverages, and (to a lesser extent) Carnation Breakfast Bars (Lemont Consulting Group 1983).

Carnation has targeted middle income housewives with children aged seven to eighteen for its marketing efforts (Lemont 1983). According to a marketing study, the key to CIB usage is the presence of children, especially teenagers, in the household. The product is initially bought for use by children but then begins to be drunk by adults, especially mothers. The primary consumers of CIB, therefore, are adult women and teenagers (both male and female) (Lemont Consulting Group 1983).

Households using CIB tend to be upscale: the female head is likely to be college educated and employed full or part-time (Lemont Consulting Group 1983). CIB sales are highest in the South and West, and lower elsewhere (Gallup Organization 1986). There is also some seasonal variation to CIB demand, with higher sales during the fall months. This can be attributed to the start of the school year as parents look once again for fast and nutritious breakfast foods. Increases in advertising tied to the start of school also contribute to sales in the fall (Cohn 1985).

**Mighty Dog.** Dog food was first commercially produced in England in the 1860s. The available dog foods at that time were dry, biscuit type products. During the 1930s, dry meat meal dog foods were introduced. The selection of these dry dog foods was expanded during the 1950s. Then in the 1960s, many varieties of canned dog foods and new semi-moist products were introduced. As of 1985, the dog food market offered four types of products: dry, canned, semi-moist, and treats. In 1985, dry dog food accounted for 56 percent of total dog food sales. Canned dog food ranked second at 27 percent of the category sales (Pet Food Institute 1987).

In 1985, Carnation ranked second out of seven major pet food market manufacturers with revenues of $660 million. The Mighty Dog brand is Carnation's leading gourmet canned dog food. Carnation ranked third in the canned dog food segment with 13 percent of total sales in 1985. Grand Met's Alpo brand leads the category with a 19 percent market share and Mars' Kal Kan ranks second with a 16 percent market share (Business Trend Analysts 1987). Other competitors in the canned dog food market include Anderson Clayton's Cycle and Quaker Oats' Ken-L-Ration.

Nearly all dog owners buy dog food (with the exception of a small number of outdoor-only dogs), suggesting that growth in the total dog food market depends on growth in the dog population. The percentage of households owning dogs remained constant at 38 percent between 1980 and 1985 (Plante 1988), while the total number of dogs in the United States increased slowly due to a steady increase in the number of households.

The demographic profile of a typical dog owner is a middle income or above family with teenage children who own their own home. Dog ownership was highest in 1981 in households with incomes between twenty and thirty thousand and somewhat lower in households with incomes below that level. In general, any household that included children was more likely to have a dog. Among those households that did have children, those with children between ages thirteen and seventeen tended to own dogs more often than those with younger children. Families living in multi-family housing or renters had much lower than average rates of dog ownership (Pet Food Institute 1993).

These profile differences may lead to regional effects which can be controlled in the analysis. For example, the East South Central, West South Central, and Mountain regions all had higher than average dog ownership rates in 1981. The New England and Mid-Atlantic regions exhibited the lowest dog ownership rates. Within regions, the most rural areas had the highest rate of dog ownership and the ownership rate consistently declined as county population increased (Pet Food Institute 1993).

It is important to identify relevant market segments within the dog food market. For instance, this market appears to be segmented by distinctions between dry and canned foods, and gourmet and maintenance products. Owners who purchase primarily canned dog food tend to have different dog ownership patterns than those who purchase only dry dog food. According to a 1980–81 survey, consumers buying gourmet canned dog food tended to own between one and two dogs, each weighing less than forty pounds. Additionally, the dogs tended to be older, live primarily indoors, exceed normal weight ranges, and not be used for hunting purposes (Management Science Associates 1982).

The most significant difference in dog characteristics between those dogs whose owners purchased canned and dry food was dog size. Dry dog food consumers generally owned dogs weighing more than forty pounds. Within the canned dog food user group, dog size was most significant for Mighty Dog consumers. The 1980–81 study found that 64 percent of Mighty Dog volume was consumed by dogs weighing twenty-five pounds or less, compared to 35 percent and 23 percent for Alpo and Kal Kan respectively. A total of 86 percent of Mighty Dog volume was consumed by dogs weighing forty pounds or less. Again, this rate was much lower for the Alpo and Kal Kan brands at 60 percent and 46 percent, respectively (Management Science Associates 1982).

The dog food market can also be categorized by classifying brands as either gourmet or maintenance types of dog food. As the names imply, consumers who purchase maintenance products focus on satisfying their dog's hunger at a low cost while gourmet consumers focus on trying to please their dogs and will pay a higher price to do so.

Although a brand loyalty variable is not used in the demand analysis, it is useful to note that Mighty Dog has a more loyal consumer/buyer base than any other canned gourmet brand. Thirty-five percent of Mighty Dog purchasers were considered highly loyal, compared to 30 percent for Alpo and 25 percent for Kal Kan. Mighty Dog's highly loyal group and medium loyal group both purchased less volume on deals than Kal Kan (Management Decision Systems, Inc. 1982). (No information on Alpo's rate of purchases on deals was reported.)

**Fancy Feast.** In recent years cats have increased in popularity as pets. Between 1981 and 1985 the cat population increased 38 percent, while the number of dogs increased only 7 percent during the same period (Progressive Grocer 1987). With changes in pet population, sales of cat food have risen sharply. With greater consumption of cat food has come the creation of new brands. Carnation was responsible for the creation of a new type of cat food, a super gourmet brand, Fancy Feast.

Carnation's introduction of Fancy Feast in 1981 expanded the gourmet cat food category upward in price, quality perception, and variety. Nine Lives, Buffet, and Kal Kan were the upper end of the cat food market before the introduction of Fancy Feast. With its three ounce size, lined can with pull-tab lid (which eased product removal), pureed texture, and premium pricing, Fancy Feast defined a new category—the super premium or gourmet cat food (Georgia Bender Research 1984).

Fancy Feast appears to be fresh, soft, moist, and juicy, and consumers assumed it has fewer by-products and fillers. Its more pleasant aroma and consistent appearance gives consumers a perception of a high-quality product. Even the higher price (sometimes nearly twice as much as conventional canned cat food) helps to convey the image of a significantly better product and to make consumers feel they are rewarding or pampering their pets. These are important considerations to many consumers who want to provide their cats with better food and care (Georgia Bender Research 1984). These observations lead us to anticipate that the demand for Fancy Feast will be different than for some of its competition.

In many respects cat owners are similar to dog owners. In fact, nearly half of all cat owners also have a dog (Crispell 1991). Families with children, especially older children, are more likely to have cats, and there is a slightly higher concentration of cats in the western United States. Historically, homeowners have been more likely than renters to have cats, but this difference has eroded recently (Pet Food Institute 1993). The typical Fancy Feast buyer is a female head of household who is employed full time, has no children, and has household income in excess of thirty-five thousand dollars. Fancy Feast has a loyal following. These observations are suggestive of possible regional variations in Fancy Feast purchases.

There appears to be strong market segmentation in the cat food market. According to marketing studies ("PSA: Preference Structure Analysis of Cat Foods" 1981), the cat food purchase decision begins with a choice by the consumer as to which form of food (dry, canned, semi-moist) to feed a pet. Once a form has been decided on, the size of the product is selected, and finally a brand is chosen that is available in the consumer's preferred type, size, and flavor. This decision process has significant implications for how products compete with one another. For example dry brands will not compete strongly with either canned or semi-moist brands, and canned will not compete strongly with semi-moist. Consequently, Fancy Feast's main competitors fall into a fairly narrow product category (other canned gourmet cat foods). One conclusion that can be drawn from the brand preference analysis is that brand name, followed by package size, are the most important attributes within the gourmet cat food decision-making process ("PSA: Preference Structure Analysis of Cat Foods" 1981).

# 5 THE DEMAND FOR RECREATIONAL FISHING IN MONTANA

## 5.1 Introduction

The Clark Fork River, located in southwestern Montana, is a tributary of the Columbia River in the northwestern United States. The Upper Clark Fork River area is known for its cold-water trout fishing. The Upper Clark Fork River from the Butte and Anaconda area to the Milltown Reservoir is contaminated with several heavy metals primarily from historical mining activities. The Silver Bow Creek, the Upper Clark Fork River, and Milltown Reservoir have been designated as Superfund sites by the U.S. Environmental Protection Area. Scientific studies indicate that the trout in these areas are at high risk from elevated metal concentrations due to their contaminated diet.

The objective of this chapter is to develop an econometric model of natural resource damage to fishing resulting from hypothetical injuries to the Upper Clark Fork River in Montana. The model designed in this chapter yields a variety of information. It employs survey data, objective and consistent measures of distance between city of residence and fishing site, and data on stream characteristics to determine those factors which affect an individual's choice of fishing site. The econometric method employed in this chapter is based on the multinomial logit choice model (MNL). I use the MNL technique to estimate the probability that an individual will choose to fish at a certain river based on both the characteristics of the individual and of the rivers available. The model is then used to estimate changes in the predicted probability of choosing a specific river when certain river characteristics are hypothetically altered. These differences in probabilities are translated into an aggregate measure of reduced fishing, which is then used to calculate the natural resource damage resulting from injuries to the Upper Clark Fork River.

Placing a dollar value on the welfare loss to individuals resulting from changes in their opportunities to enjoy natural resources (in this case, natural resource damage to fishing resulting from river injuries) has long occupied the attention of applied economists.

The appropriate methodology for assessing natural resource damage is well-known. A demand curve which includes some measure of price, as well as characteristics of the natural resource, and attributes of the individual, must be estimated. If a competitive market exists, the appropriate measure of price is simply the market price. If no competitive market exists, other price-like factors which directly affect the demand for the natural resource must be found. In the case of rivers, a natural price-like factor is an individual's travel cost.

Once the demand curve is estimated, the appropriate welfare calculations can be conducted using consumer surplus. Where a competitive market exists, consumer surplus is based on changes in the market price. In a case where no competitive market exists but, for example, travel costs are measurable, consumer surplus can be based on changes in travel costs.

These procedures are not always straightforward. A variety of modeling decisions and assumptions regarding data must be made. In particular, the researcher must choose a technique for estimating demand and must assemble a database suitable for estimating demand via the chosen technique. This chapter is based on the multinomial logit choice model, which has been used to estimate a diverse set of consumer demand issues, including transportation mode choice, the demand for consumer durables, and individual voting behavior, to name a few. Part of the data used to estimate this model combines independent surveys regarding river destination choices in Montana. As a result, an adjustment must be made in the calculations of damages to allow for the fact that the resulting survey instruments rely on "choice-based-sampling" techniques.

The multinomial logit choice model estimates the probability that an individual will choose a given river based on characteristics of both the individual and the river. The model is able to provide estimates of the change in the probability that an individual would choose a given river as characteristics of the river, such as the abundance of fish, change. I translate the changes in predicted probabilities into an aggregate measure of lost usage associated with reduced fishing quality and apply this measure to estimate the damages under various scenarios.

Section 5.2 of this chapter reviews techniques for estimating natural resource damage. In particular, it compares simultaneous equation approaches to discrete choice approaches, such as the multinomial logit choice model. Section 5.3 specifies and estimates the particular multinomial logit choice model used in this study. It begins with a discussion of the discrete choice methodology, including a development of the equations that are subsequently estimated. It then discusses data sources and explains the construction of certain key variables. It also explains the correction needed for choice-based sampling required by the combined use of separate surveys. Finally, it presents the results of the estimation based on the multinomial logit choice model. Section 5.4 uses the results of section 5.3 to calculate potential yearly damage to individuals associated with hypothetical injury to the Upper Clark Fork River in Montana. Section 5.5 aggregates these yearly damage estimates to yield a total damage estimate. A number of calculations are presented, under different assumptions regarding discount rates, extent of alleged injury, and the rate of recovery of the rivers.

## 5.2 Techniques for Estimating Natural Resource Damage

### 5.2.1 *Market and Non-Market Valuation*

A discrete choice model or logit model is only one of the techniques that can be used to estimate the demand for recreational goods or services. This section discusses how the discrete choice model compares to the alternative techniques, distinguishing strengths and weaknesses of each method.

In economic terms, the damage resulting from an alleged injury to a natural resource is equivalent to the net change in economic welfare, as measured by consumer surplus. Where natural resources are traded in organized markets and information about these markets is available, the calculation of the loss in consumer surplus associated with damage to a natural resource from some particular alleged injury is straightforward and well known.

For example, suppose $D(p; x, y)$ is an individual's demand curve where $p$ is market price, $x$ is a vector of individual attributes and $y$ is a vector of attributes describing the natural resource. At price $p^*$ consumer surplus is the area under $D(p; x, y)$ above $p^*$. If, for example, some reduction in supply increases price to $p^{**}$, then the welfare loss is given by the difference between consumer surplus at $p^*$ and consumer surplus at $p^{**}$. Of course, to the extent that substitutes for the natural resource are available, gains in consumer surplus associated with increases in demand for them will offset, to some extent, the magnitude of the welfare loss.

Similarly, if a change in some attribute of the natural resource reduces demand (represented by a shift from $y$ to $\hat{y}$), price will typically fall, say to $\hat{p}$, but so will consumer surplus, because even though $\hat{p}$ is less than $p^*$, the demand curve has shifted downward. Thus the area below the new demand curve $D(p; x, \hat{y})$ above $\hat{p}$ will be less than the area below the old demand curve $D(p; x, y)$ above $p^*$. However, to the extent that substitutes are available, gains in consumer surplus associated with increases in the demand for them must be taken into account.

Where organized markets do not exist, there is no market price and therefore the above calculation is impossible; other techniques must be devised to determine changes in the value of the natural resource to users.[1] Fortunately, in the case of river destination choice, a natural price-type variable exists, namely travel cost, which can be used in a manner analogous to market price to calculate consumer surplus. This procedure is explained in more detail below. It is important to recognize that it is still necessary to take account of substitutes in the net welfare calculation even when competitive markets fail to exist. In fact, one of the major problems in estimating the value of damage to a natural resource is the question of substitution of other natural resources. If it is assumed, a priori, that substitutes for a natural resource do not exist, or are very scarce, then it makes sense to use a single equation approach to calculate potential welfare losses. If the natural resource has numerous substitutes, and if these substitutes vary according to the travel costs of the user, it makes sense to use an approach which recognizes the substitution possibilities. Such a method normally relies on a system of simultaneous equations. Two variants are used: one is a simultaneous equation version of the typical single equation approach; the other, discrete choice, measures the likelihood that individual consumers will choose particular recreation sites.

The latter two approaches are outlined below. Both make use of the existence of multiple substitutes which vary according to the origin of the resource user. The simultaneous equation approach estimates a system of demand functions wherein travel cost replaces competitive price, and uses these demand functions to calculate consumer surplus. The key difference is that the discrete choice approach works directly from the utility maximization process via the individual utility function to calculate consumer surplus. Furthermore, the discrete choice approach can utilize individual-level data in a way that the simultaneous equation approach cannot, while avoiding problems associated with aggregation.

### 5.2.2 *The Travel Cost Method*

The most well known of the non-market approaches to measuring the welfare loss from "injured" natural resources is the travel cost method. This method had its conceptual origin in 1947 when Harold Hotelling mentioned in a letter to the director of the National Park Service that a demand curve for a given recreational site could be estimated by observing the extent to which visit rates decline as costs of travel increase. The first practical application of this model was by Clawson and Knetsch (1966).

In the standard travel cost model, individuals demand the services of a recreational site. The quantity they consume is measured by the visit rate, i.e., the proportion of people in a particular origin zone that go to the recreational site. The price of a person's consumption of a recreational site is therefore the

[1] There is no reason why the services of national resources cannot be traded in competitive markets. In the present case, the rights to fish on reaches of Montana rivers could be owned by private firms. See Clarke (1968) for a discussion of the private ownership of fishing rights in England.

cost of traveling to the site.[2] Travel costs are generally a large proportion of the total expense of recreation and it is reasonable to assume that individuals' decisions about which site to visit will be influenced considerably by the extent of these costs.

Travel costs depend on a variety of factors such as fuel costs per mile, incidental expenses, and expenses on goods which are inputs to the recreational activity.[3] However, the greatest single factor is the distance traveled. Another important determinant is the opportunity cost of time: the time spent traveling to a recreation site could have been spent on some other activity, such as work. A standard travel cost model regresses the visit rates from various origin zones to a site, against the cost of travel, income and other relevant variables.

Once a demand equation has been estimated for a site, a value of consumer surplus for a particular origin can be obtained, for example, by performing the following calculation:

$$CS_j = \int_{TC_j}^{\infty} D_j(TC, x, y)dTC$$

where $D_j(TC_j, x, y)$ is the estimated demand curve for origin $j$, $x_j$ is a vector of average characteristics of an individual from origin $j$, $y$ is a vector of resource-specific characteristics, and $TC_j$ is some measure of average travel cost for individuals from origin $j$. Summing across all origins gives an estimate of total consumer surplus.

Environmental damage to a recreation site is equivalent to a decrease in some component of the vector $y$ of resource-specific characteristics.[4] As in the case of market-traded resources, the welfare loss from such a change is given by the resulting decrease in $CS_j$, adjusted for any increase in the consumer surplus associated with changes in the demand for substitutes.[5]

The main insights of the travel cost method are the recognition that the lack of an "explicit price" does not mean that individuals do not pay to consume a non-market good; and the relevant "implicit price" can be used to calculate changes in welfare associated with changes in the demand for non-market goods. However, since environmental damage to a recreation site does not affect all origin zones equally (because of different substitution possibilities) a proper loss analysis using the travel cost method still requires a multiple equation framework incorporating substitution effects across zones.

---

[2]Individuals from different origin zones will have different costs of travel. However, these costs are given by the location of the site relative to the origin zone.

[3]For example, costs of buying bait if one is going fishing, or the cost of renting skis and boots if one is going skiing.

[4]See also Kolstad and Braden (1991) for a discussion of environmental demand theory.

[5]In some ways, the calculation for the non-market case is simpler than the calculation for the market case since travel costs $TC_j$ do not change in the former (unlike the market price in the latter). On the other hand, all consumers face the same price in the market case so there is no issue of which price to use in calculating consumer surplus. In the non-market case, since aggregate data is often utilized, some assumption must be made regarding the appropriate value of $TC_j$ to be used in calculating $CS_j$.

### *5.2.3 Simultaneous Equations Models*

The principle of the travel cost method has been applied within a multi-equation framework by several economists. The estimation of demand equations within this framework gives rise to an explicit and theoretically consistent introduction of substitution possibilities.

Recreationists travel to a site for a specific purpose. If individuals are assumed to "produce" recreation, then a site can be viewed simply as an input to the production process. An individual chooses a site which maximizes the satisfaction of recreation for any given level of costs. One outcome from this process is a set of derived demand functions for the alternative sites.

Using this conceptual base, Cicchetti, Fisher, and Smith (1976) attempt to place a value on the development of a new skiing site, Mineral King in California. The demand for the skiing site is determined by its special characteristics compared to other sites, such as relative travel times, quality of snow, and ancillary skiing facilities. If the cost per unit of time is the same at whichever site one is traveling to, then one can compare alternative sites according to their associated travel time. Assuming uniform travel speeds and costs, distance can be used as a proxy for the price of sites.

In the study by Cicchetti, et al. the quantity variable is measured by the visit rate to each site from each of the fifty-eight counties in California. This rate is interpreted as the "expected level of participation in some recreation activity at a site for a representative individual."[6]

Naturally, the visit rates and the distances to sites vary across counties, but what is to be measured is how the two are related across the sites. Cicchetti, et al. assumes a simple linear relationship between visit rates and prices and estimates simultaneously the parameters of six ski site demand equations.[7] The final step in the Cicchetti, et al. analysis is to introduce the possibility of a seventh ski facility (Mineral King).

Several comments on the Cicchetti study are in order. First, the demand system Cicchetti estimates implicitly requires aggregation, in this case, to the county level. Furthermore, no variables other than travel cost are significant in the estimated system of equations described. This may be because the necessity of using aggregate data means that some individual-level information is lost.[8] In any event, the insignificance of non-travel cost variables means that it is not possible to analyze the effects of environmental degradation in Cicchetti's framework. Discrete choice methods, on the other hand, allow the

---

[6]See Cicchetti, et al. (1976), p. 1265.

[7]It would be unrealistic to assume that the visit rates depend solely on the price vector. Recognizing this, Cicchetti, et al. tested for the effects of income and socioeconomic determinants of demand but found that the non-price variables' coefficients were not statistically significant.

[8]Indeed, Cicchetti observes that the insignificance of non-travel cost variables "does not imply that the income or socioeconomic characteristics of the visitors are not important determinants of demand. Rather, they conclude that the only measures available–county demographic statistics–are not significant determinants of visit rates (1976, p. 1265).

use of individual-level data, and thus make it more likely that non-travel cost variables will be significant in the estimated demand equations.

### 5.2.4 *The Discrete Choice Model*

Anglers can only go to one river site at a time. Thus, in order to obtain a non-discrete measure of demand for river sites (a "visit rate") some aggregation of individual-level data is necessary. Such aggregation raises many issues: the appropriate level of aggregation, the definition of variables such as travel costs which describe a "representative individual," and the loss of explanatory power due to the implicit reduction in sample size.

An alternative approach is to recognize that river site choice is inherently discrete and to work with the data in that form. Rather than estimating a visit rate for river sites, the model yields estimates of the probability of visiting each of the available river sites. Presumably, one of the explanatory variables used to generate these probabilities will be travel costs. For anglers, other explanatory variables will likely include fishing characteristics at each river site.

A potential problem with the discrete choice methodology is that it does not yield demand curves which can be used to calculate consumer surplus measures (whether or not market prices are available). Nonetheless, for the multinomial logit choice model it is possible to calculate welfare measures directly from the estimated parameters of the model. Furthermore, if at least one explanatory variable is measured in dollars (e.g., travel cost), the welfare measures can also be expressed in dollars.

This procedure has several advantages:

- It makes full use of available data since observations are at the individual level. No information is wasted.
- It not only allows for the possibility of substitution, it is based on the concept.
- It avoids the need to make arbitrary decisions about the level and form of aggregation.
- It avoids the need to make what are sometimes arbitrary decisions about what values to use in the construction of consumer surplus measures, and
- It allows survey data to be incorporated easily into the analysis.

As with any method, the discrete choice method has some structural requirements of its own which, if not met, reduce its power and accuracy. Foremost among these is the requirement that the substitutes for the good in question be available in elastic supply. That is, supply is expected to be able to expand in step with demand at essentially constant prices.[9]

[9]In the present analysis, this amounts to the assumption that there are no capacity constraints at any of the river sites in the study.

Nevertheless, because the discrete choice method makes full use of individual-level data, it may avoid generating false conclusions about the relevance of non-price variables on choice behavior, which can occur when data are aggregated. This can reduce or even eliminate the need to make additional arbitrary decisions about appropriate substitutes for a given site when the estimated model is applied to the calculation of damage.

### *5.2.5 The Discrete-Continuous Choice Model*

A weakness of both the simultaneous equations model and the discrete choice model is that they assume that the intensity with which a resource is used is the same for all consumers or classes of consumers. In practice, this may not always be a valid assumption. The discrete-continuous choice model tries to capture this intensity factor.

The estimation technique that is normally used for estimating the discrete-continuous choice model is called Limited Information Maximum Likelihood. In this technique, the analyst first estimates the parameters of the choice probabilities. The estimates from the choice model are then used to adjust the estimates of the parameters of the demand equations to account for the simultaneity of the two decisions.[10] Once a satisfactory set of demand equations, including choice probabilities, has been estimated, the demand for the good in question can be estimated as the weighted average of the demands at alternative sites.

## 5.3 Specification and Estimation of a Discrete Choice Model for River Destination

Economists assume that individuals choose between various alternatives by selecting the alternative that provides the greatest satisfaction. If, for example, an angler is faced with the choice of fishing at two different sites on a river, economists predict the angler will go to the site where he or she expects to catch more fish, to encounter fewer people, where natural beauty is greater, or simply is closest. It will generally be the case that satisfaction (i.e., utility) is determined by a number of factors, and that the relative importance of each will vary across individuals.

The objective of estimation is to determine what factors affect the actual choices made by individuals. Before estimation can proceed, however, a model describing the selection of various alternatives must be specified. In the case of discrete choices (i.e., the choice of one and only one of $j$ alternatives), the model must describe the probability of the selection of various alternatives.

In this section, the multinomial logit choice model, which allows for the discrete nature of river site selection, is specified and estimated. Subsection 5.3.1 begins with a detailed discussion of the discrete choice methodology, leading up to a description of the equations that are subsequently estimated. Subsection

[10] See Dubin and McFadden (1984) for details.

5.3.2 discusses data sources and subsection 5.3.3 explains the construction of two key variables based on those data sources. Subsection 5.3.4 explains corrections necessitated by the combined use of independent surveys, subsection 5.3.5 discusses the calculation of predicted probabilities and consumer surplus, and subsection 5.3.6 presents the econometric estimates.

### 5.3.1 *The Discrete Choice Methodology*

Let $U_i$ represent the utility an individual derives from alternative $i$ out of a set of several alternatives. By assumption, alternative $i$ will be chosen if and only if $U_i$ is the highest within the set of alternatives, that is, if $U_i > U_j$ for all $j \neq i$. Also by assumption, $U_i$ depends on several factors. This can be expressed mathematically by the following function:

$$U_i = U_i(p_i, Z_i, S)$$

where $p_i$ is the price of the underlying good (e.g., the travel cost of going fishing at site $i$), $Z_i$ is a set of factors that are specific to alternative $i$, and $S$ is a set of factors that are specific to the individual but do not depend on alternative $i$.[11] The vector $Z_i$ might include the natural beauty of site $i$ or the number of fish available at site $i$, while the vector $S$ might include the individual's age or education, or the purpose of the trip (to go boating or fishing, for example).

Not all factors which influence utility are observable. It is assumed that utility can be partitioned into two components: one which is based on observable factors, $V_i(p_i, Z_i, S)$, and one which is the unobservable, $\omega_i$, with

$$U_i = V_i(p_i, Z_i, S) + \omega_i.$$

The probability that alternative $i$ is chosen is

$$P_i = Prob(U_i > U_j, \ \ \forall j \neq i).$$

Substituting for $U_i$ from above and rearranging terms, the probability of selecting alternative $i$ from the set of alternatives available to the individual is

$$P_i = Prob(\omega_j - \omega_i \leq V_i - V_j, \ \ \forall j \neq i)$$

If it is assumed that unobservable components of utility, $\omega_i$, are randomly distributed in the population, then the above expression can be operationalized by making additional assumptions with respect to (1) the distributional form for $\omega_i$ and (2) the specification of the function, $V_i$. In particular, under the assumption that $\omega_i$ are independent extreme value distributed, $P_i$ is given by the multinomial logit model:

[11]The function $U_i$ is an indirect utility function since it depends on prices and attributes rather than the actual quantities consumed. It gives the maximum level of utility achievable for an individual who faces fixed prices and income.

$$P_i = \frac{e^{V_i}}{\sum_j e^{V_j}}.$$

In order to estimate the functional form for indirect utility, the method of maximum likelihood is employed. This calculates the parameters of the indirect utility function, maximizing the sample log-likelihood function.

In practice the parametric specification of the indirect utility function embodies certain inconsequential normalizations. Since

$$\begin{aligned} P_i &= Prob(U_i > U_j, \ \forall j \neq i) \\ &= Prob(\omega_j - \omega_i \leq V_i - V_j, \ \forall j \neq i) \end{aligned}$$

it is clear that only the difference in utilities affects the probability that a given alternative will be selected. Therefore, any alternative can be used as the basis for normalization. Without loss of generality, the last alternative $J$ is selected. The multinomial logit model can be rewritten as

$$P_j = \frac{e^{V_j}}{\sum_k e^{V_k}} = \frac{e^{(V_j - V_J)}}{\sum_k e^{(V_k - V_J)}}.$$

If we assume that $V_j$ is linear in its arguments with

$$V_j = X\beta_j + W_j\gamma$$

where $X$ is a vector of factors that do not depend on the alternative, $\beta_j$ are the unknown weights attached to those factors, $W_j$ is a vector of factors that do depend on the alternative, and $\gamma$ are the weights attached to those factors, then the differences in indirect utility from the normalizing alternative can be written as

$$V_j - V_J = X(\beta_j - \beta_J) + (W_j - W_J)\gamma.$$

As the parameters $\beta_j$ enter the formula for $V_j - V_J$ as differences, only these differences are identifiable. If $\lambda_j$ denotes the difference $\beta_j - \beta_J$ then the parameters to be determined are $\lambda_j, j = 1, 2, \ldots,$ J-1 since $\lambda_J$ is identically zero. When the vector $X$ contains a constant term, the logit choice model will determine the levels of J-1 alternative specific constants. These are referred to as "alternative-specific effects."

Observed utility, in our model of river choice, is assumed to be a function of the alternative-specific effects just described and a travel cost variable. Thus $W_j$ is comprised of a single element, amounting to a measure of travel cost per fish caught. This "dollars-per-fish" (*DPF*) variable is calculated using measured distances between the individual's origin and the alternative rivers, the individual' s skill level, and the abundance of fish in the alternative rivers.[12]

[12]The specification for observed utility (for non-anglers) is similar to that just described for anglers, except that the distance cost is not adjusted for the number of fish caught.

These specifications for observed utility, are quite parsimonious. Nevertheless, they fit individual behavior in both a logical and significant fashion. The construction of the variables which measure travel costs and travel costs per expected catch require several steps. In the next subsection, the data sources for the components of the variables are reviewed.

### *5.3.2 Data*

The data used to construct the variables used in the logistic choice model are taken from three sources: an Angler Preference Survey designed and administered by the Montana Department of Fish, Wildlife & Parks (DFWP); origin-destination distances from standard Automobile Association of America (AAA) maps; and an Interagency Stream Database.

**Angler Preference Survey.** In general, there are two kinds of demand information that are captured in surveys: preferences and behaviors. Surveys seek to determine whether people have participated in certain activities in the past, whether they do so now, and whether they expect to do so in the future. In addition to this factual type of information, surveys often seek to find out why people have made certain choices and how they value different recreational opportunities.

Thus, a recreation survey may seek to find out how many users have visited particular sites, where they came from, and what they did at the site. Such information is akin to what a census taker might measure at the time the recreationindexrecreation site was actually being used. One of the primary problems with surveys is accuracy. People do not always measure their mileage accurately, nor do they record the dates and times of all their trips. Thus travel cost surveys may reflect some errors in people's recollections.[13]

In 1986, the Montana DFWP conducted an Angler Preference Survey to uncover the economic value of sport fishing in Montana and to assess the attitudes and preferences of the anglers who fish for trout in the state's rivers and streams. The survey was directed at trout stream anglers who had visited nineteen Montana rivers and streams. The sample was constructed using a list of residents and nonresidents who had purchased Montana fishing licenses and had been previously contacted in the DFWP's annual fishing pressure survey.

The questionnaire asked anglers about their most recent trip to one of the nineteen target rivers (Beaverhead, Big Hole, Bighorn, Bitterroot, Blackfoot, Boulder, Upper Clark Fork, Lower Clark Fork, Flathead, South Fork Flathead, Gallatin, Kootenai, Madison, Missouri, Rock Creek, Smith, Stillwater, Upper

[13]Some surveys also ask respondents what they might do if conditions at the site were different. This latter information is called "contingent behavior" questioning and is at the heart of contingent value surveys and contingent valuation methods. There is ongoing controversy over whether such surveys accurately reflect the willingness of users to pay for various states of nature or of a resource. For further discussion see Dubin, Cicchetti, and Wilde, (1991).

Yellowstone, and Lower Yellowstone). The sample size was targeted at approximately two hundred people for each river included in the study.

Responses to the Angler Preference Survey were obtained from the state of Montana. The Angler Preference surveys were processed for each river separately and the resulting databases were then merged to form a single database composed of all nineteen rivers.

**Map Distances.** A crucial element of the estimated choice model is distance traveled from a respondent's home to the nearest fishing location on the nineteen rivers in the sample. Although the Angler Preference Survey asked the respondent to report the distance traveled to the chosen river, there is not enough information in the entire sample to extrapolate estimated distances to the other rivers. In any event, objective measures are generally preferred to self-reported measures. Thus, distances from rivers to Montana cities are obtained "by hand" from the AAA Idaho-Montana map.

**Interagency Stream Database.** The calculation of expected fish catch as used in the choice model requires supplemental data on each river. The main source for additional data is the Interagency Stream Database. This database was compiled in the late 1970s as a part of the Pacific Northwest Rivers Study.[14] When the database was constructed, its purpose was to assess river segments (reaches) in the region with respect to a variety of attributes: fish, wildlife, wilderness, recreationindexrecreation, and cultural resources. The agency responsible for the database in Montana is the Department of Fish, Wildlife and Parks.

I use the Interagency Stream Database to obtain measures of: length of the reach, upper and lower boundaries for each reach, fishing pressure (fishermen days per every ten km), fish abundance for trout and non-trout species, aesthetics rating, and ingress rating.

In order to make the data from the Interagency Stream Database compatible with those from the Angler Preference Survey, it is necessary to aggregate the reach-specific data from the Interagency Stream Database into values for each river in its entirety. The reach specific data are weighted either according to fishing pressure or reach lengths.

[14]The Interagency Stream Database represents data gathering efforts undertaken in the late 1970s, with continued efforts to refine and update the database through the mid-1980s. The next major update to the Interagency Stream Database is not expected until the mid-1990s. More recent data on fish abundance and angler pressure come from other sources, most notably the Angler Preference Survey. In addition, the state of Montana undertakes periodic updates to the Interagency Stream Database for selected rivers. However, since these updates are sporadic and incomplete, they could not be used.

### 5.3.3 Explanatory Variables

Two models are estimated, one for anglers and one for non-anglers. Each model represents the choices of individuals among seventeen of the nineteen sampled rivers. The Lower Yellowstone River was eliminated from the sample since no reliable biomass information was available for this river from the Interagency Stream Database. South Fork Flathead River was also eliminated because the survey responses do not contain a sufficient number of Montana residents who chose this river.

The choice models are specified to include a full compliment of alternative-specific constants. These constants, denoted ALT1 through ALT16, represent alternative-specific effects and capture any pure preference for each river above and beyond that explained by the travel cost variable.[15] In the angler model, the travel cost variable, denoted by *DPF*, measures the costs incurred in travel to each river divided by the expected catch. For non-anglers, a similar variable, denoted by *DISTCST*, measures the cost to reach a given river, but ignores the adjustment for expected catch. The construction of the explanatory variables DPF and *DISTCST* is presented next.

***DISTCST.*** Travel costs incurred to reach river $j$ from origin $t$, $DISTCST_{tj}$, play a major role in river site choice: the further one must travel to a river site, the less attractive that river site becomes. However, the monetization of distance is often a complex calculation. For the purposes of this analysis, a simple approximation is used where total travel costs are calculated using estimates of transportation and travel time costs, and measured round-trip distance from an individual's origin to the nearest site on river $j$. As both are a function of distance, transportation costs and the cost of travel time are combined. The calculation of $DISTCST_{tj}$ takes the form

$$DISTCST_{tj} = \left(TC + \frac{W}{MPH}\right) Distance_{tj}$$

where

| | | |
|---|---|---|
| $TC$ | = | Transportation costs, estimated at \$0.0817 per mile[16] |
| $W$ | = | Average hourly wage, \$8.33[17] |
| $MPH$ | = | Average speed forty-five miles per hour[18] |

[15]Without loss of generality, the alternative-specific effect for the last alternative (Upper Yellowstone River) can be omitted; this alternative is selected as the normalizing alternative, a choice which has no effect on the results. See subsection 5.3.1 above.

[16]*Statistical Abstract of the United States* (1984) estimates the age of the average car at 7.4 years. Department of Transportation, "Cost of Owning and Operating Automobiles and Vans," (1984) estimates the cost of driving a seven-year-old large vehicle at \$.0817 per mile for gas and taxes, which assumes seventeen miles per gallon with gas at \$1.389 per gallon. These are the same estimates used by Duffield, Loomis, and Brooks (1987).

[17]*Statistical Abstract of the United States* (1984). Average household income is \$27,735; average hourly wage is \$8.33.

[18]See Duffield (1981).

| | | |
|---|---|---|
| $Distance_{tj}$ | = | Measured round-trip distance from the origin of individual to nearest site on river $j$. |

**DPF.** For anglers, travel costs are normalized by the expected number of fish caught. This variable ($DPF_{tj}$) can be interpreted as a "price" for each expected fish caught. The numerator of $DPF_{tj}$ is $DISTCST_{tj}$, the travel cost estimate calculated above. The construction of the denominator for $DPF_{tj}$, "expected fish," is based on a measure of an individual's fishing skill. The individual's self-reported trout catch is divided by the number of hours spent fishing on the surveyed trip, producing a "fish-per-hour" ($FPH$) calculation for the chosen river. Since it is easier to catch a fish in rivers where fish are more abundant, the $FPH$ calculation was corrected to reflect the difficulty of catching a fish in the chosen river, thereby producing a relative measure of trout production. This is accomplished by dividing $FPH$ by a measure of fish abundance.

The measure of fish abundance that I have utilized reflects a respondent's preference or non-preference for trout: the weighted abundance of trout is used for those anglers for whom catching many trout is important, while the weighted total fish abundance is used for those anglers who are indifferent to catching many trout. This skill estimate can be extended beyond the chosen river to calculate the expected catch in river $j$ by simply multiplying by a measure of fish abundance in river $j$. Thus, the "expected fish" for each river provides an estimate of how many fish per hour an individual is expected to catch at each of the available rivers.

The derivation of $DPF$ takes the form

$$DPF_{tj} = \frac{DISTCST_{tj}}{(WTA_j\, Skill_t)}$$

where

| | | |
|---|---|---|
| $DISTCST_{tj}$ | = | Round-trip travel costs in dollars from origin $t$ to destination $j$ |
| $WTA_j$ | = | Weighted total abundance of fish in river $j$ |
| $Skill_t$ | = | Fish catching skill measure for individual $t$. |

The variable $Skill_t$ is calculated by the equation

$$Skill_t = \frac{FPH_t}{WFA_t} = \frac{\left(\frac{Catch_t}{(Trip_t\, HPD_t)}\right)}{WFA_t}$$

where

| | | |
|---|---|---|
| $Catch_t$ | = | Self-reported catch for individual $t$ |
| $WFA_t$ | = | Weighted fish abundance in river chosen by individual $t$ |
| $Trip_t$ | = | Number of days individual $t$ fished on surveyed trip |
| $HPD_t$ | = | Hours per day fished by individual $t$. |

Descriptive statistics for $DPF$ and $DISTCST$ are presented in tables 5.1 and 5.2, respectively.[19]

**Table 5.1.** Mean and Standard Deviation of DPF By Alternative

| ALTERNATIVE | MEAN | STANDARD DEVIATION |
|---|---|---|
| Beaverhead | 16.77 | 50.76 |
| Big Hole | 37.67 | 79.23 |
| Bitterroot | 14.96 | 65.14 |
| Blackfoot | 6.63 | 12.62 |
| Boulder | 59.77 | 96.61 |
| Bighorn | 37.31 | 62.66 |
| Upper Clark Fork | 163.25 | 862.62 |
| Clark Fork | 18.18 | 65.08 |
| Flathead | 56.78 | 125.15 |
| Gallatin | 21.58 | 52.27 |
| Kootenai | 5.55 | 19.41 |
| Madison | 28.96 | 48.65 |
| Missouri | 13.58 | 42.27 |
| Rock Creek | 31.12 | 82.73 |
| Smith | 76.99 | 232.07 |
| Stillwater | 45.34 | 111.59 |
| Upper Yellowstone | 17.54 | 81.73 |

### 5.3.4 *Correction for Choice Based Sampling*

The Angler Preference Survey was designed to interview approximately two hundred individuals at each of the nineteen rivers; combining the responses from these surveys provides a sample of roughly twenty-one hundred cases.[20] The individual survey designs, which sought roughly equal numbers of individuals for each study river, lead to an underrepresentation of the actual demand at some rivers. For example, the Upper Clark Fork has an actual pressure (usage) of approximately 4.2 percent of all anglers. However, the sample of Montana residents who were surveyed at the Upper Clark Fork was only 2.1 percent.

[19]The variable $DPF_{tj}$ can be expressed as

$$DPF_{it} = \frac{DISTCST_{tj}}{FPH_t} \frac{WFA_t}{WTA_j}.$$

It can therefore be re-interpreted as a measure of "dollars-per-fish" adjusted for the relative abundance of fish.

[20]The response rate averaged 81 percent across the study rivers. See Allen (1988).

**Table 5.2.** Mean and Standard Deviation of DISTCST By Alternative

| ALTERNATIVE | MEAN | STANDARD DEVIATION |
|---|---|---|
| Beaverhead | 20.28 | 39.20 |
| Big Hole | 26.20 | 35.98 |
| Bitterroot | 11.37 | 35.80 |
| Blackfoot | 8.99 | 18.73 |
| Boulder | 43.92 | 28.14 |
| Bighorn | 25.85 | 20.25 |
| Upper Clark Fork | 5.31 | 11.85 |
| Clark Fork | 21.95 | 34.14 |
| Flathead | 39.58 | 37.79 |
| Gallatin | 24.72 | 41.67 |
| Kootenai | 12.25 | 29.88 |
| Madison | 34.64 | 41.54 |
| Missouri | 8.21 | 17.91 |
| Rock Creek | 25.25 | 35.94 |
| Smith | 27.82 | 29.54 |
| Stillwater | 33.06 | 40.36 |
| Upper Yellowstone | 13.65 | 30.56 |

When samples of individuals are drawn based on their actual choices (i.e., sampling approximately two hundred individuals who chose to fish at the Clark), the resultant population has a property known as choice-based sampling.

Correcting the estimation for choice-based sampling requires knowledge of both the true population frequency of usage at each river, $Q_j$, as well as the frequency of usage provided by the sample at each river, $H_j$. Suppose that standard maximum likelihood methods were used to fit the unknown parameters in the sample log-likelihood,

$$\pounds = \sum_{t=1}^{T} \sum_{j=1}^{J} \delta_{jt} \log \mathrm{P_{jt}} \quad (1)$$

where $\delta_{jt}$, denotes an indicator variable which is one if and only if person $t$ chooses alternative $j$, and where $P_{jt}$ is the probability that individual $t$ chooses alternative $j$. As is well known, this will lead to inconsistent estimates of the unknown parameters when the sample is choice-based. Instead, one can achieve consistent parameter estimates using the weighted exogenous sample maximum likelihood estimator (WESML). Equation (1) is modified as

$$\pounds^* = \sum_{t=1}^{T} \sum_{j=1}^{J} \left(\frac{Q_j}{H_j}\right) \delta_{jt} \mathrm{logP_{jt}} \tag{2}$$

Manski and McFadden (1981)[21] demonstrate that maximum likelihood methods applied to equation (2) will yield consistent estimates of the unknown parameters.

While this procedure is straightforward, some care must be taken in the calculation of the weighting parameters, $Q_j$ and $H_j$. Since $H_j$ represents the frequency of usage of river $j$ in the estimation sample, it is simply the number of individuals observed to choose river $j$ divided by the total number of individuals in the sample. The calculation of $Q_j$ requires auxiliary data on the actual usage of river $j$ in the population.

Again I rely on the Interagency Stream Database to calculate the fishing pressure at each river. This requires the aggregation of river reach data to a total river value. The pressures reported on each three hundred meter reach are added for the entire length of the river in order to obtain its total pressure. The estimate of $Q_j$ is then the pressure at river $j$ divided by the total pressure on all seventeen rivers.

While maximum likelihood methods applied to equation (2) yield consistent estimates of the structural parameters, further adjustments are required to obtain estimates of the probability that an individual will choose a river, as well as aggregate predictions of river usage. In the next section I develop the required modifications for consumer surplus calculations in multinomial logit models when choice based sampling is present.

### 5.3.5 *Calculation of Predicted Probabilities and Consumer Surplus*

In order to estimate the usage at a given river under alternative assumptions regarding changing fish biomass, estimates of the predicted probability that an individual will choose a given river are needed, as well as an aggregate prediction of the use of that river. The first step in this calculation is the calibration of the likelihood function using the WESML method. Given the parameter estimates, one can find the predicted probabilities for each individual that he or she will choose a given river. As discussed above the probability of choosing river $j$ is given by the multinomial logit expression

$$P_{jt} = \frac{e^{V_{jt}}}{\sum_{k=1}^{J} e^{V_{kt}}} \tag{3}$$

where the utility $V_{jt}$ is assumed to be linear in parameters with $V_{jt} = X_{jt}\beta$. $X_{jt}$ denotes a vector of explanatory variables, which are both individual alternative-specific (such as distance traveled by individual $t$ from his or her origin to the

[21]See Manski and McFadden (1981), Chapter 3.

river $j$), and $\beta$ denotes a corresponding vector of weights assigned to those variables.

It is well known that as long as the specified probability model contains alternative-specific constants, the average predicted probability will equal the average frequency of choice for a given alternative in the population. This is a desirable property of the multinomial logit model and is similar to the good practice of having linear regression models pass through the average of the data. A similar property, demonstrated below, holds for weighted logit models and provides the necessary ingredients for forming aggregate predicted probabilities and other aggregate calculations.

Suppose the multinomial logit models contain an alternative-specific constant for the first alternative. If $X_{jt}^{(1)}$ denotes the alternative-specific constant for alternative one (without loss of generality, this is taken to be the first component of the vector of explanatory variables, denoted by the superscript (1)) then $X_{jt}^{(1)} = 1$ if and only if $j = 1$.

The key step in the derivation requires inspection of the first-order conditions for maximum likelihood of the modified likelihood function given in equation (2):

$$\pounds^* = \sum_{t=1}^{T} \sum_{j=1}^{J} \left(\frac{Q_j}{H_j}\right) \delta_{jt} \log \mathrm{P_{jt}}. \tag{4}$$

Maximum likelihood estimation requires that

$$\frac{\partial \pounds^*}{\partial \beta} = 0$$

at the maximum. Using equations (1) and (2) yields

$$\frac{\partial \pounds^*}{\partial \beta} = \sum_{t} \sum_{j} \left(\frac{Q_j}{H_j}\right) \delta_{jt} \frac{\partial \log \mathrm{P_{jt}}}{\partial \beta}$$

so that

$$0 = \sum_{t} \sum_{j} \left(\frac{Q_j}{H_j}\right) \delta_{jt} \left[X_{jt} - \sum_{k=1}^{J} X_{kt} P_{kt}\right].$$

From the first component of the gradient, we obtain:

$$0 = \sum_{t} \sum_{j} \left(\frac{Q_j}{H_j}\right) \delta_{jt} \left[X_{jt}^{(1)} - \sum_{k=1}^{J} X_{kt}^{(1)} P_{kt}\right]$$

$$= \sum_{t} \sum_{j} \left(\frac{Q_j}{H_j}\right) \delta_{jt} \left[X_{jt}^{(1)} - P_{1t}\right]$$

$$= \sum_t \sum_j \left(\frac{Q_j}{H_j}\right) \delta_{jt} X_{jt}^{(1)} - \sum_t \sum_j \left(\frac{Q_j}{H_j}\right) \delta_{jt} P_{1t}.$$

This implies that

$$\frac{1}{T} \sum_t \left(\frac{Q_1}{H_1}\right) \delta_{1t} = \frac{1}{T} \sum_t P_{1t} \left( \sum_j \left(\frac{Q_j}{H_j}\right) \delta_{jt} \right),$$

where $T$ is the number of individuals in the sample. But $H_1$ is given by

$$H_1 = \frac{1}{T} \sum_t \delta_{1t}$$

so that

$$Q_1 = \frac{1}{T} \sum_t P_{1t} \left( \sum_j \left(\frac{Q_j}{H_j}\right) \delta_{jt} \right). \tag{5}$$

In the usual multinomial logit model without choice-based sampling, $Q_j = H_j$ so that

$$\sum_j \left(\frac{Q_j}{H_j}\right) \delta_{jt} = \sum_j \delta_{jt} = 1$$

and equation (5) reduces to

$$H_1 = Q_1 = \frac{1}{T} \sum_t P_{1t}.$$

This is the well-known result referred to above. In the multinomial logit model without choice-based sampling the average predicted probability is equal to the population frequency for a given alternative. The formula derived above shows that for WESML estimation of multinomial logit models, the population frequency of choosing an alternative is a weighted average of the predicted probability of choosing that alternative.

To further understand the nature of the weighting process, equation (5) can be written as

$$Q_1 = \frac{1}{T} \sum_t \sum_j \left(\frac{Q_j}{H_j}\right) P_{jt} \delta_{jt}$$

$$= \frac{1}{T} \sum_k \sum_{t \ni \delta_{kt}=1} \sum_j \left(\frac{Q_j}{H_j}\right) P_{1t} \delta_{jt}$$

$$= \frac{1}{T} \sum_{k} \sum_{t \ni \delta_{kt}=1} P_{1t} \left( \frac{Q_k}{H_k} \right).$$

Thus, the weighting scheme amounts to averaging the predicted probabilities, depending on the relative likelihood represented by the observation. Therefore, any individual who chooses river one will have his or her probability weighted by $(Q_1/H_1)$ in the aggregation. This corrects for the under (or over) sampling of the alternative in the sample relative to its true frequency in the population.

When other predicted quantities need to be aggregated, a scheme is employed as suggested by equation (5). For example, if $CS_t$ denotes the consumer surplus from angler $t$, then the total consumer surplus will be given by

$$\frac{1}{T} \sum_{t} CS_t \left( \sum_{j} \left( \frac{Q_j}{H_j} \right) \delta_{jt} \right) \tag{6}$$

rather than the usual formula

$$\frac{1}{T} \sum_{t} CS_t.$$

### 5.3.6 *Econometric Results*

Individuals in the sample are divided into anglers and non-anglers based on two criteria. To be identified as an angler both criteria must apply: first, that fishing is the main purpose of the trip in question (given by a survey response) and, second, that the individual's catch rate is at least one fish caught per twelve hours of fishing. Since an average fishing day is approximately 5.3 hours, this amounts to the requirement that at least one fish is caught in 2.2 days, which is the average trip length. It is thus required that "anglers" catch at least one fish per trip.

Table 5.3 presents the estimated multinomial choice model for anglers. Table 5.4 presents the estimated multinomial choice model for non-anglers. The productivity adjusted travel cost variable ($DPF$) is quite significant in the angler model with a $t$-statistic of over ten in absolute value. The variable enters the model such that an increase in the travel cost of a given river from the angler's origin decreases the probability of going to that river and an increase in the expected fish caught at a river increases the likelihood of going to that river.

The alternative-specific constants reveal a further pattern of preference. Above and beyond the travel cost and expected catch criteria, anglers show a significant preference for the Big Hole, Madison, and Bighorn rivers, while a significant non-preference is revealed for the Blackfoot, Boulder, and Smith rivers. These comparisons are relative to a comparison river (chosen arbitrarily to be Upper Yellowstone River). The model fits the choice of individuals among all seventeen rivers. The percentage of cases that are correctly predicted is about 27 percent. Pure guessing would produce a correct classification only

**Table 5.3.** Weighted Multinomial Logit Choice Model: Anglers

| ALTERNATIVE | RIVER | COUNT | PERCENT |
|---|---|---|---|
| 1 | Beaverhead | 56 | 5.91 |
| 2 | Big Hole | 86 | 9.07 |
| 3 | Bitterroot | 58 | 6.12 |
| 4 | Blackfoot | 56 | 5.91 |
| 5 | Boulder | 43 | 4.54 |
| 6 | Bighorn | 91 | 9.60 |
| 7 | Upper Clark Fork | 20 | 2.11 |
| 8 | Clark Fork | 52 | 5.49 |
| 9 | Flathead | 30 | 3.16 |
| 10 | Gallatin | 77 | 8.12 |
| 11 | Kootenai | 30 | 3.16 |
| 12 | Madison | 42 | 4.43 |
| 13 | Missouri | 98 | 10.34 |
| 14 | Rock Creek | 47 | 4.96 |
| 15 | Smith | 23 | 2.43 |
| 16 | Stillwater | 71 | 7.49 |
| 17 | Upper Yellowstone | 68 | 7.17 |

| INDEPENDENT VARIABLE | ESTIMATED COEFFICIENT | *t*-STATISTIC |
|---|---|---|
| ALT1 | -0.45758 | -1.63305 |
| ALT2 | 0.55492 | 2.00128 |
| ALT3 | 0.10024 | 0.30084 |
| ALT4 | -0.57633 | -1.83550 |
| ALT5 | -0.58586 | -2.93210 |
| ALT6 | 0.57157 | 2.49758 |
| ALT7 | -0.61604 | -1.42452 |
| ALT8 | 0.38699 | 1.10598 |
| ALT9 | -0.44536 | -1.21818 |
| ALT10 | 0.18123 | 0.78822 |
| ALT11 | -0.68838 | -1.24851 |
| ALT12 | 1.29733 | 3.21018 |
| ALT13 | 0.34666 | 1.22209 |
| ALT14 | -0.42241 | -1.38253 |
| ALT15 | -1.05831 | -3.31710 |
| ALT16 | -0.13597 | 0.65596 |
| *DPF* | -0.02118 | -10.06954 |
| Log Likelihood at Convergence | | -1799 |
| Number of Observations | | 948 |

one in seventeen times (5.9 percent), while a constant probability model (equivalent to using only alternative-specific constants) would achieve only 10 percent classification.

The estimated model for non-anglers reveals a similar goodness of fit and shows a significant preference for the Madison River and non-preference for the Smith River (relative to the Upper Yellowstone). The cost variable, *DISTCST*, is quite significant with a *t*-statistic of over 7.9 in absolute value.

**Table 5.4.** Weighted Multinomial Logit Choice Model: Non-Anglers

| ALTERNATIVE | RIVER | COUNT | PERCENT |
|---|---|---|---|
| 1 | Beaverhead | 13 | 3.40 |
| 2 | Big Hole | 23 | 6.02 |
| 3 | Bitterroot | 34 | 8.90 |
| 4 | Blackfoot | 23 | 6.02 |
| 5 | Boulder | 14 | 3.66 |
| 6 | Bighorn | 22 | 5.76 |
| 7 | Upper Clark Fork | 8 | 2.09 |
| 8 | Clark Fork | 34 | 8.90 |
| 9 | Flathead | 27 | 7.07 |
| 10 | Gallatin | 26 | 6.81 |
| 11 | Kootenai | 16 | 4.19 |
| 12 | Madison | 18 | 4.71 |
| 13 | Missouri | 35 | 9.16 |
| 14 | Rock Creek | 12 | 3.14 |
| 15 | Smith | 11 | 2.88 |
| 16 | Stillwater | 40 | 10.47 |
| 17 | Upper Yellowstone | 26 | 6.81 |

| INDEPENDENT VARIABLE | ESTIMATED COEFFICIENT | *t*-STATISTIC |
|---|---|---|
| ALT1 | 0.10504 | 0.20303 |
| ALT2 | 0.95797 | 1.77791 |
| ALT3 | -0.01940 | -0.03015 |
| ALT4 | -0.65501 | -1.07402 |
| ALT5 | -0.53664 | -1.58246 |
| ALT6 | 0.20379 | 0.58250 |
| ALT7 | -0.58219 | -0.75562 |
| ALT8 | 0.19065 | 0.28796 |
| ALT9 | -0.56073 | -0.79286 |
| ALT10 | 0.64105 | 1.60317 |
| ALT11 | -1.46426 | -1.72414 |
| ALT12 | 1.86403 | 2.99406 |
| ALT13 | 0.44821 | 0.87781 |
| ALT14 | -0.34912 | -0.51996 |
| ALT15 | -1.35588 | -2.67897 |
| ALT16 | -0.08958 | -0.30785 |
| DSTCST | -0.03011 | -7.90072 |
| Log Likelihood at Convergence | | -733.5 |
| Number of Observations | | 382 |

Having successfully estimated both the angler and non-angler models, it is possible to use them to construct estimates of damage associated with hypothetical injuries that might affect the abundance of fish. These estimates are developed in the next section.

## 5.4 Simulation of Estimated Models

Estimates of potential damage to recreationists on the Upper Clark Fork River are based on simulation results of the probability that anglers will choose to fish the Upper Clark Fork River. There are two different estimates of the consumer surplus that users of a river enjoy. The first estimate is the measure of the consumer surplus at current levels of fish biomass. The second estimate of consumer surplus is based on the assumption that restoration efforts result in a change in the fish biomass at the river. Since both estimates require a calculation of consumer surplus based on the estimated models, it is useful to begin with a discussion of consumer surplus measures for multinomial logit models. Subsequently, the actual calculation of damage for the two scenarios is discussed.

### *5.4.1 Estimation of Consumer Surplus*

For the multinomial logit model, McFadden[22] has derived the formula for consumer surplus. In the context of this analysis, the formula is

$$\begin{aligned} CS &= expected\ maximum\ utility/marginal\ utility\ of\ income \\ &= \log\left(\sum_{j-1}^{J} e^{V_j}\right) / \hat{\beta} \qquad (7) \end{aligned}$$

where $\hat{\beta}$ is the marginal utility of income. For non-anglers, $V_j$ is given by:

$$V_j = \alpha_j - \beta\, DISTCST_j;$$

where $\alpha_j$ denotes attribute specific components of utility for alternative $j$ and $DISTCST_j$ is the distance cost of alternative $j$. Since $DISTCST_j$ is measured in dollars, for the non-anglers models $\beta$ is equal to the marginal utility of income (i.e., $\hat{\beta} = \beta$).

The anglers model specifies a somewhat more complicated relationship for the observable utility $V_j$

$$V_j = \alpha_j - \beta(DSTCST_j\ /\ expected\ fish\ catch\ at\ river\ j).$$

The conversion from dollars to utils in the anglers model therefore is given by $\hat{\beta} = \beta/(expected\, fish\, catch\, at\, river\, j)$. Since in this case the dollar to util relationship is river dependent, the conversion factor is derived for a preselected river. This guarantees that total consumer surplus is measured in a consistent manner throughout the analysis.

Using the appropriate $\hat{\beta}$, the observable utility for each individual at each river can be calculated, as well as the consumer surplus for each individual.

---

[22]See Manski and McFadden (1981), Chapter 5. See also Small and Rosen (1981).

Lastly, total consumer surplus is determined by the appropriate aggregation, correcting for choice-based sampling. The consumer surplus for all anglers at all streams is calculated to be $66,548,900 per year with an average value of $83.80 per angler (1984 dollars). This amount does not include the surplus derived from the seventeen rivers by the population of non-anglers who visit the rivers for reasons other than fishing.

### *5.4.2 Potential Natural Resource Damage Calculation from the Discrete Choice Model*

Using the estimates summarized in subsection 5.3.6 and the consumer surplus formulas given in subsection 5.4.1., this section estimates potential natural resource damage to anglers in 1984 on the Upper Clark Fork River.[23] The hypothetical pre-injury carrying capacity of the Upper Clark Fork River (referred to as the baseline) is assumed to represent a 100 percent increase in the fish population over existing levels (referred to as the status quo).[24] Total consumer surplus is calculated for the baseline level of fish biomass and for the status quo level of fish biomass. The difference between these two measures of consumer surplus represents the additional costs that anglers suffer as they choose to fish in other, more costly (i.e., distant) rivers due to the reduced fish population at the Upper Clark Fork River.

The results of the choice model summarized in subsection 5.3.6 yield average values of consumer surplus for anglers. Using pressure data from the Interagency Stream Database, population values are derived by extrapolating from the sample to the whole population.

To illustrate the nature of the calculations involved, a respondent whose surveyed trip was to the Upper Clark Fork River is examined in some detail. This individual was chosen randomly among the survey respondents and is not meant to be representative of the population at large.

Under baseline conditions, the model estimates the selected respondent's probability of fishing at any one of the surveyed rivers, as shown in table 5.5. This respondent has a predicted probability of 10.686 percent of choosing the Upper Clark Fork River. The "dollars-per-expected fish" for this respondent are also presented in table 5.5.

To simulate a hypothetical injury to the fish population of the Upper Clark Fork River, assume that the weighted fish biomass for all fish types were halved compared to the baseline (this represents a return to the status quo). This will have the effect of making the Upper Clark Fork River less attractive to this respondent, relative to the other alternatives. Halving the fish population of the Upper Clark Fork River has no effect on the "dollars-per-expected fish" estimates for any river other than the Upper Clark Fork, as shown in table 5.5. It does, however, affect the selected respondent's probability of choosing

[23]These loss estimates thus ignore damages to non-anglers, if present.

[24]The status quo measure of the fish biomass is taken from the Interagency Stream Database.

**Table 5.5.** Comparison of Base Case and Simulated Injury Predicted Probabilities and "Dollars-per-Fish" for a Randomly Selected Individual

| RIVER | BASE CASE | | SIMULATED INJURY | |
|---|---|---|---|---|
| | Predicted Probability | Dollars-per-Fish | Predicted Probability | Dollars-per-Fish |
| Beaverhead | 0.713% | 139.78 | 0.720% | 139.78 |
| Big Hole | 8.519% | 70.50 | 8.603% | 70.50 |
| Bitterroot | 23.687% | 0.76 | 23.921% | 0.76 |
| Blackfoot | 9.108% | 13.94 | 9.198% | 13.94 |
| Boulder | 0.139% | 210.93 | 0.140% | 210.93 |
| Bighorn | 0.148% | 262.64 | 0.149% | 262.64 |
| Upper Clark Fork | 10.686% | 4.53 | 9.805% | 9.05 |
| Clark Fork | 18.679% | 25.51 | 18.864% | 25.51 |
| Flathead | 4.607% | 52.29 | 4.653% | 52.29 |
| Gallatin | 1.117% | 146.52 | 1.183% | 146.52 |
| Kootenai | 0.404% | 155.75 | 0.408% | 155.75 |
| Madison | 0.739% | 112.26 | 0.746% | 112.26 |
| Missouri | 5.021% | 85.62 | 5.070% | 85.62 |
| Rock Creek | 8.873% | 22.44 | 8.960% | 22.44 |
| Smith | 0.102% | 203.30 | 0.103% | 203.30 |
| Stillwater | 0.314% | 206.59 | 0.317% | 206.59 |
| Upper Yellowstone | 0.440% | 184.16 | 0.445% | 184.16 |

the Upper Clark Fork River, thereby affecting the probability of choosing other rivers. In this case, the selected respondent's probability of choosing the Upper Clark Fork River falls from 10.686 percent to 9.8 percent. In addition, the selected respondent's probability of choosing all other rivers has increased.

The selected respondent's observable utility for each river, $V_j$, can be calculated by:

$$V_j = \alpha_j - \beta(DISTCST_j \; / \; expected\ fish\ catch\ at\ river\ j).$$

Using the values for $\alpha_j$ and $\beta$ presented in table 5.3 shows that the selected respondent's observable utility for the first alternative, the Beaverhead River, is

$$\begin{aligned} V_1 &= \alpha_1 - \beta \mathrm{DPF}_1 \\ &= -0.46 - 0.02 * 139.78 \\ &= -3.26\ utils. \end{aligned}$$

Similar calculations provide the observable utility for the other alternatives. These utilities are then used to determine this respondent's consumer surplus using the formula:

$$CS = \log \left( \sum_{j=1}^{J} e^{V_j} \right) \cdot [expected\ fish\ catch\ at\ Upper\ Clark\ Fork].$$

This calculation produces an estimated consumer surplus of $46.69.

Calculating this respondent's consumer surplus in the injury simulation is analogous. The only exception is that the *DPF* estimate for the Upper Clark Fork River is higher in the injury scenario. This will produce a lower observable utility for fishing at the Upper Clark Fork River for the selected respondent. This causes the respondent's consumer surplus to decline to $46.39, a difference of thirty cents. This change in consumer surplus represents the added cost this respondent would incur in travel costs to fish at a river which provides the same level of utility as the Upper Clark Fork River before the hypothetical injury.

Expanding these calculations to the entire angler population requires an estimate of the total number of anglers at a river. To do this, the total number of people who use each river must first be determined. It is estimated that approximately 1.2 million people use the seventeen rivers included in the choice model. Of those, 65.9 percent or 790,800 are estimated to be anglers. To determine how many of the anglers select the Upper Clark Fork River, the model first estimates the average probability of selecting the Upper Clark Fork River among all anglers who were surveyed. As discussed above, to correct for choice-based sampling, this average probability must be weighted to reflect the true population.

The weighted average probability of choosing the Upper Clark Fork River is 6.2 percent. This means that at the baseline level of fish biomass, approximately 49,187 anglers will fish at the Upper Clark Fork River in a given year. However, under the hypothetical injury scenario, the weighted average probability declines from 6.2 percent to 4.2 percent, which represents approximately 15,625 fewer anglers.

The calculation of the total consumer surplus for the sample is similar to that for the selected respondent, except that the estimate of consumer surplus, like the predicted probabilities, must be averaged and weighted to reflect the true population of anglers. In the baseline scenario, average consumer surplus is estimated to be $84.45 per angler. Total consumer surplus would then be $67,063,200. However, a decrease of half the total fish population in the Upper Clark Fork River would result in a change of consumer surplus to $83.80, a decrease of approximately sixty-five cents per angler. Total consumer surplus decreases by $514,300 to $66,548,900. Therefore, if an injury to the Upper Clark Fork River were to half the total baseline fish population, then the costs to anglers on the whole would rise $514,300 per year.

## 5.5 Present Value of Natural Resource Damage

### *5.5.1 Methodology*

The present value analysis translates annual natural resource damage estimates into present value terms. Since travel costs are measured in 1984 dollars, the estimates of consumer surplus for anglers are also calculated in 1984 dollars. These estimates are then adjusted to nominal values for each of the other years in the period 1981-1989. The calculations of the travel costs are given in table 5.6.[25] All final monetary values are expressed in 1989 dollars.

**Table 5.6.** Calculation of Travel Cost

| YEAR | WAGE | | GASOLINE | | TOTAL | |
|---|---|---|---|---|---|---|
| | $/hour | $/mile | $/gal | $/mile | $/mile | INDEX |
| 1981 | 7.25 | 0.1611 | 1.540 | 0.0906 | 0.2517 | 0.943 |
| 1982 | 7.68 | 0.1707 | 1.459 | 0.0858 | 0.2565 | 0.961 |
| 1983 | 8.02 | 0.1782 | 1.410 | 0.0829 | 0.2612 | 0.979 |
| 1984 | 8.33 | 0.1851 | 1.389 | 0.0817 | 0.2668 | 1.000 |
| 1985 | 8.57 | 0.1904 | 1.400 | 0.0824 | 0.2728 | 1.022 |
| 1986 | 8.76 | 0.1947 | 1.094 | 0.0644 | 0.2590 | 0.971 |
| 1987 | 8.98 | 0.1996 | 1.138 | 0.0669 | 0.2665 | 0.999 |
| 1988 | 9.29 | 0.2064 | 1.148 | 0.0675 | 0.2740 | 1.027 |
| 1989 | 9.66 | 0.2147 | 1.256 | 0.0739 | 0.2885 | 1.081 |

The calculation of present values for potential natural resource damage has two distinct elements, past and future, which must be treated differently from a discounting or compounding perspective. Discount rates may or may not account for risk and uncertainty. Moreover, there is already a government recommendation on the appropriate discount rate to use.[26] For compounding, some courts have considered 0 percent appropriate, while others have accepted the use of some non-zero, risk-free compounding rate.

In the calculations presented, a (three-year) average of three-month Treasury bills (normally considered a measure of the risk-free rate of interest) is used to determine the pre-1990 damage due to the hypothetical injury. After 1990, the present value of damage in all scenarios is calculated with interest rates of 5 percent and 10 percent. The 10 percent rate is the one mandated by the DOI; the 5 percent rate has been used for comparison purposes.

[25] *Economic Report of the President* (1990), tables C-44 and C-59. The calculations of travel cost are made assuming an average speed of forty-five miles per hour and average fuel efficiency of seventeen miles per gallon.

[26] See U.S. Department of the Interior's Type B Regulations, Issues 1 August 1986 (Federal Register 27726, 2 August 1986).

Using the 5 percent and 10 percent rates, future damage is discounted to January 1, 1990 under two scenarios. In Scenario I it is assumed that there is no recovery of the river (i.e., the annual damage from the injury remains constant in real terms). In Scenario II, the river is assumed to fully recover its pre-injury level of fish biomass over a thirty-year period. The results for each scenario are given in tables 5.7 and 5.8, respectively. Each table shows the present discounted value of total damage using both a 5 percent and a 10 percent discount rate. Each also considers two alternative levels of injury: "low injury" representing a loss of 25 percent of the baseline level of fish biomass, and "high injury" representing a loss of 50 percent of the baseline level of fish biomass.

### *5.5.2 Scenario I: No Natural Recovery*

Scenario I assumes no natural recovery of the Upper Clark Fork River; a 10 percent discount rate for the post-1990 damage; and the three-month treasury average for the 1981-1989 period. As shown in table 5.7, the present values of post-1990 damage are $2.449 and $5.566 million for the low and high injury cases, respectively. Adding the 1981-1989 figures of $2.972 and $6.755 million gives a total ranging from $5.422 million to $12.321 million in present value terms.

**Table 5.7.** Scenario I (No Recovery): Estimated Total Potential Natural Resource Damage for Lost Fishing (thousands of 1989 dollars)

| Item | Low Injury | High Injury |
|---|---|---|
| Value of 1981-1989 Damage Compounded to 1990 | 2,972.43 | 6,755.29 |
| Present Value from 1990 @ 10% Discount Rate | 2,449.08 | 5,565.90 |
| Present Value from 1990 @ 5% Discount Rate | 4,898.16 | 11,131.80 |
| Total Damage, 10% Discount Rate | 5,421.51 | 12,321.18 |
| Total Damage, 5% Discount Rate | 7,870.59 | 17,887.07 |

Reducing the discount rate to 5 percent increases the present value of the future damage, presumed to continue indefinitely, by 100 percent to $4.898 and $11.131 million, respectively. In the total damage calculation, using a 5 percent discount rate increases the figure by 45 percent to $7.870 and $17.887 million for the two cases, respectively.

### *5.5.3 Scenario II: Full Recovery*

In Scenario I, constant estimates of real damage from 1990 to perpetuity are used. However, there are a number of factors which could influence the estimated level of damage in the future. Remediation, restoration, and natural recovery of the Upper Clark Fork River, singly or in combination, would all reduce hypothetical future damages. Other factors which could also change the damage estimates include increased angler days, increased fishing pressure, improved access to substitute sites, and congestion. The first of these four would act to raise the estimated damage figure, while the other three would reduce the estimated damage figure.[27]

In Scenario II the Upper Clark Fork River experiences full recovery of its fish biomass to its baseline levels. No presumptions are made in this analysis as to how the recovery comes about, whether through remediation, restoration, natural recovery, or any combination of the three. Appropriate assumptions are made to generate the following scenario:

- Damage remains constant at its real 1990 levels for five years;
- Recovery due to intensive restoration or remediation activities commences in year six;
- By year ten, recovery has proceeded such that damage has fallen to about 10 percent of the real 1990 damage level, and
- By year fifteen, the real value of damage is about zero.[28]

As in Scenario I, a 10-percent discount rate for the post-1990 damage, and the three-month treasury average for the 1981-1989 period are also assumed. As shown in table 5.8, the present values of post-1990 damage are \$1.148 and \$2.609 million for the low and high injury cases, respectively. Adding the 1981-1989 figures of \$2.972 million and \$6.755 million gives a total ranging from \$.120 million to \$9.364 million in present value terms.

Dropping the discount rate to 5 percent has the effect of increasing the present value of future damage to \$1.372 million and \$3.118 million, respectively. In the total damage calculation, using a 5 percent discount rate increases the figure by 45 percent to \$4.345 and \$9.874 million for the two cases, respectively.

[27]Congestion reduces consumer surplus by inducing some users to go to alternative sights. In other words, it raises the costs for some users. Similarly, increased angler pressure reduces the fish biomass of the river, inducing some anglers to fish elsewhere. Improved access to substitute sites reduces damages by decreasing the cost of using such substitutes. As the cost of substitutes falls, the change in consumer surplus diminishes.

[28]The described rate of recovery is generated by assuming a 35 percent annual decline in damages after year five.

**Table 5.8.** Scenario II (Full Recovery): Estimated Total Potential Natural Resource Damage for Lost Fishing (thousands of 1989 dollars)

| Item | Low Injury | High Injury |
|---|---|---|
| Value of 1981-1989 Damage Compounded to 1990 | $2,972.43 | $6,755.29 |
| Present Value from 1990 @ 10% Discount Rate | $1,148.05 | $2,609.11 |
| Present Value from 1990 @ 5% Discount Rate | $1,372.15 | $3,118.40 |
| Total Damage, 10% Discount Rate | $4,120.48 | $9,364.40 |
| Total Damage, 5% Discount Rate | $4,344.58 | $9,873.69 |
| Total as Percent of Scenario I, 10% Discount Rate | 76.00% | 76.00% |
| Total as Percent of Scenario I, 5% Discount Rate | 55.00% | 55.00% |

## 5.6 Conclusions

As a comparison with table 5.7 shows, full restoration even at a relatively slow rate, can have a significant effect on the present discounted value of damage. For this reason, engineering studies and cost estimation for several different degrees of restoration can help to establish what is a proportionate and disproportionate response for a particular resource.

# 6 THE DEMAND FOR COMMERCIAL FISHING IN CALIFORNIA

## 6.1 Introduction

From the late 1940s to the late 1070s, the chemicals DDT and PCB were deposited off the coast of Los Angeles. The DDT came to be located in the sediments as a result of manufacturing activities when DDT was directly discharged into the Los Angeles County sewer system. The manufacturing waste passed through a sewage treatment facility but was eventually discharged into the ocean through outfall pipes. PCB's were released by other sources and also entered the marine environment. These chemicals are alleged to have adversely affected various animals that live along the South Coast and in the area of the Los Angeles basin (*Draft Injury Determination Plan*, 1991). At present, all but four species have completely recovered from the effects of the dumping while the four are expected to fully recover over the next fifty years. In an attempt to recover compensation for the damage, the state of California has brought forward a suit against the companies who were responsible for the dumping. The state, under the law, must restrict its claim for compensation to the lost use and non-use of the harbor.

The purpose of this chapter is first to develop a model that explains commercial fishermen's choices among ocean areas and species of fish. I then derive hypothetical damage estimates using the results of the model, assuming that there were damages to commercial fishing as a result of contamination of the coast waters near Palos Verdes Peninsula, the Los Angeles-Long Beach Harbor area, and two ocean disposal sites in the San Pedro Channel. The hypothetically contaminated areas are shown in figure 6.1.

Damages are calculated by estimating the loss in producer surplus to commercial fishermen, assuming that they could not fish in the two polychlorinated biphenyl (PCB) dump sites areas, or near the Palos Verdes Peninsula during the period 1969 through 1983. The lost producer surplus for commercial fishermen represents lost profits due to increased travel costs. In this respect, I extend the traditional travel cost model as discussed in chapter 5 to a model of "travel profit."

Damage estimates are limited to two fish species: jack mackerel and northern anchovy. Although northern anchovies are not listed in the United States' *Draft Injury Determination Plan*, these two species are a reliable measure of the presence or absence of damages since they represent close to 70 percent of the catch during the time period in the coastal waters delineated in the *Draft Injury Determination Plan.*

### *6.1.1 Model Employed*

A nested logit model is used in this study. The nested logit model consists of three parts: a model of the choice of ocean area (or block) given that particular species are fished, a model of the choice of species fished, and a model of the choice between commercial fishing and other activities.[1]

The models I estimate are consistent with standard economic theory because they relate commercial fishermen's choices to profit. The characteristics that affect commercial fishermen's costs such as the distance of the fishing area to port are included in the block choice model; the output prices which affect commercial fishermen's revenues are included in the species choice model.

### *6.1.2 Model Simulation*

I derive an estimate of damages for jack mackerel and northern anchovy assuming that injury to these two species could be proven and that this injury actually had an effect on commercial catch. My damage estimate is derived by assuming that fish can not be caught in the ocean areas in which the two PCB dump sites and the municipal outfalls mentioned in the *Draft Injury Determination Plan* are located. However, both northern anchovy and jack mackerel were caught by commercial fishermen in these areas, and I have no evidence that commercial fishermen have shifted from fishing in these areas to others.

The damage estimates equal the additional costs incurred by commercial vessels per fishing trip for northern anchovy and jack mackerel. Hypothetical damages on a per-trip-basis range from \$278 to \$378 for northern anchovies

[1]Fishing location choice has been previously studied in Eales and Wilen (1986). Their modelling is also regression based and relies on the distance traveled as an important determinant of location choice.

**Figure 6.1: Study Areas: Palos Verdes Shelf, Los Angeles Harbor, Long Beach Harbor, and Dump Sites One and Two**

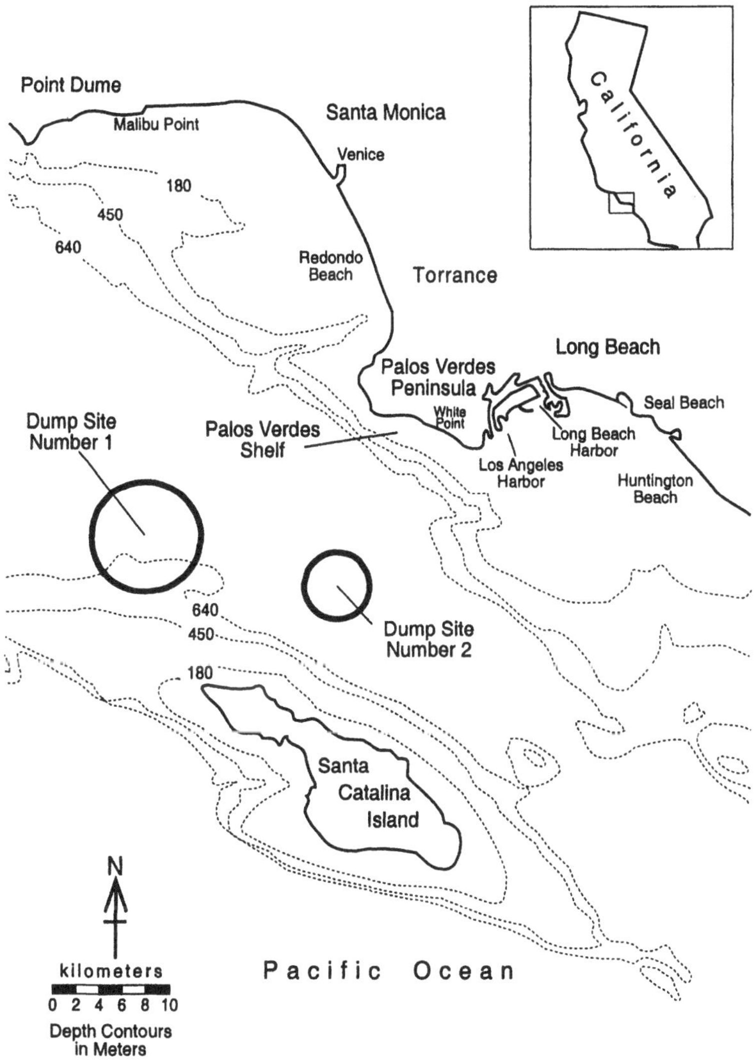


Source: "Draft Injury Determination Plan," March 8, 1991

and from $35 to $179 for jack mackerel, depending on the historical period at issue.

I find that the possibilities for substitution among ocean blocks and species limit the magnitude of potential damages from lost use. The nested logit model I estimate takes account of the substitutability of blocks and species. If one block is not available as a commercial fishery, another block with similar characteristics may be substituted. If one species of fish is not available, then other species of fish can be potentially substituted.

The remainder of the chapter is organized as follows. In section 6.2 I discuss the jack mackerel and northern anchovy fisheries. The first part of section 6.3 discusses the nested logit method used in the empirical part of this chapter. A more detailed description of the nested logit technique is presented in appendix 6.6.1. I then describe the block choice model and the species choice model, including the models estimated, the variables included in the models, and the results of the estimation. In section 6.4, I discuss the method used for estimating damages resulting from PCB and dichloro-diphenyl-trichloro-ethane (DDT) contamination and obtain an estimate of per-trip damages for northern anchovy and jack mackerel.

## 6.2 The Northern Anchovy and Jack Mackerel Fisheries

Between 1969 and 1983, the northern anchovy and jack mackerel catch comprised an average of 68 percent of the total catch in the 271 blocks[2] in the Southern California bight (table 6.1). For nearly half of these years, these two species accounted for more than 80 percent of the catch. Both northern anchovy and jack mackerel are fished by the wetfish fleet, using purse seine nets.

### *6.2.1 Purse Seine Fishing*

Over the last fifteen to twenty years, the San Pedro-Port Hueneme purse seine wetfish fleet has consisted of between forty and fifty vessels rigged with purse seine nets. Purse seines are long, wall-like nets that encircle relatively shallow schools of fish. The fish are trapped by "pursing" or pulling in a drawstring that runs around the bottom of the net. After closing the net, the trapped fish are dragged onto the vessel and stored in an unrefrigerated hold. The term "wetfish" is used since the fish are unloaded wet, rather than cold.

The wetfish fleet shifts from species to species as prices, regulations, populations, and fish availability change. Since the 1930s, the fleet has shifted its focus from sardines to Pacific and jack mackerel, to jack mackerel and northern anchovy, to jack mackerel and Pacific mackerel. Over the past ten years the

[2]See footnote 9, infra, for the definition of ocean blocks.

**Table 6.1.** Percentages of Jack Mackerel and Northern Anchovy In Southern California Commercial Catch

| Year | Jack Mackerel Percent | Northern Anchovy Percent | Jack Mackerel and Northern Anchovy Percent |
|---|---|---|---|
| 1969 | 23.0 | 58.2 | 81.2 |
| 1970 | 16.6 | 66.8 | 83.4 |
| 1971 | 31.2 | 73.8 | 77.6 |
| 1972 | 22.0 | 59.0 | 81.0 |
| 1973 | 6.1 | 77.7 | 83.8 |
| 1974 | 11.0 | 66.6 | 77.6 |
| 1975 | 9.4 | 77.4 | 86.8 |
| 1976 | 12.5 | 71.2 | 83.7 |
| 1977 | 26.5 | 53.6 | 80.1 |
| 1978 | 41.2 | 12.8 | 54.0 |
| 1979 | 17.2 | 34.4 | 51.7 |
| 1980 | 19.1 | 31.2 | 50.3 |
| 1981 | 11.8 | 31.8 | 43.6 |
| 1982 | 22.4 | 29.8 | 52.2 |
| 1983 | 17.3 | 3.3 | 20.6 |
| Source: | *1AA Annual Report of Catch by Origin/Species/Month* California Department of Fish and Game Library | | |

wetfish fleet has caught northern anchovy, bonito, squid, sardine, Pacific and jack mackerel, bluefin tuna and, when available, albacore.[3]

### *6.2.2 Northern Anchovy Fishery*

A reduction fishery for northern anchovy was established in 1965-66. In a reduction fishery, the catch is pressed to obtain oil and then ground and dried to produce fish meal. The northern anchovy fishery included the fishery in the Southern California bight and a smaller fishery in the Monterey area.

The northern anchovy biomass exploded from less than one hundred thousand tons in the early 1950s, to roughly two million tons in the mid-1970s (Methot 1989). The anchovy reduction fishery was established due to the pressure exerted by commercial fishing interests and because some fishery scientists

[3]In the late 1960s, the population of Pacific mackerel declined significantly, leading the state of California to effectively close the fishery in 1972. Beginning in 1965-1966, California established a reduction fishery for northern anchovy, which became a mainstay of the Southern California purse seine wetfish fleet. By the early 1980s, pacific mackerel stocks had returned to their former levels. At that time, the landed price of northern anchovy dropped and after 1983 the wetfish fleet abandoned the fishery. Jack mackerel remained an important component of harvest throughout the period.

believed a smaller northern anchovy population would assist the recovery of the sardine.[4]

Northern anchovy landings were made at reduction plants located at Port Hueneme and in the Los Angeles Harbor area. Landed prices reflected fish meal prices with adjustments made for the level of oil content. While overall reduction plant capacity was considerably greater than annual production, at peak landing periods the plants placed limits on boat loads. As fish meal prices and landed anchovy prices declined in the early 1980s, catch also declined. The reduction fishery virtually disappeared after 1983.

### *6.2.3 Jack Mackerel Fishery*

The jack mackerel found in the Southern California bight and harvested by the San Pedro-Port Hueneme purse seine wetfish fleet are, for the most part, juveniles and young adults. While the spawning stock is found further out to sea, the harvested stock schools around islands and banks offshore. Jack mackerel often school with Pacific mackerel and sardines.

The state of California has jurisdiction over this stock but sets no catch quotas. What restrictions apply relate to incidental catch of Pacific mackerel and sardines. Jack mackerel are landed at Port Hueneme and Los Angeles Harbor and canned for human and pet food.

## 6.3 The Nested Logit Model

### *6.3.1 The Nested Logit Methodology*

I use a nested logit model for the interdependent sequential choices made by commercial fishermen. As illustrated in figure 6.2, my model has three sets of choices: whether to engage in commercial fishing or another activity, the species to fish and, finally the choice of ocean block in which to fish for a given species.

A nested logit model is used in the first two stages of the analysis to examine the relationship between: (1) the share of commercial fishing for particular species in various ocean blocks with specific characteristics, and (2) the share of particular species caught, their relative market prices, and a measure of their relative values.[5] The first stage of my analysis, the share of catch by block, explains the portion of catch in a block for a given species, rather than the absolute amount of catch in a block. The second stage of my analysis, the share by species, explains the portion of total catch represented by a particular species, rather than the total amount of that species of fish caught in all blocks.

---

[4] Annual anchovy reduction catch quotas were initially set by the state of California. In years when the quotas were approached, the state revised them upwards. Both the state of California Fish and Game Commission and the Pacific Fisheries Management Council have set quotas since 1978.

[5] The nested logit model as applied to commercial fishing model is presented in appendix 6.6.1.

**Figure 6.2: Nested Logit Model: Choice Heirarchy**

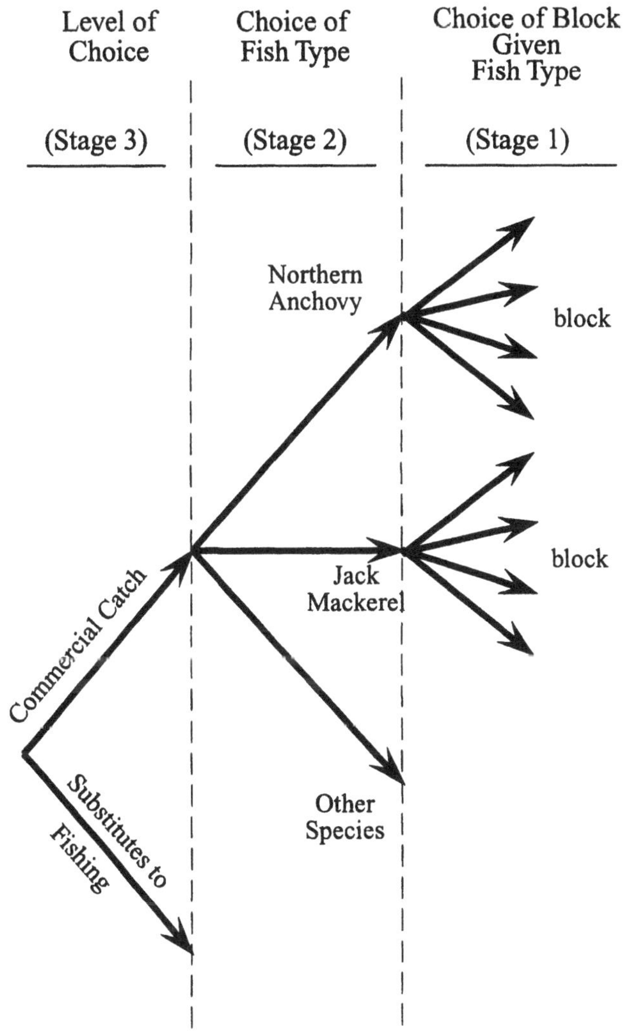

The final stage of my analysis is illustrated as Stage 3 in figure 6.2. A logit model is not used in this part of my analysis since I estimated the relationship between various factors and the level of total commercial fishing, and not the relationship between these factors and the share of commercial fishing relative to all substitute activities.

### 6.3.2 *Stage 1: Estimation of the Block Choice Models*

Estimation proceeds sequentially but in reverse order to that of the decision process shown in figure 6.2.[6] First, I analyze the choice to fish in a specific block given that commercial fishermen are fishing for a particular species of fish. I estimate two models: one for the choice of blocks for northern anchovy fishing and one for the choice of blocks for jack mackerel fishing.[7] As discussed above, these two species together represented between approximately 43 and 87 percent of the catch of all species in the Southern California bight for the years 1972 through 1982 (on average approximately 67 percent of the catch).[8]

### 6.3.3 *Area and Time Period Covered*

The block choice models for jack mackerel and northern anchovy cover the area containing the 271 ocean blocks in the Southern California bight for which the California Department of Fish and Game (CDFG) maintains catch data on an ocean and species specific basis.[9] Using the catch data for these 271 blocks, I determine, for both the jack mackerel and northern anchovy choice models, which blocks accounted for the majority of northern anchovy and jack mackerel catch. I limit my analysis to the relationship between catch in these subsets of the 271 blocks and various block characteristics. The blocks included in the northern anchovy and jack mackerel models are the same for each year.

[6]My analysis is limited to the northern anchovy and jack mackerel species. Other fish species of less total value were excluded from the second stage of my model. It is not necessary to include all alternatives in the logit model in order to obtain consistent estimates of the degree of substitutability among blocks or in order to calculate the damages which should be apportioned to the northern anchovy versus jack mackerel fisheries.

[7]The nested logit model emphasizes both the hierarchy of decisions and the relative substitutability of the choices being made. Once it has been decided to catch northern anchovy, specific blocks relevant for northern anchovy fishing are grouped together. Blocks which are more similar to one another for catching jack mackerel are similarly grouped together.

[8]In 1983, the catch of northern anchovies represented only 3.3 percent of total catch reported for 271 blocks in the Southern California bight. In 1983 the market for northern anchovies collapsed. However, eliminating data for 1983 did not materially affect the estimation of the nested logit model, nor did it affect the qualitative results.

[9]The CDFG uses a system of numbered blocks to track fin fish, shellfish and other marine life caught in California waters. Most of offshore California is divided into ocean blocks, which are roughly ten miles square. The catch data used below includes blocks located from south of Point Piedras Blancas (just north of San Simeon) to Bishop Rock, which is roughly one hundred miles west south west of San Diego. Two sets of blocks are larger than standard blocks. These are island group blocks and far offshore fringe blocks.

Blocks in which there was not a significant amount of jack mackerel or northern anchovy catch are excluded from the estimation because these models are intended to explain the share of catch among blocks. If there is little or no fishing for a particular species in a block, then this block is not a good substitute for other blocks in which commercial fishermen do catch a substantial amount of a particular species.[10] In other words, if a commercial fisherman is making a choice as to which blocks in which to fish for jack mackerel, he will not include in his choice set blocks in which he has never caught or caught only insignificant amounts of jack mackerel.

The ocean blocks included in the jack mackerel and northern anchovy choice models are listed in table 6.2 and shown in figures 6.3 and 6.4.[11]
The blocks in which there is a significant amount of anchovy catch are located adjacent and close to the coastline from Point Conception (north of Santa Barbara), south to San Clemente and surrounding Santa Catalina Island. The blocks included in the jack mackerel model include blocks in four areas which I designate as inner west blocks, inner blocks, middle blocks and outer blocks. The inner west blocks are adjacent to and west of Port Hueneme, the inner blocks roughly form a semicircle around Los Angeles Harbor, the middle blocks surround San Clemente and Santa Barbara Islands, and the outer blocks include the waters around the Cortez and Tanner banks.[12] Out of 271 blocks, 46 blocks, or approximately 17 percent, are included in the northern anchovy model and 55 or approximately 20 percent are included in the jack mackerel model. Between 80 and 98 percent of all jack mackerel caught were fished in these blocks during the period 1969 through 1983. For northern anchovies, 74 to 99 percent were caught in these blocks.

---

[10]Blocks without any catch are excluded from the estimation since the logit models are calibrated using log odds probabilities. Blocks with small catch are also excluded from the "anchovy area" since it is implausible that they are good substitutes for the historically active blocks.

[11]The choice of blocks to include in the northern anchovy model is based, to some extent, on the pattern of the actual catch by block for 1969, 1972, and 1975. Several criteria were used in selecting blocks. First, all blocks having at least one million pounds of northern anchovy catch were included. Second, blocks were included if the blocks surrounding them were major producers of anchovy catch. Finally, several narrow blocks adjacent to the coast were excluded because of the three to six-mile coastal exclusion zone applicable to the anchovy reduction fishery.

[12]The jack mackerel catch records for the years 1969, 1972, 1975, 1978, 1981, and 1982 reported in the *1AA Annual Report of Catch by Origin/Species/Month,* compiled by the CDFG, were used to establish the principal jack mackerel catch areas. Blocks comprising the principal jack mackerel catch area were included in the jack mackerel block choice model. The six reported years covered the period of study. Blocks were included in the choice set based on several criteria. The first criteria was to include all blocks having at least one year of one million pounds catch of jack mackerel. Next all blocks having multiple years of one hundred thousand pound jack mackerel catch and sharing sides with one million pounds catch jack mackerel blocks were added to the four catch areas. Blocks with one one hundred thousand pound jack mackerel catch year were included when they served either to connect a catch area or to remove a concavity in a catch area. Finally, all mainland shore blocks within the inner and inner west areas were included except those characterized exclusively as broad sand beaches.

**Figure 6.3: Blocks Included in Northern Anchovy Choice Model**

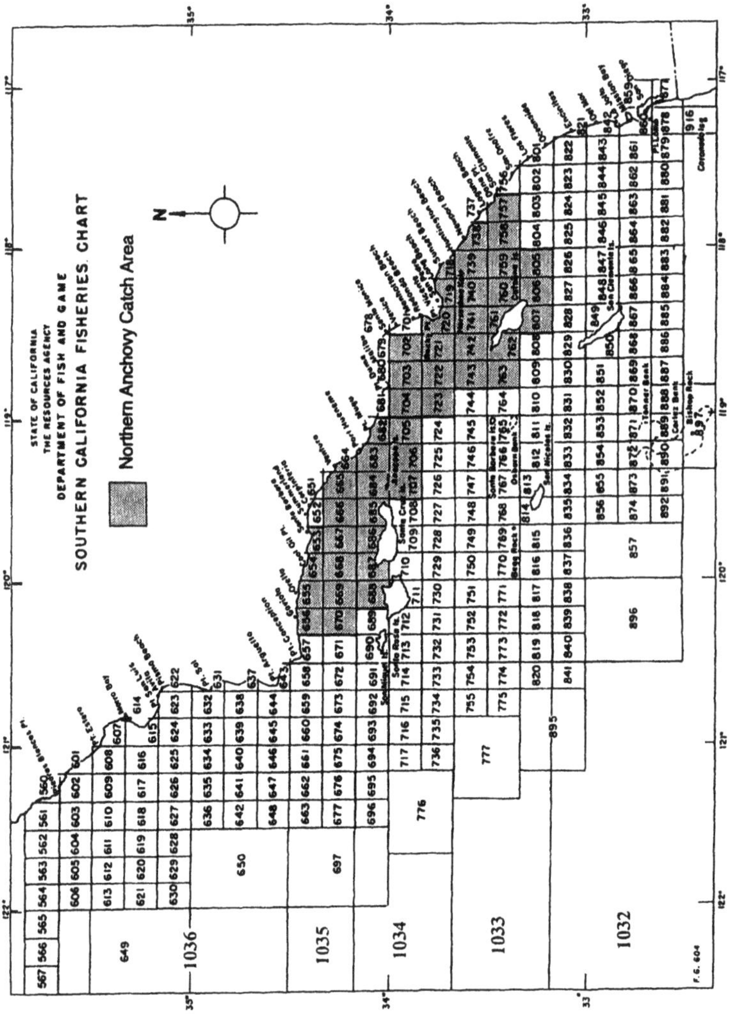

# Figure 6.4: Blocks Included in Jack Mackerel Choice Model

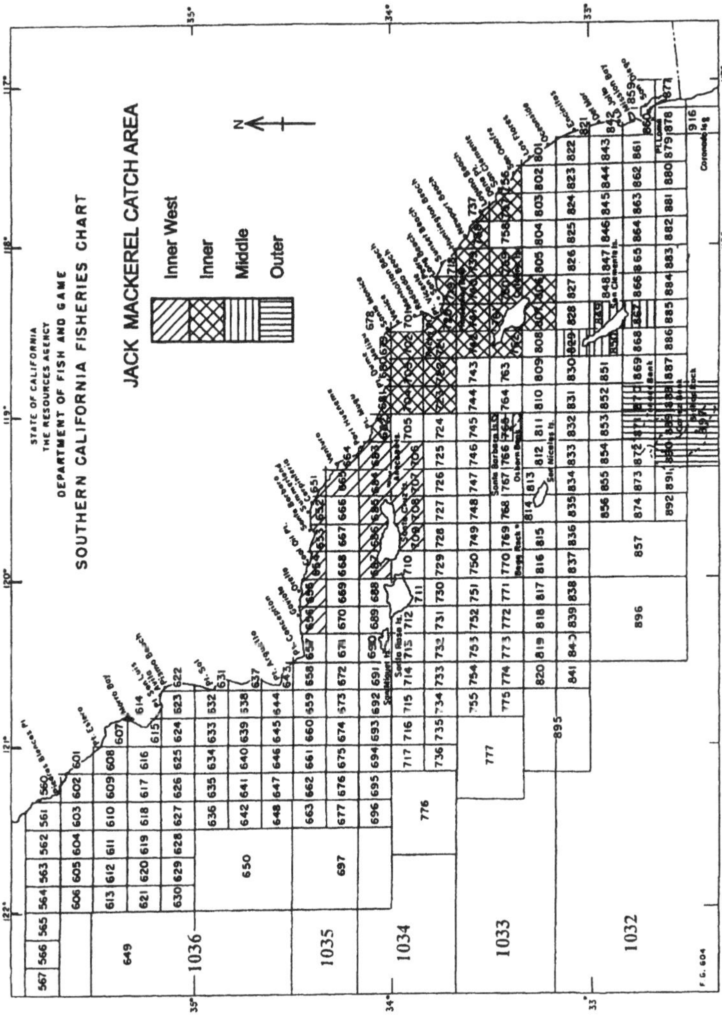

**Table 6.2.** Block Numbers of Catch Regions Included In Commercial Fishing Models

| Northern Anchovy Catch Region | | | | |
|---|---|---|---|---|
| Other Blocks | | | | Blocks Potentially Affected by PCBs and DDTs |
| 653 | 670 | 704 | 757 | 719 |
| 654 | 682 | 705 | 758 | 720 |
| 655 | 683 | 706 | 759 | 722 |
| 656 | 684 | 707 | 760 | 741 |
| 664 | 685 | 718 | 761 | 742 |
| 665 | 686 | 721 | 762 | 743 |
| 666 | 687 | 723 | 763 | |
| 667 | 688 | 738 | 805 | |
| 668 | 702 | 739 | 806 | |
| 669 | 703 | 740 | 807 | |

| Jack Mackerel Catch Region | | | | |
|---|---|---|---|---|
| | Inner | | | |
| Inner West | Blocks Potentially Affected by PCBs and DDTs | Other Blocks | Middle | Outer |
| 651 | 719 | 678 | 765 | 870 |
| 652 | 720 | 679 | 829 | 871 |
| 653 | 722 | 680 | 849 | 888 |
| 654 | 741 | 681 | 850 | 889 |
| 655 | 742 | 702 | 867 | 890 |
| 656 | | 703 | | 897 |
| 664 | | 704 | | |
| 665 | | 721 | | |
| 682 | | 723 | | |
| 683 | | 737 | | |
| 684 | | 738 | | |
| 685 | | 739 | | |
| 686 | | 740 | | |
| 687 | | 756 | | |
| 706 | | 757 | | |
| 707 | | 759 | | |
| 708 | | 760 | | |
| 709 | | 761 | | |
| | | 762 | | |
| | | 806 | | |
| | | 807 | | |

Source: *1AA Annual Report of Catch by Origin/Species/Month*, California Department of Fish and Game Library

Both the jack mackerel and the northern anchovy models cover the period from 1969 through 1983. This period was chosen for the following reasons: (1) the data on commercial catch by block was not available prior to 1969 and (2)

data on catch by block by species was not as reliable after 1983 because a larger percentage of the catch was assigned to "catch-all" blocks.[13]

The estimation of the northern anchovy model is based on a total of 690 observations, or fifteen years, 1969 through 1983, of catch data for forty-six blocks. The estimation of the jack mackerel model is also based on fifteen years but for fifty-five blocks for a total of 825 observations. Since all blocks do not have a positive catch for all years, the estimation sample for the northern anchovy model is 493 observations, and 599 observations for the jack mackerel model.[14]

### *6.3.4 The Block Choice Model for Northern Anchovy Fishing*

**Explanatory Variables.** The block choice model for northern anchovy fishing relates the share of catch of northern anchovies in a block to several block specific characteristics.[15] Explanatory variables include a measure of the stock of northern anchovies, the presence of fishing spots, the distance of the block from two processing locations at Port Hueneme and the Port of Los Angeles (San Pedro), the presence of dump sites, the presence of military sites designated as restricted or dangerous areas, and the presence of marine sanctuaries.

The concentration of northern anchovy ichthyoplankton (fish larvae) is used in the northern anchovy choice model as a measure of the stock of northern anchovies. A measure of the stock of northern anchovies is included as an explanatory factor in the estimation because commercial fishermen frequently base their choice of fishing location based on expected catch.

The use of ichthyoplankton data as a proxy for the stock of northern anchovies raises several issues.[16] First, the ichthyoplankton data used in our analysis were not collected on an ocean block basis. I therefore establish a method of assigning data from ichthyoplankton sampling stations to the vari-

---

[13]After 1984 fishermen were no longer required to assign catch to blocks other than catch-all blocks. However, my examination of the catch data showed that in 1984 significant portions of the catch data were assigned to catch-all blocks. Therefore, I have not included 1984 in the analysis.

[14]The estimation sample in the northern anchovy model falls from 690 to 493 observations after blocks with zero catch are eliminated. All blocks in the northern anchovy area (or in the jack mackerel area) are assigned values based on their characteristics using the parameters as estimated in the logit models. Thus, if some block appears in the northern anchovy catch area, but for whatever reason does not have a positive catch in any of the fifteen years used in the estimation, that block is not used in the calibration of the underlying parameters. However, that same block contributes to the inclusive value of the catch area and influences decisions by commercial fishermen to fish for one species over another.

[15]The dependent variable in the block choice model is the share of northern anchovy caught in a particular block relative to the total anchovy caught in all blocks in the northern anchovy catch area divided by the share of anchovy caught in a base block relative to the total anchovy catch. Since both the numerator and denominator are divided by total catch, the dependent variable is the amount of catch in a particular block divided by the catch in a base block. Thus a base block is selected as a normalizing alternative.

[16]These issues are discussed in greater detail in appendix 6.6.2.

ous ocean blocks.[17] Second, there is a complex relationship between the stock of adult spawning northern anchovies and catch. Third, there is not a direct relationship between northern anchovy stock and the amount of ichthyoplankton because anchovy larvae and eggs can be a significant portion of the northern anchovies' food intake. Nonetheless, other researchers have used estimates of northern anchovy stocks based in whole or in part on ichthyoplankton data (Anderson, Gress, and Mais 1982, Smith 1972).

The number of fishing spots indicates the presence of prime fishing locations in a block. Prime fishing locations may be found in the vicinity of reefs, kelp beds, banks, canyons, flats, or wrecks.[18] The prime fishing locations are obtained from the *Fishing Spot Locator*, a publication that documents the latitude and longitude of prime fishing locations in the Southern California region (Grabenstatter 1990).

Two distance measurements are included in the northern anchovy block choice model. These are the distance from the center of each block to Port Hueneme and to the Port of Los Angeles (San Pedro).[19] These two port-to-block distances are included in the analysis because facilities for processing northern anchovies exist at these two ports and landings at other ports were either nonexistent or small relative to total landings of northern anchovies at Port Hueneme and the Port of Los Angeles. As explained below, in my discussion of the model specifications, these variables are included in the northern anchovy block choice model both separately and combined.[20]

Variables denoting the presence of dump sites, military sites, or marine sanctuaries are also included in the block choice model for northern anchovies.[21] The dump sites variable denotes the existence of either dump sites containing dredged or unspecified materials. The military sites variable denotes the existence of one or more military restricted or danger areas within a block.

---

[17]The best measure of ichthyoplankton density for a given year and block is judged to be the average of the year's samples taken at the ichthyoplankton station nearest to a block.

[18]Reefs are considered prime fishing areas because they may either promote reproduction or growth, or because they attract fish. Reefs, kelp beds, and other structures may also proxy for areas of productive shallows which contain bottom dwelling flora and fauna, and nutrients washed off from the adjacent land.

[19]In measuring the port-to-block distances, I attempted to estimate the distance of the shortest route between a given port and the waters closest to the centers of the blocks. Possible "shortest routes" excluded only those waters with clearly designated obstructions. Islands, major rocks, designated wrecks, oil platforms, and naval restricted areas comprised the key obstructions.

[20]Later in the chapter I discuss the relationship between distance traveled and the costs of commercial fishing.

[21]A number of other block-specific characteristics are identified. These additional characteristics are: 1) disused chemical munitions dump sites, 2) explosives dump sites, 3) disused explosives dump sites, 4) underwater pipelines, 5) oil production platforms, and 6) underwater cables. Some of these characteristics were excluded from the commercial fishing block choice models because they did not vary in the catch regions; that is, they carried the value zero for all observations in both the northern anchovy and the jack mackerel catch areas. The remaining characteristics from the above list were excluded because they were judged to contribute little to the overall explanatory power of the model.

Restricted areas refer to hazardous areas within which vessels would have to be specially equipped in order to operate safely, whereas danger areas are passable when firing ranges are not in use. The marine sanctuary variable denotes blocks which contain portions of either the Channel Islands National Marine Sanctuary or the Sea Otter Refuge. The blocks included in the northern anchovy choice model which contain dump sites, military sites, or marine sanctuaries are listed in table 6.3.[22] The variables included in the northern anchovy and jack mackerel regressions are summarized in table 6.4.

**Table 6.3.** Blocks Containing Site Characteristics, By Catch Region

| Northern Anchovy Catch Region | | | |
|---|---|---|---|
| Dump Sites | Military Sites | Marine Sanctuaries and Refuges | |
| 683 | 682 | 668 | |
| 738 | 702 | 670 | |
| 740 | 718 | 683 | |
| 741 | 719 | 684 | |
| | 720 | 685 | |
| | 761 | 686 | |
| | | 687 | |
| | | 688 | |
| | | 706 | |
| | | 707 | |
| Jack Mackerel Catch Region | | | |
| Dump Sites | Military Sites | Marine Sanctuaries and Refuges | Offshore Blocks |
| 683 | 682 | 683 | 765 |
| 738 | 702 | 684 | 829 |
| 740 | 719 | 685 | 849 |
| 741 | 720 | 686 | 850 |
| | 761 | 687 | 867 |
| | 829 | 706 | 870 |
| | 849 | 707 | 871 |
| | 850 | 708 | 888 |
| | 867 | 709 | 889 |
| | | 765 | 890 |
| | | | 897 |
| Sources: | 1) NOAA Nautical Chart #18022.<br>2) *United States Coast Pilot, Pacific Coast: California, Oregon, Washington, and Hawaii*, 26th edition, NOAA (U.S. Department of Commerce). | | |

[22]Only portions of blocks contain dump sites, military sites, or marine sanctuaries. Obviously, some blocks have none of these characteristics. In the jack mackerel catch area, four blocks contain dump sites, nine contain military sites, and ten contain marine sanctuaries or refuges. The corresponding numbers of blocks for northern anchovies are four, six and ten.

**Table 6.4.** Variables Used in Stage 1 Regressions

| Name | Description and Source |
|---|---|
| Dependent Variable: log (Relative share of catch) | Based on annual commercial catch in pounds reported by origin block and species. Source: *1AA Annual Report of Catch by Origin/Species/Month*, California Department of Fish and Game, Long Beach, CA. (1969 through 1983). The resulting variables (one for jack mackerel and one for northern anchovy) represent the logarithms of shares of catch relative to those of the base block. |
| Number of fishing spots | Based on the latitude and longitude of prime fishing locations in the Southern California region, most of which may be found in the vicinity of reefs, kelp beds, banks, canyons, flats, or wrecks. Source: Frank Grabenstatter, *Fishing Spot Locator* (Glendale, CA: Perfect-10, 1990). This variable tallies the number of fishing locations lying either within or on the boundaries of each block. Number of fishing spots varies over blocks, but is constant over time. |
| Distance to Port of Los Angeles | Represents the minimum traveling distance, in statute miles, between the center of each block and the Port of Los Angeles. Source: National Ocean Service, NOAA Nautical Chart No. 18022, 27th edition, (May 5, 1990) Washington, DC: U.S. Department of Commerce. |
| Distance to Port Hueneme | Represents the minimum traveling distance, in statute miles, between the center of each block and Port Hueneme. Source: National Ocean Service, NOAA Nautical Chart No. 18022, 27th edition, (May 5, 1990) Washington, DC: U.S. Department of Commerce. |
| Ichthyoplankton Concentration, Northern Anchovy | Represents the degree of concentration of northern anchovy ichthyoplankton in each block. Source: "Ichthyoplankton and Station Data for California Cooperative Oceanic Fisheries Investigations Survey Cruises in (1969, 1972, 1975, 1978, 1981)," NOAA Tech. Memo., NOAA-TM-NMFS-SWFC-(100, 109, 110, 111, 112). |

**Estimation Results.** The estimated northern anchovy block choice models are presented in table 6.5. As discussed above, these models relate the share of catch in a block relative to a base block to various characteristics of the block relative to the base block.

In Model 1 both port-to-block distances for Port Hueneme and Port of Los Angeles are included and in Model 1a the distance measures are combined. In Model 1 the coefficients on the distances from either port are negative, significant, and approximately equal. Thus, Model 1 demonstrates that the value of an additional mile spent in travel from either of the two ports is not dependent on the particular port.

The amount of northern anchovy ichthyoplankton in each block (a measure of the stock of northern anchovies as discussed above) is also included in Model

**Table 6.4.** (continued) Variables Used in Stage 1 Regressions

| Name | Description and Source |
|---|---|
| Dump Sites | Denotes the existence of one or more dump sites within a block. The contents of a dump site, as defined here, consist of either dredged or unspecified material. Dump sites containing either explosives or chemical munitions are not represented by this dummy variable. Source: National Ocean Service, NOAA Nautical Charts No. 18020, 18022, 18720, 18721, 18725, 18727-18729, 18740, 18744, 18746, 18749, 18751, 18755-18757, 18762-18765, 18772-18774, Washington DC: U.S. Department of Commerce. |
| Military Sites | Denotes the existence of one or more military restricted or danger areas within a block. Restricted areas refer to locations in which vessels cannot operate safely without special authorization, whereas danger areas are passable when firing ranges are not in use. Source: National Ocean Service, NOAA Nautical Charts No. 18020, 18022, 18720, 18721, 18725, 18727-18729, 18740, 18744, 18746, 1874, 18751, 18755-18757, 18762-18765, 18772-18774, Washington DC: U.S. Department of Commerce., and United States Coast Pilot No. 7, Pacific Coast: California, Oregon, Washington, and Hawaii. Washington, DC: U.S. Department of Commerce, 1991. |
| Marine Sanctuary/ Refuge | Denotes blocks which contain portions of either the Channel Islands National Marine Sanctuary or the Sea Otter Refuge. Source: National Ocean Service, NOAA Nautical Charts No. 18020, 18022, 18720, 18721, 18725, 18727-18729, 18740, 18744, 18746, 18749, 18751, 18755-18757, 18762-18765, 18772-18774, Washington DC: U.S. Department of Commerce. |
| Offshore Blocks | Identifies offshore blocks in which jack mackerel are commercially fished in significant numbers. The particular blocks are 765, 829, 849, 850, 867, 870, 871, 888, 889, 890, and 897. Based on analysis of catch data. Source: *1AA Annual Report of Catch by Origin/Species/Month*, California Department of Fish and Game, Long Beach, CA. (1969 through 1983). |

1. The coefficient on the ichthyoplankton variable is positive, indicating that the presence of northern anchovy ichthyoplankton has a positive effect on the catch of northern anchovies in a specific block. While this effect is not quite statistically significant, it shows that northern anchovy ichthyoplankton provide a reasonable proxy for the stock of northern anchovies and that this proxy is positively associated with the desirability of a given block for the catching of northern anchovies.

The results for Model 1 also show that the presence of dump sites leads to increased catch within a given block, while areas with military restrictions lead to diminished catch. The positive relationship between the presence of a dump site and catch within a block may be explained by block characteristics which are not included in the model. The blocks in which there are dump sites

**Table 6.5.** Commercial Fishing Stage 1 Regression Results: Estimated Coefficient (*t*-statistic)

| Independent Variable | Northern Anchovy | | Jack Mackerel |
|---|---|---|---|
| | Model 1 | Model 1a | Model 2 |
| Constant | 1.198 (−4.37) | 1.160 (−4.30) | −0.261 (−0.71) |
| Number of Fishing Spots | 0.0012 (0.17) | 0.0002 (−0.03) | 0.0160 (2.30) |
| Distance to Port of Los Angeles | −0.0213 (−4.36) | −0.0234 (−5.67) | |
| Distance to Port Hueneme | −0.0257 (−5.01) | −0.0234 (−5.67) | |
| Northern Anchovy Ichthyoplankton Concentration | 0.00018 (1.64) | 0.00015 (1.45) | 0.00054 (3.87) |
| Dump Sites | 1.052 (2.79) | 1.001 (2.70) | 2.081 (4.00) |
| Military Sites | −1.049 (−3.08) | −1.080 (−3.20) | 0.769 (1.99) |
| Marine Sanctuaries and Refuges | −0.488 (−1.49) | 0.375 (−1.28) | 0.958 (2.39) |
| Offshore Blocks | | | 2.244 (6.27) |
| Observations | 493 | 493 | 599 |

Dependent Variable: Natural logarithm of the block's share relative to the share of a base block.

are located in shallow coastal areas and/or contain submarine canyons and escarpments (underwater cliffs and canyons). The size of anchovy schools is typically larger in shallow coastal areas and areas containing submarine canyons and escarpments (Mais 1974).

The number of "prime" fishing spots is not significantly related to the share of catch in a block. This result may be due to a variety of factors. First, many of the blocks containing reefs also are adjacent to the coastline and anchovy reduction fishing is restricted within either three or six miles of the coast. Second, many of the reefs lie beyond the area in which anchovies are fished. Third, kelp beds (included in the definition of prime fishing locations) may hinder purse seine fishing. However, kelp beds may indicate prime fishing areas for other species (Miller and Geibel 1973).

Model 1a in table 6.5 is identical to Model 1, with one exception. In Model 1a the two distance measures are added together. The pattern of results is very similar to the results for Model 1. In Model 1a, the combined effect of distance is quite significant with a $t$-statistic of -5.7.[23]

### *6.3.5 The Block Choice Model for Jack Mackerel Fishing*

**Explanatory Variables.** Most of the variables included in the jack mackerel block choice model regression were also included in the northern anchovy model and are discussed above. These include: the presence of fishing spots, the presence of dump sites, the presence of military sites, the presence of marine sanctuaries and refuges, and the amount of northern anchovy ichthyoplankton. However, in the jack mackerel model I do not include the amount of jack mackerel ichthyoplankton or the port-to-block distances for Port Hueneme and the Port of Los Angeles.

The use of jack mackerel ichthyoplankton as an appropriate measure of the stock of mackerel in specific blocks requires that certain conditions be met. First, the catch must consist of adult jack mackerel. The amount of ichthyoplankton can be used as a proxy for the adult spawning population, but not as a proxy for the non-spawning juvenile population. Second, it is necessary that the adult spawning population spawn and be caught within a small area (in my model, an ocean block). Neither of these conditions are met for jack mackerel. Non-spawning juvenile jack mackerel (not the adult jack mackerel) are caught in the blocks included in the model. But adult jack mackerel are located far offshore and rarely spawn within the area included in the model. In addition, jack mackerel are pelagic; that is, they cover a wide area of ocean and it is unlikely that jack mackerel caught in a particular area also spawn in that area (Kramer and Smith 1970).

Although the amount of jack mackerel ichthyoplankton may not be a good proxy for the stock of jack mackerel, the amount of northern anchovy is an indirect measure of the stock of jack mackerel. One of the main predators of northern anchovies is jack mackerel (Methot 1982, Pacific Fishery Management Council and National Marine Fisheries Service 1983, Parrish and MacCall 1978). Jack mackerel concentrate on anchovy schools to feed, so that the highest concentrations of jack mackerel should be found in close proximity to the highest concentrations of northern anchovies. Therefore, I work from the assumption that the amount of northern anchovy ichthyoplankton which is a proxy for the stock of northern anchovies will also be a good proxy for the stock of jack mackerel.

[23] Since the regression results are presented in terms of the log-odds, the interpretation of goodness-of-fit for these equations is somewhat difficult. I have used the estimated model to predict the fraction of catch which would occur in each block in each year, and have compared that to the actual fraction of catch which did occur in each block in each year. The correlation between these two measures provides a measure of goodness-of-fit. For the northern anchovy model, I find a correlation of 34 percent between predicted and actual allocations.

The further inclusion of a variable indicating whether the catch was in an offshore block instead of port-to-block distance measures (as in the northern anchovy model) is discussed below.

**Estimation Results.** Model 2 in table 6.5 shows the results of jack mackerel block choice model. In this model the catch by block is a function of the number of fishing spots, northern anchovy ichthyoplankton, the presence of dump sites, the presence of military sites, the presence of marine sanctuaries and refuges, and a dummy variable which indicates those major catch sites which are furthest away from the inner harbor area.

Distance from port-to-block is not included in this model because the stock of jack mackerel increases as the distance from shore increases; that is, there is an inverse relationship between the distance from shore and the stock of jack mackerel. The port-to-block distance variable would measure the effect of stock on catch, rather than the effect of distance on catch.[24] On the other hand, the offshore block variable indicates that the outer ocean reaches are more valuable for the catch of jack mackerel.[25] The offshore blocks include the blocks in middle and outer areas as shown in figure 6.4.

Unlike the results of the northern anchovy model, I find that the presence of reefs is a very significant indicator of jack mackerel catch. Middle and outer, as well as in-shore blocks in which there is high jack mackerel catch, frequently contain numerous reefs. I also find that northern anchovy ichthyoplankton, military sites, marine sanctuaries, and areas in which dumping of dredged or unspecified materials occur are all positively associated with jack mackerel catch.[26]

### *6.3.6 Stage 2: Estimation of the Species Choice Model*

In the second stage of the nested logit model, I analyze the choice of species fished. The choice of species fished is related to (1) the value of fishing different species, calculated using the results from the block choice models estimated in Stage 1 and (2) the market prices of the species included in Stage 1. Since I estimate block choice models for jack mackerel and northern anchovy, the species choice model relates the choice between these two species to their rel-

[24]When the combined distance from port-to-block for Port Hueneme and the Port of Los Angeles was included in the regression, the coefficient on this variable was positive, indicating that it was not more costly to travel to more distant blocks. In order to model the relationship between jack mackerel catch by block and distance traveled, I would need to obtain additional information on jack mackerel catch for areas beyond the 271 ocean blocks for which I have data.

[25]Jack mackerel stocks are probably larger in the blocks more distant from the shore. Often the greatest concentrations of jack mackerel are found off the coasts of the outer Channel Islands and especially off the distant Cortez and Tanner banks. Jack mackerel are also found in mid-ocean areas.

[26]For the jack mackerel model, the correlation of predicted and actual allocations is about 19 percent.

ative values and prices. The species choice model explains the distribution of catch between northern anchovies and jack mackerel.

**Explanatory Variables.** The value of fishing for jack mackerel or northern anchovies is calculated using the results from the block choice models. The inclusive value of all blocks in the catch area is calculated by an exponential average of the individual values for each block in the catch area. First, the value of the block characteristics that affect commercial fishermen's choices between blocks for jack mackerel and northern anchovies is calculated. Second, the values of the blocks associated with the catch of a particular species are aggregated to arrive at a separate inclusive value for jack mackerel and northern anchovies.

Although not included in the model for reasons discussed below, market price information was obtained and analyzed for jack mackerel and northern anchovies. The jack mackerel prices obtained are average annual prices and are based on the payments made to vessel operators for jack mackerel landed at the dock and intended for canning, reduction, and for retail sales. The northern anchovy prices obtained are also average annual prices based on payments to vessel operators.[27] The variables included in the species choice model are described in table 6.6.

**Table 6.6.** Names and Descriptions of Variables Used In Stage 2 Regressions

| Variable Name | Description and Source |
|---|---|
| Dependent Variable: log (Catch in Northern Anchovy Catch Region / Catch in Jack Mackerel Catch Region | Based on catch data. Source: *1AA Annual Report of Catch by Origin/Species/Month*, California Department of Fish and Game, Long Beach, CA. (1969 through 1983). |
| Time Trend | |
| Difference in inclusive values from block choice model | Based on first-stage logistic regression. |
| Constant | |

**Econometric Results.** The estimated species choice model is presented in table 6.7. The dependent variable in this model is the natural logarithm of the ratio of northern anchovy catch to jack mackerel catch.

[27]Price information was obtained from the CDFG publication entitled "The Marine Fish Catch of California/California Marine Fish Landings."

**Table 6.7.** Commercial Fishing Stage 2 Regression Results: Estimated Coefficient (*t*-statistic)

| Independent Variable | Coefficient |
|---|---|
| Constant | 27.966<br>(3.84) |
| Time Trend | -0.136<br>(-2.90) |
| Difference in inclusive value from block choice model | 2.851<br>(2.52) |
| Observations | 15 |
| R-squared | 0.573 |
| Dependent Variable: Natural logarithm of the ratio of total northern anchovy catch in the northern anchovy catch area to total jack mackerel catch in the jack mackerel catch area, by year. | |

The independent variables include the difference of the inclusive values from the northern anchovy and jack mackerel block choice models, a constant term for northern anchovies, and a time trend.[28]

According to economic theory, the difference in the output prices of northern anchovy and jack mackerel should also appear in the species choice model. Figure 6.5 displays the real time trends for northern anchovy and jack mackerel prices. In the model specification (in which the difference between output prices for northern anchovies and jack mackerel, the difference in inclusive values, and a simple time trend are included) I find that the difference between output prices for northern anchovies and jack mackerel is insignificant. I therefore omit the price difference, but retain the time trend to capture general time effects.

Inspection of table 6.7 shows that the difference in inclusive values between northern anchovy and jack mackerel is positively related to the ratio of the catch of anchovy to the catch of mackerel. The *t*-statistic shows that the inclusive value coefficient is significantly different from zero, but based on its standard error is not significantly different from one. I noted above that the nested logit model groups together alternatives which are more similar to one another than they are to other alternatives. The inclusive value coefficient measures this degree of similarity. As with a simple correlation, the inclusive value coefficient should have a value between zero and one. Estimated values out of this range indicate misspecification of the model.

[28]Since the species choice model depends only on time-specific factors it is based on fifteen observations, one for each year from 1969 to 1983.

**Figure 6.5: Real Price for Northern Anchovy and Jack Mackerel, by Year (1982 $ / Metric Ton)**

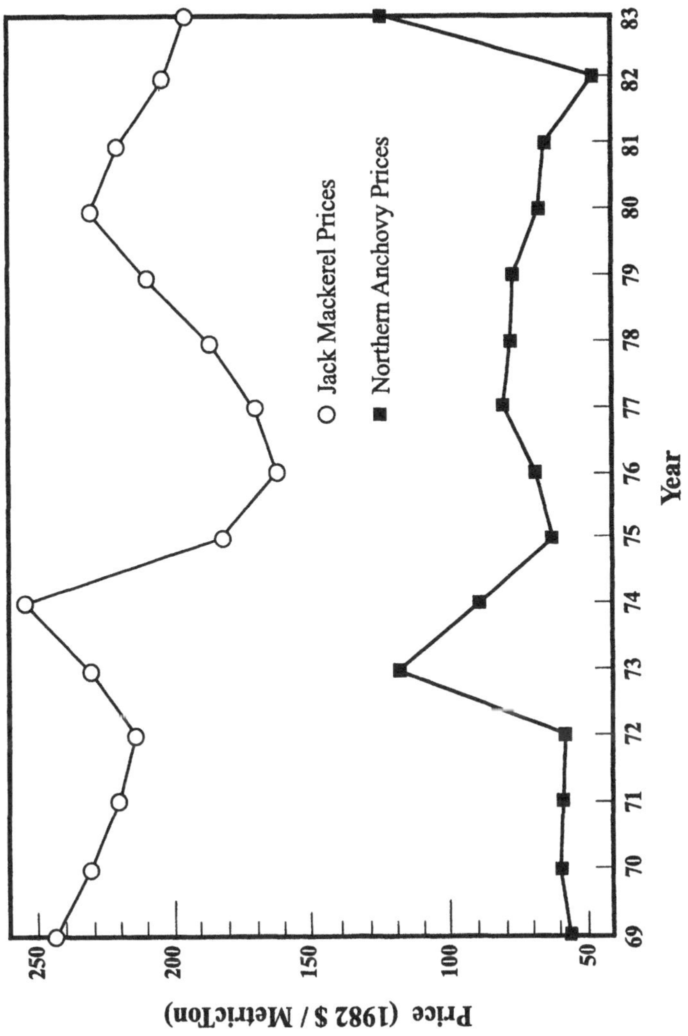


Sources: Economic Report of the President, February 1990, Table C-58. "California Marine Fish Landings", Fish Bulletins 161, 163, 166, 168, 170 (Tables 15); Fish Bulletin 173 (Tables 4-10), California Department of Fish and Game.

If the inclusive value coefficient has a value of one, the nested logit model reduces to a multinomial logit model without any grouping or nesting of the alternatives. When the inclusive value coefficient has a value of zero, the choice model treats alternatives within a subgroup as if they contained only a single alternative with a value equal to the maximum of the values of all alternatives in the subgroup. Since the inclusive value coefficient has an estimated value near one, there is no evidence that the model is misspecified. The coefficient of the time trend variable indicates a significant trend away from anchovy fishing and in favor of jack mackerel fishing.

To illustrate the predictive ability of the second stage model, I show in figure 6.6 the predicted and actual shares of northern anchovy and jack mackerel catch by year. For the Stage 2 species choice model, the correlation between predicted and actual allocations is about 75 percent.

## 6.4 Natural Resource Damage Estimates Based on the Nested Logit Model

In this section, a hypothetical damage estimate is derived by comparing producer surplus for commercial fishermen assuming that they can or cannot fish in particular ocean blocks. The lost surplus is then converted into a dollar figure which is my estimate of hypothetical damages. The damage estimate is hypothetical since no injury has actually been proven to exist in these areas.

### *6.4.1 Simulation of Potential Damages*

I now turn to the use of the nested logit model for the purposes of simulating potential damage to the commercial fishing fleet. I ask the question, "What would be the effect on commercial fishing if specific blocks of the ocean were not available to commercial fishermen?" To answer this question, I first estimate the inclusive value of commercial fishing based upon actual conditions. I then recalculate the inclusive value of northern anchovy fishing and jack mackerel fishing after removing the hypothetically lost ocean blocks.

In losing the opportunity to fish or harvest or catch fish in specific blocks, the commercial fishery will suffer some loss in total surplus. This loss can be intuitively understood as the added average distance the fishery must go to fish in other locations. If blocks of high value for northern anchovy catch are lost, but these same blocks are of little value for the catch of jack mackerel, then I would expect that some substitution would occur between northern anchovy and jack mackerel fishing. However, if the lost blocks are valuable both for the catch of northern anchovies and jack mackerel, then there is likely to be a simultaneous loss of surplus from both components, which might lead to substitution toward the catch of other species or to a diminution in the magnitude of total catch.

The specific damage calculation proceeds as follows. First, I recalculate the inclusive values of northern anchovy fishing and jack mackerel fishing after removing the hypothetically contaminated blocks. These blocks, shown in fig-

**Figure 6.6: Predicted versus Actual Northern Anchovy to Jack Mackerel Catch by Year**

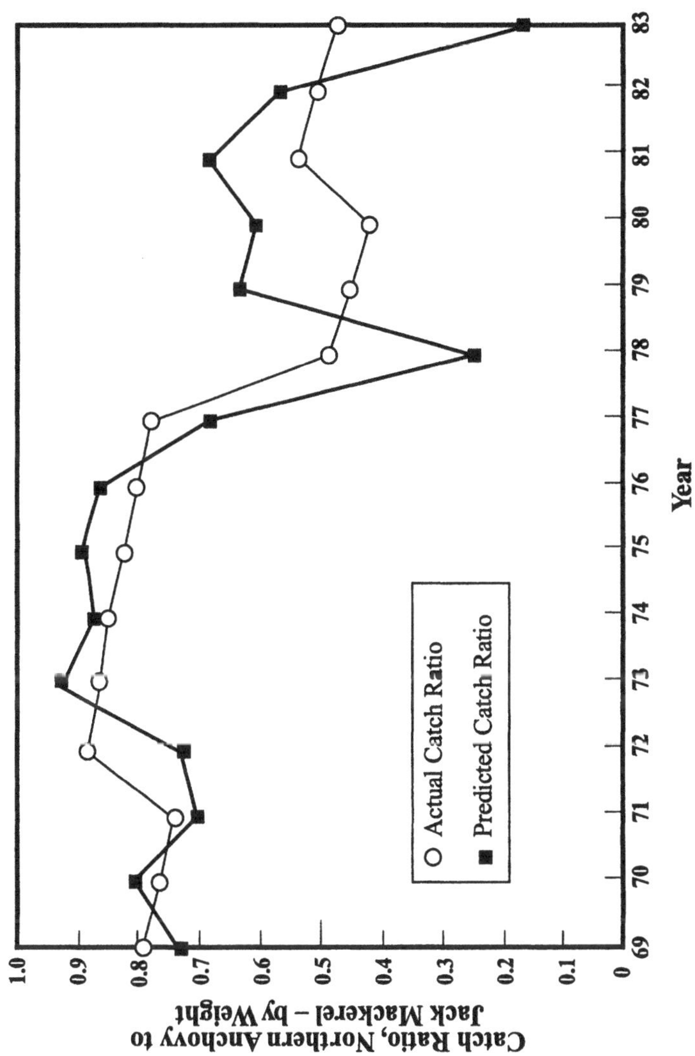

ures 6.7 and 6.8, are assumed to be those into which the Joint Water Pollution Control Plant municipal discharge facilities discharged effluent (blocks 719 and 720), and those in which the PCB dump sites mentioned in the *Draft Injury Determination Plan* are located (blocks 741, 742, 743, and 722). These recalculated inclusive values are then subtracted from the surplus values calculated using the Stage 1 logistic regression results to form an estimate of lost producer surplus. Second, I convert the lost surplus values which are valued in terms of utility into dollars. The presence of the distance variable in the block choice model permits the translation of utility into miles; that is, the coefficient of the distance variable provides the conversion factor between utility and miles. Thus, lost surplus can be translated into the additional miles that must be traveled by the fleet to compensate for the lost blocks.

Once lost surplus is translated into mileage terms, a dollar value can be calculated by multiplying the average increase in miles by the marginal cost per mile traveled.[29] My specific damage estimates are presented below. However, my damage calculation could be affected by several factors. First, I do not consider the choice of any fish species besides northern anchovies or jack mackerel. If the hypothetically damaged blocks affect the value of the catch of other species besides northern anchovy and jack mackerel (absent or including the effects of substitution), then it is possible that I understate the damages arising from these lost blocks. Second, if blocks are not totally lost but only partially damaged, I may overstate the damage to the commercial fleet. A partially lost block should be treated in this analysis differently than the discrete loss of an alternative.[30] Finally, it is possible that commercial fishermen could reduce their own activity, leading to lower catch levels and presumably some lost revenue. This component of hypothetical damage is not measured.

### 6.4.2 A Hypothetical Damage Calculation

As discussed above, the damage calculation proceeds by removing the six hypothetically affected blocks and requires the calculation of differences in surplus under the status quo and under the hypothetical. In table 6.8, I display the time series of predicted damages to commercial fisheries from the loss of the six blocks for northern anchovy, and five blocks for jack mackerel.[31]

In 1983, the damage to fishermen involved in the northern anchovy catch is calculated at \$378 per trip and \$179 per trip for those fishing for jack mack-

[29] In appendix 6.6.4, I provide an estimate of the marginal cost per mile traveled for the commercial fishing fleet.

[30] A partially lost or damaged block could appear in the block choice model using variables which measure block specific pollution. These measurements would require an engineering model which allocates pollution to specific blocks. My model, therefore, cannot measure the partial impacts of pollution on multiple blocks. Instead the hypothetical damage calculation assumes the complete loss of the six specific blocks.

[31] Only five of the six blocks that we assume are affected by PCB and DDT contamination are also blocks that are in the jack mackerel catch area. Therefore, in the damage simulation I remove five, not six, blocks from the jack mackerel catch area.

**Figure 6.7: Blocks Hypothetically Contaminated by PCBs and DDTs within Jack Mackerel Catch Area.**

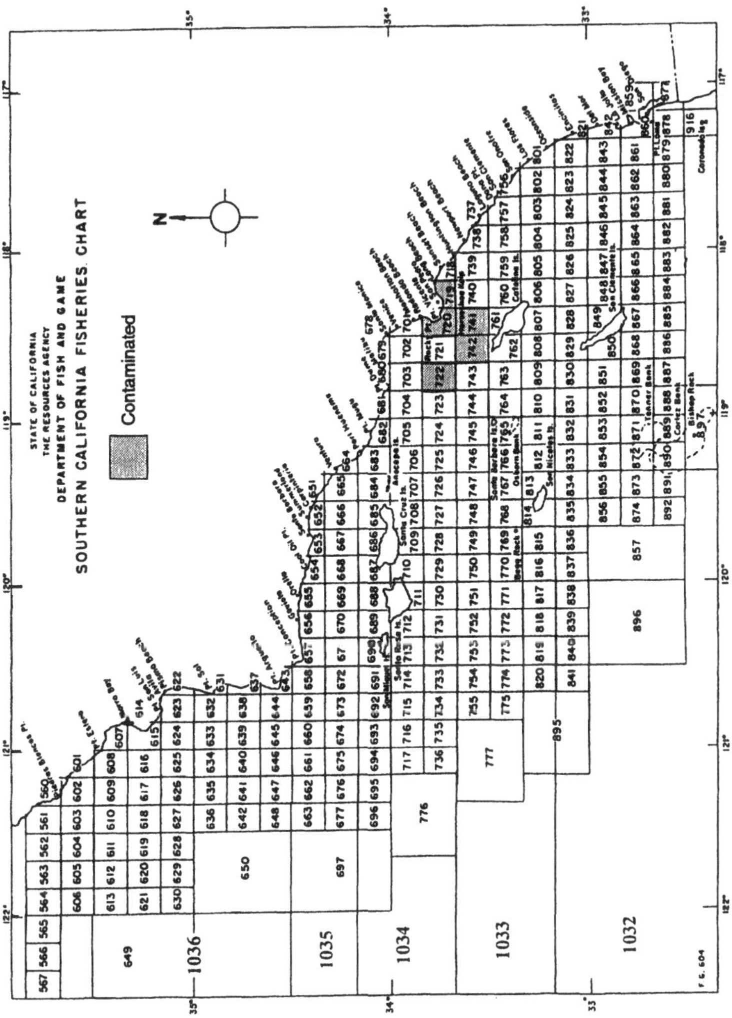

**Figure 6.8: Blocks Hypothetically Contaminated by PCBs and DDTs within Northern Anchovy Catch Area.**

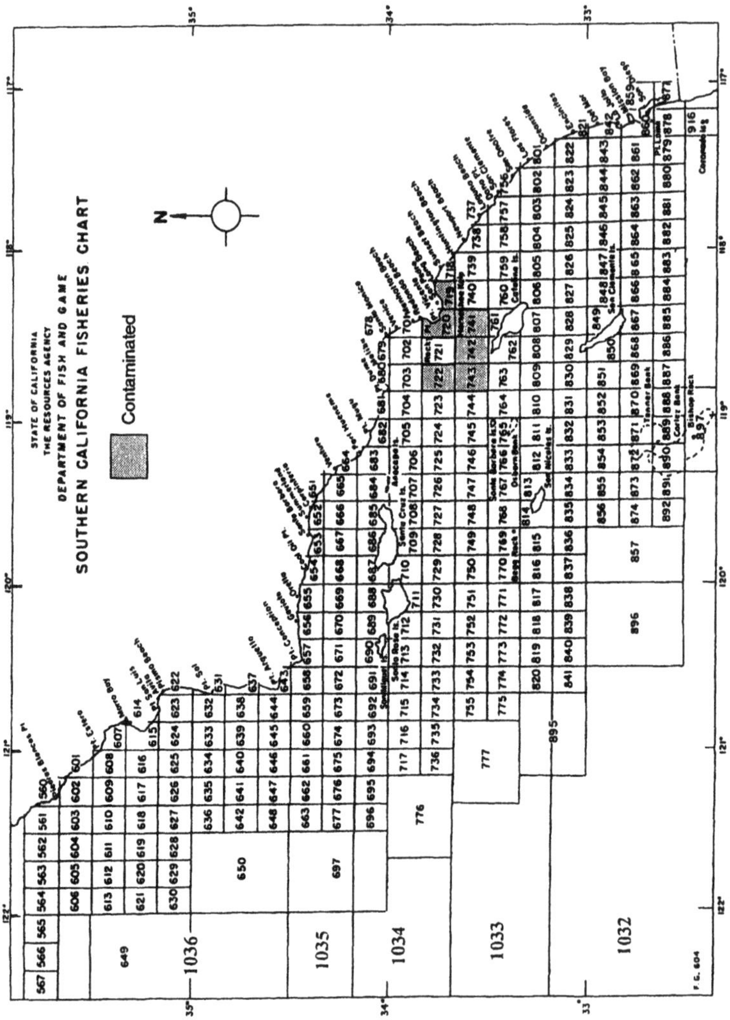

**Table 6.8.** Commercial Fishing Models Per-Trip-Losses Due to Increased Travel Costs

| Year | Northern Anchovy | Jack Mackerel |
|---|---|---|
| 1969 | $278 | $35 |
| 1970 | 278 | 35 |
| 1971 | 278 | 35 |
| 1972 | 290 | 42 |
| 1973 | 290 | 42 |
| 1974 | 290 | 42 |
| 1975 | 307 | 50 |
| 1976 | 307 | 50 |
| 1977 | 307 | 50 |
| 1978 | 284 | 46 |
| 1979 | 284 | 46 |
| 1980 | 284 | 46 |
| 1981 | 378 | 179 |
| 1982 | 378 | 179 |
| 1983 | 378 | 179 |

erel. The damage simulation further demonstrates an approximately 18 percent drop-off of anchovy fishing in favor of mackerel fishing after accounting for the effects of time. Overall, predicted anchovy share declines from 67 percent to approximately 57 percent. This is expected since the predicted lost surplus for the anchovy fishing segment is $378 compared with the lost surplus of $179 for mackerel. Therefore, the model predicts substitution away from the alternative which has increased most in fishing cost due to the loss of the six blocks.

In table 6.9, I present the calculation of the approximate number of trips taken per year by the commercial fleet for northern anchovy. This calculation is based on the total catch of northern anchovy by year, an estimate of the catch rate in pounds per hour, and an average trip length of twelve hours per trip. Although the number of trips varied considerably from year to year, I use an estimate of one thousand total trips per year for northern anchovy fishing to calculate hypothetical annual damages. If per trip loss is on the order of $378 per trip, the annual damage attributable to the loss of the six hypothetically affected blocks is $378,000 per year.

The estimation of the choice of species model does not directly contribute to the damage calculation I present. The importance of the Stage 2 model, however, is threefold. First, estimation of the Stage 2 models provides a test for the internal consistency of the nested logit structure. As noted above, I found no evidence of misspecification using the inclusive values as estimated in the block choice model. Second, the degree of substitution among blocks is only identified at the second stage. The degree of substitution among blocks provides insight into the distribution of potential damages among the species

**Table 6.9.** Commercial Fishing Vessel Trips for Northern Anchovy

| Year | Total Catch (Metric tons) | Catch (1,000 lbs) | Catch Rate (Metric tons /Hr) | Hours Fishing | Trips |
|---|---|---|---|---|---|
| 1967 | 29,346 | 64,696 | 2.01 | 14,600 | 1,217 |
| 1968 | 12,515 | 27,591 | 2.40 | 5,215 | 435 |
| 1969 | 59,153 | 130,409 | 6.22 | 9,510 | 793 |
| 1970 | 84,328 | 185,911 | 5.74 | 14,691 | 1,224 |
| 1971 | 39,601 | 87,305 | 5.79 | 6,840 | 570 |
| 1972 | 60,435 | 133,236 | 3.55 | 17,024 | 1,419 |
| 1973 | 118,432 | 261,098 | 5.86 | 20,210 | 1,684 |
| 1974 | 73,400 | 161,819 | 6.53 | 11,240 | 937 |
| 1975 | 141,586 | 312,144 | 7.08 | 19,998 | 1,667 |
| 1976 | 112,270 | 247,513 | 4.81 | 23,341 | 1,945 |
| 1977 | 99,674 | 219,741 | 4.91 | 20,300 | 1,692 |
| 1978 | 10,339 | 22,793 | 2.20 | 4,700 | 392 |
| 1979 | 47,408 | 104,516 | 6.00 | 7,901 | 658 |

Sources: 1) Sixth Amendment to the Northern Anchovy Fishery Management Plan, Pacific Fishery Management Council, Portland, Oregon, November 1990.
2) Assumes twelve hours per trip, Jacobson and Thomson (1991): p. 15.

caught by the commercial fishing industry. Hypothetical damage to a block lying in the jack mackerel catch area and not in the northern anchovy catch area could cause substitution by jack mackerel fishermen into other blocks in the jack mackerel catch area. Alternatively, it could cause some substitution into fishing for northern anchovy in place of jack mackerel fishing. The second stage model and the estimated inclusive value coefficient indicate what forms of substitution are most likely. Finally, the second stage estimates are required to complete the final stage of the estimation for total commercial catch. I use the nested logit model to measure the cost of the increased distance that fishermen must travel to compensate for the loss of the six blocks. An alternative calculation allows me to approximate the magnitude of these added costs and serves as a double-check on the magnitude of estimated damages. Using 1983 data, I calculate the weighted distance traveled by the commercial fleet to catch northern anchovy. The weighting is proportional to the fraction of catch that arises in different blocks. For all blocks in the northern anchovy catch area, the weighted average distance in 1983 is approximately eighty-seven miles. If I exclude the six blocks mentioned above and recalculate the weighted distance to the remaining blocks, I find that the weighted distance traveled increases to ninety-nine miles. Therefore, the loss of the six blocks implies an approximate twelve-mile increase in travel per trip. At $30 per mile for round trip costs, this entails a loss or extra cost of $360 per trip. This compares fairly closely to the nested logit model damage estimate of $378 per trip.

This estimate differs from the damage estimate based on the block choice model because the block choice model takes account of other characteristics affecting the share of catch in particular blocks. The fact that the nested logit model produces a slightly higher damage figure reflects the fact that the features of the blocks remaining in the choice set are somewhat less valuable than those lost in the hypothetically contaminated blocks, although this difference is somewhat minor for 1983.

## 6.5 Conclusions

In the nested logit model, substitution can occur through changes in utilization of blocks, changes in the mix of fish caught, or through a decrease in the level of commercial fishing activity. The degree to which one form of substitution dominates, depends on the estimated inclusive value coefficient. Since the estimated inclusive value coefficient in the second stage model is nearly one, it follows that the loss of one block will be shared approximately proportionately by all other blocks in the northern anchovy and jack mackerel catch areas. In 1983 the total tonnage of northern anchovy caught in the anchovy catch area was approximately seven million pounds. If the six blocks are removed from the northern anchovy catch area this figure declines to approximately six million pounds. The lost catch of northern anchovy in the six blocks is therefore about one million pounds.

## 6.6 Appendices

### *6.6.1 A Nested Logit Model of Commercial Fishing*

A nested logit model for commercial fishing begins with the strict utility $V$ for fish type $f$ in block $b$ at time period $t$.

$$V_{fb}^{t} = x_{fb}^{t}\beta + z_{f}^{t}\gamma \tag{1}$$

Here $V$ is assumed to be a linear function of characteristics of the block that are specific to the type of fish under consideration and specific to the time period, denoted by the vector $x$, and additional factors $z$, which are specific to the fish type and time period but which are not block specific. The conditional probability (conditional on type of fish) or fraction of catch arising from a given block is given by the multinomial logit model:

$$P_{b|f}^{t} = e^{x_{fb}^{t}\beta} / e^{I_{f}^{t}} \tag{2}$$

The log of the denominator of equation (2) is the inclusive value for fish type $f$ at time period $t$. The inclusive value is given by:

$$I_{f}^{t} = \log\left(\sum_{b=1}^{N_f} e^{x_{fb}^{t}\beta}\right) \tag{3}$$

The inclusive value is an exponentially weighted average of the values of variables which characterize specific blocks for specific fish types. Note that the conditional choice probability for a specific block given a specific fish type is not a function of variables which do not vary by block (e.g., the $z$ factors). Differences in strict utility which are not block specific at this point in the model, are not estimable. Therefore, the supply price of jack mackerel would not influence the block choice decisions since this price is presumably invariant to which block the fish are found.

The unconditional probability of fishing fish type $f$ in period $t$ is also given by a multinomial logit model where the inclusive values from the previous stage appear as additional explanatory variables. The unconditional probability has the form:

$$P_{f}^{t} = e^{z_{f}^{t}\gamma + (1-\sigma)I_{f}^{t}} / \sum_{t} e^{z_{f}^{t}\gamma + (1-\sigma)I_{f}^{t}} \tag{4}$$

The inclusive value coefficient is (1-$\sigma$). The nested logit model is consistent with random utility maximization if the random utility of a given block is assumed to equal the strict utility observed to the analyst $V$ plus an additively separable random component $\epsilon$ unobserved to the analyst:

$$U^t_{fb} = V^t_{fb} + \epsilon^t_{fb} \tag{5}$$

Under the assumption that the unobserved components are distributed as a multivariate generalized extreme value with generating function given by:

$$G(y) = \sum_f \left( \sum_b y_{fb}^{\frac{1}{1-\sigma}} \right)^{1-\sigma} \tag{6}$$

the probability of fish type and block selection is nested logit (McFadden 1978).

The total surplus attached to the joint choice of fish type and block location given fish type is given by:

$$S = \log \sum_f e^{z^t_f \gamma + (1-\sigma) I^t_f}. \tag{7}$$

Equation (7) is the log of the denominator of the multinomial logit model as specified in equation (4). Total surplus depends on both variables specific to the type of fish, and on the inclusive values as estimated from the block choice model.

The use of aggregate data allows the estimation to be accomplished using weighted regression (i.e., minimum chi-squared techniques). Specifically, I define: $F^t_{b|f}$ = percentage of fish type $f$ caught in block $b$ at time period $t$ and, $F^t_f$ = percentage of fish of type $f$ caught at time period $t$. These fractions are used as estimates of the true probabilities of selection as given by equations (2) and (4). To facilitate estimation by regression techniques, I rewrite equation (2) as the log odds of the probability of selecting a given block, conditional on fishing a given type of fish, relative to that of an arbitrarily selected base block:

$$\log \left( \frac{P^t_{b|f}}{P^t_{b_o|f}} \right) = \left( x^t_{fb} - x^t_{fb_o} \right) \beta \tag{8}$$

The log odds of the relative fraction of catch of a given fish within a given block relative to the base block is given by the difference of the explanatory variables which are block specific. Equation (8) illustrates how variables which are not block specific do not appear at this level of the estimation. Since equation (8) is linear in its parameters, it can be estimated by linear regression techniques. The estimated block characteristic weights (the coefficients $\beta$) are used to construct the inclusive values given by equation (3). These inclusive values are then used in the estimation of the log odds analogue of equation (4):

$$\log \left( \frac{P^t_f}{P^t_{f_o}} \right) = \left( z^t_f - z^t_{f_o} \right) \gamma + (1-\sigma) \left( I^t_f - I^t_{f_o} \right) \tag{9}$$

This equation is also linear in parameters and therefore can be estimated by weighted regression techniques. Estimation of equation (9) identifies the inclusive value coefficient (1-$\sigma$). Estimation of the aggregate nested logit model and issues of appropriate weighting are further discussed in Dubin, Graetz, Udell, and Wilde (1992).

### *6.6.2 Ichthyoplankton*

**Ichthyoplankton Data.** The California Cooperative Fisheries Investigation (CALCOFI) represents a major source of information regarding ichthyoplankton. A joint activity of National Marine Fishery Service (NMFS), Southwest Fisheries Center at La Jolla, California, CDFG, and Scripps Institute of Oceanography, it was established to investigate the demise of the California sardine fishery in the late 1940s and early 1950s. Since 1951, CALCOFI has conducted surveys of the ocean adjacent to California and Baja California. These studies use counts of fish eggs and larvae (ichthyoplankton) in conjunction with physical measures, such as water temperatures and salinity, to understand the population dynamics of the Pacific ocean. The eggs and larvae allow researchers to identify spawning areas, as well as to make estimates of spawning biomass.[32]

The CALCOFI ichthyoplankton data set summarizes the numbers of fish larvae and eggs collected by species or larger grouping. The fish larvae are collected by research vessels trolling with special fine mesh nets using a standardized set of locations (stations) organized in lines extending for several hundred miles out from the coast. Research vessels on such cruises follow these lines, sampling at each station on that line. Collection cruises were made every year from 1951 until 1969, and every third year thereafter. Larvae counts by species group, station, and year are available up to 1984 for all species except the northern anchovy, which is available through 1990.

**Pacific and Jack Mackerel.** Increasing stocks of the Pacific mackerel in the late 1970s are implicated in an increase in anchovy natural mortality and the consequent reduction in anchovy biomass (Methot 1982). The northern anchovy fishery management plan estimates that the 1981 Pacific mackerel biomass (166,000 tons) might annually consume 450,000 tons of northern anchovy (Pacific Fishery Management Council, and National Marine Fisheries Service 1983). Peak northern anchovy biomass was on the order of two million tons.[33]

---

[32]Fish larvae are hatchlings that have not reached the juvenile stage. A juvenile exhibits all the characteristics of the adult fish, for example, the placement and number of fins or the placement of the eyes.

[33]The following analysis, which explicitly discusses Pacific mackerel, can be applied to jack mackerel since it is well established that jack and Pacific mackerel school together (Parrish and MacCall [1978]).

Because of its dependence on the anchovy, the adult Pacific mackerel stock depends on the recent history of northern anchovy stocks. Catch, however, depends both on the size of the stock and on its availability to fishermen; that is, its degree of concentration.

**Northern Anchovy.** The levels of northern anchovy ichthyoplankton have been used by marine biologists to estimate the stock of spawning northern anchovies. However, there are several potential problems with using the level of northern anchovy ichthyoplankton to estimate the stock of northern anchovies in a particular block. First, anchovies change their schooling behavior after they spawn, and catch occurs in those blocks in which schools of anchovies are found. Second, one of the major food sources for anchovies is their own ichthyoplankton. Therefore, there is not necessarily a direct relationship between the amount of northern anchovy ichthyoplankton and the amount of northern anchovy stock (Loukashian 1970, Hunter and Kimbrell 1980, and MacCall 1980). However, to the extent that the spawning stock in a particular ocean block is correlated with the stock available for harvest in a particular ocean block, the current year's level of northern anchovy ichthyoplankton should be related to the current year's anchovy catch in a particular ocean block.

In addition, the stock of northern anchovies is also related to the concentrations of total ichthyoplankton.[34] Therefore, anchovy catch in particular blocks should also be related to the density of total ichthyoplankton within a block.

### *6.6.3 Incremental Costs Associated With Distance Traveled*

In order to estimate the cost of going an additional mile from port, I use estimates of the cost which vary with distance. In studying the Southern California wetfish fleet, researchers have used 1990 business records to obtain costs that vary with time at sea (Jacobson and Thomson 1991). These costs include fuel cost, ship-to-shore telephone costs, and an opportunity cost of labor. The researchers obtained an average fuel consumption of 37.8 gallons per hour from interviews with fishermen. Ship-to-shore telephone expenses averaged approximately $6.80 per hour (Jacobson and Thomson 1991).

I assume that fishing vessels going to fishing areas and returning to port (with a hold full of fish) travel an average of eight nautical miles per hour.[35] I use the average of outbound and inbound speeds, six nautical miles per hour (9.2 miles per hour) as the overall speed of the purse seiners. This results in consumption of 4.11 gallons of fuel per mile. Given $0.90 per gallon for marine diesel fuel, the one way cost is $3.70 per mile, or $7.40 per mile for both ways.[36]

[34] Anchovies feed on all types of zooplankton of which fish larvae (ichthyoplankton) are one component.

[35] Conversation with an employee at Mike's Main Channel Marine, Long Beach, California, 1993.

[36] Note that all distance measurements are made one way in this study so that it is necessary to double the costs to reflect the round trip. The 1990 nationwide average retail price for

At $6.80 per hour ship-to-shore telephone service is $0.74 per mile one way, or $1.48 per mile both ways.

Purse seine crew members work, as do most fishermen, on a share basis. Jacobson and Thomson (1991) estimate an opportunity cost for traditional crewmen of between $6.06 per hour to $14.33 per hour. They also note that average gross earnings for a crew member were $17,000 in 1990, or $8.50 per hour for a two thousand-hour work year. In this study I assume $10 per hour as a crew member's wage. Using the estimate of 8.9 crewmen per vessel, I obtain a labor cost of $9.67 per mile one way, or $19.35 per mile both ways. The total of fuel cost, ship-to-shore telephone costs and the labor cost proxy is $28.22 per mile both ways. I round this to $30 per mile. Thus, I assume the incremental cost associated with fishing an added mile from port is $30.

### *6.6.4 Commercial Fishing Data Sources*

**Regulation of Commercial Fishing.** Government agencies compile most of the available fishery and oceanographic data. Historically state agencies have collected the bulk of fishery statistics. Early fisheries were local, and therefore it was left to the states to manage and regulate them.

The "Wholesale Dealer's License Act" incorporated into the California Fish and Game Laws of 1911 required the licensing of fish dealers. Legislation passed in 1915 additionally required dealers and processors to record monthly purchases by species. Further legislation passed in 1917 required the recording of every transaction between dealer, or processor, and fishermen. In 1933 the various fish and game laws were revised and consolidated into the Fish and Game Code.

Over the years reporting requirements were expanded. In 1933 the origin block system was adopted, dividing California waters into ten mile square blocks to cover catch, and out of state waters into much larger blocks to cover landings not reflecting catch. The Fish and Game Code requires commercial fishermen to assign catch by species to one of these blocks.

The California Department of Fish and Game was formed in 1940. The CDFG regulates sport species and certain commercial species and administers and enforces the Fish and Game Code. Regulations include closed seasons, area closures, equipment regulations, size limits, entry restrictions, incidental catch restrictions, restrictions on the ultimate use of catch, and recreational daily catch or bag limits. Such regulations are published annually in the *Digest of California Commercial Fish Laws* and *California Sport Fishing Regulations.*

The California Department of Fish and Game collects data on catch (pounds of fish caught in California waters) and landings (pounds of fish landed at California ports) for licensed fishing boats. These records are an outgrowth

---

#2 diesel fuel ranged from fifty-four cents per gallon in June to $1.01 per gallon in October (Price, Retail, Refinery and Gas Plant Sales. DOE/EIA Petroleum Marketing Monthly). Ninety cents per gallon was quoted as the current price, inclusive of taxes, and was taken as roughly consistent with 1990 prices.

of the development of fisheries regulation in the state of California (California Department of Fish and Game, Bureau of Marine Fisheries 1952).

The Magnuson Fishery Conservation and Management Act of 1976 (Public Law 94-265) sets up a fishery conservation zone extending from the three mile limit out to the two hundred mile limit. Regional councils (for the Pacific Coast, the Pacific Fishery Management Council) are required to develop fishery management plans which outline the setting of quotas and other regulations. The state of California, however, retains the regulation of most coastal pelagic fish. Coastal pelagic fish are schooling fish found relatively close to land. These include Pacific mackerel, jack mackerel, northern anchovy, Pacific sardine, bonito, and market squid.

**Data Sets.** The economic side of commercial fisheries involves landed prices for fish, fishermen's costs, vessel and processing capacities, and actual fishing effort. Landed fish prices are available for California by region, species, and year. Information on cost, capacity, and effort, where they exist, are limited in scope or not published.

### Annual 1AA Fish Catch Report

This report provides monthly commercial catch by species (both fin and shellfish) and block. Approximately three hundred blocks partition the ocean off Southern California. Barely legible microfiche reports exist for the period from 1953 to 1968. From 1969 to 1988 reproduction is good and organization is consistent. After 1985, however, reporting standards were relaxed with much of the catch being assigned to one of five regions rather than to blocks.[37]

### Department of Fish and Game *Fish Bulletin*: The Marine Fish Catch of California/California Marine Fish Landings from 1977 to 1986

The *Fish Bulletin* provides data on the weight and value of fish landed[38] annually for six port districts: Eureka, San Francisco, Monterey, Santa Barbara, Los Angeles, and San Diego.[39] Landings include fish caught outside state waters. One table separates in-state from out-of-state landings, but only for the overall state totals. The species reported include both fin and shellfish. Reports are available from the 1930s through 1986.

Additionally, this source gives the number of fishing vessels registered and fishermen licensed in California. For the period before 1977 the publication provides tabulations of fishing boats by length and class, and classifies licensed fishermen by area of residence: Eureka, San Francisco, Monterey, Santa Bar-

[37]The five regions are Morro Bay, Santa Barbara, Los Angeles, Orange County, and San Diego.

[38]These reports also include shipments into the state.

[39]Before 1977 catch is also recorded by month for each district, and by port (roughly thirty in number) for each year.

bara, Los Angeles, San Diego, Sacramento, and out of state. Out-of-state fishermen make up roughly 5 to 7 percent of the total. Neither boat-by-size, nor fishermen-by-residence tables have been prepared since the 1976 report.

### Pacific Coast Fisheries Information Network

This provides monthly landings for federally regulated species along with some rudimentary effort in summarizing and tabulating regulatory and financial variables. This data set covers the period 1981 to 1990.

### Commercial Fishing Vessel Logs

CDFG collects catch data for all licensed commercial fishing boats and recreational party boats. Operators of both kinds of fishing vessels must file a report for each trip. Commercial fishing boat operators report pounds of fish by species and by location of catch. These logs provide the information compiled in the department's reports and publications. Logs of the Southern California wetfish fleet are available at the CDFG's offices.

### Ichthyoplankton Station Data for California Cooperative Oceanic Fisheries Investigations Survey Cruises

The CALCOFI ichthyoplankton data set is discussed in appendix 6.2 above.

### West Coast Fishing Fleet Cost-Earnings Data Base

This database contains cost information on three commercial fishing fleets: the West Coast groundfish/shrimp trawl fleet, the Southern California swordfish/shark drift gillnet fleet, and the U.S. tropical tuna purse seine fleet. Cost data come from tax forms, available for the years vessel owners participated in certain federal programs. The information includes annual cost and returns for individual vessels for some years in the period 1981 to 1985 (Herrick, Lee, and Squires 1988).

### Nautical Charts and the Coast Pilot

The charts listed in the bibliography have been extensively used in conjunction with the Coast Pilot to measure distances (National Ocean Service [NOS]).

# 7 THE DEMAND FOR CAMERAS BY CONSUMERS—A MODEL OF PURCHASE, TYPE CHOICE, AND BRAND CHOICE

## 7.1 Introduction

In 1948, Dr. Edwin Land and the Polaroid Corporation introduced its first instant camera and film. The technology involved a photograph which required that the consumer manually remove a protective peel-away layer. Consumers were also involved in the somewhat messy process of "stopping" the development and applying a protective gel. By the 1960s Polaroid had introduced an enormously successful color version of its black and white technology. In 1972, Polaroid introduced a revolutionary technology with its SX-70 instant camera and film. The technology which is similar to that sold in stores today, automatically ejected a photograph which develops before one's eyes. There was no longer any need to peel off the protective layer or to intervene in the timing of the picture development. Hailed as a major technological achievement, the SX-70 sold well despite its relatively high price as compared to conventional photography.

In March 1976, the Kodak Corporation began selling its own version of an integral instant camera system. Kodak was promptly sued by Polaroid alleging the infringement of twelve Polaroid patents. By 1985 it was decided in U.S. Federal Court that Kodak had infringed seven valid patents held by Polaroid. Kodak was issued an injunction to cease the sale of instant cameras and was forced to recall its cameras from the market. Having found Kodak liable for patent infringement, Polaroid proceeded with the damage portion of its case asking for approximately twelve billion dollars. Actual damages were estimated to be one-third of this figure as Polaroid had requested treble damages due to Kodak's willful infringements. Of the four billion dollars (pre-trebling) roughly half was for pre-judgment interest. Of the two billion in actual damages approximately half again was for the lost profits from the sale of cameras and half for the sale of film.[1]

If Polaroid had been the sole seller of instant cameras and film from 1976 to 1985, Kodak would obviously not have sold the instant cameras and film it did sell in that period. It is less obvious what would have happened to Polaroid's sales of instant cameras and film if Kodak had been in the conventional camera and film business but had not entered the instant photography business. I call the hypothetical world in which Kodak did not enter instant photography the "but for" world.

In general, Kodak's actual customers in the damage period can be divided into two groups: (1) customers who did buy Kodak instant photography products and yet who, but for Kodak, would have bought Polaroid instant photography products (the sales Polaroid would have made to these customers represent "business diversion" from Polaroid by Kodak), and (2) customers who did buy Kodak instant photography products and who, in the "but for Kodak" world, would *not* have bought Polaroid instant photography products. These customers would instead have used a conventional photographic system or had fewer cameras in their household. The sales Kodak made to these customers are not business diversion but rather "market expansion" by Kodak.

Kodak instant photography customers thus consisted in part of people who would have been Polaroid instant photography customers in the "but for Kodak" world, and in part of people who would not. The total purchases of these two groups add up to Kodak's actual sales of instant photography products. Only the sales that Polaroid *would have made* to the first group represent a loss to Polaroid caused by Kodak's infringement of Polaroid's patents. My economic analysis of business diversion and market expansion is an attempt to determine the size of each of these two groups.

The purpose of this chapter is to explain the economic assumptions and logic relevant to the assessment of business diversion and market expansion and to describe in detail a nested logit model of camera purchases which reveals the structure of preference and allows us to quantify the extent of business diversion and market expansion by Kodak.

## 7.2 Heterogeneity in Households' Preferences for Systems

Analysis of the demand for different camera and film products must take "product differentiation" as its point of departure. Manufacturers of cameras and film do not all produce the same products and compete only on price. In-

[1]The Polaroid-Kodak patent infringement case has been summarized in Hammonds (1990) and Frankel (1991) and has received analytic attention in Bettis and Weeks (1987) and Mahajan, Subhash, and Buzzell (1993).

stead, they use a variety of technical and product design features to make their products different. They use advertising and other marketing strategies to communicate these differences to consumers.[2] Cameras and film are typically grouped into market "segments" such as 35mm, disc, instant, etc., on technical grounds.[3] However, even products within a given segment can vary considerably in their features, and in the way consumers perceive those features. Brand names may also be valuable to sellers in product-differentiated markets, such as those for cameras and film. Consumers base their choices of particular cameras and film in part on their perception of the manufacturer's brand. This is the phenomenon known as "brand loyalty."

Households vary in their circumstances, in their needs and desires for taking pictures, and in their perceptions of different photography products and brands. This heterogeneity influences the actual choices that consumers make regarding instant and conventional photography. For example, different households' circumstances may provide more or fewer picture taking situations in which instant photography is the preferred alternative. Different households may value the instant arrival of the image differently. Also, different households may have different perceptions of the Kodak and Polaroid brand names and of instant and conventional photography.[4]

In the real world, households are heterogeneous in their circumstances, needs, and perceptions. This heterogeneity means that different households make different choices. During the damage period, for example, some chose Polaroid instant, others chose Kodak instant, and others chose conventional photography, while some chose not to own a camera. Before and after the damage period, some households selected a (Polaroid) instant, others a conventional camera, and others none at all; none chose Kodak instant, because it was not available.

Now consider the hypothetical world. What would the group of households that actually chose Kodak instant have done in the "but for" world? In the actual world, these households had a Kodak instant camera and film, and used them to chronicle particular life events. These were their instant picture taking situations. In the but for world, they might have responded to these situations in any of a variety of ways. Some would have acquired and used a Polaroid instant system. Others would have used conventional photography. Still others would have taken no pictures at all. The latter two groups would have had no need for a Polaroid instant photography system.

---

[2]For the purposes of an analysis of market expansion and business diversion, it is not important whether camera and film product differentiation involves genuine differences among products or not. What is important is that consumers' make choices as if the products are different.

[3]A more recent classification would be different and would presumably include digital and disposable camera types.

[4]These perceptions have their origins in a variety of sources including advertising, the past experience of the household with particular brands or types of cameras, and so on. It is the effects of these perceptions, not their origins, which are relevant here.

The relative frequency with which households would have made these different choices is determined by the distribution of perceived photography needs and characteristics of the population of households. Some households had a strong preference for instant photography per se. If they did not have the opportunity to select a Kodak instant camera, they would have chosen Polaroid. Other households had a strong preference for the Kodak brand name. In the but for world, they would have responded to conventional camera and film brand names, as well as to the prices, features, and advertisement of conventional photography options.

Since different households made different choices in the real world, this heterogeneity of tastes and perceptions is fundamental to understanding photography demand. The analysis of market expansion as opposed to business diversion uncovers the nature of this heterogeneity. In particular, the goal of my analysis is to learn about the relative frequency of households of different types (different tastes and perceptions). Since I cannot observe tastes and perceptions, directly I instead measure differences in behavior attributable to things I can observe. The things I can observe are indicators of household differences in tastes and perceptions.

The point of the empirical analysis presented below is to uncover the structure of the heterogeneity underlying household behavior by observing households choices in the real world.

## 7.3 Data

The basic data for the analysis presented in this chapter come from micro-level, that is, consumer-level surveys. These surveys were conducted by National Family Opinion, Inc., (NFO) contemporaneously with the damage period and were purchased by Kodak as part of its marketing research.

### *7.3.1 The NFO Database*

NFO provides households with packets of response cards ("multicards") asking for specific information on their purchase and use of a large variety of products, as well as for information about the characteristics of the household itself. Among the products surveyed in this manner are cameras and film products. For camera products, information is gathered annually, shortly after the new year, on the existing stock of cameras in use by the household and on camera purchases in the year immediately prior to the survey.

The sampling objective pursued by NFO is to assemble a set of households that will be representative of the American population. A comparison of the NFO multicard to other public data sources is presented in table 7.1. The particular survey method employed makes it difficult to achieve this goal precisely. Because the compensation provided to households is in kind rather than cash and is modest, the most affluent households are underrepresented in the survey. Similarly, the survey underrepresents racial minorities, single-member households, younger households, and households living in apartments.[5]

An analysis of these data must account for the sample limitations. In practice, there are two areas that deserve attention. First, the underrepresentation of black households is so severe as to prevent any separate treatment of their camera and film demand behavior. There is, however, no basis for the belief that black households' demand behavior is very different from that of white households. Second, there is the issue raised by the fact that NFO households are more likely to be retired, to live in houses, and to own their own housing unit than is the population at large. These differences do not affect the utility of the NFO dataset for analysis. To the extent that these variables are important predictors of camera and film demand behavior, the differences need to be taken into account in extrapolating from the behavior of the NFO households to the behavior of the population at large. In the analyses reported below, I reweight all of the NFO results to make them comparable to the entire population of the United States. Generally, the reweighting has little impact on the results. This confirms the representativeness of the NFO data sets.

**Table 7.1.** 1983 NFO Multicard Compared to Public-Source Data[1]

| | NFO Multicard | CPS[2] | CHS[3] | CPR[4] | E&E[5] |
|---|---|---|---|---|---|
| One Person Household | 23.8% | 23.8% | | | |
| Married | 62.7% | 60.3% | | | |
| Live in house | 74.6% | | 67.1% | | |
| Own home | 74.4% | | 64.4% | | |
| White | 96.0% | | | 84.7% | |
| He works | 73.9% | | | | 68.8% |
| She works | 50.2% | | | | 48.0% |

[1] All figures taken from the 1987 *Statistical Abstract of the United States.*
[2] Current Population Survey.
[3] Current Housing Survey.
[4] Current Population Reports.
[5] Employment and Earnings.

[5]Kodak marketing personnel regarded these representation problems as modest limitations on the value of the survey for understanding consumer behavior. They regularly relied on and renewed the contract for NFO services over the years to provide information for Kodak's marketing efforts. The cost to Kodak of this information was in excess of two million dollars annually, a significant investment for marketing information.

### *7.3.2 Matching of Households Across Time and the Construction of Panel Data Sets*

Table 7.2 provides information on the total number of households and the number of households that had identical household identification numbers for various years. Analysis of the household survey data indicates that the identification numbers were unique. Households from different years' data sets with the same identifiers are therefore "matched households." Concern about the possibility of eventual reuse of individual identifiers after several years and the small number of such matches made it desirable to confine analysis to "year-to-year" or "year-to-year-after-next" pairs. A number of such matches are developed for the purpose of analysis. They include adjacent year matches on 1982–83, 1983–84, 1984–85, 1985–86, and 1986–87.

**Table 7.2.** Numbers and Match Rates of Households in NFO Database

| |
|---|
| Households appearing in only a single year are the most frequent case. Of 143,792 household observations, 105,519 or 73.4 percent appear only once (17,964 in 1982, 19,356 in 1983, 16,131 in 1984, 16,354 in 1985, 15,964 in 1986, and 19,750 in 1987). |
| Households appearing in two adjacent years are the next most frequent case. Of 143,792 household observations, 18,387 or 12.8 percent appear in two adjacent years (5,838 in 1982–83, 106 in 1983–84, 5,008 in 1984–85, 3,312 in 1985–86, and 4,123 in 1986–87). |
| Households appearing in both 1985 and 1987 number 3774, or 2.6 percent. |

Matching years creates almost double the number of variables that can be observed on a household. The individual identifier, of course, remaines the same. Other variables are year specific and are available for the purpose of checking the consistency of the match. The ability to observe the changing stock of cameras in use from year to year is one of the many observational possibilities allowed by this matching procedure.

### *7.3.3 Derivation of Additional Variables*

I also construct variables reflecting each household's acquisition and use of cameras in each year the household is present in a panel data set. The NFO multicard survey records the year of acquisition of cameras that are in use and which were acquired in years prior to the date of the survey, and the month of acquisition of cameras acquired in the year of the survey. In addition, information is available on the type (i.e., types include instant and 35mm SLR for example) and brand of camera. Variables are constructed that tabulate the cameras of a given type in the household. Other variables are constructed that reflected the types of cameras acquired. In the case of Kodak and Polaroid instant cameras, this procedure was extended to tabulate the number of Kodak instant and the number of Polaroid instant cameras in a household.

Some of the information from the NFO surveys is used to create new variables for the statistical analysis. For example, I create a variable to indicate the presence of a male or female head of household, equal to one if the male or female head-of-household's year of birth was reported in the survey.

For each of the matched households, there is information on the characteristics of household members. First, one can check whether a female or male head of household (or both) is present. In this sample, 89 percent of the households surveyed have a female head of household, while roughly 73 percent have a male head of household. The average age of the female head is about 50.5 years and the average age of the male head is about 50.7 years.

In addition to the information on individuals in the household, the survey also reports the household's income (in thousands of dollars) and size (in numbers of members, either one through seven, or eight and above). The mean income of surveyed households in 1985 (in 1985 dollars) was $27,500 and the mean size of a household was 2.5 individuals, including the head(s).

### *7.3.4 Categorical Variables*

Also provided in the survey are both the female and male head of household's education and employment status. Education levels fit into one of seven categories. Possible educations levels are elementary: zero to seven years, elementary: eight years (graduate), high school: one to three years, high school: four years (graduate), college: one to three years, college: four years (college graduate), and college: post-graduate studies. Possible employment categories are full time, part time, retired, and not employed.

Home ownership status, marital status, type of residence, and location by state were collected in the survey as well. Ownership status can have four values: own, rent, live with relatives, and other. Marital status categories are married, never married (female), divorced (female), widowed (female), separated (female), never married (male), divorced (male), widowed (male), and separated (male). Type of residence refers to the type of dwelling occupied by the respondents, whether house, apartment, mobile home, condominium, duplex, or other.

The survey indicates that 62 percent of the heads of household surveyed were married and that the majority of the respondents, 73 percent, occupied a house.

### *7.3.5 Camera Use Variables*

The NFO survey provides information on the use of seven cameras by household. For each household, for each year, and for up to seven cameras, the survey reports: the type of camera, the brand or "make" of the camera, the age of the camera, the month of acquisition, and the year of acquisition. Camera types are roll, cartridge, disc, 35mm, instant, video, movie, and other. Another variable gives even more detailed information on the cameras. This variable takes on the following values: 110, 126, disc, SLR, non-SLR, wet, dry-rigid, dry-folding, and miscellaneous.

There are fifty-four different makes of camera in the data. For analysis, I have aggregated these brands into three categories: Kodak, Polaroid, and all other firms. I have also changed the camera type variable for purposes of analysis. In addition to the eight categories mentioned above, I created a 35mm SLR and a 35mm non-SLR camera type.

The NFO data record, for each household, whether a camera was acquired during the survey year and, if so, what type of camera. The data also indicate what cameras are held by each household in each year. The holdings variables can take on a value anywhere from zero, if the household surveyed did not own a particular camera type, up to the number of cameras of each type held. The maximum number of Kodak Disc cameras held by a household in 1985, for example, was six. The maximum number of Polaroid Instants held was three.

## 7.4 The Nested Logit Model of Camera Acquisition

Forecasting the market shares of alternative camera brands and types is complicated by the great variety of cameras offered to consumers. My analysis focuses on the decision to buy cameras, the decision to buy cameras of a given brand (e.g., Kodak or Polaroid for instant camera types), and the type of cameras to buy (e.g., 35mm or disc technology). These decisions are essentially discrete in nature, that is, the dependent variable may take on only a limited number of values. Other examples of discrete outcomes are whether an individual will vote yes or no in an election, whether or not to use public transportation, whether a given dosage of a drug causes mortality in a laboratory animal, and whether or not to replace an automobile in a given period. As standard multivariate regression analysis presumes a continuous dependent variable, the qualitative nature of discrete outcomes leads to special estimation issues.

If the dependent variable for the outcomes in these examples is coded as a dummy variable with zero representing the answer 'No' and one representing the answer 'Yes,' then a regression of these variables on explanatory variables will lead to predictions that mainly fall in the zero-one interval. The interpretation of the predicted values in these cases is that of a probability. Indeed, the mathematical expectation of the dummy dependent variable is the probability that the event occurs and the regression provides a basis to estimate this expectation.

Formally, I represent individual $i$'s response by an indicator variable, $y_i$, which I code as one for 'Yes' and zero for 'No'. The probability that a 'Yes' occurs is defined by:

$$\text{Prob}[y_i = 1] = \phi_i. \tag{1}$$

The statistical problem is to assess the dependence of $\phi_i$ on explanatory variables representing characteristics of the choice process. An obvious possibility is to apply the method of ordinary least squares, which assumes that the expectation of $y_i$ is a linear function of the explanatory variables:

$$\phi_i = E[y_i] = \sum_{s=1}^{K} x_{is}\beta_s = x_i\beta \tag{2}$$

where $x_{is}$ is the $i^{th}$ observation on explanatory variable $s$ and $\beta_s$ is the unobserved weight attached to this variable. In matrix notation $x_i = (x_{is})$ and $\beta = (\beta_1, \beta_2, \ldots, \beta_K)'$.

The method of least squares estimates the expectation in equation (2) with the regression:

$$y_i = x_i\beta + \epsilon_i \tag{3}$$

where $\epsilon_i$ is a disturbance representing characteristics which are not observable or are idiosyncratic to the decision maker.

Two problems arise in the application of least squares to equation (3). First, the variance of $y_i$ equals $\phi_i(1 - \phi_i)$ as $y_i^2 = y_i$. The regression in equation (3) therefore violates a basic assumption of the Gauss-Markov theorem—the disturbances $\epsilon_i$ should have constant variance if least squares is to be the best linear unbiased estimator. While this is not in itself a serious drawback (a correction may be made in equation (3) to improve efficiency), a more fundamental difficulty arises from the condition that $\phi_i$ is a probability, that is, $0 \leq \phi_i \leq 1$. Second, least squares estimates of $\beta$ can lead to predicted values of $\phi_i$ which fall outside the unit interval. Again this problem is easy to circumvent. The predicted values that lie outside the unit interval are simply recoded to the closest boundary value. This procedure, in conjunction with equation (3), is known as the 'linear probability model'.

A related issue (and one that applies to the linear probability model) is that the estimated parameters of the model in equation (3) have a limited range of validity; in particular the linear approximation does not behave well in the tails of the probability distribution.

Rather than employ a model with recognized limitations, I instead choose a functional form for $\phi_i$ which embodies the restriction $0 \leq \phi_i \leq 1$.

The binary logit model, for example, assumes that a logistic transformation of the probability, $\phi_i$, (i.e., the log-odds) is itself linear in parameters:

$$\log\left(\frac{\phi_i}{1 - \phi_i}\right) = x_i\beta. \tag{4}$$

In this case, the probability $\phi_i$ satisfies:

$$\phi_i = \text{Prob}[\text{y}_\text{i} = 1] = \exp(\text{x}_\text{i}\beta)/\left(1 + \exp(\text{x}_\text{i}\beta)\right). \tag{5}$$

One could estimate equation (5) using least squares techniques after a suitable adjustment for the non-constant variance of the disturbance. A more efficient estimation method is provided by the maximum likelihood method. The likelihood function for a sample of $N$ independent observations is:

$$L = \prod_{i=1}^{N} \phi_i^{y_i}(1-\phi_i)^{(1-y_i)} \tag{6}$$

$$= \prod_{i=1}^{N} \frac{\exp(\mathrm{y_i x_i}\beta)}{(1+\exp(\mathrm{x_i}\beta))}. \tag{7}$$

Estimation of the unknown parameters can then be accomplished by an iterative search technique such as Gauss-Newton.

Scaling methods other than logit exist which transform the unit probability interval to a continuous range. A common alternative employs the inverse cumulative normal distribution and leads to the probit model. The logistic transformation has had wide spread application in a variety of empirical applications because of its excellent numerical properties and the ease by which the method generalizes from binary to multiple outcomes. For models in which the choice set is large, multinomial logit (the generalization of binary logit to multiple alternatives) provides the only practical estimation method; alternatives such as multinomial probit require the evaluation of high-dimensional indefinite integrals which is difficult computationally.

Techniques such as multinomial logit, commonly applied in both marketing and economics, are not however appropriate in applications where the perceived similarities of alternatives have a significant influence on market shares. However, to present the econometric procedure employed below, we first discuss the multinomial logit model and demonstrate its limitations for the present study.[6]

The rest of this subsection contains a concise explanation of the multinomial logit model and of the nested multinomial logit model. The nested multinomial logit model has been used to measure consumer choice behavior in the U.S. camera market. Section 7.5 discusses the results obtained using this model.

The multinomial logit model expresses the probability that alternative $i$ is chosen as

$$P_i = e^{V_i} / \sum_{j=1}^{N} e^{V_j} \tag{8}$$

where alternatives are indexed $j = 1, 2, \cdots N$. $V_i$ is termed the strict-utility alternative of $i$ and is a measure of the desirability of the alternative. In

[6] Introductory surveys on the theory and application of discrete choice models are given in McFadden (1976) and Amemiya (1981). More rigorous treatments are given in McFadden (1981, 1982).

common application, $V_i$ is assumed to be linear-in-parameters with

$$V_i = \sum_{l=1}^{L} \beta_l x_{li} = \beta' x_i, \tag{9}$$

where the last term is simply a vector representation of the second. The observed covariates $x_{li}$ include both attributes of the alternatives and characteristics of the decision maker. The unobserved parameters $\beta_l$ are the weights assigned to these covariates by the decision maker.

The multinomial logit model is particularly attractive for application in choice modeling contexts, given that it can be derived from a basic theory of economics known as random utility maximization. The random utility model assumes that individuals, in making choices, maximize their preferences. The pattern of observed market shares is reflective of heterogeneity in both households and the alternatives they select among.

Suppose the utility derived from alternative $i$ by a given individual or household is separated into systematic and random components with $u_i = V_i + \epsilon_i$ where $V_i$ is the strict utility of the alternative and $\epsilon_i$ is an unobserved factor (unobserved at least from the point of view of the econometrician) which is idiosyncratic to the decision maker. McFadden (1973) has shown that if the $\epsilon_i$ have independent extreme-value distributions $\text{Prob}(\epsilon_i \leq \epsilon) = \exp\,(-e^{-\epsilon})$ then the probability that alternative $i$ will be selected is:

$$\begin{aligned} P_i &= \text{Prob}[u_i \geq u_j, \forall j \neq i] \\ &= \text{Prob}[\epsilon_j - \epsilon_i \leq V_i - V_j, \forall j \neq i] \\ &= e^{V_i} / \textstyle\sum_{j=1}^{N} e^{V_j} \end{aligned}$$

i.e., the multinomial logit model of equation (8).

From the point of view of thc dccision maker the choice of the best alternative (the alternative that maximizes his or her preference) is a deterministic problem. From the point of view of the econometrician, the selection or choice is random with outcomes that obey a simple probabilistic rule. Correlating the observations of choices with the attributes of the decision maker, as well as the attributes of the choice set, permits estimation of the unobserved parameters $\beta_l$. The technique by which this estimation is performed is known as maximum likelihood estimation. The maximum likelihood method attempts to match the probability that an outcome is selected by a decision maker with the actual choice made. The procedure does, however, allow for discrepancies and permits otherwise identical households (identical in observable characteristics and choice possibilities, but not necessarily tastes) to make different selections.

It follows from equation (8) that the log-odds of choice $i$ to choice $j$ depends only on the attributes of these two alternatives:

$$\log(P_i/P_j) = V_i - V_j. \tag{10}$$

This is the *independence from irrelevant alternatives* (IIA) property of the multinomial logit model. An implication of the IIA property is that all cross-elasticities are equal:[7]

$$\epsilon(P_i, x_{lj}) = \frac{\partial \log P_i}{\partial \log x_{lj}} = -\beta_l x_{lj} P_j. \tag{11}$$

In the present circumstance, this implies that any change in observable factors that makes one alternative less attractive will make all other alternatives more attractive by exactly the same degree. This assumption is not likely to hold when the set of alternatives is sufficiently heterogeneous that choices are made hierarchically, or when there is a natural structure of similarity among subsets of choices. In the marketing context, Punj and Staelin (1978) and Silk and Urban (1978) have recognized the inherent limitations of using the multinomial logit model for forecasting market share.

To relax the IIA assumption, my empirical analysis uses a family of nested logit models developed by McFadden (1978). The nested logit specification was selected based on its simplicity in estimation and its consistency with the theory of random utility maximization.

I first illustrate the derivation of a two-level nested logit model where a decision is made to enter the camera market and then a type of camera is selected. Let $Y_{mt}$ denote a positive measure of the desirability of alternatives indexed by $mt$, where $m$ denotes the decision to enter the camera market and $t$ indicates the type of camera purchased (if any). McFadden (1978, 1981) has shown that a class of generating functions $G(\langle Z_j \rangle) = G(Z_1, Z_2, \cdots, Z_N)$ exist for which the probability of choosing alternative $k, P_k$, is $\partial\ lnG/\partial\ lnZ_k$.[8] To construct a two-level nested logit model I compose the generating functions at each level. Specifically, let

$$G^{t|m}(\langle Y_t \rangle) = (\sum_t Y_t^{\frac{1}{1-\sigma}})^{1-\sigma} \tag{12}$$

$$\text{and} \quad G^{m}(\langle Y_m \rangle) = (\sum_m Y_m) \tag{13}$$

be generating functions for the camera type choice and for the market purchase decision respectively.

The generating functions in equations (12) and (13) are in logistic form so that the conditional probability of choosing $t$ given $m$, $P_{t|m}$ and the unconditional probabilities of purchasing some camera $P_m$ are each in the form of

---

[7] In general, $\epsilon(P_i, x_{lj}) = \beta_l x_{lj}(1 - P_j)$ if $i = j$ and $\epsilon(P_i, x_{lj}) = -\beta_l x_{lj} P_j$ otherwise.

[8] A nested logit generating function $G[\langle Z_j \rangle]$ is a positive homogeneous of degree one function whose mixed partial derivatives alternate in sign as their order increases, $\partial G/\partial Z_j \rangle 0$, and $\lim_{Z_j \to \infty} G[\langle Z_j \rangle] = +\infty$. The best known examples of these functions are $G[\langle Z_j \rangle] = \sum_j Z_j$ and $G[\langle Z_j \rangle] = (\sum_j Z_j^{1/\theta})^{\theta}$.

multinomial logit models. The unobserved scale parameter $\sigma$ measures the degree to which alternatives within the choice set are similar to one another as I show below. A generating function for the two-level model is

$$\begin{aligned} G[\langle Y_{mt}\rangle] &= G^m\left[\langle G^{t|m}[\langle Y_{mt}\rangle]\rangle\right] \\ &= \sum_m(\sum_t Y_{mt}^{\frac{1}{1-\sigma}})^{1-\sigma}. \end{aligned} \tag{14}$$

The probability of choosing combination $(mt)$, $P_{mt}$, is then:

$$\begin{aligned} P_{mt} &= \partial\, lnG/\partial\, lnY_{mt} \\ &= (\partial\, lnG^m/\partial\, lnG^{t|m})\cdot(\partial\, lnG^{t|m}/\partial\, lnY_{mt}) \\ &= P_m \cdot P_{t|m}. \end{aligned} \tag{15}$$

In other words, the generating function for the composition implies a node probability that may be separated into the product of the probabilities at each level of the tree.

McFadden (1981) demonstrates that the probabilistic choice model in equation (15) is consistent with a random utility theory of preference maximization. Specifically, the decision maker may be viewed as choosing the alternative $(mt)$ with largest utility $u_{mt} = V_{mt}+\epsilon_{mt}$ where $V_{mt} = lnY_{mt}$ and $\langle\epsilon_{mt}\rangle$ has a generalized extreme value distribution. If I adopt a linear-in-parameters representation of strict utility $V_{mt}$ with

$$V_{mt} = \sum_{k=1}^{K}\beta_k x_{kmt} + \sum_{l=1}^{L}\alpha_l y_{lm} = \beta' x_{mt} + \alpha' y_m \tag{16}$$

then

$$\begin{aligned} P_{t|m} &= \frac{e^{\tilde{\beta}' x_{mt}}}{\sum_t e^{\tilde{\beta}' x_{mt}}} \\ P_m &= \frac{e^{[\alpha' y_m + J_m(1-\sigma)]}}{\sum_m e^{[\alpha' y_m + J_m(1-\sigma)]}} \end{aligned} \tag{17}$$

where $J_m = ln(\sum_t e^{\tilde{\beta}' x_{mt}})$ is the inclusive value for type of camera choice and $\tilde{\beta} = \beta/(1-\sigma)$. The quantity $(1-\sigma)$ is known as the inclusive value coefficient and will obey $0 \leq \sigma \leq 1$ if the function $F(\langle\epsilon_{mt}\rangle) = \exp\left[-G[\langle e^{-\epsilon_{mt}}\rangle]\right]$ is the cumulative distribution function for $\epsilon_{mt}$.

When $\sigma = 0$, the nested multinomial logit model for $P_{mt}$ reduces to the standard joint multinomial logit model. For $\sigma$ in the interval $(0,1)$, the nested model treats the camera type alternatives as more alike (more alike than not buying any camera). Thus, $\sigma$ maybe viewed as an indicator of the similarity of alternatives within the type-choice branch. The structural similarity of alternatives also changes the formula for the cross-elasticities:

$$\epsilon(P_{mt}, x_{kij}) = \partial \, lnP_{mt}/\partial \, lnx_{kij} \quad = \tag{18}$$

$$\begin{array}{lll} - & (1-\sigma)\tilde{\beta}_k x_{kij} P_{ij} & \text{if } i \neq m \\ - & (1-\sigma)\tilde{\beta}_k x_{kij} P_{ij} - \sigma\tilde{\beta}_k x_{kij} P_{j|i} - \tilde{\beta}_k x_{kij} & \text{if } i = m, j = t \\ - & (1-\sigma)\tilde{\beta}_k x_{kij} P_{ij} - \sigma\tilde{\beta}_k x_{kij} P_{j|i} & \text{if } i = m, j \neq t. \end{array}$$

For $\sigma$ in the unit interval, the cross-elasticity between camera types, given the decision to buy some camera, is larger in magnitude than the cross-elasticity across purchase decision nodes.

### *7.4.1 Model Specification*

Formulating a more general model of camera choice which adds the complexity of brand decisions to the types of cameras purchased (or indeed to camera models within brands) requires the econometrician to compare alternative non-nested hierarchical decision models. Figures 7.1 and 7.2 illustrate two such models of camera purchase.

Figure 7.1 illustrates a three stage choice process. In the first stage, the market decision—whether to buy a camera or not—is considered. In the second stage, the type of camera (here instant, 35mm, or other) is decided, and finally the brand of camera is selected for a given type.[9] These three stages are broadly labeled MARKET, TYPE, and BRAND. Figure 7.2 illustrates a contrasting process of camera selection. Here the BRAND decision is made before the TYPE decision, rather than the reverse. Each ordering is representative of a very different structure for the perceived similarities among alternatives.

Figure 7.1 represents a nesting in which brands of cameras are closer substitutes than types of cameras. Figure 7.2, by contrast, assumes that types of cameras within brands are closer substitutes. In this case, a decrease in the utility of Kodak instant cameras will result in an increase in the demand for other Kodak type cameras. Either structure is consistent with models of the camera choice process. My analysis assumes the structure illustrated in Figure 7.1. This choice is supported both by the empirical evidence and a review of the relevant marketing studies.

[9]For expositional purposes, I illustrate the instant camera brand choice segment in figures 7.1 and 7.2. In the post-damage period, only Polaroid instant cameras may be selected, so choosing instant photography and choosing a Polaroid instant are identical decisions. Thus in the post-damage period the instant brand choice segment would not be present. I further note that the empirical analysis examines camera model choice within brands although this is not shown in the figures.

**Figure 7.1: Camera Choice by Market, Type, and Brand**

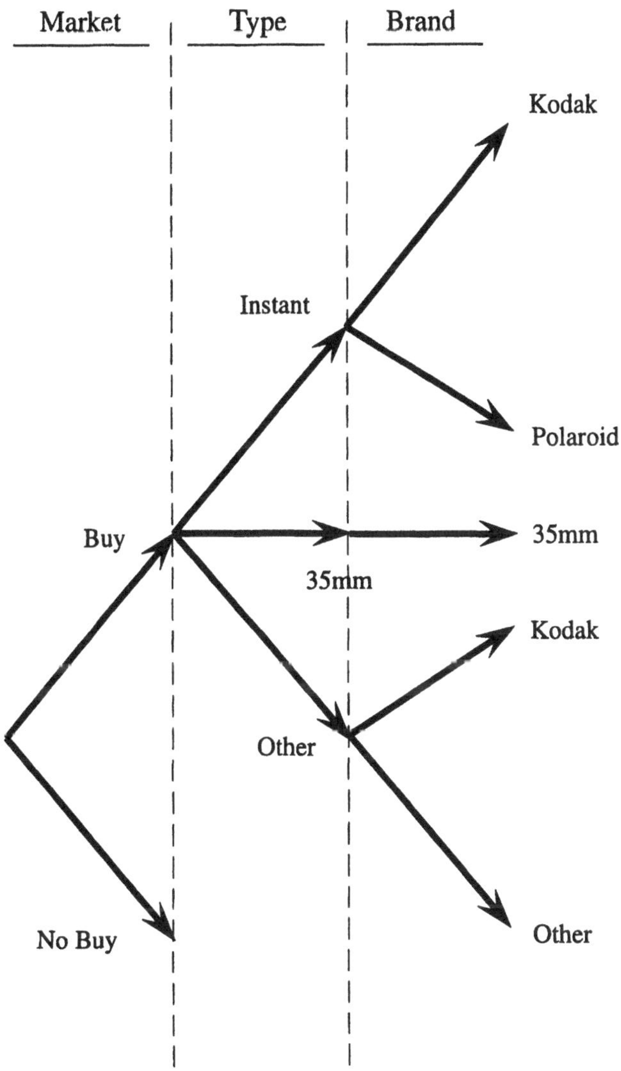

**Figure 7.2: Camera Choice by Market, Brand, and Type**

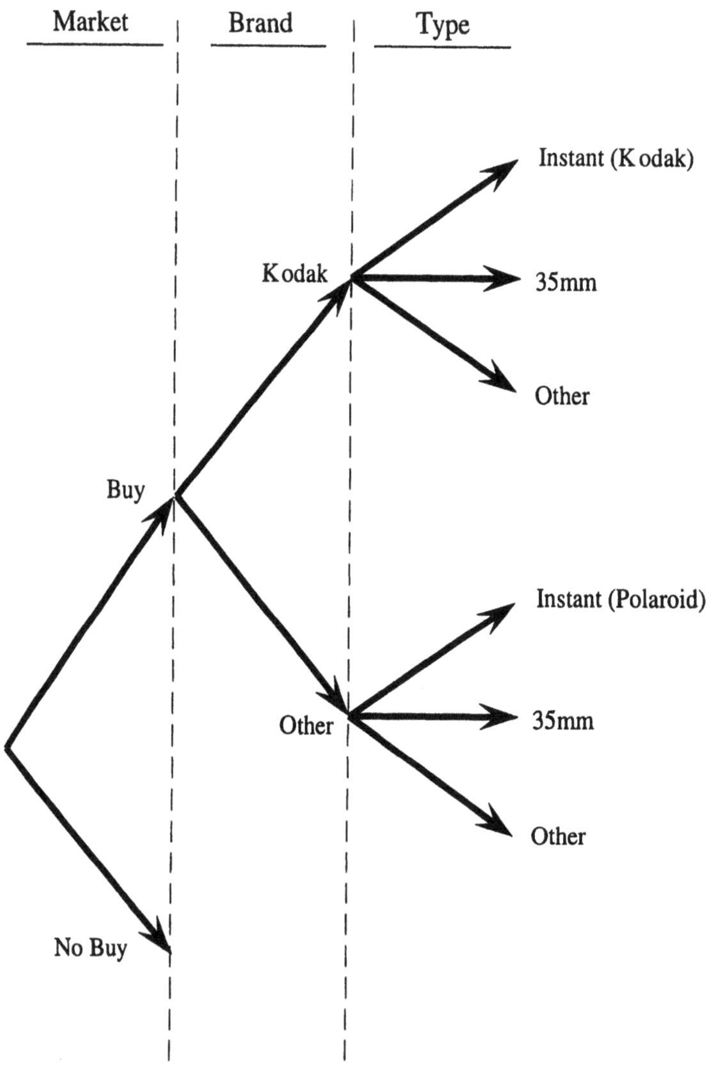

In the center of the tree illustrated in figure 7.1, the dependent variable is whether the household acquired an instant, 35mm, or other (still) camera.[10] This is the camera market segment level of the tree. The probability that the household will buy in one of the three segments is modeled as depending on demographic and economic features of the household and on the measured attractiveness of the brands within the market segment. Finally, to the leftmost part of the tree, the dependent variable is whether the household acquired any (still) camera at all.[11] At each of these levels of the tree, the basic building block of the model is a prediction about the fraction of households of any given type that make any particular choice.

The structure of the tree imposes implicit assumptions about the nature of substitution among different cameras. In particular, the tree has brand choice farther to the right than type choice. This imposes the assumption that cameras of different brands in the same market segment are closer substitutes than cameras of different types.[12] The degree of substitutability is determined by the econometric estimation. The model permits cameras that are on the same branch to be much closer substitutes than cameras on different branches, but it also permits them to be only slightly closer substitutes. Let us call the extent to which cameras in the same market segment are closer substitutes than cameras in different segments the degree of "segment-specific substitutability."

The idea that goods can be substitutes in demand, and the treatment of the degree of substitution among particular goods or groups of goods, is a familiar theme in economic analysis. "Close substitutes" in demand are goods for which, if the price of one were to rise slightly, the vast majority of consumers would switch to the other. "Poor substitutes" in demand are goods for which few customers would switch even if the price of one were to change substantially. The idea of substitution is typically thought of in terms of price, just as I have stated. One could also think of consumers' response to changes in other variables, such as the advertising, availability, quality, etc. of the goods. Large responses to small changes in these variables are associated with very close substitutes, while small changes in the response following large changes in these variables are associated with poor substitutes. The general concept, then, is

[10] I treat households that made multiple acquisitions within the year as follows. A household which acquired an instant camera is coded as "instant," even if it also acquired other types. This preserves the largest possible number of instant camera choosing households for analysis. Among those households which did not acquire an instant, all those that acquired a 35mm camera are coded as "35mm," even if they acquired another still camera. Finally, households which acquired a still camera, but not an instant or a 35mm, are coded as "other."

[11] It would be slightly more precise to say "acquired and used" throughout the text. This usage, continually repeated, will grow tedious, so I use "acquired" as a shorthand. What I observe is a year end report on cameras in use, and count as acquired any camera in use with an acquisition date in the last year.

[12] More precisely, the tree structure in figure 7.1 and in the analysis rules out the possibility that cameras of the same brand in different market segments could be closer substitutes than cameras of different brands in the same segment. It does permit, as a limiting case, the possibility that cameras of the same brand in different market segments are exactly as close substitutes as cameras of different brands in the same segment.

this: products are close or poor substitutes in demand as consumers' response to a change in the relative attractiveness of the products is large or small.

In a product differentiated industry such as photography, there is a close link between the form of consumer heterogeneity and product substitutability. By "the form of consumer heterogeneity" I mean the ways in which households tend systematically to be alike or different: Do most of the households that value Kodak instant cameras highly also like Polaroid, or do most of them value other Kodak products highly?

First, suppose that households differ only in the strength of their desire for instant photography. That is, any household which has a strong liking for Polaroid instant photography also has a strong liking for Kodak instant photography. A household which prefers some conventional alternative, say 35mm, over Kodak instant will also prefer a 35mm over Polaroid instant. Given this form of consumer heterogeneity, the two instant brands will be close substitutes in demand. Either instant alternative will be a much weaker substitute for conventional cameras. A decline in the attractiveness of Kodak instant photography (either through an increase in price or a change in another important variable) would lead to a reduction in the sales of Kodak instant, and an offsetting increase in the sales of Polaroid instant. There would be little effect on conventional camera demand. Similarly, increases in the attractiveness of any particular conventional photography alternative would draw customers from Kodak instant and Polaroid instant in proportion, rather than disproportionately from either one.

As a second hypothetical example, suppose that households differ in two ways. Some households are like those just described, and treat instant photography as a field of photography in itself; they either like or dislike the whole field, not any particular brand within it. Other households are partially motivated by brand loyalty. To keep the hypothetical example simple, suppose that some but not all households like and trust the Kodak brand name, and would be swayed to Kodak products, while other households respond far less to particular brand names. This kind of heterogeneity of household preferences leads to a somewhat different substitution pattern. If I were now to change the price or other attractiveness attributes of Kodak instant, some customers would behave as before and simply switch to Polaroid. But those customers with particularly strong Kodak brand loyalty and no great desire for instant photography per se would shift to Kodak conventional photography systems. In this example, the two brands of instant photography are less close substitutes for each other, and substitution between conventional and instant photography is more important.

Of course, the real world is more complex than either of these two simple examples, and a great many forces interact to determine the actual substitutability of different types of photography. The intuition underlying the two extreme cases is useful nonetheless. The stronger is the force of type loyalty, the more important is within type substitutability and the less important is between type substitutability. This is illustrated by the first hypothetical. The stronger is the force of brand loyalty, the weaker is within type substitutability and the stronger is between type substitutability for cameras of the same brand, as the second hypothetical indicates.

The same points can be made in the language of market definition, familiar from antitrust analysis. The assertion that all of Kodak's instant photography customers were business diversion is equivalent to the statement that the relevant market for instant photography products is extremely narrow. In fact, it means that the relevant market contains only instant photography products. If the correct market definition is broader, Kodak's introduction of a new brand of instant photography products would have diverted some sales from other (conventional) photography types as well as from Polaroid instant photography systems. A broader market definition thus implies market expansion as a result of Kodak entry.

It is unreasonable to assume a priori that the correct market definition is instant photography products. The correct market definition will be broader to the extent that competitive conditions in conventional photography affect the demand for instant products. Similarly, it is unreasonable to assume a priori that there is no substitutability between cameras of different types and brands. It is an empirical question whether Kodak instant products were substitutes only for Polaroid instant products, or whether Kodak instant products were also substitutes for the conventional cameras and film of Kodak or of other firms.

In order to assess what would have happened in the "but for Kodak" world, I estimate actual brand loyalty, type loyalty, and demand substitutability of cameras of different types and brands using the nested logit analysis. In my empirical analysis, I find that Kodak instant cameras are closer substitutes for Polaroid instant cameras than for any other cameras. Under this model the procedures are, if anything, biased toward finding larger business diversion and smaller market expansion.

## 7.5 Empirical Results

### *7.5.1 Selection of Estimation Sample*

The estimation of an econometric model of camera purchase requires observation of households over time. To gather these observations, the multicard datasets are linked together across adjacent years as discussed in section 7.3.2.

The paired years provide information about change in household composition, camera holdings, and camera purchases.[13] Each pair of years was treated in an identical fashion. The first year was termed the base year and was used to construct the demographic characteristics of the household. These include edu-

[13]I observe in the multicard data the acquisition and subsequent use of cameras. The reported cameras can be obtained either by purchase, as gifts, or as premiums; from 1985 onward the household reports whether or not the camera was a "premium" model. Cameras which the household acquires but does not use are not reported.

cation—measured as years of school attended by the head of household; retirement status—whether the head of household is retired; residence type—whether the household lives in a house; residence ownership—whether the household owns its residence; income—household income measured in thousands of dollars; and number of children—measured by the number of household residents other than the household heads.

I selected these variables for two reasons. First, a review of the marketing literature suggests their potential importance as indicators of population heterogeneity. Second, some of the variables may be significant in controlling for possible differences between the NFO sample and the population at large. For example, the fraction of households that own their residence is not identical in NFO samples and in the U.S. population. The NFO surveys, as I have used them, are formed into short panels wherein households are matched between adjacent years. This sub-sample is likely to include more stable (less mobile) households who are also more likely to own their homes. If home ownership is significant in the decision to purchase cameras (perhaps as an alternative indicator of household wealth), then omitting this explanatory variable could lead to bias in the estimation or to bias in the forecasted market shares.

### *7.5.2 Data from the NFO Multicards*

The data for the analysis is a panel dataset of households with records in two adjacent years. For example, the 1983 multicard data set was searched to find all the households with the same APPNUM as households in the 1982 multicard dataset. This led to 5,838 matches between the 1982 and 1983 datasets. The same procedure led to 106 matches between the 1983 and 1984 datasets, and 5,008 matches between the 1984 and 1985 datasets. Since the datasets from before 1982 do not survive in usable form, these are the three feasible adjacent-year matches during the damage period.

The 106 households matching from the 1983–1984 datasets were not used at all in the analysis because they were so few. For the analysis below, I merge the base years 1982 and 1984 into a single large data set. This data set has 10,846 (5,008 + 5,838) observations with nearly half the cases consisting of individuals observed in base year 1982 and then again in decision year 1983. The other cases selected for this sample are based on individuals observed in base year 1984 and again in decision year 1985. Combining the samples, however, does not amount to the assumption that 1982 and 1984 (or 1983 and 1985) are identical, since I allow for differences among years in the estimation procedure.

As discussed above, the dataset contains information about the demographic and economic features of the household, and about its camera holding and acquisition. The analysis reported in this section is of the household's decision to acquire a camera, and of the choice of camera type and brand if one is chosen.

### 7.5.3 Specification of the Nested Logit Model

Figure 7.1 (in section 7.4) illustrates a process by which the choice decision is broken into three stages. In the first stage, the market decision—whether to buy a camera or not—is considered. In the second stage, the type of camera (here instant, 35mm, or another type) is decided, and in the last stage the brand of camera is selected.

At each node of the tree, the dependent variable is a camera acquisition choice by the household in the second year I observe it, either 1983 or 1985. For example, households that acquire an instant camera, whether Polaroid or Kodak, enter into the analysis of the top right node: brand choice given choice of the instant type. For households at that node, the dependent variable is set according to whether they bought Polaroid or Kodak. The probability that they choose one versus the other will be modeled as depending on demographic and economic features of the household and on indicators of brand loyalty. By observing these variables, associated with every brand choice, it is possible statistically to infer (and estimate) the relationship between these features and brand choice. In other words, observations on a large number of households can provide systematic knowledge about what kinds of households tend to choose particular brands. The interpretation is that those households selecting specific products have greater need, desire, or knowledge of those particular brands. In other words, those households are more attracted to the brand. The BRAND level analysis yields a measure of the attractiveness to different consumers of the brands within each camera type.

Similarly, at the other nodes of the decision tree I examine other choices, namely the choice of whether or not to acquire a still camera, and if the decision to acquire a still camera is made, the type and brand of camera to acquire.

The structure of the tree imposes implicit assumptions about the nature of substitution among different cameras. In particular, the tree has brand choice farther to the right than type choice. This imposes the assumption that cameras of different brands but in the same segment are closer substitutes than cameras of different types. In this analysis, therefore, Kodak instant cameras are assumed to be closer substitutes for Polaroid instant cameras than for any other cameras. I have also investigated another tree structure, in which the ordering is MARKET, BRAND, TYPE instead of MARKET, TYPE, BRAND.

### 7.5.4 Structure of Conditional Probabilities

To derive a nested logit model for the structure given in figure 7.1, I begin with a generalized extreme value generating function:

$$G[\langle y_{mtb}\rangle] = \sum_{m} \left[ \sum_{t \epsilon B_m} \left[ \sum_{b \epsilon B_t} y_{mtb}^{\frac{1}{1-\sigma_t}} \right]^{\frac{1-\sigma_t}{1-\sigma_m}} \right]^{1-\sigma_m} \tag{19}$$

where $0 \leq \sigma_m \leq \sigma_t \leq 1$. The notation should be understood in the following way. The levels of the tree are indexed by $m$ for 'market decision,' $t$ for 'type of camera,' and $b$ for 'brand of camera.' The sets $B_t$ and $B_m$ are allowed to vary by alternative and the constants $\sigma_t$ and $\sigma_m$ may vary across nodes. Utility of alternative $mtb$, $u_{mtb}$, is assumed to be separable into random and systematic components with $u_{mtb} = V_{mtb} + \epsilon_{mtb}$. The random component $\epsilon_{mtb}$ is distributed as $F(\langle\epsilon_{mtb}\rangle) = \exp[-G[\langle e^{-\epsilon_{mtb}}\rangle]\ ]$ and strict utility $V_{mtb}$ is assumed to be linear-in-parameters with $V_{mtb} = \beta' x_{mtb} + \gamma' y_{mt} + \alpha' z_m$. Under these assumptions the following hold:

$$P_{mtb} = P_m \cdot P_{t|m} \cdot P_{b|mt} \tag{20}$$

$$P_{b|mt} = \frac{e^{\beta' x_{mtb}/(1-\sigma)}}{\sum_b e^{\beta' x_{mtb}/(1-\sigma)}} \tag{21}$$

$$I_{mt} = \log \sum_b e^{\beta' x_{mtb}/(1-\sigma)} \tag{22}$$

$$P_{t|m} = \frac{e^{[\gamma' y_{mt} + (1-\sigma) I_{mt}]/(1-\theta)}}{\sum_t e^{[\gamma' y_{mt} + (1-\sigma) I_{mt}]/(1-\theta)}} \tag{23}$$

$$I_m = \log \sum_t e^{[\gamma' y_{mt} + (1-\sigma) I_{mt}]/(1-\theta)} \tag{24}$$

$$P_m = \frac{e^{\alpha' z_m + (1-\theta) I_m}}{\sum_m e^{\alpha' z_m + (1-\theta) I_m}} \tag{25}$$

where for simplicity I have taken $\sigma = \sigma_t$ for all $t$ and $\theta = \sigma_m$ for all $m$. Each conditional probability follows the multinomial logit specification with linear-in-parameters log odds:

$$\log(P_{b|mt}/P_{b'|mt}) = \beta'(x_{mtb} - x_{mtb'})/(1-\sigma) \tag{26}$$

$$\begin{aligned} \log(P_{t|m}/P_{t|m'}) &= [\gamma' y_{mt} + (1-\sigma) I_{mt}]/(1-\theta) \\ &- [\gamma' y_{m't} + (1-\sigma) I_{m't}]/(1-\theta) \end{aligned} \tag{27}$$

$$\begin{aligned} \log(P_m/P_{m'}) &= [\alpha' Z_m + (1-\theta) I_m] \\ &- [\alpha' Z_{m'} + (1-\theta) I_{m'}] \end{aligned} \tag{28}$$

### *7.5.5 Interpretation of the Model*

As I have demonstrated above, a measure of brand substitutability is the inclusive value coefficient for the brand choice branch of the nested logit tree. An inclusive value coefficient for brand choice that is between zero and one will imply that anything that decreases the utility of Kodak instant cameras (relative to Polaroid) may lead to an increase in the demand for Polaroid instants, and to an increase in the demand for other types of cameras. The degree to which demand is shifted to Polaroid instants rather than other types of cameras depends on the substitutability of Polaroid and Kodak instant cameras. When the inclusive value coefficient is zero, the two types of instant cameras are weakest substitutes and most of the increase in camera demand will be seen among other types of cameras. If the inclusive value coefficient is one, the two types of instant cameras are closest substitutes

The coefficients of primary interest are those measuring brand loyalty and segment-specific substitutability. The estimates show both considerable brand loyalty and an intermediate level of segment- specific substitutability. I next discuss these estimates.

### *7.5.6 Estimation Results*

Table 7.3 gives the results of the binary logit model for type of 35mm camera. This model is based on the selections of 588 households who bought some type of 35mm camera in the decision year. A glossary accompanies each table to provide definitions of the variables used in that specification. The summary statistics at the bottom of table 7.3 show that 39 percent of the households selected single-lens reflex cameras while 61 percent chose non-single-lens reflex cameras. Remembering that a coefficient is statistically different from zero at the five percent significance level when its $t$-statistic is larger than 1.96 in absolute value, I note that the variables ALT, HELD, and RETIR are significant while other effects are not statistically significant.

ALT is the constant term for the first alternative and forces the estimated logit to have an average predicted probability identical to that which occurs in the population. HELD is an alternative specific variable for type of 35mm camera holdings in the base period. The value of HELD in the first alternative is the number of SLR 35mm cameras held by the household in the base year. The value of HELD in the second alternative is the number of non-SLR 35mm cameras held in the base year. The positive coefficient estimated for the variable HELD indicates that having a SLR type camera of a given type increases the probability that this type will be purchased again (if any 35mm is purchased).

The effect of prior holdings of 35mm camera types is assumed to be equal for both types of cameras. This need not have been the case. I tried other specifications in which the effect of having a non-SLR type camera was distinguished from the effect of having a SLR camera in the base period. This alternative specification was statistically similar to the one presented in table 7.3. Thus, having a non-SLR 35mm camera increases the probability of buying another non-SLR, rather than increasing the probability of buying the SLR type. I also note that the sign of the RETIR coefficient indicates that if the head of the household is retired then the household is more likely to buy a non-SLR camera. The variable D84 is an indicator for the set of observations whose base year is 1984. Its presence controls for a possible shift between 1982 and 1984 in the propensity to buy a given type of 35mm camera. Table 7.3 indicates that there is a shift away from single-lens reflex 35mm cameras in favor of non-single lens reflex 35mm cameras that is not accounted for by other variables. The effect is, however, at the borderline of statistical significance. The type of residence and its ownership status, the level of education, income, and children are not statistically significant in this model.

Table 7.4 presents the results of the binary logit model for brand of instant camera purchased. This model fits the conditional probability of selecting a Kodak instant camera versus the probability of selecting a Polaroid instant camera given that some instant camera is purchased. Of the 10,846 households, exactly 189 chose instant cameras in the decision year. Of the 189 households, 26.5 percent chose Kodak and 73.5 percent chose Polaroid. The estimated model shows a general insignificance of socioeconomic characteristics in explaining which households buy Kodak versus Polaroid instant cameras. Indeed, only the presence of a larger number of children gives consumers a preference for the Kodak brand. The HELD variable is, however, highly significant and shows that the prior holdings of either Kodak or Polaroid instants leads to the purchase of this brand again. Previous experience with instant photography (measured by having an instant camera of a particular brand in use in the base year) leads to an increase in the probability that a household will choose that brand of instant again.

I interpret this result as demonstrating a considerable brand loyalty. Those customers who have previously revealed themselves to favor Kodak (demonstrated by previously purchasing a Kodak instant camera) will tend to choose Kodak instant photography again if they chose to buy any instant camera at all in the decision year. Finally, the insignificance of the shift indicator for base year 1984 (variable D84) shows no additional preference for Kodak or Polaroid instant cameras between 1982 and 1984.

Table 7.5 presents the results of the estimation of the binary logit model for brand of camera choice for cameras other than 35mm and instant types. Here I distinguish between the choice of the Kodak brand versus the choice of non-Kodak cameras. The table shows that 565 households made this selection and, of these, 70.4 percent preferred the Kodak brand. In this model the conditional probability of purchasing a Kodak camera is increased among those households with fewer children (although this result is only weakly significant) and for households with larger incomes. Also, I note that a brand preference for Kodak cameras is demonstrated by a significant positive effect of having previously owned and used a Kodak camera of the "other" type. None of the other socioeconomic variables reveal significant effects on distinguishing Kodak versus other brand choice.

I have used the results of the estimated models given in tables 7.3, 7.4, and 7.5 to calculate for all households an inclusive value that summarizes the expected maximum utility of purchase within the relevant branch. The inclusive value of instant camera purchase, for example, is equal to the expected maximum utility that a household would receive if it were to buy some instant camera. The inclusive value variables calculated at this level become explanatory variables in the type choice model at the next level.

Table 7.6 presents the results of the estimated trinary logit model for camera type choice. In the sample, 1,294 households acquired some type of camera (instant, 35mm, or other still camera). Of these, 10 percent chose instant photography, while the remaining 90 percent were split nearly evenly between

35mm and other still cameras. The multinomial logit choice model for type of camera purchased is somewhat more complicated to interpret.

Socioeconomic variables such as education and household residence type have two displayed effects and one implied effect on the choice probability. EDUC2, for example, is the education of the household head as it affects the probability of buying a 35mm camera. EDUC3 gives the effect of education on the purchase of instant cameras. The effect of education on the probability of buying another type of still camera is implied by the previous two effects since the conditional probabilities of buying *some* type of camera add to one.

In table 7.6, I note that households who live in houses have a higher probability of selecting a 35mm camera. Households with higher incomes are also more likely to select a 35mm (if they purchase any camera). Households with more children are less likely to purchase 35mm cameras and less likely to purchase instant cameras. Taken together the significance of these two effects implies that households with more children are more likely to purchase a non-instant, non-35mm still camera. Table 7.6 also shows that the inclusive value coefficients for 35mm type choice and instant brand choice are both significant, while the inclusive value coefficient for non-instant non-35mm cameras is not. This pattern of significance is consistent with the random utility maximization theory for each branch except the 35mm branch where the inclusive value coefficient is greater than one.[14] The point estimate for the instant branch inclusive value is 0.65 and contains the unit interval more than 99 percent of the time. The coefficient of D842 shows a marked increase in the tendency to purchase 35mm cameras between 1982 and 1984.

In table 7.7 I present the results of the binary logit model for purchasing some camera. This estimation is based on the full sample of 10,846 households, each of which makes the decision to acquire a camera. Of these households, approximately 12 percent buy some camera in the decision year. I note from the table that more children lead to a greater likelihood that the household will acquire a camera. Retired households are less likely to acquire cameras. The other socioeconomic effects are not statistically significant (education, residence type, and ownership form). The inclusive value from the type choice model is significant and has a coefficient estimated to be within theoretical limits. The coefficient on D84 shows a decrease in the overall probability of buying a camera between 1982 and 1984.

[14] An estimated inclusive value coefficient greater than one can be inconsistent with the random utility maximization paradigm for consumer behavior. As a purely statistical matter, the inclusive value coefficient indicates the relative substitutability among the nodes in the choice set. The estimated value of the inclusive value coefficient in the 35mm branch indicates an extremely low degree of substitutability between SLR and non-SLR 35mm cameras. Empirically it is therefore not possible to distinguish the type and model components of 35mm camera demand within this time period.

### *7.5.7 Implications of the Estimates*

The nested logit model is successful at providing a predictive model of camera choice. There is clearly a systematic relationship between some variables I expected to be significant a priori, notably those measuring brand loyalty and the choice of camera. While cameras within the same market segment are closer substitutes than those in different market segments, this effect is not extremely strong. The degree of segment-specific substitutability takes on an intermediate value. This implies that type loyalty is present in photography system choice, but not that it is the dominant force; brand loyalty is important as well.

In appendix 7.7 I examine these results in the context of a nested logit model which allows for heteroscedasticity in the preference structure. The structural results obtained in this section are showed to hold under more general conditions.

**Table 7.3.** Binary Logit Model for Type of 35mm Camera 1982–1985

| Independent Variable | Estimated Coefficient | $t$– Statistic |
|---|---|---|
| ALT | −1.0714 | −2.1756 |
| HELD | 0.4104 | 3.7841 |
| EDUC | 0.0395 | 1.3362 |
| HOUSE | −0.0737 | 0.2645 |
| OWNRES | 0.3149 | 1.0837 |
| INC | −0.00009 | −0.0084 |
| KIDS | 0.0208 | 0.2685 |
| RETIR | −0.8692 | −2.5117 |
| D84 | −0.3552 | −1.8387 |
| Number of observations | | 588 |
| Percent correctly predicted | | 62.9 |
| Log likelihood at convergence | | −375.9 |

| | | |
|---|---|---|
| Alternative 1 | SLR 35mm camera | 38.9% |
| Alternative 2 | Non-SLR 35mm camera | 61.1% |

**Glossary**

| | |
|---|---|
| ALT | Constant term (Alt. one) |
| HELD | Base year holdings by type of 35mm camera (had in use a SLR camera—Alt. one; had in use a non-SRL camera—Alt. two) |
| EDUC | Education of household head (Alt. one) |
| HOUSE | Residence is a house (Alt. one) |
| OWNRES | Owns residence (Alt. one) |
| INC | Income (Alt. one) |
| KIDS | Persons in home other than heads (Alt. one) |
| RETIR | Head of household is retired (Alt. one) |
| D84 | One if base year is 1984 and decision year is 1985, and zero if base year is 1982 and decision year is 1983 (Alt. one) |

**Table 7.4.** Binary Logit Model for Brand of Instant Camera 1982–1985

| Independent Variable | Estimated Coefficient | $t-$ Statistic |
|---|---|---|
| ALT | −0.3919 | −0.4861 |
| HELD | 1.2981 | 2.8213 |
| EDUC | −0.0080 | −0.1556 |
| HOUSE | −0.5604 | −1.1383 |
| OWNRES | −0.4426 | −0.8204 |
| INC | 0.0007 | 0.0317 |
| KIDS | 0.2841 | 2.0212 |
| RETIR | 0.2347 | 0.4507 |
| D84 | 0.0326 | 0.0767 |
| Number of observations | | 189 |
| Percent correctly predicted | | 75.1 |
| Log likelihood at convergence | | −99.8 |

| | | |
|---|---|---|
| Alternative 1 | Kodak | 26.5% |
| Alternative 2 | Polaroid | 73.5% |

**Glossary**

| | |
|---|---|
| ALT | Constant term (Alt. one) |
| HELD | Holdings of instant camera in base year (had in use a Kodak instant camera in base year—Alt. one; had in use a Polaroid instant camera in base year—Alt. two) |
| EDUC | Education of household head (Alt. one) |
| HOUSE | Residence is a house (Alt. one) |
| OWNRES | Owns residence (Alt. one) |
| INC | Income (Alt. one) |
| KIDS | Persons in home other than heads (Alt. one) |
| RETIR | Head of household is retired (Alt. one) |
| D84 | One if base year is 1984 and decision year is 1985, and zero if base year is 1982 and decision year is 1983 (Alt. one) |

**Table 7.5.** Binary Logit Model for Brand of 'Other' Camera 1982–1985

| Independent Variable | Estimated Coefficient | $t-$ Statistic |
|---|---|---|
| ALT | 0.8334 | 1.9374 |
| HELD | 0.2582 | 3.3328 |
| EDUC | −0.0318 | −1.0355 |
| HOUSE | −0.1352 | −0.4955 |
| OWNRES | 0.0568 | 0.2050 |
| INC | 0.0349 | 3.0022 |
| KIDS | −0.1237 | −1.6793 |
| RETIR | 0.0311 | 0.1090 |
| D84 | 0.0859 | 0.3911 |
| Number of observations | | 565 |
| Percent correctly predicted | | 71.3 |
| Log likelihood at convergence | | −331.9 |

| | | |
|---|---|---|
| Alternative 1 | Kodak | 70.4% |
| Alternative 2 | Polaroid | 29.6% |

**Glossary**

| | |
|---|---|
| ALT | Constant term (Alt. one) |
| HELD | Base year holdings by brand of 'Other' camera (had in use a Kodak 'Other' camera—Alt. one; had in use a non-Kodak 'Other' camera—Alt. two) |
| EDUC | Education of household head (Alt. one) |
| HOUSE | Residence is a house (Alt. one) |
| OWNRES | Owns residence (Alt. one) |
| INC | Income (Alt. one) |
| KIDS | Persons in home other than heads (Alt. one) |
| RETIR | Head of household is retired (Alt. one) |
| D84 | One if base year is 1984 and decision year is 1985, and zero if base year is 1982 and decision year is 1983 (Alt. one) |

**Table 7.6.** Trinary Logit Model for Type of Camera 1982–1985

| Independent Variable | Estimated Coefficient | t– Statistic |
|---|---|---|
| ALT2 | −1.9266 | −3.0641 |
| ALT3 | −1.5025 | −2.0953 |
| EDUC2 | 0.0093 | 0.3816 |
| EDUC3 | 0.0066 | 0.2104 |
| HOUSE2 | 0.3641 | 1.8666 |
| HOUSE3 | −0.0451 | −0.1687 |
| OWNRES2 | −0.3179 | −1.5612 |
| OWNRES3 | 0.2067 | 0.7257 |
| INC2 | 0.0463 | 3.4582 |
| INC3 | 0.0156 | 0.9922 |
| KIDS2 | −0.2888 | −4.7623 |
| KIDS3 | −0.3301 | −3.5958 |
| RETIR2 | 0.0752 | 0.3373 |
| RETIR3 | −0.0202 | −0.0755 |
| INCV1 | 0.2067 | 0.4876 |
| INCV2 | 1.9924 | 5.1501 |
| INCV3 | 0.4595 | 2.8861 |
| D842 | 0.6543 | 4.3023 |
| D843 | −0.1605 | −0.7108 |
| Number of observations | | 1294 |
| Percent correctly predicted | | 56.8 |
| Log likelihood at convergence | | −1154.7 |

| | | |
|---|---|---|
| Alternative 1 | Still | 43.6% |
| Alternative 2 | 35mm | 45.5% |
| Alternative 3 | Instant | 10.9% |

**Glossary to Table 7.6**

| | |
|---|---|
| ALT2 | Constant term (Alt. two) |
| ALT3 | Constant term (Alt. three) |
| EDUC2 | Education of household head (Alt. two) |
| EDUC3 | Education of household head (Alt. three) |
| HOUSE2 | Residence is a house (Alt. two) |
| HOUSE3 | Residence is a house (Alt. three) |
| OWNRES2 | Owns residence (Alt. two) |
| OWNRES3 | Owns residence (Alt. three) |
| INC2 | Income (Alt. two) |
| INC3 | Income (Alt. three) |
| KIDS2 | Persons in home other than heads (Alt. two) |
| KIDS3 | Persons in home other than heads (Alt. two) |
| RETIR2 | Head of household is retired (Alt. two) |
| RETIR3 | Head of household is retired (Alt. three) |
| INCV1 | Inclusive value of 'Other' brand choice (Alt. one) |
| INCV2 | Inclusive value of 35mm model choice (Alt. two) |
| INCV3 | Inclusive value of Instant brand choice (Alt. three) |
| D842 | One if base year is 1984 and decision year is 1985 (Alt. two) |
| D843 | One if base year is 1984 and decision year is 1985 (Alt. three) |

**Table 7.7.** Binary Logit Model for Camera Acquisition 1982–1985

| Independent Variable | Estimated Coefficient | $t$– Statistic |
|---|---|---|
| ONE | −2.8508 | −18.3627 |
| INC | −0.0009 | −0.1688 |
| EDUC | −0.0017 | −0.1695 |
| KIDS | 0.3258 | 9.7436 |
| HOUSE | −0.0675 | −0.7450 |
| OWNRES | −0.0767 | 0.8359 |
| RETIR | −0.2461 | −2.5623 |
| INCV | 0.8117 | 5.5341 |
| D84 | −0.8368 | −12.2266 |
| Number of observations | | 10,846 |
| Percent correctly predicted | | 88.1 |
| Log likelihood at convergence | | −3767.3 |

| | | |
|---|---|---|
| Alternative 1 | Buy | 11.9% |
| Alternative 2 | Don't Buy | 88.1% |

**Glossary**

| | |
|---|---|
| ONE | Constant term (Alt. one) |
| INC | Income (Alt. one) |
| EDUC | Education of household head (Alt. one) |
| KIDS | Persons in home other than heads (Alt. one) |
| HOUSE | Residence is a house (Alt. one) |
| OWNRES | Owns residence (Alt. one) |
| RETIR | Head of household is retired (Alt. one) |
| INCV | Inclusive value from type choice model (Alt. one) |
| D84 | One if base year is 1984 and decision year is 1985 and zero otherwise (Alt. one) |

### *7.5.8 Simulation of "But for Kodak" World*

The implications of the estimation can best be understood by a simulation of the hypothetical but for world. I perform this simulation by hypothetically reducing the attractiveness of Kodak instant cameras until the model predicts no household will acquire one. This corresponds to an extreme increase in the price of Kodak instant photography, or an extreme decrease in its availability. I then use the model to predict the choice behavior of households in the but for world. This simulation is reported in table 7.8.

The first column reports the actual behavior of the sample of 10,846 households in 1983 and 1985.[15] The most common choice in any given year (at just over 88 percent) is to buy no camera. The next most common choice is 35mm, followed by "other" and instant, at 1.28 percent. The model's predictions about behavior before I change the attractiveness of Kodak instant are given in the second column. The model does a good job of predicting the actual world. The model's predictions for the but for world, after I change the attractiveness of the Kodak instant alternative, are given in the next column. The final column gives the predicted effect of removing Kodak from the instant segment. This is the difference between the previous two columns.

**Table 7.8.** 1983–1985 Predicted Camera Purchase Behavior in Real and But-for Worlds

| | Real World | Model | But For | Change |
|---|---|---|---|---|
| %Instant | 1.28 | 1.28 | 1.07 | –.21 |
| %Other | 5.19 | 5.19 | 5.28 | .09 |
| %35mm | 5.46 | 5.46 | 5.54 | .08 |
| %None | 88.07 | 88.07 | 88.11 | .04 |
| %PRD | .94 | .94 | 1.07 | .13 |
| %EKI | .34 | .34 | 0.0 | –.34 |
| Market Expansion: | | 62% | | |
| Business Diversion: | | 38% | (.13/.34) | |

The simulation predicts that, in the but for world, the instant market segment would contract to 83.6 percent (1.07/1.28) of its size in the actual world. Both the "other" and 35mm market segments would be larger in the but for world, and a slightly larger fraction of consumers would buy no camera. Substitution into the other camera segments is quantitatively more important in the simulation than substitution into not buying any camera: 81 percent ((.09 + .08)/.21) of the households that switch out of buying an instant switch

[15]Note that the first two columns of table 7.8 are identical. The statistical model I am using has the property that it always correctly predicts the sample probability of each outcome.

into one of the other market segments. By construction, Polaroid's share in the instant market segment is predicted to rise to 100 percent, and Kodak's to fall to 0 percent. Note that Polaroid's share in aggregate behavior is predicted to rise from 0.94 percent to 1.07 percent, a rise of 0.13 percent. Kodak instant falls from 0.34 percent to nothing. Thus 0.21 percent of the 0.34 percent decline in Kodak instant represents switches out of the instant market segment. Only 38 percent of Kodak's fall in market share is regained by Polaroid. Thus, there is a business diversion effect of 38 percent.

The effect of the actual levels of substitutability across segments and brands, as revealed by the heterogeneous behavior of photography consumers, is to imply a substantial market expansion effect of 62 percent. This applies to the variable actually reported in the multicard surveys, cameras in use.

## 7.6 Conclusions

Consumers' experience within the damage period differs from their experience after the end of the damage period. Within the damage period, consumers were choosing between Polaroid and Kodak instant photography systems at the same time. Thus, the within-damage period data presents an opportunity to study that choice directly.

This chapter has presented a detailed analysis of the choices made during the damage period. The degree of substitution revealed by the nested logit model implies a 38 percent business diversion from Kodak's entry into the instant photography market.

## 7.7 Appendix

### 7.7.1 The Heterogeneous Logit Model

The purpose of this appendix is to provide an extension of the generalized extreme value (GEV) family which allows non-constancy of the similarity parameters in the nested logit model and which introduces non-homoscedasticity in the underlying random components of utility. While the heteroscedastic form of the logit model has appeared before in the literature, it has not been identified as a member of the GEV family. This appendix makes this connection and further extends the GEV family to include logit models with heteroscedasticity across alternatives.

The GEV family allows a relatively flexible pattern of correlation among the unobserved components of random utility. In this regard it bears some similarity to the covariance probit model of Hausman and Wise (1978). The GEV class however, unlike the covariance probit model, embodies two restrictions. First, the unobserved components of utility are assumed to be homoscedastic across individuals and alternatives. Second, the similarity coefficients are also assumed to be constant across individuals. Neither of these restrictions is desirable. Moreover, when heterogeneity is present, maximum likelihood estimation of models within the GEV class is likely to be inconsistent.

I begin with a population of $T$ decision makers, each choosing among $I$ discrete alternatives. Alternative $i$ is assumed to provide utility $u_{it}$ to individual $t$ which consists of a deterministic component $v_{it}$ and an unobserved random component $\epsilon_{it}$ with $u_{it} = v_{it} + \epsilon_{it}$. Under the assumption of random utility maximization, individual $t$ chooses alternative $i$ whenever $u_{it} \geq u_{jt}$, $\forall j \neq i$. The probability of this event is

$$p_{it} = \text{Prob } (v_{it} + \epsilon_{it} > v_{jt} + \epsilon_{jt}, \ \forall j \neq i) \tag{29}$$

$$= \int_{-\infty}^{\infty} \int_{-\infty}^{v_{it}+\epsilon_{it}-v_{1t}} \cdots \int_{-\infty}^{v_{it}+\epsilon_{it}-v_{It}} f(\epsilon_{1t}, \ldots, \epsilon_{It}) d\epsilon_{It} \ldots d\epsilon_{1t} d\epsilon_{it} \tag{30}$$

where $f(\epsilon_{1t}, \ldots, \epsilon_{It})$ is the joint density of the $\epsilon_{it}$. Equation (30) implies that

$$p_{it} = \int_{-\infty}^{\infty} F_i(v_{it} + \epsilon_{it} - v_{1t}, \ldots, \epsilon_{it}, \ldots, v_{it} + \epsilon_{it} - v_{It}) d\epsilon_{it} \tag{31}$$

where $F(\epsilon_{1t}, \ldots, \epsilon_{It})$ is the cumulative distribution of the $\epsilon_{it}$ and where $F_i$ denotes the partial derivative of $F$ with respect to its $i^{th}$ argument.

The GEV probabilistic choice family is obtained by assuming that the distribution function $F$ takes the form

$$F(\epsilon_{1t}, \ldots, \epsilon_{It}) = \exp(-G(e^{-\epsilon_{1t}}, \ldots, e^{-\epsilon_{It}})) \tag{32}$$

where $G(Y_1, \ldots, Y_I)$ is a non-negative, homogeneous of degree one function on $\Re_I^+$ with $\lim_{Y_i \to \infty} G = +\infty$, and the $l^{th}$ order cross-partial derivatives of $G$

with respect to distinct $Y_i$'s non-negative if $l$ is odd and nonpositive if $l$ is even. Under these conditions, McFadden (1978) shows that equation (31) defines a multivariate extreme value distribution with

$$p_{it} = e^{v_{it}} G_i(e^{v_{1t}}, \ldots, e^{v_{It}}) / G(e^{v_{1t}}, \ldots, e^{v_{It}}). \tag{33}$$

The GEV class contains the multinomial and nested logit models as special cases. For example, when $G(\cdot) = \sum_{i=1}^{I} Y_i$, equation (33) is the multinomial logit model with $p_{it} = e^{v_{it}} / \sum e^{v_{jt}}$. The nested logit model groups the $I$ alternatives into $J$ subsets with each subset containing alternatives that are similar. For example, the two-level nested logit model results from

$$G = \sum_{k=1}^{J} \Big( \sum_{i \in C_k} Y_i^{1/\sigma_k} \Big)^{\sigma_k},$$

where

$$C_k \subset \{1, 2, \ldots, I\}, \cup_{k=1}^{J} C_k = \{1, 2, \ldots, I\}, \text{ and } 0 < \sigma_k \leq 1.$$

Here, $\sigma_k$ measures the similarity of the random components of utility within subset $C_k$. For this $G$ function, the probabilities in equation (33) can be written as the product of two probabilities each in standard logit form:

$$p_j = \frac{e^{v_j/\sigma_k}}{\sum_{i \in C_k} e^{v_i/\sigma_k}} \cdot \frac{e^{\sigma_k I_k}}{\sum_{k=1}^{J} e^{\sigma_k I_k}}, \quad j \in C_k$$

where $I_k = \log \sum_{i \in C_k} e^{v_i/\sigma_k}$ defines the inclusive value of alternatives in subset $C_k$.

Models in the GEV class embody two important restrictions. First, the marginal distribution of each random disturbance has constant variance. To see this, note that the marginal distribution of $\epsilon_{it}$ is given by

$$\begin{aligned} F^i(\epsilon_{it}) &= F(\infty, \ldots, \epsilon_{it}, \ldots, \infty) \\ &= \exp(-G(0, \ldots, e^{-\epsilon_{it}}, \ldots, 0)) = \exp(-a_i e^{\epsilon_{it}}) \end{aligned} \tag{34}$$

where $a_i = G(\delta_{i1}, \ldots, \delta_{iI})$ and where $\delta_{ij} = 1$ if $i = j$ and 0 otherwise.[16] But $F^i(\epsilon_{it})$ is the cumulative distribution function of an extreme value random variable with location parameter $ln a_i$ and variance $\pi^2/6$.[17] Therefore the variance of the marginal distribution is independent of the functional form of the GEV generating function. Second, the similarity coefficients (in the case of nested

[16] The last equality in equation (34) uses the linear homogeneity of $G$.

[17] The extreme-value distribution has cumulative distribution functions $F(\epsilon) = exp(-e^{-(\epsilon-\xi)/\theta})$ with $E(\epsilon) = \xi + \theta\gamma$ and $\text{var}(\epsilon) = (\pi^2/6)\theta^2$ where $\gamma$ is Euler's constant.

logit models) are assumed to be constant across individuals, that is, decision makers are assumed to have identical perceptions about the degree of similarity among alternatives. In the following section I show that it is possible to introduce heteroscedasticity through a scale parameter which depends on the individual and the alternative.[18]

### *7.7.2 Heteroscedastic Errors*

Following Dubin (1995, p. 221) observe that if $G(Y_1, \ldots, Y_I)$ is a proper GEV function, and if $\theta_{it} > 0$ then

$$\tilde{F}(\epsilon_{1t}, \ldots, \epsilon_{It}) = \exp(-G(< e^{-\epsilon_{jt}\theta_{jt}} >)) \tag{35}$$

is multivariate extreme-value distributed.[19] The marginal distributions are of the form:

$$\begin{aligned} \tilde{F}^i = \tilde{F}(\infty, \ldots, \epsilon_{it}, \ldots, \infty) &= \exp(-G(0, \ldots, e^{-\epsilon_{it}\theta_{it}}, \ldots 0)) \\ &= \exp(-a_i e^{-e_{it}\theta_{it}}) \end{aligned} \tag{36}$$

and are extreme-value distributed with variance $(\pi^2/6)(1/\theta_{it}^2)$.

Under random utility maximization, the choice probabilities corresponding to equation (35) satisfy equation (30). In this case,

$$\tilde{F}_i = \theta_{it} e^{-\epsilon_{it}\theta_{it}} G_i(\cdot) \exp(-G(< e^{-\epsilon_{it}\theta_{it}} >)),$$

implies

$$\begin{aligned} p_{it} &= \int_{-\infty}^{\infty} \theta_{it} e^{-\epsilon\theta_{it}} \\ &\quad \cdot G_i(e^{-(v_{it}+\epsilon-v_{1t})\theta_{1t}}, \ldots, e^{-\epsilon\theta_{it}}, \ldots, e^{-(v_{it}+\epsilon-v_{It})\theta_{It}}) \\ &\quad \cdot e^{-G(\cdot)} d\epsilon. \end{aligned} \tag{37}$$

When heteroscedasticity is present across individuals, but not alternatives, $\theta_{it} = \theta_t$, and equation (37) becomes

$$\begin{aligned} p_{it} &= \int_{-\infty}^{\infty} \theta_t e^{-\epsilon\theta_t} G_i(< e^{v_{jt}\theta_t} >) \exp\{-e^{-(v_{it}+\epsilon)\theta_t} G(< e^{v_{jt}\theta_t} >)\} d\epsilon \\ &= e^{v_{it}\theta_t} G_i(< e^{v_{it}\theta_t} >)/G(< e^{v_{it}\theta_t} >). \end{aligned} \tag{38}$$

---

[18] Dubin and Zeng (1991) demonstrate specific results for the nested logit model with varying similarity coefficients.

[19] Observe that $\tilde{F}(\epsilon_1, \ldots, \epsilon_I) = F(\epsilon_1\theta_1, \ldots, \epsilon_I\theta_I)$ where $F(\cdot)$ is the cumulative distribution function given in equation (32). Therefore $\tilde{F}$ is also a cumulative distribution function. This may be verified by directly checking the conditions given in McFadden (1978) or in Smith (1984). Dubin (1985) considers the distribution $\tilde{F}(\epsilon_1, \ldots, \epsilon_I) = F(\epsilon_1\theta, \ldots, \epsilon_I\theta)$ which provides individual level (but not alternative specific) heterogeneity.

In the special case, $G(\cdot) = \sum_{i=1}^{I} Y_i$, equation (38) is a multinomial logit model with heteroscedasticity across individuals:

$$p_{it} = e^{v_{it}\theta_t} / \sum_{j=1}^{I} e^{v_{jt}\theta_t}. \tag{39}$$

Equation (39) exhibits heteroscedasticity in the multinomial logit model. I have therefore shown that this form of heteroscedasticity is consistent with random utility maximization.

### 7.7.3 *Heteroscedasticity in the Demand for Cameras*

To investigate the consequences of heteroscedasticity for the models of camera choice considered in this chapter, I examine the selections made from among three broad types of cameras: 35mm, instant, and still cameras. The data are taken from surveys of households conducted in 1982 and 1983 by National Family Opinion, Inc. (NFO). I selected the sample for analysis based on three criteria (1) the household is interviewed in both 1982 and 1983, (2) the household buys some type of camera in 1983, and (3) complete data is available for all household characteristics in the 1982 base year. The model I estimate is a somewhat simplified version of those previously discussed in this chapter. In particular the choice model has been collapsed to its non-nested form where only the camera type choice decision is developed. The estimation sample contains 875 households.

The utility of a given camera type is modeled as a function of four socioeconomic characteristics: education, income, presence of children, and marital status and a variable which measures the stock of cameras held by the household in the base year. The latter variable is alternative specific. The explanatory variables are defined as follows: EDUC, the number of years of education for the head of household; INC, household income in thousands of dollars; HKIDS, one if the household has children; MARITAL, one if the head of household is married; and HELD, the number of cameras of each type (35mm, instant, or still) present in the household in the base year.

Variable definitions and summary statistics are given in table 7.9. In this sample, roughly equal numbers of households choose the 35mm and still formats (41 and 43 percent respectively), while the remainder choose instant photography (16 percent). Nearly 90 percent of the households used some camera in the base year.

The results of the estimation for a standard multinomial logit model are presented in table 7.10.[20] The alternative specific constant terms show significant preference for the still format as compared with either 35mm or instant type cameras. Households with higher income are more likely to choose 35mm cameras over still and instant formats. This is consistent with the fact that

[20]Without loss of generality, I have used the "still" alternative as the basis for normalization.

35mm cameras were more expensive than other types of cameras in the early 1980s. Households with children were significantly less likely to purchase instant cameras, instead preferring other still formats. Higher education increases the probability of purchasing 35mm cameras. This is consistent with the then commonly held view that 35mm cameras are more complicated to use than other types of cameras.[21] Households in which the head is married do not reveal any significant preference among the camera types. Finally, the presence of cameras of a given type in the base year significantly increases the probability of repurchasing that type in the year of camera acquisition. Households therefore reveal significant "type" loyalty.

To test whether heteroscedasticity is present in the logit choice model I estimate the heteroscedastic logit model, derived in the previous section, using the specification $\log(\theta_t) = \alpha \cdot \mathrm{SIZE}_t$. The results of this estimation are also shown in table 7.10. Comparing the standard and heteroscedastic logit estimates I observe relative stability in the estimated coefficients and only modest changes in the levels of statistical significance. The most prominently affected coefficient is that of HKIDS. This might have been expected since the scale effect is modeled in terms of family size and family size increases when children are present. The implication of this finding is that larger families may have a greater diversity of camera needs arising from their larger and potentially more diverse constituency.

Results similar to these were also obtained for the nested logit models specified in the chapter. While some degree of heteroscedasticity may be evident, the estimated coefficients were similar in both magnitude and significance. Therefore, my conclusions regarding brand loyalty, substitution, and the degree of business diversion are robust to household level heteroscedasticity.

[21] Recall that in 1982 few, if any, 35mm cameras provided automatic focusing, automatic shutter control, or self-winding film.

**Table 7.9.** Variable Definitions and Summary Statistics

| Variable | Description | Mean | Standard Deviation |
|---|---|---|---|
| EDUC | head of household's education in years | 13.59 | 3.49 |
| INC | household's income in thousands | 21.54 | 9.39 |
| HKIDS | one if household has children | 0.58 | 0.49 |
| MARITAL | one if head of household is married | 0.69 | 0.46 |
| HELD 35mm | number of 35mm cameras in use in base year | 0.47 | 0.81 |
| HELD instant | number of instant cameras in use in base year | 0.24 | 0.49 |
| HELD other | number of still cameras in use in base year | 0.80 | 0.76 |
| SIZE | number of people in household | 2.87 | 1.49 |

**Table 7.10.** Standard and Heteroscedastic Multinomial Logit Models for Camera Type Choice (asymptotic $t$-values in parentheses)

| Explanatory Variable | Model | |
|---|---|---|
| | *Standard* | *Heteroscedastic* |
| *35mm Alternative* | | |
| CONSTANT | −1.53 | −2.44 |
| | (−4.26) | (−3.56) |
| INC | 0.044 | 0.063 |
| | (4.54) | (3.58) |
| HKIDS | −0.275 | −0.345 |
| | (−1.68) | (−1.38) |
| EDUC | 0.066 | 0.111 |
| | (2.67) | (2.67) |
| MARITAL | −0.22 | −0.27 |
| | (−1.18) | (−1.02) |
| *Instant Alternative* | | |
| CONSTANT | −0.88 | −1.10 |
| | (−2.10) | (−1.79) |
| INC | 0.014 | 0.021 |
| | (1.15) | (1.12) |
| HKIDS | −0.462 | −1.04 |
| | (−2.24) | (−2.16) |
| EDUC | 0.017 | 0.029 |
| | (0.57) | (0.65) |
| MARITAL | −0.31 | −0.66 |
| | (−1.37) | (−1.76) |
| *Alternative Specific Variables* | | |
| HELD | 0.201 | 0.333 |
| | (3.32) | (2.94) |
| *Heteroscedasticity Factor* | | |
| SIZE | | −0.151 |
| | | (−2.05) |
| Log-likelihood at convergence | −860.0 | −858.2 |

# 8 THE DEMAND FOR TRANSPORTATION SERVICES IN NATURAL GAS MARKETS–THE MARKET POWER OF A NATURAL GAS PIPELINE

## 8.1 Introduction

Koch Gateway Pipeline (Koch) is an interstate natural gas transmission system operating over 9,000 miles of pipeline. The system extends from South Texas through Louisiana, Mississippi, southern Alabama, and southern Florida. Koch is located in one of the nation's largest natural gas producing areas and is tied into a number of the largest gas producing regions. The Koch system is best visualized as a giant hub rather than a traditional longline interstate pipeline.

In 1996, Koch applied before the Federal Energy Regulating Commission (FERC) for market-based rates for its transportation services. Before that filing Koch, like other interstate pipelines, had been subject to regulation under a cost of service rate schedule. Koch argued before the FERC that it operates in a highly competitive environment which disciplines its pricing behavior. Koch presented evidence of its market power using traditional market concentration studies and by identifying specific pipeline alternatives to its system at metering points. Koch offered evidence of its historical discounting behavior which demonstrated the conditions under which it discounted historical rates in order to raise revenues. Additionally, Koch presented an elasticity of demand study to examine the likelihood that absent regulation it would be more likely to raise prices rather than to lower them. Finally, Koch presented evidence that its system functions as a swing or peaking system and that the capacity held by marketers and other gas suppliers competed with Koch in the marketplace. Koch's filing was the first of its kind and broad in scope.

In this chapter I discuss the elasticity and discounting analysis performed for the Koch Gateway Pipeline Company. I estimate the historical demand for Koch's transportation service and an econometric model of Koch's historical discounting behavior. In these analyses I rely on the actual transactions occurring on the Koch system for the period from April 1989 through December 1994. This time period effectively covers Koch's transition from a pipeline offering a bundled product, consisting of natural gas sales and transportation, to one offering primarily a transportation service.

The empirical analysis proceeds in two steps. First, I specify and estimate binary logit models to predict Koch's discounting practices for interruptible transportation rates (i.e., spot rates) in four markets. The results derived from the logit models are then used in the second part of my analysis, a market demand regression analysis. The second part of my analysis is used to estimate the mean demand elasticity faced by Koch for its transportation services in four primary markets. Those markets are: natural gas deliveries to industrial firms and power plants; receipts from "upstream" pipelines; deliveries to "downstream" pipelines; and, receipts from production fields.

As demonstrated below, for the 1989-1994 period, these segments comprised 91 percent of the firm (contract based) and interruptible (spot based) transportation volume through Koch's system (industrials/power plants with 20 percent; pipelines receipts with 21 percent; pipeline deliveries with 25 percent; and production fields with 25 percent). The remaining 9 percent includes aspects of Koch's business such as sales to government facilities and other pipelines using gas for compressors and storage facility operations. I further break transportation services into firm and interruptible transportation. As I show below, for the 1989 through 1994 period, of the firm transportation and interruptible transportation transactions analyzed, 71 percent of the volume is interruptible and 29 percent of the volume is firm.

In the next section I discuss issues of theory and model specification. I then review the data sources and present the econometric results. Finally I present results for the models of Koch's historical discounting behavior and for the demand for Koch's transportation services.

## 8.2 Theory

In economic theory, elastic demand operates as the primary constraint on a firm's market power. Elasticity measures a firm's ability to raise prices without losing sales. Even if a firm is the sole producer of a good or service, it will not have significant market power if demand for that good or service is sufficiently elastic. For example, many products are protected by patents which establish a legal monopoly. However, patents differ enormously in the amount of market power that they confer upon their holders because the elasticity of demand for products varies.

The market in which Koch operates is not perfectly competitive, very few markets are. However, the relevant issue is not whether the market is perfectly competitive, but whether demand is sufficiently elastic to prevent Koch from raising prices significantly and sustaining those price increases. The answer to this question depends on the elasticity of demand for Koch transportation services.

For a pipeline such as Koch which has high fixed costs and low variable costs, price increases which decrease the pipeline's total revenues are unlikely to be profitable. An elasticity coefficient greater than one indicates that increases in unit sales prices are more than offset by decreases in unit sales quantities. Therefore, increasing prices decreases total revenue. In conjunction with the high fixed to variable cost ratio, elastic demand effectively prevents Koch from raising prices.

Econometrically analyzing a firm's demand elasticity in its product and geographic markets requires collecting transaction-level historical data for the firm. Potential price endogeneity in the demand analysis requires that the analysis control for the firm's behavior with respect to the discounts it offers on its historically regulated tariff prices.

The basic demand equation has the form:

$$Q = Z\gamma_i + v \tag{1}$$

where $Q$ = quantity of transportation services demanded, $Z$ = vector of explanatory factors affecting the quantity demanded, $\gamma_i$ = vector of parameters associated with the explanatory factors when the firm is discounting prices ($i = 1$) or when the firm is not discounting ($i = 0$), and $v$ = random disturbance affecting the quantity demanded.

The vector $Z$ includes those factors which influence demand such as transportation prices, industrial production indices, the economic agent procuring service (power plants versus industrials), and so forth.

A discrete-choice model for Koch's decision to discount and the continuous demand model specified in equation (1) form a discrete-continuous system. To allow for a potential correlation between the unobservable factors that influence the decision to discount (e.g., unobservable influences affecting market competitiveness) and the unobservable factors that influence demand, the conditional expectation $E[v|i]$ can be estimated and included as an additional explanatory factor in the demand model. Dubin and McFadden (1984) have shown that this will yield consistent estimates of the parameters with ordinary least squares regression. Following Dubin and McFadden and assuming that the probability model for $P_1$ is logistic, I obtain:

$$\begin{aligned} E[v|i] &= [(P_1 - \delta_1)] \cdot \mathrm{log P_1}/(1 - \mathrm{P_1}) \\ &- [(1 - P_1) - (1 - \delta_1)] \cdot \mathrm{log(1 - P_1)/P_1} \\ &= (P_1 - \delta_1) \cdot \frac{[P_1 \mathrm{log P_1} + (1 - \mathrm{P_1}) \mathrm{log(1 - P_1)}]}{[P_1 \mathrm{log P_1} + (1 - \mathrm{P_1}) \mathrm{log(1 - P_1)}] / P_1 (1 - P_1)} \end{aligned}$$

where $P_1$ = probability of discounting, and $\delta_1$ = indicator for discounting, which is one if a discount is offered and zero otherwise.

The term $E[v|i]$ is estimated using the predicted probabilities from the logit model. Including the selectivity correction factor in the regression model transforms equation (1) into:

$$Q = Z\gamma_i + E[v|i] + \tilde{v}. \tag{2}$$

Ordinary least squares, when applied to equation (2), will yield consistent estimates of the parameters $\gamma_i$. The probability model is estimated by maximum likelihood. In the next section I present the data used in estimating the discrete-continuous demand system.

## 8.3 Data

The data used to conduct this analysis can be broken down into three categories: Koch system data, which includes historical transaction data and descriptive data on individual metering points on the Koch system; market concentration data, which includes information on Koch and competitive pipelines and shippers organized according to several different market definitions; and ancillary data used to model large-scale trends in the demand for natural gas services, including macroeconomic and climatic data series.

### *8.3.1 Koch's Historical Transaction Data*

I use historical transportation transaction data for the period from April 1989 through December 1994. The data is organized by year, month, station location number (SLN), and contract type. Each SLN is a single metering point on the Koch system. Each observation in the analysis represents an aggregation of all transactions of a specific contract type occurring at an SLN during one month. Thus, in the majority of cases, this is equivalent to aggregating across distinct shippers at an SLN. Contract types are defined by the unique combination of the discrete variables listed in table 8.1.

A summary of the historical transaction data file is provided in table 8.2.

**Table 8.1.** Koch's Contract Types

| Variable | Name | Description |
|---|---|---|
| year | Year | Year of transaction |
| month | Month | Month of transaction |
| coflow | Contract Flow | Indicates whether transaction was a receipt or delivery |
| ratesc | Rate Schedule | Distinguishes between firm and interruptible rate types |
| gathdi | Gathering Discount Indicator | Indicates discounted gathering rate |
| comddi | Commodity Discount Indicator | Indicates discounted commodity rate |
| gathtp | Gathering Take-or-Pay Indicator | Indicates take-or-pay credit on gathering rate |
| comdtp | Commodity Take-or-Pay Indicator | Indicates take-or-pay credit on commodity rate |
| tier | Tier | Indicates the rate schedule tier for the transaction |

The number of transactions and corresponding volumes are given in tables 8.3, 8.4, and 8.5.

Some features of the summaries provided in tables 8.3 through 8.5 should be noted. First, 1989 is a partial year, commencing in April. Thus, the totals represent data for five years and nine months, and the annual figures listed for 1989 are only partial totals. Second, there is a double counting issue inherent in this data summarization. In the Koch accounting system, natural gas flowing on Koch's system is counted, or metered, once when it is received by Koch and once when it is delivered. This means, in effect, that the volumes shown in these tables are nearly double the actual gas volumes which moved through the Koch system.[1]

[1]Some gas which is received by Koch is consumed in compressors and for other uses. Therefore, the "double counting" does not result in an exact doubling of the volume received by

**Table 8.2.** Historical Transaction Data Set

| Variable | Name | Description |
|---|---|---|
| sln | Station Location Number (SLN) | The number designation assigned by Koch to each point on the system for accounting or measurement purposes |
| coflow | Contract Flow | A code that indicates whether Koch contractually received or delivered gas through an SLN for a contract: R = receipt, D = delivery |
| ratesc | Rate Schedule | The rate schedule used to determine the commodity charge: ITS = interruptible transportation service, FTS = firm transportation service |
| year, month | Production Date | The calendar year and month of the transaction |
| gathdi | Gathering Discount Indicator | Indicates whether the gathering rate, if applicable, was discounted. |
| comddi | Commodity Discount Indicator | This indicates whether the commodity rate, if applicable, was discounted. |
| gathtp | Gathering Take-or-Pay Indicator | This indicates whether the gathering rate includes a take-or-pay credit. |
| comdtp | Commodity Take-or-Pay Indicator | This indicates whether the commodity rate includes a take-or-pay credit. |

Within the data I analyze, firm and interruptible transportation services are represented by 90,468 transactions. Of these, 20,235 are delivery transactions, representing 22 percent of total transactions and 70,233 are receipt transactions, representing 78 percent of all transactions. Firm service accounts for 2,477 of the delivery transactions or 3 percent of all transactions. Interruptible service accounts for 17,758 of the delivery transactions, or 20 percent of all transactions. Firm service accounts for 18,230 of the receipt transactions, or 20 percent of all transactions. Interruptible service accounts for 52,003 of the receipt transactions, or 57 percent of all transactions. Thus, firm service totals

Koch. Also, this data includes only natural gas volumes associated with the firm and interruptible transportation services analyzed, and excludes deliveries to local delivery companies (LDCs) altogether. For these reasons, the summarization is not an exact "double counting."

**Table 8.2.** (continued) Historical Transaction Data Set

| Variable | Name | Description |
|---|---|---|
| tier | Tier | This indicates the length of haul for a transaction and is used to determine the appropriate commodity rate from the rate schedule:<br>1 0-100 miles<br>2 101-200 miles<br>3 201-300 miles<br>4 301-400 miles<br>5 401-500 miles<br>6 >500 miles<br>0 Not related to any rate type |
| mcf | MCF @ 14.73 psi | Volume of gas in transaction (million cubic feet) |
| mmbtu | MMBTU | Heating value of gas in transaction (million British thermal units) |
| gathrt | Gathering Rate | The rate charged for gathering services, if applicable (dollars per MMBTU) |
| comdlp | Commodity Rate with Add-ons | The effectively charged rate, including any GRI or AGA dues (dollars per MMBTU) |
| demdlf | Demand Rate 100% Load Factor | The effectively charged demand rate, not including GRI or AGA dues at 100% load factor (dollars per MMBTU) |

**Table 8.3.** Firm and Interruptible Transportation Volumes

| Year | Transactions | Volume (mmbtu) |
|---|---|---|
| 1989 | 12,470 | 747,334,000 |
| 1990 | 18,157 | 1,076,850,000 |
| 1991 | 16,232 | 812,517,000 |
| 1992 | 15,268 | 831,636,000 |
| 1993 | 14,195 | 949,623,000 |
| 1994 | 14,146 | 972,535,000 |
| Total | 90,468 | 5,390,490,000 |

20,707 transactions, or 23 percent of all transactions. Interruptible transportation service totals 69,761 transactions, or the remaining 77 percent of the total firm and interruptible transactions.

The transaction data also show which transactions had been discounted by Koch. For the 1989-1994 period, Koch discounted 5,578 of its interruptible

**Table 8.4.** Firm Transportation Volumes

| Year | Transactions | Volume (mmbtu) |
|---|---|---|
| 1989 | 1,978 | 164,915,000 |
| 1990 | 3,961 | 336,613,000 |
| 1991 | 4,253 | 248,118,000 |
| 1992 | 3,459 | 230,228,000 |
| 1993 | 3,530 | 254,228,000 |
| 1994 | 3,526 | 319,610,000 |
| Total | 20,707 | 1,553,710,000 |

**Table 8.5.** Interruptible Transportation Volumes

| Year | Transactions | Volume (mmbtu) |
|---|---|---|
| 1989 | 10,492 | 582,419,000 |
| 1990 | 14,196 | 740,237,000 |
| 1991 | 11,979 | 564,399,000 |
| 1992 | 11,809 | 601,408,000 |
| 1993 | 10,665 | 695,394,000 |
| 1994 | 10,620 | 652,925,000 |
| Total | 69,761 | 3,836,780,000 |

(deliveries) transactions and 14,009 of its interruptible (receipts) transactions. Therefore, 21 percent of all transactions during this period were discounted interruptible transportation. Similarly, Koch discounted 1,740 of its firm (deliveries) transactions and 13,203 of its firm (receipts) transactions. Therefore, 17 percent of all transactions during this period were discounted firm transactions.

In volumetric terms, firm and interruptible transportation transactions total 5,390,490,000 mmbtu. Deliveries represent 47 percent of this volume and receipts represent 53 percent. Interruptible transportation (deliveries) constitute 33 percent and firm transportation (deliveries) constitute 14 percent of the total volume. Interruptible services (receipts) constitute 38 percent and firm services (receipts) constitute 15 percent of the total volume.[2]

[2]The volumetric data also reveal the discounting behavior. For the 1989-1994 period, Koch discounted 60 percent of the total firm and interruptible gas volume it transported. Koch discounted 79 percent of its firm (deliveries) volume and 74 percent of its firm (receipts) volume. Similarly, 57 percent of its interruptible (deliveries) and 50 percent of its interruptible (receipts) volumes were discounted. This data indicates that although Koch discounted 38

### *8.3.2 SLN Specific Data*

Along with the transaction data, I obtained supplemental information from Koch for each SLN appearing in the transaction data. The population of SLNs for which this additional data are available excludes several categories of points on the Koch system. Excluded SLNs include: local delivery company (LDC) delivery points, SLNs locked on location, SLNs with meters removed, offsystem lateral SLNs, and SLNs flowing company-used gas. There are 1,588 SLNs represented in this analysis. A summary of this information is provided in table 8.6.

Using the Koch indicator known as Main Flow Designator Code (mfd), SLNs were classified into four primary groups for further analysis: industrials and power plants (deliveries), pipeline receipts, pipeline deliveries, and production fields (receipts). The total number of SLNs in each group is presented in table 8.7.

These four groups represent 96 percent of all delivery and receipt SLNs contained in the SLN data. There are certain SLNs which do not fall into one of these four categories. This remaining 4 percent of SLNs, labeled "Other" in the table, include delivery points at government facilities, receipt and delivery points at storage facilities, and receipt and delivery points at gas processing plants. This group of SLNs, which were not analyzed in this study, corresponds to 9 percent of the total firm and interruptible volumes on the Koch system during the period from 1989 to 1994.

### *8.3.3 Market Concentration Data*

Koch prepared a data file containing Koch's diameter-squared flow capabilities (the cross-sectional area of the pipe) at the SLN and data on all "alternative" pipelines within a five mile radius of the SLN. This data is shown in table 8.8. Each record in this file corresponds to a single Koch SLN and contains information on as many as fifteen alternative pipelines passing within five miles of the SLN. Data for each alternative pipeline includes: its company code, its diameter-squared flow capabilities, its distance from the Koch SLN, and an estimated cost to connect the SLN to the alternative pipeline.

There are 1,448 SLNs in the "alternative" pipeline data set. This represents all SLNs present in the transaction data set described earlier, less those SLNs which are interconnection points between Koch and other pipelines. Koch did not conduct field surveys or compile data from digitized mapping systems for these interconnect SLNs. There were eighty-nine distinct pipelines appearing in the data set. The maximum number of alternative pipelines present at a single SLN is fifteen, the minimum is zero, and the average is just under five.

Using the diameter-squared flow capability data for all pipelines present within each SLN's five-mile radius, I calculate market shares for Koch and all

---

percent of its total firm and interruptible transactions, these transactions account for 60 percent of Koch's firm and interruptible transportation volume.

**Table 8.6.** SLN Data

| Variable | Name | Description |
|---|---|---|
| sln | Station Location Number (SLN) | The number designation assigned by Koch to each point on the system for accounting or measurement purposes |
| state | State | The state in which the SLN is located |
| mfd | Main Flow Designator (MFD) | A code which represents the primary source/disposition of the gas flowing through the SLN |
| slncus | SLN Custody | A code which represents the primary customer at the SLN |
| field | Field Code | A code which represents the producing field, if applicable, from which the SLN is receiving gas |
| curta | Capacity Allocation Area Code | A code which represents an area on Koch's pipeline which is used in scheduling gas on Koch's system |
| slnfl | Delivery Point Type Code | A code that indicates whether Koch receives or delivers gas through the SLN: R = receipt, D = delivery |
| pmcf89 | Peak Volume 1989 | The largest volume which passed through the SLN on any day during the calendar year 1989 in MCF 14.73 psi |
| pmcf90 | Peak Volume 1990 | The largest volume which passed through the SLN on any day during the calendar year 1990 in MCF 14.73 psi |
| pmcf91 | Peak Volume 1991 | The largest volume which passed through the SLN on any day during the calendar year 1991 in MCF 14.73 psi |
| pmcf92 | Peak Volume 1992 | The largest volume which passed through the SLN on any day during the calendar year 1992 in MCF 14.73 psi |
| pmcf93 | Peak Volume 1993 | The largest volume which passed through the SLN on any day during the calendar year 1993 in MCF 14.73 psi |
| pmcf94 | Peak Volume 1994 | The largest volume which passed through the SLN on any day during the calendar year 1994 in MCF 14.73 psi |

**Table 8.7.** Grouping of Koch's SLNs

| Group | Description | Number of SLNs | Percent |
|---|---|---|---|
| 1 | Industrials/Power Plants | 198 | 12 |
| 2 | Pipeline Receipts | 80 | 5 |
| 3 | Pipeline Deliveries | 60 | 4 |
| 4 | Production Fields | 1,183 | 75 |
| | Other | 67 | 4 |
| Total | | 1,588 | 100 |

alternatives at each SLN. Additionally, I create a Hirschman-Herfindahl concentration index (HHI) for the area within a five-mile radius of the SLN as the sum of the squares of all market shares.[3] The HHI at each SLN is represented by the variable sln_hhi. Koch's market share at an SLN is represented by the explanatory variable ksln_shr.

Using the distance and connection cost data, variables are calculated measuring the average distance (avg_dis) and minimum distance (min_dis) from each SLN to an alternative pipeline and the minimum estimated cost to connect an SLN to an alternative pipeline. Similarly, the variable min_cos is set equal to the smallest estimated connection cost at each SLN.

Shipper-level market concentration measures are calculated using the same source data used to compile the SLN-level measures. Shippers on Koch include all non-pipeline and non-LDC shippers or customers served by Koch at any location on the Koch system. A single SLN on Koch's system might handle business for multiple shippers. In other words, multiple customers can flow gas through a single metering point. Multiple shipper-level market concentration measures are combined at a single point by calculating a weighted average shipper HHI. The gas volumes moved through the SLN by each shipper are used to calculate a weighting factor. The volumes of all shippers using the SLN constitutes this fraction's denominator. The numerator is created by an individual shipper's volume.[4]

The weighted flow capabilities for each alternative pipeline that could serve a shipper are then summed to arrive at total flow capabilities for the shipper's market. Market shares are calculated by dividing the total flow capabilities of

[3]For a review of the Hirschman-Herfindahl index of other measures of concentration, see Encaoua and Jaquemin (1980), Saving (1970), Ordover et al. (1982), Hause (1977), and Dansby and Willig (1979).

[4]Thus, to calculate the HHI for an individual shipper, first the group of relevant SLNs on the Koch system where a specific shipper moved gas is determined. Second, the flow capabilities of Koch and all pipelines within a five-mile radius of each of these SLNs is weighted by the ratio of the volume moved by the shipper through the SLN to that moved by the shipper at all points on Koch's system. Volume weights are calculated for the period January 1990 through December 1994.

**Table 8.8.** Alternative Pipeline Data Set

| Variable | Description |
|---|---|
| sln | Koch station location number |
| koch_cap | Koch diameter-squared flow capability at SLN, in square inches |
| alt1...20 | Code for alternative pipelines within 5 miles of SLN (maximum of 20) |
| dist1...20 | Distance from SLN to alternative pipelines within 5 miles of SLN, in feet |
| cap1...20 | Diameter-squared flow capability of alternative pipelines within 5 miles of SLN, in square inches |
| cost1...20 | Cost to connect SLN to alternative pipelines, in dollars |
| avg_dis | Average distance from SLN to alternative pipelines, in feet |
| min_dis | Minimum distance from SLN to alternative pipelines, in feet |
| min_cos | Minimum cost to connect SLN to alternative pipelines, in dollars |
| num_alt | Total number of alternative pipelines within 5 miles of SLN |
| ksln_shr | Koch share of total flow capability within 5 miles of SLN |
| sln_hhi | Flow capability-based HHI for area within 5 miles of SLN |

| Variable | Obs | Mean | Min | Max |
|---|---|---|---|---|
| avg_dis | 1,325 | 11,973 | 0 | 26,388 |
| min_dis | 1,325 | 5,326 | 0 | 26,388 |
| min_cos | 1,325 | 118,809 | 0 | 1,554,360 |
| num_alt | 1,448 | 4.95 | 0 | 15 |
| koch_cap | 1,448 | 429 | 4 | 3,284 |
| ksln_shr | 1,448 | 28.57 | 0.08 | 100 |
| sln_hhi | 1,448 | 4,486 | 1,012 | 10,000 |

each competing pipeline by the total flow capabilities of all pipelines within the shipper's market. Using these market shares, an HHI is calculated for each shipper. This weighted average HHI, calculated for each SLN, is represented by the explanatory variable shp_hhi.

### 8.3.4 *Ancillary Data*

To model large-scale trends in natural gas transportation demand and to control for changes in the derived demand for natural gas transportation services, I utilize macroeconomic and climatic data.

To capture the weather's effect on the demand for Koch's transportation services and on Koch's discounting behavior, a data series of monthly, statewide, heating degree days prepared by the National Climatic Data Center's (NCDC) staff is used.[5] This series covers the period from January 1989 through December 1994. Heating degree day values are calculated from a base temperature of sixty-five degrees Fahrenheit. State averages are obtained by weighting heating degree day figures recorded by individual NOAA divisional stations within the state by the corresponding state population percentage. Each record in the data file provided by NCDC includes year, month, state, and average heating degree days. The heating degree data explanatory variable is denoted heat_dd.

To measure variations in production levels across different customer classes and the consequent effect on the derived demand for natural gas transportation services, a series of Industrial Production Indices prepared by the U. S. Federal Reserve Board is used. These industry-wide monthly indices are prepared along Standard Industrial Classification (SIC) code groupings, with a base year of 1987. Data series for relevant industries are identified and extracted using a software package developed by the Interindustry Economic Research Fund. Monthly series are extracted for fifteen industrial classes for the period from 1989 through 1994. A combined factor, ip, is defined for each transaction according to the industry classification contained in the main flow designator code for each transaction.

To develop an average transportation rate on interstate pipelines, historical data from FERC Form 11 filings are used. The data are compiled from line sixteen, "Revenues From Transportation of Gas of Others (489)," of the Form 11 filings for the monthly period from 1989 through 1994. Revenues and volumes for companies operating in Koch's territory are summed across the interstate pipelines by month. An average transportation rate is then calculated and is denoted by tranpric.

Fuel oil No. 6 price is used to capture the effect on natural gas transportation demand caused by price variations in alternative fuels. The price for fuel oil No. 6 is identified by the explanatory variable roil6.

[5]The NCDC is a division of the National Oceanic and Atmospheric Administration (NOAA). The series I used is published by the NCDC as "Historical Climatology Series 5-1, Monthly State, Regional and National Heating Degree Days Weighted by Population."

To form real prices, the monthly producer price index (PPI) series, as reported by the Federal Reserve Board for the period 1989 through 1994, is used. This series is organized by year and month with 1987 as the base year. The producer price index is identified by the explanatory variable ppi_ieg. Koch's real transportation price, rkpric, is then created by dividing the effectively charged commodity rate (comdlp) on the transportation transaction by the producer price index. I similarly adjust all other prices in real terms.

In addition to the inflation-adjusted price variables, I create several other explanatory variables. Explanatory variables used in the logit discount models are summarized in table 8.9, while explanatory variables used in the regression demand models are summarized in table 8.10.

## 8.4 Koch's Historical Discounting Behavior

Koch's decision to charge a rate for its transportation services lower than the full tariff rate was, of course, governed by Koch. This decision was pursued by Koch when deemed to be in its economic interest or because it was an economic necessity.

It should be expected that economic agents purchasing Koch's services face a different economic regime when prices are discounted than when they are not. To test this difference in regimes, a discrete choice model for Koch's propensity to discount as a function of several market characteristics, including the HHI in these markets, is specified and estimated.[6] For example, it is expected that Koch is less likely to discount in markets where the HHI is high and where Koch's market concentration is large. Conversely, it is expected that Koch is more likely to discount its prices in markets where it faces many physically or economically close competitors. These hypotheses are empirically testable.[7] To measure Koch's propensity to discount, a logit model is utilized.

### *8.4.1 Results of the Logit Analysis*

As discussed, the empirical analysis is separated into four categories: industrial and powerplant deliveries, receipts from interconnected pipelines, deliveries to interconnected pipelines, and receipts from fields. I discuss each of these in turn.

**Industrials and Power Plants.** The summary statistics used in the industrial and power plant discount logit model are presented in table 8.11. The logit model estimates for industrial and power plant deliveries (interruptible transportation) are presented in table 8.12. For these models, several alterna-

[6]The HHI regime approach has been explored by Daskin and Wolken (1989), Dalton and Penn (1976), and White (1976).

[7]Empirical tests of the HHI as a measure of competitiveness have been considered by other authors. See for example, Cohen and Sullivan (1983), Cowling and Waterson (1976), Jones,, Laudadio, and Percy (1973), McFertridge (1973), and Stigler (1964).

**Table 8.9. Logit Model Variable Glossary**

| Variable Name | Description |
|---|---|
| avg_dis | Average distance to alternative pipelines from SLN |
| comddi | Commodity discount indicator; true if commodity rate is discounted from full tariff level |
| curt1 | Dummy variable for SLN located in Curtailment Area 1 |
| curt2 | Dummy variable for SLN located in Curtailment Area 2 |
| curt3 | Dummy variable for SLN located in Curtailment Area 3 |
| curt4 | Dummy variable for SLN located in Curtailment Area 4 |
| curt5 | Dummy variable for SLN located in Curtailment Area 5 |
| curt6 | Dummy variable for SLN located in Curtailment Area 6 |
| curt7 | Dummy variable for SLN located in Curtailment Area 7 |
| curt8 | Dummy variable for SLN located in Curtailment Area 8 |
| curt9 | Dummy variable for SLN located in Curtailment Area 9 |
| curt10 | Dummy variable for SLN located in Curtailment Area 10 |
| gathdi | Gathering discount indicator; true if gathering rate is discounted from full tariff level |
| heat_dd | Heating Degree Days |
| koch_100 | Dummy variable; true if no alternative pipelines are within 5 miles of SLN |
| ksln_shr | Koch flow capability-based market share at an SLN |
| min_dis | Minimum distance to alternative pipelines from SLN |
| min_cos | Minimum cost to connect an alternative pipeline to SLN |
| num_alt | Number of alternative pipelines within 5 miles of SLN |
| constant | Constant term = 1 |
| roil6 | Real price of fuel oil No. 6 |
| shp_hhi | Weighted-average capacity-based shipper-level HHI at SLN |
| sln_hhi | Flow capability-based HHI at SLN |
| state_al | Dummy variable for SLN located in Alabama |
| state_fl | Dummy variable for SLN located in Florida |
| state_la | Dummy variable for SLN located in Louisiana |
| state_ms | Dummy variable for SLN located in Mississippi |
| state_tx | Dummy variable for SLN located in Texas |
| tier | Koch rate schedule item corresponding to distance transported |
| trend | Continuous time-trend variable |

**Table 8.10.** Regression Model Variable Glossary

| Variable Name | Description |
|---|---|
| comddi | Commodity discount indicator; true if commodity rate is discounted from full tariff level |
| comdlp | Effectively charged rate on the transportation transaction |
| curt1 | Dummy variable for SLN located in Curtailment Area 1 |
| curt2 | Dummy variable for SLN located in Curtailment Area 2 |
| curt3 | Dummy variable for SLN located in Curtailment Area 3 |
| curt4 | Dummy variable for SLN located in Curtailment Area 4 |
| curt5 | Dummy variable for SLN located in Curtailment Area 5 |
| curt6 | Dummy variable for SLN located in Curtailment Area 6 |
| curt7 | Dummy variable for SLN located in Curtailment Area 7 |
| curt8 | Dummy variable for SLN located in Curtailment Area 8 |
| curt9 | Dummy variable for SLN located in Curtailment Area 9 |
| curt10 | Dummy variable for SLN located in Curtailment Area 10 |
| gathdi | Gathering discount indicator; true if gathering rate is discounted from full tariff level |
| gathrt | Gathering rate |
| ip_index | Industrial Production Index, matched to primary customer at SLN |
| mmbtu | Volume transported in mmbtu |
| constant | Constant term = 1 |
| peakmcf | Annual peak-day volume (Mcf), matched to year of transaction |
| powrplnt | Dummy variable for SLN connected to an electric generating plant |
| ppi_ieg | Producer price index |
| roil6 | Real price of fuel oil No. 6 |
| rkpric | Real Koch transportation rate or price |
| rtrnpric | Real average interstate pipeline transportation rate |
| state_al | Dummy variable for SLN located in Alabama |
| state_fl | Dummy variable for SLN located in Florida |
| state_la | Dummy variable for SLN located in Louisiana |
| state_ms | Dummy variable for SLN located in Mississippi |
| state_tx | Dummy variable for SLN located in Texas |
| trend | Continuous time-trend variable |

tive competitiveness measures are considered. The first two measures utilize the interaction of Koch's market share at an SLN with an HHI calculated for the market containing that SLN. Two HHI measures are considered, the first measured with respect to the shipper market (represented by shp_hhi) (table 8.12, model 1) and the second with respect to alternatives present at the SLN (represented by sln_hhi) (table 8.12, model 2). These interactions are denoted by the products (ksln_shr * shp_hhi) and (ksln_shr * sln_hhi), respectively.

Generally, I expected that in markets where the HHI is high and where Koch has a large market share, Koch will act less competitively. In these situations, all other factors held equal, I expect that Koch will be less likely to discount. The estimated results in table 8.12, models 1 and 2, prove this to be the case since the estimated coefficient on the market share HHI factor is negative.

Other competitiveness measures could plausibly explain Koch's propensity to discount. In table 8.12, model 3, Koch's market share (represented by ksln_shr) is negatively related to its discounting probability. Thus, as expected, an increase in Koch's market share at an SLN decreases the likelihood that it will discount. This type of market is less competitive than others where Koch has a lower market share. Similarly, in table 8.12, model 4, more available alternatives (represented by num_alt), equate to a higher probability that Koch will discount because Koch again faces more competition in this particular market situation. An indicator is also constructed for situations in which Koch controls 100 percent of an SLN level market. These are situations in which there are no alternative pipelines within a five-mile radius of an operating Koch SLN. Table 8.12, model 5 demonstrates that in these markets (indicated by the explanatory variable koch_100) Koch is less likely to discount its transportation services.

Similarly, in table 8.12, model 6, average distance to alternatives in the five-mile circle around the SLN is considered. This factor can only be examined when Koch faces some competition from alternative pipelines within the five-mile radius circle around an SLN. Therefore, the average distance factor is introduced into the logit model as the interaction of the koch_100 indicator when it is zero and the avg_dis factor. I find that as the average distance to a competitor increases, Koch's propensity to discount decreases. Similarly, when Koch possesses 100 percent of a specific SLN level market, Koch also shows a lessened propensity to discount. Therefore, as Koch's competitors become more distant in a physical or economic sense, Koch faces lower competition and is, therefore, less likely to discount.

Similarly, factors for minimum distance to a competitor (min_dis) and minimum cost to connect (min_cos) are considered. Table 8.12, models 7 and 8 produce qualitatively similar results.

**Table 8.11.** Logit Model Variables: Industrial and Powerplant Deliveries

| Variable | Obs | Mean | Min | Max | Std. Dev. |
|---|---|---|---|---|---|
| comddi | 9,727 | 0.33 | 0.00 | 1.00 | 0.47 |
| constant | 9,727 | 1.00 | 1.00 | 1.00 | 0.00 |
| (ksln_shr*shp_hhi) | 9,727 | 73,589 | 126 | 313,085 | 63,351 |
| state_al | na | na | na | na | na |
| state_fl | 9,727 | 0.10 | 0.00 | 1.00 | 0.30 |
| state_la | 9,727 | 0.52 | 0.00 | 1.00 | 0.30 |
| state_ms | 9,727 | 0.23 | 0.00 | 1.00 | 0.42 |
| state_tx | 9,727 | 0.07 | 0.00 | 1.00 | 0.26 |
| roil6 | 9,727 | 0.0301 | 0.0213 | 0.0451 | 0.0052 |
| heat_dd | 9,727 | 155.45 | 0.00 | 853.00 | 192.85 |
| tier | 9,727 | 2.64 | 1.00 | 6.00 | 1.58 |
| trend | 9,727 | 92.39 | 89.25 | 94.92 | 1.62 |
| Additional Variables | | | | | |
| koch_100 | 9,739 | 0.22 | 0.00 | 1.00 | 0.41 |
| (!koch_100*avg_dis) | 9,739 | 6,713 | 0 | 25,145 | 6,434 |
| (!koch_100*min_dis) | 9,739 | 3,475 | 0 | 25,145 | 5,482 |
| (!koch_100*min_cos) | 9,739 | 88,713 | 0 | 1,554,360 | 233,702 |
| (ksln_shr*sln_hhi) | 9,739 | 373,508 | 752 | 100,000 | 380,870 |
| ksln_shr | 9,739 | 50.47 | 0.08 | 100.00 | 35.82 |
| num_alt | 9,739 | 2.53 | 0.00 | 10.00 | 2.47 |

**Table 8.12.** Industrial and Powerplant Logit Models

**Model 1: Probability of Discounting Industrial and Power Plant Deliveries Dependent Variable: comddi**

| Variable | Coefficient | *t*-Stat |
|---|---|---|
| constant | -3.32E+00 | -1.990 |
| (ksln_shr*shp_hhi) | -1.52E-06 | -3.867 |
| state_al | na | na |
| state_fl | 1.92E-01 | 1.689 |
| state_la | 6.22E-01 | 6.425 |
| state_ms | 6.26E-01 | 0.631 |
| state_tx | 1.34E-01 | 1.080 |
| roil6 | -1.38E+01 | -2.588 |
| heat_dd | -5.00E-04 | -4.119 |
| tier | 8.10E-02 | 5.631 |
| trend | 2.84E-02 | 1.688 |
| Observations | | 9,727 |
| % Correctly Predicted | | 67 |
| % Discounted | | 33 |

**Model 2: Probability of Discounting Industrial and Power Plant Deliveries Dependent Variable: comddi**

| Variable | Coefficient | *t*-Stat |
|---|---|---|
| constant | -2.02E+00 | -1.206 |
| (ksln_shr*sln_hhi) | -8.96E-07 | -12.185 |
| state_al | na | na |
| state_fl | -6.11E-02 | -0.526 |
| state_la | 1.44E-01 | 1.387 |
| state_ms | -2.19E-01 | -2.125 |
| state_tx | -3.08E-01 | -2.373 |
| roil6 | -1.49E+01 | -2.770 |
| heat_dd | -5.15E-04 | -4.213 |
| tier | 8.48E-02 | 5.864 |
| trend | 2.10E-02 | 1.237 |
| Observations | | 9,739 |
| % Correctly Predicted | | 67 |
| % Discounted | | 33 |

**Model 3: Probability of Discounting Industrial and Power Plant Deliveries Dependent Variable: comddi**

| Variable | Coefficient | *t*-Stat |
|---|---|---|
| constant | -3.07E+00 | -1.838 |
| ksln_shr | -4.22E-03 | -5.813 |
| state_al | na | na |
| state_fl | 1.99E-01 | 1.759 |
| state_la | 5.22E-01 | 5.274 |
| state_ms | 2.32E-02 | 0.233 |
| state_tx | 3.21E-02 | 0.254 |
| roil6 | -1.41E+01 | -2.653 |
| heat_dd | -5.06E-04 | -4.170 |
| tier | 8.34E-02 | 5.806 |
| trend | 2.76E-02 | 1.637 |
| Observations | | 9,739 |
| % Correctly Predicted | | 67 |
| % Discounted | | 33 |

**Model 4: Probability of Discounting Industrial and Power Plant Deliveries Dependent Variable: comddi**

| Variable | Coefficient | *t*-Stat |
|---|---|---|
| constant | -3.02E+00 | -1.807 |
| num_alt | 1.04E-01 | 9.229 |
| state_al | na | na |
| state_fl | 1.74E-01 | 1.539 |
| state_la | 3.35E-01 | 3.292 |
| state_ms | 4.76E-02 | 0.485 |
| state_tx | 1.03E-02 | 0.083 |
| roil6 | -1.38E+01 | -2.584 |
| heat_dd | -4.91E-04 | -4.033 |
| tier | 7.58E-02 | 5.247 |
| trend | 2.30E-02 | 1.359 |
| Observations | | 9,739 |
| % Correctly Predicted | | 66 |
| % Discounted | | 33 |

**Model 5: Probability of Discounting Industrial and Power Plant Deliveries Dependent Variable: comddi**

| Variable | Coefficient | t-Stat |
|---|---|---|
| constant | -1.75E+00 | -1.040 |
| koch_100 | -1.12E+00 | -14.794 |
| state_al | na | na |
| state_fl | -6.21E-01 | -4.823 |
| state_la | -1.29E-01 | -1.172 |
| state_ms | -5.20E-01 | -4.729 |
| state_tx | -6.37E-01 | -4.687 |
| roil6 | -1.48E+01 | -2.737 |
| heat_dd | -5.21E-04 | -4.241 |
| tier | 8.99E-02 | 6.199 |
| trend | 1.98E-02 | 1.166 |
| Observations | | 9,739 |
| % Correctly Predicted | | 67 |
| % Discounted | | 33 |

**Model 6: Probability of Discounting Industrial and Power Plant Deliveries Dependent Variable: comddi**

| Variable | Coefficient | t-Stat |
|---|---|---|
| constant | -8.10E-01 | -0.477 |
| koch_100 | -1.57E+00 | -18.832 |
| (!koch_100*avg_dis) | -5.87E-05 | -12.326 |
| state_al | na | na |
| state_fl | -9.92E-01 | -7.424 |
| state_la | 3.95E-02 | 0.356 |
| state_ms | -4.58E-01 | -4.132 |
| state_tx | -3.93E-01 | -2.851 |
| roil6 | -1.47E+01 | -2.713 |
| heat_dd | -4.94E-04 | -3.980 |
| tier | 8.71E-02 | 5.959 |
| trend | 1.40E-02 | 0.815 |
| Observations | | 9,739 |
| % Correctly Predicted | | 68 |
| % Discounted | | 33 |

**Model 7: Probability of Discounting Industrial and Power Plant Deliveries Dependent Variable: comddi**

| Variable | Coefficient | *t*-Stat |
|---|---|---|
| constant | -3.11E-01 | -0.182 |
| koch_100 | -1.41E+00 | -18.165 |
| (!koch_100*min_dis) | -7.30E-05 | -14.809 |
| state_al | na | na |
| state_fl | -8.63E-01 | -6.612 |
| state_la | -8.32E-02 | -0.757 |
| state_ms | -4.65E-01 | -4.222 |
| state_tx | -4.16E-01 | -3.028 |
| roil6 | -1.55E+01 | -2.835 |
| heat_dd | -4.71E-04 | -3.785 |
| tier | 8.02E-02 | 5.450 |
| trend | 7.57E-03 | 0.439 |
| Observations | | 9,739 |
| % Correctly Predicted | | 67 |
| % Discounted | | 33 |

**Model 8: Probability of Discounting Industrial and Power Plant Deliveries Dependent Variable: comddi**

| Variable | Coefficient | *t*-Stat |
|---|---|---|
| constant | -6.90E-01 | -0.407 |
| koch_100 | -1.26E+00 | -16.359 |
| (!koch_100*min_cos) | -1.23E-06 | -10.013 |
| state_al | na | na |
| state_fl | -7.44E-01 | -5.739 |
| state_la | -1.38E-01 | -1.255 |
| state_ms | -5.00E-01 | -4.548 |
| state_tx | -6.32E-01 | -4.642 |
| roil6 | -1.55E+01 | -2.850 |
| heat_dd | -4.89E-04 | -3.955 |
| tier | 8.14E-02 | 5.565 |
| trend | 1.02E-02 | 0.598 |
| Observations | | 9,739 |
| % Correctly Predicted | | 67 |
| % Discounted | | 33 |

Several additional explanatory variables are included in the logit models to control for factors other than market concentration and competitiveness. For instance, as fuel oil No. 6 prices (represented by roil6) increased, Koch was less likely to discount its service. Here, we see that as the real cost of fuel oil increased, the demand for natural gas increased. This led to a concomitant increase in demand for transportation services. Faced with stronger underlying demand, Koch was less likely to discount its services.

Similarly, Koch was less likely to discount as the weather became more severe. Colder days (represented by increases in heat_dd) increased the demand for natural gas and, consequently, increased the demand for natural gas transportation. Again, faced with stronger demand, Koch was less likely to discount its services.

Additionally, the haul length (represented by tier) was a significant factor influencing the discounting decision. Higher tier values are associated with longer hauls by Koch. Koch, therefore, tended to provide lower prices to its customers when hauls were longer.

Trends over time (represented by trend) show that Koch was more likely to discount its transactions over time, all other factors held constant. Geographic differences in the propensity to discount are controlled by the state indicators state_al, state_fl, state_la, state_ms and state_tx. As a normalization the indicator for Alabama was excluded from the set of treatment indicators.

**Pipeline Receipts and Deliveries.** The summary statistics used in the logit models for pipeline receipts are presented in table 8.13, and the summary statistics for Pipeline deliveries are presented in table 8.14. The logit models are presented in table 8.15, models 1-2. Table 8.15, models 1 and 2 show the discounting probability for the upstream and downstream pipeline markets. Receipts and deliveries are considered separately in these tables.

The results obtained are similar to those for the power plant and industrials market. An increase in the real price of fuel oil No. 6 (represented by roil6) decreases the likelihood that Koch will discount its transportation services. An increase in heating degree days (represented by heat_dd) also decreases the discounting probability. An increase in discounting, over time, is evidenced by the positive trend coefficient. The tier factor shows that longer hauls (an increase in tier) resulted in greater discounting. The state indicators (represented by state_al, state_fl, state_la, state_ms and state_tx), control for geographic differences in the propensity to discount.[8]

**Production Fields.** The logit model developed for the discounting likelihood for field receipts is constructed in a fashion similar to that previously described for both power plants and industrials and pipelines. There are two exceptions.

[8] A competitiveness measure, such as the one used for the power plant and industrials market, was not used in these models as Koch did not collect survey-type data for pipeline interconnect points.

**Table 8.13.** Logit Model Variables: Pipeline Receipts

| Variable | Obs | Mean | Min | Max | Std. Dev. |
|---|---|---|---|---|---|
| comddi | 4,105 | 0.52 | 0.00 | 1.00 | 0.50 |
| constant | 4,105 | 1.00 | 1.00 | 1.00 | 0.00 |
| state_al | na | na | na | na | na |
| state_fl | na | na | na | na | na |
| state_la | 4,105 | 0.42 | 0.00 | 1.00 | 0.49 |
| state_ms | na | na | na | na | na |
| state_tx | 4,105 | 0.39 | 0.00 | 1.00 | 0.49 |
| heat_dd | 4,105 | 171.76 | 0.00 | 853.00 | 198.60 |
| roil6 | 4,105 | 0.0298 | 0.0213 | 0.0451 | 0.0048 |
| tier | 4,105 | 2.92 | 1.00 | 6.00 | 1.64 |
| trend | 4,105 | 92.53 | 89.25 | 94.92 | 1.56 |

**Table 8.14.** Logit Model Variables: Pipeline Deliveries

| Variable | Obs | Mean | Min | Max | Std. Dev. |
|---|---|---|---|---|---|
| comddi | 4,220 | 0.45 | 0.00 | 1.00 | 0.50 |
| constant | 4,220 | 1.00 | 1.00 | 1.00 | 0.00 |
| state_al | na | na | na | na | na |
| state_fl | na | na | na | na | na |
| state_la | 4,220 | 0.67 | 0.00 | 1.00 | 0.47 |
| state_ms | 4,220 | 0.20 | 0.00 | 1.00 | 0.40 |
| state_tx | 4,220 | 0.13 | 0.00 | 1.00 | 0.33 |
| heat_dd | 4,220 | 192.81 | 0.00 | 827.00 | 200.21 |
| roil6 | 4,220 | 0.0302 | 0.0213 | 0.0451 | 0.0051 |
| tier | 4,220 | 2.60 | 1.00 | 6.00 | 1.49 |
| trend | 4,220 | 92.38 | 89.25 | 94.92 | 1.63 |

First, rather than use state indicators, capacity allocation area indicators control for geographic effects. There are ten definable capacity allocation areas on the Koch system. These are identified with the indicators curt1 through curt10. Given that the model contains a constant term, the capacity allocation indicators measure the separate effect of each curtailment area relative to one baseline category, which in this analysis is curt10. Similar normalization with respect to the state indicators appears in the other logit models.

The second difference in this model is that the dependent variable is defined based upon whether either the commodity charge, comddi, or the gathering indicator, gathdi, reveals discounting. While this is not a logical concern in the other logit models, when considering receipts from fields, it is necessary to examine discounting if either the commodity rate component, comddi, or the gathering rate component, gathdi, reveals discounting. The dependent variable is therefore defined by (comddi | gathdi), indicating that discounting had occurred for either of these reasons.

**Table 8.15.** Pipeline Logit Models

**Model 1: Probability of Discounting Pipeline Receipts Dependent Variable: comddi**

| Variable | Coefficient | *t*-Stat |
|---|---|---|
| constant | -6.44E+00 | -2.596 |
| state_al | na | na |
| state_fl | na | na |
| state_la | 2.09E-01 | 2.359 |
| state_ms | na | na |
| state_tx | 3.24E-01 | 3.474 |
| roil6 | -1.76E+01 | -2.202 |
| heat_dd | -3.38E-04 | -2.105 |
| tier | -5.90E-04 | -0.026 |
| trend | 7.47E-02 | 2.975 |
| Observations | | 4,105 |
| % Correctly Predicted | | 55 |
| % Discounted | | 53 |

**Model 2: Probability of Discounting Pipeline Deliveries Dependent Variable: comddi**

| Variable | Coefficient | *t*-Stat |
|---|---|---|
| constant | -1.65E+01 | -5.834 |
| state_al | na | na |
| state_fl | na | na |
| state_la | 1.74E+00 | 1.607 |
| state_ms | 1.73E+00 | 1.600 |
| state_tx | 1.69E+00 | 1.558 |
| roil6 | -1.44E+01 | -1.711 |
| heat_dd | -9.17E-04 | -5.595 |
| tier | 2.49E-01 | 11.163 |
| trend | 1.58E-01 | 5.989 |
| Observations | | 4,220 |
| % Correctly Predicted | | 61 |
| % Discounted | | 45 |

The summary statistics used in the field level receipts logit model are presented in table 8.16. The logit analysis is presented in table 8.17. The results are again similar to those obtained in the previously discussed market segments.

The market share-HHI factor (identified by (kslnshr*shp_hhi)) is again negative and significant in this model. This demonstrates that as competitiveness declined in a production field area, as measured by the market share-HHI interaction, Koch was less likely to discount its price for transportation services. Conversely, as competitiveness increased in an area, Koch was more likely to discount its prices.

**Table 8.16.** Logit Model Variables: Production Field Receipts

| Variable | Obs | Mean | Min | Max | Std. Dev. |
|---|---|---|---|---|---|
| (comddi\|gathdi) | 36,217 | 0.28 | 0.00 | 1.00 | 0.45 |
| constant | 36,217 | 1.00 | 1.00 | 1.00 | 0.00 |
| (ksln_shr*shp_hhi) | 36,217 | 34,463 | 34,463 | 331,300 | 43,523 |
| curt1 | 36,217 | 0.04 | 0.00 | 1.00 | 0.19 |
| curt2 | 36,217 | 0.02 | 0.00 | 1.00 | 0.13 |
| curt3 | na | na | na | na | na |
| curt5 | 36,217 | 0.05 | 0.00 | 1.00 | 0.22 |
| curt6 | na | na | na | na | na |
| curt7 | 36,217 | 0.15 | 0.00 | 1.00 | 0.36 |
| curt8 | 36,217 | 0.44 | 0.00 | 1.00 | 0.50 |
| curt9 | 36,217 | 0.09 | 0.00 | 1.00 | 0.29 |
| curt10 | na | na | na | na | na |
| roil6 | 36,217 | 0.0317 | 0.0213 | 0.0451 | 0.0059 |
| heat_dd | 36,217 | 154.30 | 0.00 | 1,358.00 | 194.93 |
| tier | 36,217 | 3.00 | 1.00 | 6.00 | 1.77 |
| trend | 36,217 | 91.59 | 89.25 | 94.92 | 1.60 |

### *8.4.2 Discussion*

The analysis of Koch's historical discounting demonstrates that Koch faces competition in the markets in which it operates. In each of the market segments I analyze, I find that the more concentrated the market or the longer that Koch was in that market, the less likely Koch was to discount. Historically, over fifty percent of Koch's transportation volume has been discounted. Discounting is generally inconsistent with inelastic demand. If demand were generally inelastic, Koch would have had little incentive to discount its prices below the maximum tariff. With inelastic demand, a price decrease does not increase volume enough to increase total revenues. As long as variable costs are not negative, higher volumes increase total cost, so discounting can only decrease profits. In the next section I turn to the empirical determination of Koch's demand elasticity.

## 8.5 Koch's Historical Demand for Transportation Service

I construct regression models for industrial and power plant deliveries, pipeline receipts, pipeline deliveries, and field receipts. The summary statistics for the regression models for industrial and power plant deliveries are presented in

**Table 8.17.** Probability of Discounting Field Receipts–Dependent Variable: comddi | gathdi

| Variable | Coefficient | t-Stat |
|---|---|---|
| constant | 1.94E+00 | 2.111 |
| (ksln_shr*shp_hhi) | -1.79E-06 | -5.793 |
| curt1 | -4.09E-02 | -0.505 |
| curt2 | na | na |
| curt3 | 3.26E-01 | 5.936 |
| curt4 | na | na |
| curt5 | 7.49E-01 | 10.856 |
| curt6 | na | na |
| curt7 | 3.12E-01 | 5.640 |
| curt8 | 1.23E-01 | 2.453 |
| curt9 | 3.45E-02 | 0.547 |
| curt10 | na | na |
| roil6 | -4.22E+01 | -16.106 |
| heat_dd | 6.45E-05 | 1.050 |
| tier | 5.59E-02 | 7.424 |
| trend | -2.06E-02 | -2.188 |
| Observations | | 36,217 |
| % Correctly Predicted | | 72 |
| % Discounted | | 28 |

table 8.18; for pipeline receipts in table 8.20; for pipeline deliveries in table 8.22; and for production field receipts in table 8.24. The regression models for industrial and power plant deliveries are presented in table 8.19; for pipeline receipts in table 8.21; for pipeline deliveries in table 8.23; and for production field receipts in table 8.25.[9]

Table 8.19 presents the estimated regression model for industrial and power plant interruptible transportation deliveries. The dependent variable in this model is the demand for transportation services. Each observation in the regression analysis represents the demand for interruptible transportation by an industrial firm or a power plant at an SLN in a particular year and month. The estimated model shows that the price Koch charged for its interruptible transportation services is negatively related to the demand for its services.

[9]The four estimated probability models, (table 8.12, model 1; table 8.15, model 1; table 8.15, model 2; and table 8.17), are used to predict the probability that Koch would discount. These predicted probabilities are then used to estimate the selection correction term $E[v|i]$ described above. The selection correction terms, denoted by H, are included in each of the corresponding regression models.

The coefficient of the explanatory variable rkpric is used to calculate the mean elasticity.[10]

Natural gas volumes delivered to power plants (powrplnt), controlling for all other factors, were lower than volumes delivered to industrials. Discounted transactions (comddi) are found to result in higher demand. The real price of fuel oil No. 6 (roil6), and the real transportation cost (rtrnpric), measure the effect of substitution possibilities. I find that as alternative fuel prices or other transportation service prices increased, Koch's service became relatively more attractive and the demand for its services increased.

Transactions in which the industrial production index, ip_index, is greater leads to higher demand. Additionally, the trend in demand for Koch interruptible transportation services is decreasing (shown by the coefficient on trend). A variable is included (represented by peakmcf) for the annual peak-day volume at an SLN to capture absolute magnitude differences in volumes across SLNs. As should be expected, this variable has a positive and significant influence on demand. Finally, the model includes a constant term and state indicators to control for geographic differences.

The estimated mean elasticity for Koch's transportation service, with respect to the effective transportation price, is measured at -3.182 and is statistically significant. This result will be discussed further below.

The estimated models presented in tables 8.21 (pipeline receipts) and 8.23 (pipeline deliveries) are similar to table 8.19. The estimated mean elasticity for Koch's transportation service, with respect to the effective price of its transportation service, is measured at -1.119 for pipeline receipts and -2.860 for pipeline deliveries. Again, the estimated price elasticities are statistically significant.

The results presented in table 8.25 for the field receipts demand model are also similar to those for tables 8.19, 8.21, and 8.23. The estimated mean elasticity for Koch's transportation services, with respect to the effective price of its transportation service, is measured at -3.106. Again, the price effect is statistically significant. In other respects, the model in table 8.25 quantitatively produces similar results to those reported in tables 8.19, 8.21, and 8.23.[11]

---

[10]In constructing the econometric models, the very smallest transactions, which taken together account for only 0.25 percent of the interruptible volume, are not used. This exclusion rule is enforced in each of the product markets. Thus, 6,741 production field transactions, 768 pipeline receipt transactions, 807 pipeline delivery transactions, and 2,324 industrial and power plant transactions are excluded. Some observations are also left out due to missing data. Thus, an additional 148 production field transactions and 12 industrial and power plant transactions are excluded. Typically, these small quantity transactions represented accounting adjustments rather than actual volumes transported.

[11]The regression model for field receipts is specified in a manner similar to those for power plants/industrials and pipelines. There are three exceptions to this general statement. First, discounting is identified by either discounted commodity rates or gathering rates as indicated by the explanatory factors comddi and gathdi. This parallels the development in the logit model for field receipts. Second, the price variable is defined as the full cost of transportation services price for field receipts. This is achieved by summing the commodity rate and the gathering rate (comdlp+gathrt). This sum is then converted to real terms using the price

A selectivity correction variable is included in each regression model. This variable, which controls for the potential simultaneity of the discounting decision, is significant in the power plant/industrials model, insignificant in the pipeline receipts and delivery models, and insignificant in the field receipt model. The signs on the selectivity correction factor are identical across the models and indicate that, all other things being equal, Koch was more likely to discount when it expected demand to be below average. However, once the discount was offered, the customer had increased demand.

**Table 8.18.** Demand Regression Variables: Industrial and Power Plant Deliveries

| Variable | Obs | Mean | Min | Max | Std. Dev. |
|---|---|---|---|---|---|
| mmbtu | 9,727 | 92,820 | 2,532 | 2,442,250 | 170,846 |
| rkpric | 9,727 | 0.0019 | 0.0000 | 0.0053 | 0.0010 |
| constant | 9,727 | 1.00 | 1.00 | 1.00 | 0 |
| powrplnt | 9,727 | 0.20 | 0 | 1.00 | 0.40 |
| comddi | 9,727 | 0.33 | 0 | 1.00 | 0.47 |
| state_al | na | na | na | na | na |
| state_fl | 9,727 | 0.10 | 0 | 1.00 | 0.30 |
| state_la | 9,727 | 0.52 | 0 | 1.00 | 0.30 |
| state_ms | 9,727 | 0.23 | 0 | 1.00 | 0.42 |
| state_tx | 9,727 | 0.07 | 0 | 1.00 | 0.26 |
| roil6 | 9,727 | 0.0034 | 0.0213 | 0.0451 | 0.0006 |
| rtrnpric | 9,727 | 0.0342 | 0.0225 | 0.0511 | 0.0006 |
| ip_index | 9,727 | 110.98 | 81.18 | 128.93 | 6.88 |
| H | 9,727 | 0.0003 | -1.4067 | 2.8299 | 1.3404 |
| trend | 9,727 | 92.39 | 89.25 | 94.92 | 1.62 |
| peakmcf | 9,727 | 27,360 | 0 | 190,331 | 37,805 |

deflator ppi_ieg. The resulting variable appears in the first row of table 8.25. Third, the field level model employs capacity allocation indicators (curt1 through curt 10) as opposed to state indicators for geographic effects. Again, this corresponds to the development in the field logit model.

**Table 8.19.** Demand for Transportation: Industrial and Power Plant Deliveries–Dependent Variable: mmbtu

| Variable | Coefficient | *t*-Stat |
|---|---|---|
| rkpric | -2.09E+07 | -9.076 |
| constant | 1.17E+06 | 7.742 |
| powrplnt | -3.46E+04 | -5.819 |
| comddi | 1.74E+05 | 4.443 |
| state_al | na | na |
| state_fl | 9.06E+03 | 1.171 |
| state_la | 4.97E+03 | 0.579 |
| state_ms | 2.00E+04 | 3.175 |
| state_tx | 9.39E+03 | 1.179 |
| roil6 | 1.13E+06 | 2.918 |
| rtrnpric | 9.48E+06 | 2.454 |
| ip_index | 1.28E+03 | 4.582 |
| H | -4.46E+04 | -3.216 |
| trend | -1.47E+04 | -8.434 |
| peakmcf | 2.00E+00 | 31.639 |
| Observations | | 9,727 |
| R-Squared | | 0.248 |
| Mean Elasticity | | -3.182 |
| Mean of Dep. Variable | | 92,820 |

**Table 8.20.** Demand Regression Variables: Pipeline Receipts

| Variable | Obs | Mean | Min | Max | Std. Dev. |
|---|---|---|---|---|---|
| mmbtu | 4,105 | 1,638 | 6,004 | 5,511,720 | 359,422 |
| rkpric | 4,105 | 0.00164 | 0.00005 | 0.00520 | 0.00099 |
| constant | 4,105 | 1.00 | 1.00 | 1.00 | 0 |
| comddi | 4,105 | 0.53 | 0 | 1.00 | 0.50 |
| state_al | na | na | na | na | na |
| state_fl | na | na | na | na | na |
| state_la | 4,105 | 0.42 | 0 | 1.00 | 0.49 |
| state_ms | na | na | na | na | na |
| state_tx | 4,105 | 0.39 | 0 | 1.00 | 0.49 |
| roil6 | 4,105 | 0.02984 | 0.02130 | 0.04506 | 0.00482 |
| rtrnpric | 4,105 | 0.00344 | 0.00225 | 0.00511 | 0.00056 |
| ip_index | 4,105 | 113.67 | 98.31 | 128.93 | 6.13 |
| H | 4,105 | 0 | -1.75 | 1.91 | 1.38 |
| trend | 4,105 | 92.53 | 89.25 | 94.92 | 1.56 |
| peakmcf | 4,105 | 359,824 | 0 | 6,514,120 | 900,264 |

**Table 8.21.** Demand for Transportation: Pipeline Receipts–Dependent Variable: mmbtu

| Variable | Coefficient | *t*-Stat |
|---|---|---|
| rkpric | -1.88E+07 | -2.311 |
| constant | 3.92E+06 | 5.550 |
| comddi | 5.55E+05 | 1.610 |
| state_al | na | na |
| state_fl | na | na |
| state_la | -2.28E+05 | -9.305 |
| state_ms | na | na |
| state_tx | -2.10E+05 | -6.537 |
| roil6 | 4.14E+06 | 2.143 |
| rtrnpric | 9.68E+07 | 6.688 |
| ip_index | 1.73E+03 | 1.439 |
| H | -1.47E+05 | -1.189 |
| trend | -4.83E+04 | -4.892 |
| peakmcf | 2.25E-02 | 3.601 |
| Observations | | 4,105 |
| R-Squared | | 0.100 |
| Mean Elasticity | | -1.119 |
| Mean of Dep. Variable | | 194,438 |

**Table 8.22.** Demand Regression Variables: Pipeline Deliveries

| Variable | Obs | Mean | Min | Max | Std. Dev. |
|---|---|---|---|---|---|
| mmbtu | 4,220 | 180,495 | 5,516 | 5,708,170 | 362,799 |
| rkpric | 4,220 | 0.00158 | 0.00003 | 0.00516 | 0.00094 |
| constant | 4,220 | 1.00 | 1.00 | 1.00 | 0 |
| comddi | 4,220 | 0.45 | 0 | 1.00 | 0.50 |
| state_al | na | na | na | na | na |
| state_fl | na | na | na | na | na |
| state_la | 4,220 | 0.67 | 0 | 1.00 | 0.47 |
| state_ms | na | na | na | na | na |
| state_tx | 4,220 | 0.20 | 0 | 1.00 | 0.40 |
| roil6 | 4,220 | 0.03022 | 0.02130 | 0.04506 | 0.00507 |
| rtrnpric | 4,220 | 0.00342 | 0.00225 | 0.00511 | 0.00057 |
| ip_index | 4,220 | 113.96 | 98.31 | 128.93 | 6.48 |
| H | 4,220 | 0 | -2.19 | 2.99 | 1.37 |
| trend | 4,220 | 92.38 | 89.25 | 94.92 | 1.63 |
| peakmcf | 4,220 | 202,059 | 0 | 6,514,120 | 440,561 |

**Table 8.23.** Demand for Transportation: Pipeline Deliveries–Dependent Variable: mmbtu

| Variable | Coefficient | *t*-Stat |
|---|---|---|
| rkpric | -4.89E+07 | -5.483 |
| constant | 6.28E+06 | 11.050 |
| comddi | 1.46E+05 | 2.632 |
| state_al | na | na |
| state_fl | na | na |
| state_la | 6.06E+04 | 3.824 |
| state_ms | 2.46E+05 | 12.716 |
| state_tx | na | na |
| roil6 | 1.69E+06 | 1.216 |
| rtrnpric | 1.10E+08 | 8.548 |
| ip_index | 1.94E+03 | 1.861 |
| H | -2.10E+04 | -0.992 |
| trend | -7.40E+04 | -11.156 |
| peakmcf | 3.74E-02 | 3.093 |
| Observations | | 4,220 |
| R-Squared | | 0.144 |
| Mean Elasticity | | -2.860 |
| Mean of Dep. Variable | | 180,495 |

**Table 8.24.** Demand Regression Variables: Production Field Receipts

| Variable | Obs | Mean | Min | Max | Std. Dev. |
|---|---|---|---|---|---|
| mmbtu | 36,217 | 27,228 | 833 | 3,740,500 | 90,430 |
| (comdlp+gathrt) /ppi_ieg | 36,217 | 0.00221 | 0.00007 | 0.00533 | 0.01283 |
| constant | 36,217 | 1.00 | 1.00 | 1.00 | 0 |
| comddi | 36,217 | 0.25 | 0 | 1.00 | 0.43 |
| gathdi | 36,217 | 0.08 | 0 | 1.00 | 0.27 |
| curt1 | 36,217 | 0.04 | 0 | 1.00 | 0.19 |
| curt2 | na | na | na | na | na |
| curt3 | 36,217 | 0.15 | 0 | 1.00 | 0.36 |
| curt4 | na | na | na | na | na |
| curt5 | 36,217 | 0.05 | 0 | 1.00 | 0.22 |
| curt6 | na | na | na | na | na |
| curt7 | 36,217 | 0.15 | 0 | 1.00 | 0.36 |
| curt8 | 36,217 | 0.44 | 0 | 1.00 | 0.50 |
| curt9 | 36,217 | 0.09 | 0 | 1.00 | 0.29 |
| curt10 | na | na | na | na | na |
| roil6 | 36,217 | 0.03 | 0.02 | 0.05 | 0.01 |
| rtrnpric | 36,217 | 0 | 0 | 0.01 | 0 |
| ip_index | 36,217 | 107.80 | 101.44 | 115.33 | 3.19 |
| H | 36,217 | 0 | -1.53 | 3.14 | 1.31 |
| trend | 36,217 | 91.59 | 89.25 | 94.92 | 1.60 |
| peakmcf | 36,217 | 6,050 | 0 | 876,709 | 28,948 |

Table 8.25. Demand for Transportation: Field Receipts–Dependent Variable: mmbtu

| Variable | Coefficient | *t*-Stat |
|---|---|---|
| ((comdlp+gathrt)/ppi_ieg) | -5.28E+06 | -13.263 |
| constant | 3.61E+05 | 9.652 |
| comddi | 4.21E+03 | 1.277 |
| gathddi | 7.70E+03 | 3.659 |
| curt1 | 6.39E+03 | 2.316 |
| curt2 | na | na |
| curt3 | 1.50E+04 | 7.612 |
| curt4 | na | na |
| curt5 | 9.37E+04 | 35.953 |
| curt6 | na | na |
| curt7 | -2.29E+03 | -1.157 |
| curt8 | -9.26E+03 | -5.269 |
| curt9 | -7.18E+03 | -3.276 |
| curt10 | na | na |
| roil6 | 5.15E+04 | 0.494 |
| rtrnpric | 9.11E+05 | 0.929 |
| ip_index | 8.54E+02 | 3.653 |
| H | -1.09E+03 | -0.934 |
| trend | -4.66E+03 | -8.543 |
| peakmcf | 7.80E-01 | 49.365 |
| Observations | | 36,217 |
| R-Squared | | 0.177 |
| Mean Elasticity | | -3.106 |
| Mean of Dep. Variable | | 27,228 |

## 8.6 Conclusions

Roughly one-third of all industrial and power plant transactions were historically discounted. We have learned from the logit analysis that observations which occur at discounted prices generally indicate the presence of competition. For those transactions which did not occur at discount, I am able to calculate the percentage of cases that the demand model determined were in the elastic portion of the demand curve. For the industrial and power plant market segment, I find that a substantial fraction of the transactions that did not occur at a discount are classified as elastic. In total, 90 percent of all transactions were either discounted historically or had elastic demand.[12]

Thus a substantial fraction of Koch's historical sales have occurred at discount (i.e., below tariff prices). As demonstrated in my analysis of Koch's discounting decision, Koch historically granted discounts for a variety of reasons including the extent and prevalence of competition. I show that whether competitiveness is measured by the presence of a competitor within five miles, the cost of connecting the next closest competitor, the number of competitors within five miles, or by a Herfindahl measure that reflects the fact that Koch does business with the same shipper at many points on its system, competition was a key factor in determining the likelihood that Koch would offer a discount. Even when Koch did not discount, it was often faced with elastic demand. Taken together, the picture that emerges is one of a workably competitive environment with a substantial fraction of the system either transacting at discount or in a range of price elasticity in which substantial, sustained price increases are unlikely.

Of course, it is not possible to conclude that Koch would never raise its prices at any point on its system or at any time absent regulation. However, the preponderance of the data for the interruptible segment of Koch's market indicates that competition will constrain Koch from systematically raising its prices. Moreover, in those instances in which Koch does attempt price increases, it is unlikely that they will be sustainable given that inelasticity on its system is frequently synonymous with peak-load demand.[13]

[12]For Industrials and Power Plants, 90 percent of transactions or 74 percent of the volume was provided at discount or was provided at no discount but elastically demanded. For Production Fields, these percentages were 74 percent of transactions or 44 percent of volume. For Pipeline Receipts the percentages were 87 percent of transactions, or 77 percent of volume. And for Pipeline Deliveries, 68 percent of transactions, or 66 percent of volume.

[13]Koch's market is characterized by users who swing onto and off the system. These users, as opposed to being captive by Koch, apparently find readily available alternatives to using Koch's transportation system. The transactions that I have analyzed do not record the transactions of the swing customers when they swing off the system. In effect, these customers present zero demand to Koch. While I cannot calculate demand elasticity at zero quantities and while these zero quantity customers would receive no weight in a volumetric comparison, they nonetheless reveal very large elasticity of demand for Koch's services.

# References

Allen, Stewart. 1988. *Montana Bioeconomics Study: Results of the Trout Stream Angler Preference Survey*, mimeo.

Almon, Shirley. 1965. "The Distributed Lag Between Capital Appropriations and Net Expenditure," *Econometrica*, January, 178–96.

Amemiya, T. 1981. "Qualitative Response Models: A Survey." *Journal of Economic Literature* 19 (4), pp. 483–536.

Anderson, Daniel W., Franklin Gress, and Kenneth F. Mais. 1982. "Brown Pelicans: Influence of Food Supply on Reproduction," *Oikos*, 39 (1), pp. 23–31.

Barnett, Arnold L. 1976. "More on a Market Share Theorem." *Journal of Marketing Research*, 13, pp. 104–09.

Bass, F. M. and D. Clark. 1972. "Testing Distributed Lag Models of Advertising Effects," *Journal of Marketing Research*, 9, pp. 298–308.

Becker, G. S. 1971. "Economic Theory," Knopf, New York.

Bell, David E., Ralph L. Keeney, and John D. C. Little. 1975. "A Market Share Theorem." *Journal of Marketing Research* 12, pp. 136–41.

Bellizi, Joseph A., Harry Krueckebery, John Hamilton, and Warren Martin. 1981. "Consumer Perceptions of National, Private, and Generic Brands," *Journal of Retailing*, 57 (4), pp. 56–70.

Bettis, Richard and David Weeks. 1987. "Financial Returns and Strategic Interaction: The Case of Instant Photography," *Strategic Management Journal*, 8, (November-December), pp. 549–64.

Blattberg, Robert C. and Ken Wisniewski. 1985. "Analyzing Intr-Category, Inter-Brand Price Competition," Working Paper, Center for Research in Marking, University of Chicago (February).

Burke, Charles. 1979. "Plain Labels Challenge the Supermarket Establishment," *Fortune*, 3/26.

Business Trend Analysts, Inc. 1987. "The U.S. Pet Food Market." Nestlé Marketing Research Library, Glendale, CA.

California Department of Fish and Game. 1952. Bureau of Marine Fisheries. "A Description of Methods Used in Collecting and Compiling the Statistics." *Fish Bulletin* 86: 7.73.

California Department of Fish and Game. 1970. *Digest of California Commercial Fish Laws.* California Office of State Printing, 1 January.

California Department of Fish and Game. Various years. *The Marine Fish Catch of California/California Marine Fish Landings.* California Office of State Printing.

Carnation Company Marketing Research Department. 1982–1983. "A Brief Guide to the Major Marketing Services Used by the Carnation Company." Nestlé Marketing Research Library, Glendale, CA.

Carnation Company Marketing Research Department. 1987. "Findings from a Review of Evaporated Milk Research (1974–Present)." Nestlé Marketing Research Library, Glendale, CA.

Carnation Consumer Research Department. 1985. "Instant CM & P/C Promo Franchise Analysis." October, Nestlé Marketing Research Library, Glendale, CA.

Carnation Consumer Research Department. 1991. "Coffee-Mate Research Review." May, Nestlé Marketing Research Library, Glendale, CA.

Carpenter, Gregory and Donald Lehmann. 1985. "A Model of Marketing Mix, Brand Switching, and Competition," *Journal of Marketing Research*, 22, (August), pp. 318–29.

*Chemical and Engineering News*, various issues.

*Chemical Marketing Reporter*, various issues.

*Chemical Week*, various issues.

Cicchetti, Charles, Anthony Fisher, and V. Kerry Smith. 1976. "An Econometric Evaluation of a Generalized Consumer Surplus Measure: The Mineral-King Controversy." *Econometrica*, 44 (November), pp. 1259–76.

Clarke, C. H. D. 1968. "Fish and Wildlife Values in Pollution," *Proceedings of the Lakes Water Resources Conference*, Toronto.

Clawson, Marion, and Jack L. Knetsch. 1966. *Economics of Outdoor Recreation.* Baltimore: The Johns Hopkins Press.

Cohen, Neil B. and Charles A. Sullivan. 1983. "The Herfindahl-Hirschman Index and New Antitrust Merger Guidelines: Concentrating on Concentration," *Texas Law Review*, 62 (453), pp. 433–91.

Cohn, Cathy. 1985. "Starting Your Day Off Right," *Supermarket News*, (June), S50.

Connor, John M. and Everett B. Peterson. 1992. "Market-Structure Determinations of National Brand-Private Label Price Differences of Manufactured Food Products," *The Journal of Industrial Economics*, XL (June), pp. 157–71.

Connor, John M., and S. Weimer. 1986. "The Intensity of Advertising and Other Selling Expenses in Food and Tobacco Manufacturing: Measurement, Determinants, and Impacts," *Agribusiness*, 2, pp. 293–319.

Cowling, Keith and Michael Waterson. 1976. "Price-Cost Margins and Market Structure," *Econometrica*, 43 (171), pp. 267–74.

Crispell, Diane. 1991. "Pet Sounds." *American Demographics*, May, pp. 40–53.

Dalton, James A. and David W. Penn. 1976. "The Concentration-Profitability Relationship: Is There a Critical Concentration Ratio?" *Journal of Industrial Economics*, 25 (2), pp. 133–42.

Dansby, Robert E. and Robert D. Willig. 1979. "Industry Performance Gradient Indexes," *The American Economic Review*, 69 (3), pp. 249–60.

Daskin, Alan J. and John D. Wolken. 1989. "An Empirical Investigation of thc Critical Herfindahl Index in Banking," *Journal of Economics and Business*, 41, pg. 95–105.

Dohner, Robert. 1984. "Export Pricing, Flexible Exchange Rates, and Divergence in the Prices of Traded Guide," *Journal of International Economics*, 16, pp. 79–101

Dubin, Jeffery. 1995. *Consumer Durable Choice and the Demand for Electricity*, Amsterdam: North-Holland.

Dubin, Jeffrey A., C. J. Cicchetti, and L. L. Wilde. 1991. "The Use and Misuse of Surveys in Economic Analysis: Natural Resource Damage Assessment Under CERCLA," California Institute of Technology, Working Paper No. 768, July.

Dubin, Jeffrey A., M. J. Graetz, Michael A. Udell, and L. L. Wilde. 1992. "The Demand for Tax Return Preparation Services," *The Review of Economics and Statistics*, 74 (1), pp. 75–82.

Dubin, Jeffrey A. and Daniel L. McFadden. 1984. "An Econometric Analysis of Residential Electric Appliance Holdings and Consumption," *Econometrica*, 52, pp. 345–62.

Dubin, Jeffery, and Langche Zeng. 1991. "The Heterogeneous Logit Model," California Institute of Technology Working Paper #759, February.

Duffield, John. 1981. "A Preliminary Estimate of the Value of Recreational Use on the Upper Clark Fork and Its Tributaries." February 1981.

Duffield, John, John Loomis, and Rob Brooks. 1987. "The Net Economic Value of Fishing in Montana." Report for Federal Aid in Sport Fish and Wildlife Restoration Acts, August 1987. Sport Fish & Wildlife Restoration.

Eales, James, and James E. Wilen. 1986. "An Examination of Fishing Location Choice in the Pink Shrimp Fishery." *Marine Resource Economic*, 2 (4), pp. 331–51.

*Economic Report of the President*. 1990. Transmitted to the Congress, February 1990. Washington, D.C.: United States Government Printing Office.

Encaoua, David and Alexis Jaquemin (1980). "Degree of Monopoly, Indices of Concentration and Threat of Entry," *International Economic Review*, 21 (1), pp. 87–105.

Farquhar, Peter. 1989. "Managing Brand Equity," *Marketing Research*, September, pp. 24–33.

Federal Trade Commission. 1969. "Meanings Posted Octane Ratings," 14 October, pp. 179–204.

Frankel, Alison. 1991. "Great Expectations: How Polaroid won $900 Million in its Patent Case Against Kodak and Ended up Looking like the Loser," *The American Lawyer*, March, pp. 92–99.

Friend, Cynthia M. 1993. "Catalysis on Surfaces," *Scientific American*, 268 (4), pp. 74–79.

Gallup Organization. 1986. "The Gallup Study of Consumer Attitudes and Behavior Concerning Breakfast" conducted for Carnation Company. October, pp. 1–44. Nestlé Marketing Research Library, Glendale, CA.

Georgia Bender Research. 1984. "A Qualitative Look at Fancy Feast Cat Food" prepared for Carnation Company. May, Nestlé Marketing Research Library, Glendale, CA.

Giovannini, Alberto. 1988. "Exchange Rates and Traded Goods Prices," *Journal of International Economics*, 24, pp. 45–68.

Gius, Mark. 1993. "The Extent of the Market in the Liquor Industry: An Empirical Test of Localized Brand Rivalry, 1970–1988," *Review of Industrial Organization*, 8, pp. 599–608.

Grabenstatter, Frank. 1990. *Fishing Spot Locator: Angler's Lat-Long and Loran Guide to Southern California's Pacific Coast.* Glendale, CA: Perfect 10.

Grover, Rajir and V. Srinivasan. 1989. "An Approach for Tracking Within-Segment Shifts in Market Shares," *Journal of Marketing Research*, 26 (May), pp. 230–36.

Guadagni, Peter and John Little. 1983. "A Logit Model of Brand Choice," *Marketing Science*, 2, (Summer), pp. 203–38.

Gumbhir, Ashok and Christopher Rodowskos. 1974. "Consumer Price Differences between Generic and Brand Name Prescriptions," *American Journal of Public Health*, 64, p. 930.

Hammonds, Keith M. 1990. "What will Polaroid do with All That Moola?," *Business Week*, 29 (October), pp. 38.

Harris, Richard. 1964. *The Real Voice*, The MacMillan Company, New York.

Hause, John C. 1977. "The Measurement of Concentrated Industrial Structure and the Size Distribution of Firms," *Annals of Economic and Social Measurement*, 6 (1), pp. 73–107.

Hausman, Jerry A., Gregory Leonard, and J. Douglas Zona. 1991. "A Proposed Method for Analyzing Competition Among Differentiated Products," *Antitrust Law Journal*, 60 (3), pp. 889–900.

Hausman, Jerry, Gregory Leonard, and J. Douglas Zona. 1994. "Competitive Analysis with Differentiated Products," *Annales D'Économie et de Statistique*, 34, pp. 159–80.

Hausman, J. and D. Wise. 1978. "A Conditional Probit Model for Qualitative Choice: Discrete Decisions Recognizing Interdependence and Heterogeneous Preferences," *Econometrica*, 46, pp. 403–26.

Herrick, S., J. G. Lee, and Dale Squires. 1988. "Documentation for the West Coast Fishing Fleet Cost-Earnings Data Base," NMFS Southwest Fisheries Science Center, La Jolla, CA, Administrative Report W-88-04.

Hoch, Stephen, Byung-Do Kim, Alan Montgomery, and Peter Rossi. 1995. "Determinants of Store-Level Price Elasticity" *Journal of Marketing Research*, 32, (February), pp. 17–29.

Hunter, J. R., and C. A. Kimbrell. 1980. "Egg Cannibalism in the Northern Anchovy, Engraulis Mordax." *Fishery Bulletin* (U.S.) 78, pp. 811–16.

International Coffee Organization. 1987. "United States of America Coffee Drinking Study—Winter 1987," Nestlé Marketing Research Library, Glendale, CA.

*International Trade Commission*, "Preliminary Report on U.S. Production of Synthetic Organic Chemicals," various issues.

Jacobson, Larry D., and Cynthia J. Thomson. 1991. "Opportunity Costs and the Decision to Fish for Northern Anchovy." Unpublished paper. National Marine Fisheries Service, Southwest Fisheries Science Center, La Jolla, CA, May 20.

Jones, J. C. H., L. Laudadio, and M. Percy. 1973. "Market Structure and Profitability in Canadian Manufacturing Industry: Some Cross Section Results," *Canadian Journal of Economics*, 6 (3), pp. 356–68.

Kamakura, Wagner and Gary Russell. 1991. "Measuring Consumer Perceptions of Brand Quality with Scanner Data: Implications for Brand Equity," MSI Technical Working Paper #91-122, October.

Karp, Larry S., Jeffrey M. Perloff. 1989. "Estimating Market Structure and Tax Incidence: The Japanese Television Market," *Journal of Industrial Economics*, 37, pp. 225–39.

Kirk-Othmer Encyclopedia of Chemical Technology. 1983. "Vinyl Polymers (Acetate)," Vol. 23, pp. 817–47. John Wiley & Sons, New York

Kirk-Othmer Encyclopedia of Chemical Technology. 1991. "Acetic Acid and Derivatives," Vol. 1, pp. 121–37. John Wiley & Sons, New York

Kolstad, Charles and John Braden. 1991. "Environmental Demand Theory," in *Measuring the Demand for Environmental Quality*, Charles D. Kolstad and John B. Braden (Editors) Elsevier Science Publishers B.V. (North Holland).

Kramer, David, and Paul E. Smith. 1970. "Seasonal and Geographic Characteristics of Fishery Resources: California Current Region—1 Jack Mackerel," *Commercial Fisheries Review*, May, pp. 27–31.

Leading National Advertisers. 1979–1984. "LNA Multi-Media Report Service" (Class/Brand Reports). New York, NY.

Lee, Jong-Ying, Mark Brown, and Bruske Schwartz. 1986. "The Demand for National Brand and Private Label Frozen Concentrated Orange Juice: A Switching Regression Analysis," *Western Journal of Agricultural Economics*, 11(1). pp. 1–7

Lemont, Fred L., letter to Theresa Birk, 5 August 1983. Nestlé Marketing Research Library, Glendale, CA.

Lemont Consulting Group. 1983. "Proposal to Carnation for Positioning study for Carnation Instant Breakfast." February, Nestlé Marketing Research Library, Glendale, CA.

Lipman, Joanne. 1989. "British Value Brand Names—Literally," *Wall Street Journal*, February 9, B6.

Little, John. 1979. "Aggregate Advertising Models: The State of the Art," *Operations Research*, 27 (July/August), pp. 629–67.

Loukashian, A. S. 1970. "On the Diet and Feeding Behavior of the Northern Anchovy, *Engraulis Mordax* (Girard)." *Proceedings California Academy of Science*, 4th Series, 137 (13), pp. 419–58.

MacCall, A. D. 1980. "The Consequences of Cannibalism in the Stock-Recruitment Relationship of the Planktonivorous Pelagic Fish." *Intergovernmental Oceanic Committee Workshop Report*, 28, pp. 201–20.

Mahajan, Vijay, Vihala Rao, and Rajendra Srivastava. 1990. "Development, Testing, and Validation of Brand Equity Under Conditions of Acquisition and Divestment," presented at the MSI workshop on Brand Equity, (February 1), Cambridge, MA.

Mahajan, Vijay, Sharma Subhash, and Robert D. Buzzell. 1993. "Assessing the Impact of Competitive Entry on Market Expansion and Incumbent Sales," *Journal of Marketing*, 57 (July), pp. 39–52.

Mais, Kenneth F. 1974. "Pelagic Fish Surveys in the California Current." *Fish Bulletin*, (California Department of Fish and Game) 162 (1974).

Management Decision Systems, Inc. 1982. "Perceptor Analysis of the Canned Dog Food Market" prepared for Carnation Company. Nestlé Marketing Research Library, Glendale, CA.

Management Science Associates. 1982. "Dog—Graphic Analysis" prepared for Carnation Company, April. Nestlé Marketing Research Library, Glendale, CA.

Manski, Charles F. and Daniel L. McFadden. 1981. eds. *Structural Analysis of Discrete Data with Econometric Applications.* Cambridge: M.I.T. Press.

Marston, Richard. 1990. "Pricing to Market in Japanese Manufacturing," *Journal of International Economics*, 29 pp. 217–36.

McFadden, D. 1973. "Conditional Logit Analysis of Qualitative Choice Behavior." In P. Zarembka (ed.), *Frontiers of Econometrics*, New York: Academic Press.

McFadden, D. 1976. "Quantal Choice Analysis: A Survey." *Annals of Economic and Social Measurement*, 5, pp. 363–390.

McFadden, D. 1978. "Modelling the Choice of Residential Location." In A. Karlquist *et al.* (eds.), *Spatial Interaction Theory and Planning Models*, pp. 75–96. Amsterdam: North-Holland.

McFadden, D. 1981. "Econometric Models of Probabilistic Choice," in C. F. Maskin and D. McFadden (eds.), *Structural Analysis of Discrete Data with Econometric Applications*, pp. 198–271. Cambridge, Mass: MIT Press.

McFadden, D. 1982. "Qualitative Response Models." In W. Hildenbrand (ed.), *Advances in Econometrics*, pp. 1–25. Cambridge: Cambridge University Press.

McFadden, Daniel, C. Puig, and D. Kirschner. 1977. "Determinants of the Long-Run Demand for Electricity," Proceedings of the American Statistical

Association, Business and Economics Section, Part I 72, (August), pp. 109–13

McFertridge, Donald. 1973. "Market Structures and Price-Cost Margins: An Analysis of the Canadian Manufacturing Sector," *Canadian Journal of Economics*, 6 (3), pp. 344–55.

Methot, Richard D. 1982. "Age-Specific Abundance and Mortality of Northern Anchovy." Administrative Report W-82-31, National Marine Fisheries Service, Southwest Fisheries Center, La Jolla, CA.

Methot, Richard D. 1989. "Synthetic Estimates of Historical Abundance and Mortality for Northern Anchovy," *American Fisheries Society Symposium*, 6, pp. 66–82.

Miller, Daniel J. and John J. Geibel. 1973. "Summary of Blue Rockfish and Lingcod Life Histories; A Reef Ecology Study; and Giant Kelp, *Macrocystis Pyrifera*, Experiments in Monterey Bay, California." *Fish Bulletin* (California Department of Fish and Game) 158.

Montgomery, David and Alvin Silk. 1972. "Estimating Dynamic Effects of Market Communications Expenditures," *Management Science*, 18 (June) pp. 485–501.

National Ocean Service (NOM). 1991. *United States Coast Pilot No. 7, Pacific Coast California. Oregon. Washington, and Hawaii.* Washington, DC: U.S. Department of Commerce.

National Ocean Service (NOM). 1987–1990. *Nautical Charts Numbers 18720. 18721, 18725. 18727, 18728. 18729. 18740. 18744, 18746, 18749. 18751, 18755. 18755, 18756. 1875 18762. 18763. 18764. 18765, 18772, 18773, 18774, 18022, 18020.* Washington, DC: U.S. Department of Commerce.

Nelson, Phillip. 1974. "Advertising as Information," *Journal of Political Economy*, 82 (July/August), pp. 729–54.

Nickell, Stephen and David Metcalf. 1978. "Monopolistic Industries and Monopoly Products or Are Kellogg's Cornflakes overpriced," *The Economic Journal*, 88 (June), pp. 254–68.

Nielsen Research. 1979–1984. "Nielsen Research Report to Carnation Company Inc." (reports on Non-Dairy Creamer and Evaporated Milk). Hardcopy printed from microfiche which is located in the Nestlé Marketing Research Library, Glendale, CA.

Nissen, D. M. and Armando M. Lago. 1975. "Price Elasticity of the Demand for Parcel Post Mail," *Journal of Industrial Economics*, 23 (4), pp. 281–99.

Ordover, Junusz A., Alan O. Sykes, and Robert D. Willig. 1982. "Herfindahl Concentration, Rivalry and Mergers," *Harvard Law Review*, 95, pp. 1857–1874.

Pacific Fishery Management Council, and National Marine Fisheries Service. 1983. "Northern Anchovy: Fishery Management Plan, Final Supplementary Environmental Impact Statement, and Draft Regulatory Impact Reviews/Initial Regulatory Flexibility Analysis." (24 October), pp. 4–12.

Pagoulatos, Emilio and Robert Sorensen. 1986. "What Determines the Elasticity of Industry Demand," *International Journal of Industrial Organization*, 4, pp. 237–50.

Parrish, Richard H., and Alec D. MacCall. 1978. "Climatic Variation and Exploitation in the Pacific Mackerel Fishery." *Fish Bulletin* (California Department of Fish and Game) 167.

Pet Food Institute. 1987. "Fact Sheet," Nestlé Marketing Research Library, Glendale, CA.

Pet Food Institute. 1993. "Pet Incidence Report" prepared for the Carnation Company, March. Nestlé Marketing Research Library, Glendale, CA.

Plante, R. 1988. Memorandum on U.S. Dog Size Trends to J. Brown, May. Nestlé Marketing Research Library. Glendale, CA.

Progressive Grocer. 1987. "Cats Nip at Dog Food Sales," *Progressive Grocer*, July, pp. 165–66.

Prutzman, Ferdinand. 1992. "Why Lower Dollars Didn't Do the Job," *New York Times* December 1, C1.

"PSA: Preference Structure Analysis of Cat Foods" prepared for the Carnation Company. March 1981. Nestlé Marketing Research Library, Glendale, CA.

Punj, G. and R. Staelin. 1978. "The Choice Process of Graduate Business Schools." *Journal of Marketing Research*, 15, pp. 588–98.

Rhum, Amiee. 1987. *Business Opportunity Report GA-023N Beverage Industry: Markets, Players Packing Trends ISBN: 0-89336-412-6.* Norwalk, CT: Business Communications Co., Inc., February, pp. 89–113.

Ries, Al and Jack Trout. 1986. *Positioning: The Battle for Your Mind*, New York: McGraw-Hill.

Robinson, William and Claus Fornell. 1985. "Sources of Market Pioneer Advantages in Consumer Goods Industries," *Journal of Marketing Research*, 22 (August), pp. 305–17.

Russell, Gary J. and Ruth N. Bolton. 1988. "Implications of Market Structure for Elasticity Structure," *Journal of Marketing Research*, XXV (August), pp. 229-41.

Saving, Thomas R. 1970. "Concentration, Ratios and the Degree of Monopoly," *International Economic Review*, 11 (1), pp. 139–46.

Schmalensee, Richard. 1982. "Product Differentiation Advantages of Pioneering Brands," *American Economic Review*, 72 (June), pp. 349–65.

Selling Area Marketing, Inc. 1979–1984. "SAMI Basic/Special Report." (reports on Instant Breakfast, Dog Food-Wet, and Cat Food-Wet used). Hardcopy printed from microfiche which is located in the Nestlé Marketing Research Library, Glendale, CA.

Selling Areas Marketing, Inc. 1990. "SAMI Million Dollar Brand Report."

Selling Areas Marketing, Inc. 1985. "SAMI Reports: 54 Market Areas Representing 88.1% of National Food Sales," map and socio-economic statistics.

Shapouri, S., R. J. Folwell and J. L. Baritelle. 1981. "Statistical Estimation of Firm-level Demand Functions: A case study in an oligopolistic industry," *Agricultural Economic Research*, 33, pp. 18–25.

Silk, A. and G. Urban. 1978. "Pre-test Market Evaluation of New Packaged Goods: A Model and Measurement Methodology." *Journal of Marketing Research*, 15, pp. 171–91.

Simon, Carol and Marge Sullivan. 1993. "The Measurement and Determinants of Brand Equity: A Financial Approach," *Marketing Science*, 12 (1), pp. 28–52.

Small, Kenneth A. and Harvey S. Rosen. 1981. "Applied Welfare Economics with Discrete Choice Models," *Econometrica*, 49 (1), pp. 105–30.

Smith, Paul E. 1972. "The Increase in Spawning Biomass of Northern Anchovy, Engraulis Mordax," *Fisheries Bulletin*, 70 (3), pp. 849–74.

Smith, T. 1984. "A Choice Probability Characterization of Generalized Extreme Value Models," *Applied Mathematics and Computation*, 4, pp. 35–62.

Stigler, George. 1961. "The Economics of Information." *Journal of Political Economics* and *The Organization of Industry*, Homewood, IL: Irwin, 1968.

Stigler, George. 1964. "A Theory of Oligopoly," *Journal of Political Economics*, 72 (44), pp. 44–61.

Taylor, Lester D. 1993. "The Demand for First-Class Mail: An Econometric Analysis," *Review of Industrial Organization*, 8(5), pp. 523–44.

Telser, Lester. 1962. "The Demand for Branded Goods as Estimated from Consumer Panel Data," *Review of Economics and Statistics*, 4 (August), pp. 300–24.

Thomas, Lacy Glenn. 1989. "Advertising in Consumer Goods Industries: Durability, Economies of Scale, and Heterogeneity," *Journal of Law and Economics*, 32 (April), pp. 163–93.

U.S. Department of Commerce, Bureau of the Census. 1982. *State and Metropolitan Area Data Book 1982.* Washington, D.C.: Government Printing Office.

U.S. Department of Commerce, Bureau of the Census. 1986. *State and Metropolitan Area Data Book 1986.* Washington, D.C.: Government Printing Office.

U.S. Department of Commerce, Bureau of the Census. 1991. *State and Metropolitan Area Data Book 1991.* Washington, D.C.: Government Printing Office.

U.S. Department of Commerce, Bureau of the Census. 1984. *Statistical Abstract of the United States: 1984.* Washington, D.C.: United States Government Printing Office.

U.S. Department of Commerce, Bureau of the Census. 1987. *Statistical Abstract of the United States: 1987.* Washington, D.C.: United States Government Printing Office.

U.S. Department of Commerce, Bureau of the Census. 1992. *Statistical Abstract of the United States: 1992.* 112th edition Washington, D.C.: United States Government Printing Office.

U.S. Department of Labor, Bureau of Labor Statistics. 1979–1984. "Consumer Price Index Reports." Washington, D.C.

United States and the State of California. 1991. "Draft Injury Determination Plan, Damage Assessment: Los Angeles/Long Beach Harbors, Palos Verdes Shelf, and Ocean Dump Sites, March 8.

Urban, Glen L., Theresa Carter, Steven Gaskin, and Zofia Mucha. 1986. "Market Share Rewards to Pioneering Brands: An Empirical Analysis and Strategic Implications," *Management Science*, 32 (June), pp. 645–59.

Varian, Hal R. 1992. "Microeconomic Analysis." 3rd edition New York: Norton.

Wentz, Laurel and Geoffrey Martin. 1989. "How Experts Value Brands," *Advertising Age*, 24 (January 16), pp. 24–25.

Wheeler, Kevin. 1988. *Chemical Economics Handbook—Acetic Acid*, SRI International.

Wheeler, Kevin and Alfred Abshire. 1988. "Chemical Economics Handbook, Methanol, SRI International.

White, Lawrence J. 1976. "Searching for the Critical Concentration Ratio: An Application of the 'Switching of Regimes' Technique," In S. Goldfeld & R. Quandt (eds.), *Studies in Nonlinear Estimation*, Ballinger Publishing Company, Cambridge, Mass.

Wiggins, Steven and David Raboy. 1996. "Price Premia to Name Brands: An Empirical Analysis," *The Journal of Industrial Economics*, XLIV, (December), pp. 377–88.

Zufryden, Fred. 1986. "Multibrand Transition Probabilities as a Function of Explanatory Variables: Estimation by a Logit-Squared-Based Approach," *Journal of Marketing Research*, 23 (May), pp. 177–83.

# Index

# About the Author

Jeffrey A. Dubin received his A.B. in Economics from the University of California, Berkeley in 1978 and a Ph.D. in Economics from the Massachusetts Institute of Technology in 1982. In 1982, Dr. Dubin joined the faculty of the California Institute of Technology where he is currently an Associate Professor of Economics.

Dr. Dubin was Senior Advisor at Putnam, Hayes, and Bartlett from 1989 through 1992. He was Senior Economist at Arthur Andersen Economic Consulting from 1992 through 1993 and Director of Statistics and Econometric Analysis at Arthur Andersen from 1993 through 1996. In 1996, he became a co-founding partner of the Pacific Economics Group. Dr. Dubin received the Econometric Society Frisch Medal in 1986. His first book was "Consumer Durable Choice and the Demand for Electricity," published by Elsevier North-Holland in 1985.